REDISCOVERING THOMAS ADAMS

REDISCOVERING THOMAS ADAMS

Rural Planning and Development in Canada

EDITED BY WAYNE J. CALDWELL

UBCPress · Vancouver · Toronto

21 20 19 18 17 16 15 14 13 12 11   5 4 3 2 1

Printed in Canada on FSC-certified ancient-forest-free paper
(100 percent post-consumer recycled) that is processed chlorine- and acid-free.

Library and Archives Canada Cataloguing in Publication

Adams, Thomas, 1871-1940
Rediscovering Thomas Adams : rural planning and development in Canada /
edited by Wayne J. Caldwell.

Includes bibliographical references and index.
Also issued in electronic format.
ISBN 978-0-7748-1923-7 (bound); ISBN 978-0-7748-1924-4 (pbk.)

1. Adams, Thomas, 1871-1940. Rural planning and development.
2. Rural development – Canada. 3. Canada – Rural conditions.
I. Caldwell, Wayne. II. Title.

HN110.Z9C6 2011   307.72'0971   C2011-903541-3

e-book ISBNs: 978-0-7748-1925-1 (pdf); I978-0-7748-1926-8 (epub)

Canadä

UBC Press gratefully acknowledges the financial support for our publishing program
of the Government of Canada (through the Canada Book Fund),
the Canada Council for the Arts, and the British Columbia Arts Council.

UBC Press
The University of British Columbia
2029 West Mall
Vancouver, BC V6T 1Z2
www.ubcpress.ca

In memory of JEANNE WOLFE and LEN GERTLER
for their leadership in the field of planning, and
in memory of MICHAEL TROUGHTON
for his legacy and passion for all things rural.
He was a personal inspiration, friend, and mentor.

———

CONTENTS

PREFACE AND ACKNOWLEDGMENTS

Thomas Adams' *Rural Planning and Development* was first brought to my attention by Professor Michael Troughton while I was studying for my undergraduate degree at the University of Western Ontario. Over the years it became a touchstone, a measure if you like, of how rural Canada and the profession of planning have evolved over the last hundred years. It is my hope that students of rural communities and planning will come to see the value of this book for its historic and philosophic contributions.

The republishing of this book has taken a number of years to come to fruition. It is a tribute to those who contributed in one way or another – to their patience, perseverance, and commitment to this project. To the contributing authors my many thanks. There are also many students at the University of Guelph who played a hand in the reproduction of this book. They include Kate Hagerman, Elizabeth Vanstone, Laura Weir, Erin Bankes, Nicolas Brunet, Irv Marucelj, Jennifer Ball, and Therese Ludlow. At UBC Press Melissa Pitts shepherded this project to completion and Holly Keller gave this old book new life, despite what must have felt like 10,000 ancient photos and maps.

At a personal level, none of this would be possible without the support, love, and encouragement of my wife Deborah and my children Michael and Alison. Words of thanks can never fully express my gratitude.

INTRODUCTION

Wayne J. Caldwell

*[The point is] whether we stand still and talk ideals or
move forward and get as much realization of our ideals
as possible in a necessarily imperfect society, capable
only of imperfect solutions to its problems.*

— *Thomas Adams,* New Republic, *6 July 1932*

When Thomas Adams accepted an offer of employment from the Commission
of Conservation (1909-21) and landed in Canada in 1914, it was still uncertain
how much influence he would have on the newly established profession in which
he had, largely through circumstances of the moment, become involved. He was
invited to Canada because of his prior involvement in Letchworth Garden City,
an experiment that was arguably unsuccessful in its implementation, if reasonable in its scope and idea. By managing that project from 1901 to 1906, however,
Adams did acquire practical experience that made him marketable, and so he
enjoyed professional life for the next eight years as one of the earliest private
planning consultants, supplementing practice with academic study and seizing
opportunities to speak at conferences around the world.

It was therefore because of Adams' reputation and experience that he was
sought after and hired in Canada. Although he achieved some success, a number
of factors undermined his long-term goals and ultimately soured his experience.
Adams eventually left Canada for residency and employment in the United States,
but not before leaving behind several legacies. He wrote numerous publications,
the most comprehensive of which is *Rural Planning and Development: A Study
of Rural Conditions and Problems in Canada* (1917). He established the Town
Planning Institute of Canada and, finally, he ceaselessly promoted the modern
planning profession, even though his efforts were often opposed by his newly
adopted countrymen.

It is, perhaps, a testament to Adams' strength of character that he suffered
professional disappointment in both Britain and Canada, and the disappointments followed him to the United States. Because they coloured his expectations

over time, his writings tend to include details of implementation rather than rhetoric. From this perspective, he is a planner's planner: the idea may be the thing, but application of a described process accomplishes the goal.

Adams also continues to be relevant because of his ability to effectively link short-term actions with their long-term effect, to link the tactical with the strategic aspects of planning decisions. In other words, he recognized that short-term projects could either contribute to or sabotage long-term goals. Some would call Adams an idealist, but though he might have walked with his head brushing the clouds, his feet were firmly locked to that plane of earth where business, government, and other man-made institutions swirled in conflict. He could draw, and explain to others, a traversable path from the realities of his world to the standards he was attempting to espouse.

WHO WAS THOMAS ADAMS?

Thomas Adams was both a product of his times and of his personal circumstances. Having grown up on a family farm outside of Edinburgh, Scotland, Adams introduced a new concept of balance between rural and urban life to Canadian planning. Although his work was regarded highly throughout the world, he suffered the consequences of his time – a climate of war and uncertainty. As a convinced utilitarian and pragmatist, he insisted on attaining natural harmony in society and the co-operation of individuals.

In his early life, Adams had two major influences. Family, farming, and his involvement in public life allowed him to further his understanding of the social issues of his time. Distrust in the power of the state caused him to favour individual liberties (or associated individualism). His involvement in local politics became more serious when he became a local councillor at the end of the nineteenth century. This led to a career in journalism in London and involvement in the newly emerging Garden City movement.

Adams then qualified as a surveyor and became one of the first people in England to make his living entirely from planning and designing garden suburbs. In 1910, because of his growing reputation in his new profession, he became the first president of the British Town Planning Institute.

Canada's Century, 1896-1913

Meanwhile, Canada was experiencing a fifteen-year period of economic prosperity and an incredible expansion of its population. This expansion was essentially caused by wide open immigration policies that were aimed at populating the Prairies. However, Canada's rural population rose only by 17 percent while its urban population grew by 62 percent. Urban development was characterized by grid design and did not take into consideration the topography of the land.

Market forces determined land use, and single-family housing encouraged the development of new subdivisions at an alarming rate. Adams identified some major consequences of these developments.

Adams noticed that land speculation resulted in cities expanding their bound-aries to attain more land for development. However, a large proportion of this land had no prospect of being developed and would consequently become sterile. This idle land would result in increased costs for municipalities and lead to bankruptcy in some cases. Furthermore, according to Adams, land assessments were based on fictitious values. Unrealistically low densities of development, he argued, would lead to dramatic tax increases because of increased servicing costs. Residents of suburban areas would then be faced with high land and transport expenditures. Many homes would become slums because families would not be able to afford these unpredicted increases in living costs. Moreover, cities were increasingly becoming grim and dirty because of the lack of public investment in the arts and green spaces. There was little control over the exploita-tion of natural resources and land use.

Adams recognized that rural areas faced similar issues. Speculators held the best land, close to railways and off the market, and other lands were unavailable because of premature subdivisions. Settlements were scattered and lacked es-sential services such as health care, municipal services, and schools. This made the city look like a good option for rural Canadians and contributed to the de-population of rural areas.

In response, city planning became a prominent feature of Canadian progres sivism. It was believed that America's City Beautiful movement, with its well-laid-out plans and aesthetically pleasing concepts, would reduce social tension, secure property values, and promote stability and efficiency. Canadians in general, however, were not receptive to these ideas, stressing instead more urgent needs such as health care. Town planning came to be associated with luxury, and the City Scientific movement instead prioritized health, economics, and beauty (in that order). The movement was based on the British Garden City movement and, in its attempt to provide for the population at large, was oriented towards effi-ciency in the provision of services.

Canada and Thomas Adams: A Marriage Waiting to Happen

The Commission of Conservation was established in response to a growing concern about the rapid destruction of natural resources in Canada. It sought to promote scientific management principles for the conservation and economic development of natural resources. Before the arrival of Thomas Adams, Dr. Charles Hodgett, the commission's chief medical officer, along with G. Frank Beer and Colonel Jeffrey H. Burland, was the leading authority in Canadian planning. Aware of the rapid decay of the urban environment, a lobby campaigned for the appointment of a planning expert. To this end, Adams was appointed town planning adviser to the federal government in 1914 following three requests from Prime Minister Robert Borden. The British government simply could not spare Adams until that time. Adams was given a three-year contract, and he took on the new challenge in stride.

By early 1915, Adams had visited all the Canadian provinces except for Prince Edward Island. His aim was to establish planning as a central function of governments at all levels and to base it on an integrated structure of legislation, administration, public support, and professional organization, education, and expertise. Around the same time, he founded the commission's journal, *Town Planning and the Conservation of Life,* and advised many municipalities on planning problems, often through the Civic Improvement League. By 1918, five provinces had adopted new planning legislation. Early planning legislation was tame in comparison to the legislation of today because planning was usually limited to the urban fringe, not developed areas. Adams, inspired by his desire to make planning an academic discipline and his belief that little was known about Canada's environmental problems, also designed several projects. In his case study of Ottawa, he surveyed housing issues in the urban environment. He then undertook an investigation of attitudes towards urban planning and development by circulating a questionnaire in over two hundred towns. As he worked on these projects, he was also writing *Rural Planning and Development,* his first major work and possibly his most notable contribution to Canadian planning.

In 1916, Adams unveiled the first draft of an Act to ensure that new development would be regulated, that public monies would be spent in the best possible way, and, finally, that conditions in urban communities would not cause unnecessary impairment of health or loss of life. Executive responsibilities would be placed in the hands of a professional town planning surveyor, and planning would be made mandatory. Towns would adopt long-term planning schemes, while rural areas would adopt the simpler method of bylaws. His plan was criticized. Critics claimed it lacked imagination and was far too complex. The Act, therefore, was not adopted on a large scale. Adams' 1919 campaign for provincial planning legislation also had little success and came to a halt. Critics said that the legislation could not be adapted to the needs of Canada and that the British town planning scheme was not suitable for the North American context. Many provinces adopted American-style legislation, which was simpler and allowed municipalities to have comprehensive control over planning and zoning.

As a private practitioner, Adams was appointed as a consultant on a number of new Canadian communities, including Temiscaming in western Quebec, Corner Brook in Newfoundland, and the Richmond District of Halifax, which had been devastated by an explosion in the harbour in 1917. From 1922 to 1936, Welland,

Kitchener, and London each hired Adams as their town planning consultant. Kitchener's plan was the first to become law in Ontario. Adams also designed Lindenlea in Ottawa in response to demands for low-cost housing suburbs after 1918. In this case, his progressive plan was not followed, and the project was taken over by others. Although the project was completed, it never housed its target population.

The Town Planning Institute of Canada

In 1919, a group of land surveyors and engineers combined their efforts with those of Adams to create the first professional planning institute, the Town Planning Institute of Canada. This group included Noulan Cauchon, Horace Seymour, A.S. Dalzell, and James Ewing, all of whom Adams had worked with previously. The institute had fifty two members, and Adams became its first elected president, serving two terms. Members included engineers, surveyors, architects, and landscape architects.

Leaving Canada, 1920-30

In the postwar era, growth was interrupted and planning seemed irrelevant. The major preoccupations of the profession became zoning and town and highway design, and recessions and government conservatism had a detrimental effect on Adams' work. The expiration of the Civic Improvement League and the pro gressive recommendations of *Rural Planning and Development* went unnoticed. In January 1921, the Commission of Conservation was dissolved because of policy conflicts between levels of government and intra-government jealousies. Adams' influence was reduced further when the Town Planning Branch of the Commission of Conservation was transferred to the National Parks Division of the Department of the Interior. Adams, however, was appointed town planning adviser for the Town Planning Branch.

Following these events, Adams' involvement in Canadian planning issues became increasingly distant. In February 1920, Adams accepted a part-time position as chief consultant on planning for a new firm in the United States, American City Consultants. He also lectured part-time at MIT and went on to play a leading role in the establishment of US planning education. In July 1923, his contract as the town planning consultant to the Canadian government ended. In September, he was appointed chief consultant to the Committee on the Regional Plan of New York and Its Environs. Six years later, he retired after com-pleting the plan's ten volumes. At that time, he had a staff of 150 and a budget of one million dollars, a considerable amount at the time. He then went on to become associate professor of research in city planning at Harvard University.

During this period, he wrote four books: *Neighborhoods of Small Homes: Economic Density of Low-Cost Housing in America* (1931); *Recent Advances in Town Planning* (1932); *Design of Residential Areas: Basic Considerations, Principles and Methods* (1934); and *Outline of Town and City Planning: A Review of Past Efforts and Modern Aims* (1935).

Throughout his career, Adams proved to be a pioneer in modern planning. On 24 March 1940, after a lifetime of dedication to the field, he passed away in Sussex, England, after a short illness. His professional experience in Britain, Canada, and the United States included significant disappointments, but perhaps they added to the realism and urgent practicality of his writings.

THE PLANNING OF YESTERDAY, TODAY

Although *Rural Planning and Development* was written for a different age, the issues that Adams identifies in it resonate with our own times. Adams spent a great deal of effort attempting to formalize the planning profession in Canada, and we now bear the benefits of his exertions. It is now recognized that planning has its own approaches, tools, and methods. Although planning may focus on land use issues, planners also concern themselves with the local economy, labour and employment, demographics, resource management, and environmental protection (see Figure 1). They adapt to and capitalize on parallel processes, relying on community initiatives as much as on legislated processes in the implementation of their initiatives. In sum, rural planning is the process of planning for rural areas, with a focus on rural issues and from a rural perspective (implying an appreciation for the rural community, its needs and aspirations) (Caldwell 2005).

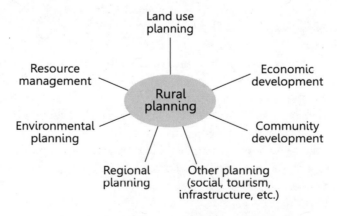

FIGURE 1   COMPONENTS OF RURAL PLANNING

Adams advises as much in *Rural Planning and Development*. Although his omission of public participation in the planning process is sometimes identified as a key difference between planning then and now, Adams does recommend comprehensive social surveys as a prerequisite to local planning (page 344). Although today's methods of eliciting community participation are not discussed explicitly in Adams' writing, it is evident that Adams was moving in that very direction with his conclusions on process and good planning. Along with his call for an integration of effort among different levels of government in planning initiatives, Adams' writing attempts to pre-empt the bureaucratization of comprehensive planning that came later.

As the designer, in the 1920s, of New York's first regional plan, Adams recognized the benefits of comprehensive planning, but he only did so in a manner that could be tolerated by residents. While Adams was open to a diversity of approaches and strategies, he was also sensitive to community aspirations with an appreciation for what the community would accept.

Adams' exploration of local character as a key to local planning solutions has been institutionalized over time, particularly in the rural context, where staying within budgetary or profitability limits can be more difficult than in the urban context. Farmers in the Okanagan Valley, for instance, face different issues than those in the Fraser Valley – the diversity of rural Canada has forced us to heed Adams' insistence on social and economic surveys in the search for realistic solutions.

Adams was also concerned about reactive government policies and public initiatives to stem urbanization. In *Rural Planning and Development,* he extensively acknowledges the challenges of rural living, the illusory ease of urban living, and the need for planners to maintain the rural-urban balance by planning rural communities that offer the same promises as their urban counterparts. The 29 November 2004 issue of *Maclean's,* which featured an article on the war between town and country, illustrates the continued currency of this issue. Canada has continued to transform from a rural to an urban country, and this shift has often meant a loss of political clout for rural communities, migrating youth, an aging population, the paving over of farmland for suburbs, and ongoing competition within urban Canada for increasingly limited resources.

Although Adams identified rural issues and outlined solutions, thoughtful and deliberate planning interventions are quite recent. There were efforts in the 1930s to respond to challenges on the farm through the Prairie Farm Rehabilitation Act, but a broader community-based focus on planning was much later in coming. Following the Second World War, the rejuvenated planning profession turned its attention to urban issues, which, in the postwar decades of rapid economic growth and relative urban prosperity, proved to be more pressing. Regional planning focused on urban regions and the debate about metropolitan management

(Hodge and Robinson 2002). This focus in turn led to questions and concerns regarding the role of the so-called rural. The Agricultural Rehabilitation and Development Act (1961) created a framework for focusing on rural issues, and within fifteen years of the publication of Ralph Krueger's seminal study of Ontario's tender fruit lands (1959), Canadian planners had developed a distinct rural perspective. The 1961 legislation was followed by the Canada Land Inventory, which also facilitated this shift in perspective by cataloguing the location and quality of agricultural lands (Crerar 1963). In the early 1970s, provincial and municipal governments increasingly focused on planning for rural areas. David Douglas (1989) notes that agriculture resurfaced as the primary rural issue in the British Columbia Land Commission (1973), in the passage in Quebec of the Act to Preserve Agricultural Land (1978), and in the Ontario Foodland Guidelines (1978). Countryside planning in Ontario proved to be influential throughout the country (MacLaren 1975). All of these studies addressed planning issues related to an increasingly industrial agricultural sector (Troughton 1982). By the mid to late 1970s, effective municipal rural planning systems existed in areas such as the County of Kings, Nova Scotia, and Huron County and Waterloo Region in Ontario.

In many respects, urbanization and suburbanization, scattered rural development, economic decline, environmental degradation, and the relationship between primary industries and their host communities drove the rural planning agenda for the next four decades. Successful rural planning responded to these issues. British Columbia's Agricultural Land Reserve program, for example, stemmed the conversion of farmland for non-agricultural uses (Smith and Haid 2004). Quebec developed an Act to Protect Agricultural Land (Bryant 1994) and, in Ontario, some agriculturally based municipalities eliminated new, scattered, rural development (Caldwell, Weir, and Thomson 2003). However, challenges remain. Although Canadian cities have achieved relatively high densities (Condon 2004), the issue of sprawl and the related loss of farmland still exist. Recent initiatives, including Greenbelt legislation, attempt to respond to these trends.

Is rural planning constantly struggling to find its niche? Why is it that after a century of planning efforts, planners continue to face the same problems? Adams' professional experience caused him to recognize the conflictual nature of planning and the need for a focused dedication to principles. In his words, "there can be no simple and ready solution of the complicated social questions dealt with in this report, and it is equally obvious that the adoption of the most perfect system of planning and developing land will not do more than provide the right foundation on which to build a solution by a slow and gradual process" (page 339). In the closing chapter of *Rural Planning and Development,* Adams sets out an agenda that continues to represent the focus of today's rural planners (page 340). Although advancements have been made since his time – particularly in the investigation of rural issues, the adoption of planning legislation, and the formalization of planning processes – the rest of the world has not waited for the planning world to implement its collective plan. As a result, the intensification of pressures has forced rural planners to constantly experiment with new strategies and to assess old tactics for their continued relevance. Given the pace of progress, it can be expected that some of today's challenges will burden the planners of the next century. And, as Adams' example shows, it is the policy of today that will prevent or ameliorate the issues of tomorrow. Again, this should not deter us from the accomplishments of *Rural Planning and Development*. Thomas Adams might have been one of the catalysts of the movement, but rural planners and those involved in rural planning but not formally of the profession also deserve credit. Rural planning in Canada has, however, continued to be a stew of challenges over the past decades.

From the Rural Planning District Commissions of New Brunswick to those who deal with the agricultural lands of Ontario and Alberta, there are planners dedicated to speaking about and addressing rural issues. As a profession, however, planners have devoted inadequate attention to rural matters. For example, a keyword search of articles in *Plan Canada* (1978-2008) yields 64 "rural" and 860 "urban" articles. Canadian planning texts make limited reference to rural or agricultural issues, yet approximately 20 percent of the country's population and more than 99 percent of the country's land is rural and remote. Thus, while a rural focus does exist in planning, it does not command a sufficient degree of attention.

One of the successes of rural planning has been a willingness to tackle diverse issues. Yet much of rural Canada remains susceptible to broad global and market trends that threaten community stability. Although the interest is there, rural planners lack the influence needed to guarantee the maintenance of rural qualities of life. Provincial governments also struggle with this issue. In Quebec, for example, the National Policy on Rurality was developed in 2006 to establish conditions conducive to ensuring that Quebec's rural areas develop and thrive.

Parts of Canada have made progress in recognizing the role of agriculture and acting to protect it. British Columbia took strong action nearly thirty years ago and continues to see dividends. Alberta is grappling with this issue. Ontario passed the Greenbelt Act in 2005 and a revised planning policy statement. Many farmers recognize that preventing scattered rural development serves the interest of agriculture. Complementary urban planning successes contribute to higher densities that, in turn, protect farmland.

Across Canada, specialized tools, techniques, and policies are used to plan for the countryside. Scattered residential development is generally discouraged. Legislation regulates land use issues associated with livestock production. Recreational and extractive uses can be accommodated. In Ontario, laws protect sensitive rural areas, including the Niagara Escarpment and the Oak Ridges Moraine. Although conflict continues, planners have attempted to use preventative and consultative strategies to facilitate decision making.

Many small towns and villages struggle with a changing economy. Although main street and heritage programs help, the decline in population and economic strength of small communities continues. Moreover, the desire for development sometimes leads to a lowering of community standards in the hope of attracting investment.

In a country as diverse as Canada, some communities have limited capacity and desire to pursue comprehensive planning. While some do not perceive a need for planning and others are reluctant to see an enhanced role for government, a wider range of communities could benefit from rural planning.

We know that most Canadians, given the option, would choose to have dynamic, healthy, and sustainable rural communities. Much as Adams did several generations ago, it is now our professional obligation to guide our surroundings toward that goal. After all, from the planners that followed Adams, we have inherited the tools and policies that make this an achievable objective; in cases where they are wanting, we have the processes in place to refocus or change them entirely.

PLANNING FOR TOMORROW

Today, there are more than eight thousand professional planners in Canada and millions of citizens who are engaged in the planning process in one way or another. In fact, everyone in the country, whether they are insulated in a condominium in the heart of our largest cities or travelling on roads in the most remote communities, have been influenced and affected by numerous planning decisions. Our transportation systems, our development standards, and, increasingly, the holistic planning of our communities (in accordance with Adams' thinking) affect how we move, live, and, ideally, thrive in our environments. Although there may not be direct linkages between all of Adams' conclusions and the planning challenges of today, Adams' critical method of investigation, recognition of (but not resignation to) realities, and openness to local perspectives all serve as excellent principles for planners to emulate.

Adams' *Rural Planning and Development* is unequivocally a milestone in Canadian planning for three reasons. First, it provides insight into rural planning a century ago. It has thus become valuable for its historical information. Adams provides us with a detailed overview of conditions in rural Canada at the turn of the last century. He draws upon census information and numerous case studies and examples from the United States, England, Australia, and elsewhere. He was witness to the development, speculation, and intolerable living and working conditions prevalent throughout rural and urban Canada, and he outspokenly condemned the trends.

Second, Adams' book provides a broad-based vision for planning. Although his work has a decidedly land use and development bias, Adams recognizes the relationship between planning and the broader connections with health, culture, education, and employment. In fact, an argument can be made that Adams offers a comprehensive vision of planning that, at times, has been lacking for the past one hundred years.

Third, the book provides an objective and rational scientific vision for planning practice. Adams' focus on numbers, standards, and statistics clearly promulgated the value that planning could bring to society. He understood the political realities of planning and how to navigate government institutions and processes to achieve success. In this context, Adams sowed the seeds for planners and the planning profession, as it is known today.

Rural Planning and Development is an important book for all Canadian planners and students of planning. It provides historical context for our profession. It provides a formative, and still relevant, vision of what planning can be. And, through understanding Adams' personal experiences, it demonstrates that planning, whether rural or urban, requires hard work and individual initiative to be successful. Planners cannot afford to simply guard and maintain the processes and policies of the past; they must strive to improve the quality of life in the communities where they operate. In today's evolving, complex society, where communities struggle to achieve "sustainability," planners must, ultimately, be courageous enough to provide leadership.

THIS BOOK

This book includes the complete text of *Rural Planning and Development*, including appendices, diagrams, and photos. None of the original work has been modified or changed in any way. Modern reflections or commentaries, however, follow each chapter.

These reflections are by leading academics and practitioners from across the country who provide their perspectives on Adams' work and the role he played in shaping communities and professional practice in Canada. The commentaries also update each chapter by reflecting on the context and, in some cases, the relevance of its conclusions in the twenty-first century. Adams' place in the history of the profession is evident in the enthusiasm that each author brings to the project.

Although each contributor offers a different perspective on Adams' influence, they all acknowledge that Adams was a product of his times, the First World War era, and heavily influenced by his background in the United Kingdom. They also recognize the thoroughness of his work and his perceptive understanding of rural conditions at the turn of the twentieth century.

Jeanne Wolfe, who passed away in 2009, in her commentary on Chapter I, notes both Adams' on-going relevance and the historical context of his work. She outlines Adams' understanding of the interplay between rural and urban conditions and shows that this interplay persists today. Her description of Adams' holistic view of planning – one that included not only prescriptive land use but also an acknowledgment of the need to address local opportunities for social development – reinforces its applicability in the intervening years.

Wolfe also notes some of Adams' deficiencies. His writings on European immigration to North America and the re-integration of returning soldiers may have less direct usefulness today. In a wider sense, however, international population movement has not been staunched in recent years, and the challenges of rapid growth and the accommodation of immigrants into economic and social life are still with us.

The late Michael Troughton of the University of Western Ontario discusses how Adams connected the lack of protection for rural issues to a focus on urban planning and the encroachment of urban land use. Troughton notes the necessity to protect rural lands and Adams' quest for rural sustainability. Both are relevant to today's rural planners.

Understanding the Canadian context in which Adams worked is also central to formulating a clear view of both the factors that drove Adams' conclusions and our modern dilemmas regarding rural and urban attention. Being able to cleave the conclusions in *Rural Planning and Development* from the outdated societal conditions in which they were formulated increases the applicability of its lessons for today.

Chapter III of Adams' text focuses on systems of surveying and planning land in rural areas. In reviewing the chapter, Hok-Lin Leung notes the legacy of these initial survey patterns in both rural and urban forms throughout Canada. He flags the resulting contradiction between this man-made system and the "natural order" because of its implications for today's settlement patterns.

In Chapter IV, Ian Wight reflects on Adams' discussion of rural transportation and distribution, both within Canada and beyond. Wight supports Adams' promotion of comprehensive planning, although he acknowledges that the omission of public participation in Adams' writings would not be in line with today's practice. He concludes by recognizing the rational nature of Adams' planning and questioning. Wight also speculates on how Adams himself would operate as a planner in today's environment of increasingly qualitative approaches.

The late Len Gertler reflects on land speculation, assessment, and development in Chapter V, "Rural Problems that Arise in Connection with Land Development." Adams' cautions regarding land speculation and its ties to real property value and development incentives are very real today in both rural and urban areas, especially on the heels of the recent housing boom. Adams' warnings about subdivision and rural land severance have gone largely unheeded, and we have now witnessed many of the consequences he warned against.

Tony Fuller examines Adams' agricultural concerns in Chapter VI. In this chapter, Adams emphasizes the role of capital and education in promoting activities in rural areas. There are parallels with the modern issue of rural credit in both the developed and developing worlds. Adams identifies types of rural industries, as well as issues regarding their incorporation into the greater community fabric. He uses the concept of distribution economy to help describe the challenges these industries face. Fuller also comments on Adams' promotion of co-operation among farmers, rural industries, and rural communities in general.

Chapter VII, "Government Policies and Land Development," delves into Adams' views on the realities planners face when they work through public administrations to accomplish their goals. Adams exposes the pressure that commercial interests can have on government decisions and the need for planners to maintain their professional stamina in the course of their work. The role that governments have in dictating planning is discussed by Jill Grant in her reflection on the chapter. She points out that Adams identified the repercussions of failing to achieve a balance between government and industry. He also discussed the role of infrastructure, primarily transportation networks, and the segments of society they promote. Grant perceptively observes that Adams' faith in scientific expertise reflected the philosophy of the progressive era, particularly its emphasis on the governments' role in achieving efficient and orderly development.

Chapter VIII, which addresses the reintegration of soldiers following the First World War, at first glance appears to be dated. In his reflections, however, John Devlin ties the issue of soldier settlement to settlement and migration in general, an issue that, in the rural-urban context, elicits as much concern today as soldier settlement did in Adams' time. At issue is the broad challenge of encouraging settlement in certain areas or certain patterns. Since overcrowding and sprawl remain problems, the details in this chapter maintain their relevance.

Adams addresses the need for planning legislation in Chapter IX. Gary Davidson notes that it was Adams' vision that set the tone for comprehensive planning legislation that covered both rural and urban areas. This was a new idea in Canada at the time, and it took time for the idea to come to fruition, even though Adams spent much effort planting the seeds in his work. Ever the pragmatist, he lays out a scheme in this chapter by which the legislation could be administered, updated, and enforced. Adams' instrumentalist, even ideological, view of planning is emphasized in Davidson's reflections. He argues that these ideas "started a planning process that has had significant negative impacts on rural communities." Although there is much to be praised in Adams' work, this critical observation is equally relevant to today's communities.

Chapter X summarizes Adams' recommendations, which I group into five themes. Government organization, or Adams' attempts to promote co-operation with and complement various levels of government on planning issues, is the first. Adams also reinforced the need for comprehensive survey during his work in Canada and beyond and, as Adams points out in Chapter IX, he believed formal legislation was critical to the sustainability and advancement of the planning profession. The need for settlements, both agricultural and industrial, free from artificial pressures, was an important pillar in Adams' rational approach. Lastly, the issue of social readjustment, in the context of returning soldiers, illustrates Adams' understanding of the many factors that need to be taken into consideration to establish a thriving community and, therefore, what constitutes good planning.

REFERENCES

Bryant, Christopher R. 1994. "Preserving Canada's Agricultural Land." *Plan Canada* (Special Edition), 4: 49-51.

Caldwell, Wayne J. 2005. "Rural Planning in Canada." *Plan Canada* 45, 3: 25-28.

Caldwell, Wayne J., Claire Weir, and Sarah Thomson. 2003. "Rural Non-Farm Development and the Future of Ontario Agriculture." *Ontario Planning Journal* 18, 6: 6-7.

Condon, Patrick. 2004. *Canadian Cities American Cities: Our Differences Are the Same.* http://www.jtc.sala.ubc.ca/.

Crerar, A.D. 1963. "The Loss of Farmland in the Metropolitan Regions of Canada." In *Regional and Resource Planning in Canada,* ed. Ralph R. Krueger, Frederic O. Sargent, Anthony De Vos, and Norman Pearson, 126-33. Toronto: Holt, Reinhart and Winston.

Douglas, David. 1989. "Note from the Guest Editor." *Plan Canada* 29, 2: 3-7.

Hodge, Gerald, and Ira M. Robinson. 2002. *Planning Canadian Regions.* Vancouver: UBC Press.

Krueger, R.R. 1959. "Changing Land-Use Patterns in the Niagara Fruit Belt." *Transactions of the Royal Canadian Institute* 32, Part 2, 67: 39-140.

MacLaren, J.F. 1975. *Countryside Planning: A Methodology and Policies for Huron County and the Province of Ontario.* Toronto: MacLaren Limited.

Maclean's. 2004. "The War between Town and Country." 29 November.

Quebec. 2006. *National Policy on Rurality, 2007-14: A Source of Strength for Quebec.* Quebec City: Government of Quebec.

Simpson, Michael. 1985. *Thomas Adams and the Modern Planning Movement: Britain, Canada and the United States.* London: Mansell Publishing.

Smith, Barry, and Susan Haid. 2004. "The Rural-Urban Connection: Growing Together in Greater Vancouver." *Plan Canada* 44, 1: 36-39.

Troughton, Michael J. 1982. "Process and Response in the Industrialization of Agriculture." In *The Effect of Modern Agriculture on Rural Development,* ed. G. Enyedi and I. Volgyes, 213-27. New York: Pergamon Press.

RURAL PLANNING AND DEVELOPMENT

A Study of Rural Conditions and Problems in Canada

BY

THOMAS ADAMS

———

WITH COMMENTARIES

PLATE I   VIEW OF RICHMOND, EASTERN TOWNSHIPS, QUEBEC

Where nature and the art of man combine to make the perfect blend of country and town.

Photo by courtesy of the Immigration Branch, Dept. of Interior

CHAPTER I

Introductory

Old problems and a new perspective | Social problems that need emphasis | Conservation and development | Readjustment after the war | Kind of results to be aimed at | Necessity for planning for the purpose of proper development | British and Canadian conditions | Land settlement in Canada | The object of production

---

OLD PROBLEMS AND A NEW PERSPECTIVE

AFTER the great war, European nations will need restoration and reconstruction, but Canada will need conservation and development. There never was a greater opportunity for wise statesmanship – for the exercise of prescience and sound judgment by the men who lead in national affairs.

The period of pioneer achievement is not over in Canada, but it has entered upon a new phase, mainly because we see things in a different light after the crowded experience of recent years. We recognize that, in the future, science and clean government must march side by side with enterprise and energy in building up national and individual prosperity. The problems we have to solve are old but our perspective is new.

We are at the opening of a new era of social construction and national expansion, and the question is not whether we will grow but how we will grow. The mistakes of the past must be ignored, except as a guide for the future. On some things, it is possible, we have spent too much of our wealth as a nation, and on other things we have spent too little. Those things on which we have spent too much are easy to criticize, because we see them and can count the cost; those things on which we have spent too little may have caused greater losses, but they are not so apparent. Economic loss may be greater as a result of leaving some things undone than as a result of doing other things extravagantly. It is not certain that we would have gained by being less spendthrift in some directions, for it does not follow that we would have been more enterprising in others.

The war, and a combination of circumstances surrounding it, has brought new ideas to our minds, and none more vividly than this – that

3

the strength of a nation depends neither on the physical, intellectual and moral character of its citizens, nor on the stability and freedom of its institutions, nor on the efficiency of its organization, but on the existence of all of these things.

We share the growing consciousness, which is everywhere apparent, that national prosperity depends on the character, stability, freedom and efficiency of the human resources of a nation, rather than on the amount of its exports or imports, or the gold it may have to its credit at a given time.* For lack of that consciousness in the past we have placed the sanctity of property on a higher level than human life and civic welfare. In that matter democratic nations are not the least blameworthy, for they are prone to exalt individual liberty above social justice, and to treat liberty as an end in itself, instead of as a means to attain the end of equal opportunity for all its citizens.†

The self-styled practical man, who has lacked ideals and vision in his outlook on life – and prided himself on the fact – has been perhaps the most potent factor in building up the organization and system in peace which has in part caused this war and been discredited by this war. Today the same man is claiming that the loss of material wealth in the war will be small as compared with the strength of soul we will gain as a result. Whatever be the truth as regards the claim, we have the important fact that the "man in the street" and the "man in the trench" have undergone a change of attitude that will have its effect in profoundly altering the course of history in the next generation. It is certain that that change will result in demands for more justice in our human relations, more efficient organization, more scientific training and higher ethical standards in public affairs, than have hitherto prevailed. We have indications that the tendency of governing bodies in Canada is to give a lead to human activity along these lines, and we may be sure that, in so far as

---

* While the conservation of natural resources and the promotion of industries are important and the development of trade has possibilities of benefit, the conservation of life and ability in the individual workers is supreme. Next to that comes the provision of conservation of opportunity for satisfactory employment. — *Report of Royal Commission on Industrial Training and Technical Education.*

† There is nothing more fatal to a people than that it should narrow its Vision to the material needs of the hour. National ideals without imagination are but as the thistles of the wilderness, fit neither for food nor fuel. A nation that depends upon them must perish. We shall need, at the end of the war, better workshops, but we shall also need more than ever every institution that will exalt the vision of the people above and beyond the workshop and the counting-house. We shall need every national tradition that will remind them that men cannot live by bread alone. — *The Right Hon. Lloyd George.*

government policies fail to recognize the growing sentiment in favour of scientific methods, as opposed to the haphazard methods of the past, they will fail in result.

RURAL PROBLEMS THAT NEED EMPHASIS

Broadly speaking, we require to lay emphasis on the following needs as a means of conserving human and natural resources in connection with any policy inaugurated in the future:

(1) The planning and development of land by methods which will secure health, amenity, convenience and efficiency, and the rejection of those methods that lead to injurious speculation.

(2) The promotion of scientific training, improved educational facilities and means of social intercourse.

(3) The establishment of an efficient government organization and improved facilities for securing co-operation, rural credit, and development of rural industries.

We have to deal primarily with the first of these needs, and only incidentally and partially with the other two – but all of them are interdependent and cannot be separated in any sound scheme for improving rural conditions.

CONSERVATION AND DEVELOPMENT

It is perhaps necessary to explain briefly why such matters, as are dealt with in this report, are regarded as problems of conservation. Briefly, the answer may be given that the land question, and all questions of conservation of natural resources, are fundamental questions, because they have to do with life. "The final aim of all effort, whether individual or social, is life itself, its preservation and increase in quantity or quality or both."* We have to ask ourselves whether the rural policy in Canada in the past has had conservation and development of life as its final aim. Conservation means economy and development at the same time. To conserve the forests means to prevent waste – for without that prevention there cannot be economy – and, simultaneously, to develop new growth. To conserve land resources means to prevent deterioration of the productive uses of the land that has already been equipped and

---

* *The Land and the People. — Times Series.*

improved, and simultaneously to develop more intensive use of such land, as well as to open up and improve new lands. To conserve human resources means to increase the quantity and quality of human activity that can be applied to production; to lessen social evils and injury to health under established conditions – a matter of economy – and simultaneously to develop conditions in the future which will remove the causes of such evils, a matter of still greater economy. Hence to conserve human and natural resources means not only to prevent waste in what we have but also to plan and develop for future growth. Considered in that sense nearly every social problem in Canada is a problem of conservation.

Out of the total area of 2,306,502,153 acres of land in Canada, it is computed that 358,162,190 acres of land are capable of being used for productive purposes.* The population of the Dominion in 1911 was 7,206,643, or 1.9 persons to each square mile of territory. We have 35,582 miles of railway, or about one mile to every 200 persons, providing means of distribution by railway in advance of the needs of commerce. The natural resources may be said to be unlimited in extent, subject to proper conservation and development; and the means of distribution by main railways may be regarded as capable of no limitation in meeting demands for many years to come. But, while there is practically an unlimited quantity of natural resources, and of railways to distribute them, we are limited in the economic use to which we can put them. *Wealth is produced not from the existence of natural resources but from the conversion of these resources into some form for human use. Canada is seriously limited in actual resources by the extent to which it lacks sufficient population to apply the human activity necessary to adequately use and distribute its resources. Hence there is nothing so vital in the interests of production in Canada as to conserve and develop human life – not merely to conserve the physical qualities, but also to develop the intellectual qualities.*

We have, perhaps, made the error that all that matters as regards population is increase in quantity. But productivity depends on quality as well as on quantity of human material – on intelligence and organization as well as on physique. If, by increase of population, we can secure a higher level of prosperity per capita we should strive for that increase; if a lower level of prosperity we should strive against it. History shows that it is possible for a population to grow in a country of ample resources and yet to diminish in productivity and prosperity as it grows. With improved methods and organization, the average level of prosperity in Ireland is probably greater today than ever in its history, notwithstanding

---

* *Census for 1911,* Vol. IV, p. 7.

its depleted population. Notwithstanding the withdrawal of a large proportion of the productive workers of Great Britain from peaceful industries during the past three years, the volume of exports from that country appears to have greatly increased during that period.* Conservation of life, so far as it implies the development of the qualities of efficiency and of the capacity to make the best economic use of the resources on the part of the people, counts most largely in increasing production. There was a period in the history of England when improved methods alone resulted in enormously developing natural resources. According to the census of 1851, the intelligence and capital devoted to the improvement of landed estates and farm stock, the formation of agricultural societies, the adoption of new processes, the drainage of marshes, the introduction of machinery, etc., and the impulse given to agricultural science in the middle of the 19th century, caused a great increase in production and population.

Whether such improvements are a cause or an effect of increase in population, the country benefits, but when an increase takes place without improvements and without proper development and organization, the increase may be injurious. Even on the basis of its present population, if Canada could retain its natural increase and properly safeguard the health of its citizens, and if it could develop its educational system and keep at home those whom it educated, it would soon enormously increase in wealth.

But do we, as a nation, pay sufficient regard to the value of promoting healthy living conditions, developing skill and conserving our educational resources? Are the rural and urban conditions of Canada such as to provide the most ample protection possible of the most valuable asset of the country – healthy and active human life? In face of the fact that labour is so limited in proportion to the natural resources at its command, is the organization of labour and of the means of production capable of improvement? Is the system of planning and developing land, and of utilizing science and expert knowledge, such as to secure the greatest industrial efficiency, and the fullest opportunity for obtaining healthy conditions, amenity, and convenience for the inhabitants? We need a national stocktaking to enable adequate answers to be given to these

---

* With millions of men called to the colours, British exports in 1916 were valued at 507 millions, as compared with 525 millions in 1913, the last full year of peace. It is true that values have risen enormously and that the figures of 1918 do not represent anything like the same quantity of goods. But the' new figures do not include the huge quantities of supplies sent wherever the British army is fighting. On the balance we have probably produced more goods than in the last year of peace. — *Westminster Gazette,* January 8, 1917.

questions, but sufficient is known to justify the attempt which is made in this report to deal with them in a preliminary way.

RE-ADJUSTMENT AFTER THE WAR

In addition to the question of conservation as a permanent problem, we have the transitory problems of re-adjustment and reorganization that will have to be faced in Canada at the close of the war. In Europe, these problems are only less important and grave than those of the war itself; in Canada they can be made of secondary importance if we proceed at once to work out a constructive policy of rural and urban development. We will have new questions to deal with, like that of reinstating the returned soldiers into the social and industrial life of the community and providing for the maimed. We will also have old questions which are the outcome of the defective organization and unhealthy speculation that existed before the war, questions which, to a large extent, have been saved from coming to a head by reason of the activities and public expenditures caused by the war itself. In the war we have been made to see that even military strength must rest, in the final analysis, on a strong civil and economic foundation; how much more then must this be the case with industrial strength. A comparatively small number – 7 per cent – of our citizens are likely to be engaged in the direct work of warfare. The able bodied citizens among the other 93 per cent are assisting the nation in proportion as they are engaged in the task of production, or in that of preparation and organization for times of peace, or in providing healthy living conditions and education for the young who will form the source of human activity for the future. During the war, and after, a great majority of the citizens of the country must continue to live in their well-administered or mal-administered towns, villages, and rural districts; must pursue their daily tasks; must worship their domestic gods in their palaces or slums; must see their children grow in strength or in weakness, and must continue to look into the future in hope or in despair. And the country will grow in wealth and prosperity in proportion as the human activities of the great body of the citizens are conserved and properly directed.

KIND OF RESULTS TO BE AIMED AT

In Canada we seem to have suffered, not so much from lack of organization as from lack of scientific methods applied to organization as a means of making the most of our limited human activities. The necessarily crude methods of the pioneer stage of development and civilization still prevail in many phases of government. Getting results still counts more with some men than getting the right results in the most efficient and economic way. We lay out towns and townships, construct buildings, roads and bridges, and colonize land without proper development schemes, on the theory that getting things done quickly is more important than getting things done efficiently and well. This theory of going blindly for results, on the principle of "hustling," is the refuge of the unscientific and unimaginative mind that is impatient of expert advice or plans, because they are presumed to waste time in preparation which ought to be given to constructive work.

NECESSITY FOR PLANNING FOR PURPOSES OF PROPER DEVELOPMENT

Yet, of all the constructive work that is done in peace or war, there is none that counts more in obtaining good results than the planning and preparation that goes before the actual performance. To those who hold fast to the theories that nothing is practical that has not been tried by experience, that immediately tangible results must be obtained whatever the outcome, that preliminary financial success must be secured whatever the ultimate effect, it is possible that many of the lessons of recent years will be lost, and that sound schemes will be dismissed as visionary and impracticable. It is hoped that the theories advanced and the suggestions made in this report are both visionary and practicable, for there is no greater heresy than that which regards these two elements as necessarily opposed to one another. It is true statesmanship to look into the future and plan for the future in the light of experience gained from the past, and there are signs that Canada is not lacking in that statesmanship, and that suggestions which are put forward to improve conditions will not be despised because they involve the exercise of some imagination. The main consideration to be borne in mind in this regard is that the planning of territory shall not be an end in itself, but only a means by which the end is to be achieved. That end shall be the proper development of land for the purpose of securing the best results from the application of human activity to natural resources.

BRITISH AND CANADIAN CONDITIONS

Broadly speaking, the land question is at the root of all social problems, both in rural and in urban territory. It is so in Great Britain, and it is so in Canada. In a recent article T. P. O'Connor, M.P., writing of the present situation in England, describes the probable change of outlook which will occur after the war in regard to the land question. He sums up the situation by saying that they have in England the evidences of a "land revolution as already an effect of the war." He quotes Lord Northcliffe as a witness to what he calls the dawn of a new era, as follows:

> *Tommy Wants His Land.* – In one of the chapters he (Lord Northcliffe) uses these remarkable words, talking of the conversation he had with the Tommies. The speaker in this instance had been a gamekeeper and a Tory when he was in civil life; but this is what he said:
>
> "The men in the dugouts talk of a good many subjects, but there is one on which they are all agreed. That is the land question. They are not going back as labourers, or as tenants, but as owners. Lots of them have used their eyes and learned much about small farming here."
>
> And this is what another Tommy said:
>
> "Many will go to Canada, some to Australia, I dare say; but I am one of those who mean to have a little bit of 'blighty' for myself. We see enough in France to know that a man and his family can manage a bit of land for themselves and live well on it."

The remarkable effects of the system of peasant proprietorship in France, which had impressed this "Tommy," are referred to in a later chapter, which goes to show that the success of that system is due as much to the rural industries and social opportunities in the rural districts of France as to the fact of ownership. It is possible that "Tommy" ascribed to mere ownership advantages which did not belong to it, although they accompany it. Ownership can be obtained in Canada as well as in France, but, in this country of wide spaces, and with the markets and social facilities so far distant from the farmer, more than mere ownership is needed. If a successful system of peasant ownership is set up in Britain after the war, and all signs point to this being achieved, the chances of securing British immigrants to Canada will lessen in proportion as Canada does not seek to provide facilities for proper planning, for co-operation, for marketing, and social intercourse.

In Great Britain the mistake which has been made in the past has been that the user of the land has not been sufficiently encouraged to own it or to improve it; he has lacked security of tenure and scope to make the most of his own improvements. We have drawn large numbers of British farmers and labourers to Canada by offering free homesteads, and this has, till recently, persuaded many to migrate to this country who were attracted by getting something which was not available at home. But in course of time the farmer has recognized that ownership is not everything, and that he has only exchanged a condition of one form of servitude for another.

Improved land in Great Britain can be rented at a sum which represents nothing more than a reasonable interest on the cost of improvements made by the owner. The writer has had personal experience in Scotland as a farmer, and spent ten years managing, inspecting and valuing rural land in England on behalf of large owners and purchasers. In 1908 he surveyed the rural conditions of three counties for the Board of Agriculture. That experience proved that bare agricultural land frequently produced no revenue to the owner. Apart, therefore, from the "magic of property," which, it is agreed, has a great value, farms can be had as cheaply in Britain as in Canada.

The British landowner has recognized that he can only keep his tenants by helping them to obtain good roads, social opportunities and cheap money, and by encouraging co-operation and improving the methods of husbandry. Moreover, he has acted as a partner with the farmer, in keeping up the productive quality of the soil by requiring proper crop rotation, in getting facilities for cheap transportation, and in obtaining government assistance to keep up a high quality of stock. In areas available for new settlers, the Canadian farmer gets ownership, but he loses other advantages which he regarded too cheaply while he had them. To make farm settlement in this country successful, therefore, we must not only give opportunities to obtain ownership, but the facilities and social conditions which go with tenancy in other countries. Thus, ownership will become an addition to the attractions which are available in these other countries, and not, as at present, an alternative.

It is as important to Great Britain as it is to Canada that more men and women of British blood, and possessing the ideals and courage of British citizens, should be attracted to Canada at the close of the war. It is important to Britain because her outlook in regard to food supply, and in regard to other matters connected with the future destiny of the British Empire, cannot be circumscribed within the narrow limits of the British Isles. Whatever Great Britain may do to improve agricultural development and to make herself more independent of foreign supplies of food it is only in a limited degree that she can artificially promote and carry out that improvement; and owing to the limited area of her land resources she must look more and more to her overseas Dominions for increased production.

It is in the direction of more intensive cultivation and more scientific production of dairy food, rather than an increased acreage of wheat, that there is most hope of building up agricultural development and a sound land policy in Britain, and for reducing importations from foreign countries without lessening demands on the overseas Dominions.

There can be no greater loyalty to Great Britain than that of persuading her to send of her best to build up Greater Britain. In the past it is probably true that the British people have not done justice to Canada, and few of them know or appreciate what Canada stands for in the Empire. They have sent too few of their fittest and best educated citizens to help in building up this country. Surely when the war is over there must be a stronger and more united effort made, both by Britain and Canada, to look more on each other as integral parts of a great whole, in which no part can benefit to the injury of the other, and no part be injured to the benefit of the other. All parts of the Empire must unite in a scheme of things in which there will be co-operation with independence; in which there will be a blending of ideals and ideas, and an interchange of citizenship. Why should there not be a greater interchange of population between Canada and Great Britain? Why should the university trained men of both countries not come and go and find a welcome in their diversified fields of labour? Perhaps Britain has revealed in connection with the war a strength and a power which Canadians who have never closely studied her institutions and her social conditions, scarcely realized as possible. Perhaps Canada has revealed resources and potency little dreamt of in Britain. Britain has had a great quality of keeping her most skilled and able men at home, and those who have gone abroad have not always done her justice, but in the future the maintenance of her strength will largely depend on spreading her talents into wider fields. On the other hand, there are men of great parts and resourcefulness in the Dominion who could find scope for their skill and energy in the Old Country. The splendidly organized means of transportation between Britain and Canada which existed before the war must be surpassed by greatly improved transportation in the future, and the linking up of the two peoples must be made more real and intimate. Canada needs the kind of human energy that Britain can give and which Britain will find it best to spare; and Britain needs the resources of the lands, the mines and the forests of which Canada has superabundance, when the labour is available to work them.

Whatever may be done in other belligerent countries to conserve population after the war, it seems as if the people of the British Empire will have to spread themselves over wider fields. But it must be done after careful thought and preparation is given to the scheme of distribution of human and material resources. Vigilance in preventing selfish exploitation of these resources, science in the system of planning and developing them for right use and, above all, conservation and development of the energy and intelligence of the people must underlie our imperial and social policies.

Land Settlement in Canada

The development of the land resources of Canada, and the skill and constructive ability which have been applied to the building up of the population and industries of the country during the past twenty years, combine to make one of the most remarkable achievements in the modern history of nations. The enormous increase in population and the settlement of the Western provinces between the years 1891 and 1914 were the result of a combination of circumstances, among which two of the most important were the development of the transportation system of the country and the skillful organization of the Canadian governments. This has to be recognized no matter to what extent it may now be found that the absence of proper planning and more scientific organization of settlement might have secured a greater measure of success in connection with the development that has taken place.

The defects in the system of land settlement in Canada have only become evident or at least pronounced in recent years. Even in the United States, where a similar system has been in operation for a much longer period of time, it is only lately that the people have begun to recognize the fact that a scientific plan of development prepared in advance of settlement is essential to enable a sound economic structure to be built up.

Whatever may be said as to the success of the system of land settlement in Canada up to a certain point, the time has come to abandon careless methods of placing people on the land without proper organization and careful planning. If the farmer is to be kept on the land he must have the kind of organization and facilities provided for him to enable him to make profitable use of the land.

In other words, the farmer requires a stronger tie than what is provided by the "magic of property" to keep him on the land. He requires the facilities and means to live as well as to exist; the enjoyment of better social conditions for his wife and family as well as for himself; the use of capital at a reasonable rate of interest, and the satisfaction that the facilities for distributing his products and for utilizing the natural resources of the country are not controlled to the disadvantage of his class. We have relied too much on the magnet of ownership to attract the labouring farmer to the soil of Canada and too little on the more enduring magnets of social amenities and efficient organization of the actual development of the land.

To keep the farmers on the land when they get there has become a greater problem than that of first attracting them to the land. They are said to be leaving the land in thousands at the present time, and we are told that millions of acres of land, which had been occupied at one time, are now deserted, and that the present system of land settlement is productive of much poverty and degradation.* Whether these statements are exaggerated or not, the fact that they are made by responsible people indicates a state of affairs that demands a remedy. Why do men now hesitate to go on the land in the first place, and find it uncongenial to stay in the second place? Why do women stay away, with the injurious consequences to rural life which is caused by their absence? The three outstanding reasons are:

First, the numerous ills caused by the holding of large areas of the best and most accessible land by speculators and the want of proper plans for the economic use and development of the land.

Second, the compelling social attractions and the educational facilities of the cities and towns, and,

Third, the lack of ready money and of adequate return for the labour of the farmer, because of want of co-operation, rural credit and of facilities for distribution of his products.

To secure any real improvement in rural life and conditions we must try to bring tracts of land held for speculative purposes into use, prepare development schemes of the land in advance of settlement, try to take part, at least, of the social and educational facilities of the cities into the rural areas, and, simultaneously, provide the co-operative financial and distributive conveniences that are necessary to give the farmer a larger share of the profits of production.

THE OBJECT OF PRODUCTION

But before embarking on any scheme of improvement, of our rural as well as of our urban conditions, we must have regard to the object we have in view in increasing production as well as the method by which we seek to attain the increase. We have, in the historic case of Germany, an instance of what appears to have been an efficient organization directed to the achievement of a bad object, with the result that forty years of wrongly directed effort in production have been largely wasted. Conservation and development under such conditions are worse than useless, for they are merely instruments in a scheme which has destruction as its ultimate aim; the aim of Germany or rather of its military party, being to destroy the development of other peoples at the risk of destroying

---

* Millions of acres of land homesteaded in Western Canada have been abandoned by men who failed as farmers. — *Farmers Advocate.*

its own. There is no danger in our democratic country of such a disaster as is befalling Germany, but the pursuit of material gain as a sole object is dangerous and futile, whether the aim be accretion of wealth or of military power. When the object of development in a state is to secure the greatest freedom and equality of opportunity for the greatest number of its citizens to enjoy the results of human labour, then the accumulation of wealth follows as a result of that freedom, and history shows that it is only on such a foundation that national prosperity can be maintained. But we must direct our policies and measures with that object and not our words only.

Freedom and equality of opportunity cannot be attained on the basis of what is sometimes misnamed individual liberty – the license for each citizen to do as he wills whether or no other citizens suffer from his actions. We recognize the principle of limiting individual liberty to do wrong in regard to certain moral issues but not so freely as we should in regard to matters affecting health and general welfare.

The needs of human life are social as well as individual or personal. The four primary human needs are food, clothing, shelter and social intercourse. All of these are essential to normal existence – although the length of time a human being can dispense with any one of them varies. In a civilized community provision for shelter is more distinctly a social than a personal need; the family being the unit corresponding to the dwelling rather than the individual citizen. Social intercourse is not always regarded as a necessity of human life, and yet no healthy and intelligent human being can do without it for any lengthy period.* If our object be to build up real national prosperity we have to see that our citizens have not only the bare necessities of food, clothing and shelter; but we must also direct the ends of government so as to secure that the shelter shall be healthy and that the desire for social intercourse, for recreation and education shall be gratified. It is after these needs are met that a progressive country obtains surplus wealth by the barter of its surplus production for things its citizens desire but cannot themselves produce. If we are only able to secure a surplus by withholding the necessities for well-being from our own people we shall lose more than we gain, in the end.

A community exists by reason of its industry in production whether the industry be agriculture or manufacture. That is the condition of its being.

---

* Marshall in *Economics of Industry* makes a distinction between "necessaries for existence" and "necessaries for efficiency," defining the latter as including good sanitary conditions, some education and recreation, etc. Social intercourse is in some degree necessary for existence and in a greater degree necessary for efficiency.

But in modern life it needs also healthy environment, efficient organization, convenience for distribution and social amenities. These are the conditions of its well-being. The aim of all government and all planning should be to promote, simultaneously, the being and the well-being of the community.

Particularly in our rural districts the conditions of well-being of the community have not been sufficiently respected in Canada – and until they are we shall lack in the essentials of real progress. Therefore, whatever scheme may be put forward to improve the methods of laying out and developing land, or to increase production, should have regard to these fundamental considerations.

CHAPTER I
INTRODUCTORY

Commentary by Jeanne M. Wolfe

Thomas Adams' introduction to *Rural Planning and Development* is strongly embedded in the time in which he wrote, the year 1917. The Great War had been raging for three years: by this time, it was felt that the tide was turning and that the end was in sight. Adams pitches his message toward a new, improved, and reconstructed future, one in which freedom, social justice, human well-being, equal opportunity, and civic welfare would necessarily prevail, arguing that "the loss of material wealth in the war will be small as compared with the strength of soul we will gain as a result" (page 4).

Part of this strength of soul would come from an acceptance of the ideas of the conservation movement, the conservation of human life and of natural resources, and the development of both in a scientific and productive manner. This focus on these ideas, of course, is an early definition of what today is referred to as the three-legged stool of sustainable development: the resolution of conflict between the needs of people, the environment, and the economy.

There is, however, one element in Adams' message that is different: in his time, conservation meant development. He believed the conservation of human resources and the natural environment would make economic development more efficient, equitable, and durable. The idea of nature for nature's sake simply did not enter into his argument. Furthermore, arguments in favour of nurturing biodiversity were not part of early nineteenth-century rhetoric.

When it comes to the careless and wasteful use of resources, Adams' text is, sadly, as pertinent today as it was when it was written. However, there are parts that do not resonate as well. First, his fierce insistence on encouraging British immigration to Canada can doubtless be attributed to the wartime situation – there were many immigrants of German origin who were regarded with suspicion and many others from eastern Europe who did not speak English and were equally a cause for concern. Some of these immigrants were interned as "undesirables" for the duration of the war.

Second, Adams tirelessly flogged British ideas about planning. Earlier publications of the Commission of Conservation – substantial annual reports, for instance – refer to examples of conservation and planning approaches from all of the Western countries, including Germany, from which early notions of North American zoning were derived. Furthermore, the then vigorous conservation movement in the United States, from which Canada borrowed so much of its agenda and terminology, is not mentioned.

Third, Adams completely disregards the opinions of the people for whom planning was to benefit. There is no discussion of popular participation in conservation and planning processes. Although he includes some fine words on democracy, there is no hint that the people should be directly consulted about their futures, much less involved in decision making. Rather, they are to be instructed, trained, and educated to behave in a scientific, rational, and prudent way.

On the other hand, although the contexts differed, many of the issues Adams identifies in the introductory chapter are as debated today as they were in the early twentieth century. Adams understood the complex interrelationships between urban and rural settlement. He deplored unhealthy living conditions in both rural and urban areas, nefarious land speculation, lack of rural educational opportunities, and defective civic organization. In *Rural Planning and Development* he calls for postwar adjustments to attack these problems, particularly planning and careful management. He blames the drift of people to cities from uneconomic, remote farms – far from services, support systems, and social interaction – for the lack of a systematic approach to land settlement, both in the subdivision of land and in the placement of settlers.

It is worth remembering that in the years before the First World War Canada received more immigrants than at any other time in its history. The peak year was 1913, when over four hundred thousand arrived at a time when the country's total population was only 7.6 million. Many went to the Prairies, where the square mile system of land subdivision meant neighbours were likely to be at least half a mile apart, making social interaction difficult. The loneliness of pioneer life and the hardships of making a living often precipitated moves into the nearest town.

Adams also found farming methods to be inadequate. He felt that a more intensive mixed cultivation, including dairying, would be a sounder agricultural practice than the blind monoculture of wheat or other crops, an observation that is only now gaining currency. In the Introduction, he also points to the need for quality educational, social, financial, and marketing infrastructures, which he considers essential to maintaining rural populations. He notes that the provision of rural-based industries and winter work could be the key to making the lives of rural settlers in closely knit communities both more viable and enjoyable.

Adams also writes about the profitable ownership of land by peasants in rural France and how British and Canadian soldiers noticed, perhaps enviously, their success while fighting overseas. He brushes this approach aside for Canada, however, because it must be supported by dense networks of markets and social facilities. But he states that the approach is a necessity in highly developed Britain, where there is a high proportion of landless peasantry. In his discussion of these options, he anticipates the current theories of Hernando de Soto's *The Mysteries of Capital* by eighty years.

Through its comprehensive approach, this introductory chapter sets the stage for the rest of the book. Despite later claims to the contrary, this first Canadian planning manual addresses not only land questions but also the social, educational, and economic attributes and consequences of planning in fostering the well-being of populations and the health of communities. Critiques of planning in later years, particularly during the late 1960s, blamed early planners for focusing on the physical and neglecting the social and economic aspects of human environments. Adams was clearly different: his approach was as holistic as that of the most dedicated planner today.

CHAPTER II

Rural Population and Production in Canada

Urban increase and rural decrease | Depopulation of homestead land | Female population | Movement of population | Bad conditions in Ontario | Physical and moral deterioration | Good conditions in Ontario | Conditions in Western Provinces | Distribution of lands | Profits of farming and values of farm products | Rural production | Mining, lumbering and fishing industries | New developments of rural industries | Water-powers | Past tendencies in industrial growth

URBAN INCREASE AND RURAL DECREASE

THE rapid growth of urban populations need not be an evil, if the urban development is properly directed and controlled, and if the urban conditions are made as healthy as the rural conditions. Neither growth of cities nor depletion of rural population is necessarily an unhealthy tendency. If the movement from the country to the town is the result of desires for greater opportunities and educational facilities and for obtaining better sanitary and social conditions, who can say that a movement so inspired is an evil? If every city and town were as healthy as the rural districts, as they could be under proper conditions of development, why deplore the natural tendency of population to migrate to the most profitable industries, so long as they remain the most profitable. We may deplore rural depopulation, but it will be futile to fight against it so long as manufacturing produces a better return to labour and capital than agriculture, and so long as there are urban opportunities for human betterment superior to those in rural districts. Indeed, we cannot have national prosperity unless human activity is applied to the most profitable fields of production – whether they be growing food, or making clothes, or building ships. One of the men who failed to make a farm pay in Northern Ontario is today managing a large and successful motor industry in Canada, and there are hundred of others who have gone through the same experience. Indirectly, that man, in making cheap motors, is a great agricultural producer; if he had remained on the soil he would have practically been a non-producer, as he would be wasting his efforts on an unprofitable business.

But what is wrong is not that that man and thousands of others have left the soil, but that the opportunities for making profitable use of their skill were not present in the country. What is wrong is that wasteful and inefficient methods have driven the most intelligent and energetic men into the towns, and, as a consequence, the absence of these men has perpetuated the wastefulness and inefficiency. What is wrong is not that people go to the cities and towns to find social opportunity, but that they are not able to get that opportunity on the farm. What is causing deterioration of mind and body in urban communities is not the growth of cities and towns, but the unnecessary overcrowding and bad sanitation which accompanies that growth as the result of laxity of government. What makes rural depopulation in Canada most serious to the rural districts themselves is the quality, rather than the quantity, of those who leave the land, and the fact that the capital and energy which have been spent to artificially promote settlement have been so largely wasted.

As a rural area becomes thinner in population the causes of migration become accentuated, social opportunities and facilities for co-operation and distribution are further lessened, and there is a consequent further lowering of the profits of production. It is usually the best of the rural population that is drawn to the city for these reasons and, where the land is of poor quality, the residue becomes more and more impaired in physique, intelligence and morals as the process of depopulation continues. The small wage of the agricultural labourer in England, which was first a cause of the best men leaving the rural districts, has become an effect of the lowered efficiency of those who have remained. May not the alleged lack of business capacity of the farmers in some of the older provinces of Canada be an effect of the low profits of the industry, before it becomes a cause? Parallel with low profits to the producer is the anomaly of high costs to the consumer. The high cost of living is a premium paid for lack of efficient development and organization of production.

It is difficult to determine to what extent Canada as a whole has suffered from movement of population. In so far as it has been encouraged by injurious speculation, by the sale of farms at high prices for purposes of subdivision, or by the opportunities of making easy money in land-gambling, it has been wholly injurious. In so far as it is the result of the settlement of land which was unsuited for agriculture and could not be put to economic use it has also been injurious. On the other hand, in so far as it may have increased production in the city at the expense of diminished production in the country, it may not have been entirely an

PLATE II   OVERCROWDING
Four-storey tenement house in a Canadian city occupied by eight families.

PLATE II   ISOLATION
Neither city life nor country life need be unhealthy. Unhealthy conditions
arise from overcrowding in the city and isolation in the country, largely due to want of
proper control of the development of land in both urban and rural areas.

evil; on the contrary, it may have been a benefit if it has meant the transfer of labour from an unprofitable to a profitable industry. Within proper limits the development of manufacturing is as important as the development of agriculture, and over-production in agriculture has to be guarded against as well as under-production. There must be a proper equilibrium maintained between the two kinds of industry. Unfortunately for the country at present the production of food has not been commensurate with the demand; because the equilibrium between the rural and the urban industries and populations has not been properly maintained.

While, however, it is wrong to jump to the conclusion that the movement of population from rural to urban districts is necessarily injurious to a country, there is no gainsaying that a large proportion of this movement in Canada has resulted from a play of forces which has left us weaker and poorer as a nation. If, by Government subsidy or other artificial means, we were to succeed in temporarily increasing rural settlement in the future, without revising our methods of planning and arranging agricultural holdings so as to improve farm revenues and obtain opportunities for better social conditions, and if we were not, at the same time, to place difficulties in the way of land-gambling, we would not succeed in arresting such injurious results as follow from the migratory tendencies of the population.

Sir Horace Plunkett has stated that the city on the American continent has been developing at the expense of the country. Would it not be more correct to say that neither the city nor the country has developed properly because of their neglect of each other? Both have suffered, because of lack of recognition of their inter-dependence.

DEPOPULATION OF HOMESTEADED LAND

Whatever question there may be as to the effects of rural depopulation, on health and production as a whole, there can be no question as to the deplorable national and social waste which must result from any failure to secure permanent rural settlement, after public money has been expended and public property has been alienated to secure that settlement under a system of free homesteading. If a costly and artificial method of opening up new territory is resorted to, if settlers have to be secured by immigration at considerable public cost,* if railways and roads have to be

---

* In five years ending 1914, the Dominion Government spent $6,725,216 to get 1,661,425 immigrants, or an expenditure of about $4 per head.

built and public lands alienated to assist the process, if the private capital of settlers is sunk in improvements, and several years of energy is applied to the task of development – if all that is done, what must be the loss if the result is anything short of permanent settlement under conditions which not only increase production, but make production profitable to the producer?

The evidence of population and other statistics, supported by the evidence of observers of social conditions in rural territory, is that all the efforts and expenditures enumerated above have been employed in developing certain areas, and that, instead of permanent settlement, there are to be found in many of these areas depleted population and unoccupied homesteads. A primary cause of this condition appears to have been the forcing into settlement of areas unsuitable for settlement. Where settlement has been successful in Canada, in spite of an indifferent system of planning and settlement, it has been largely because of three factors, first, the great fertility of the soil in areas suitable for agriculture; second, the energy and enterprise of the governments and administrations, and, third, the fine qualities of the settlers. When, as a result of these things, success has come, it has proved the best means of securing additional settlers of the right kind. When, however, in spite of these things, perhaps because of the placing of settlers on poor land, the scattered nature of settlement and the absence of co-operative and distributive facilities owing to forced homesteading, there has been failure, is it not likely that the real causes of that failure will be misunderstood and that outsiders will assume that the causes lie deeper than inefficiency of organization – that they lie in the general unproductive character of the industry?

Canada need not fear comparison with any country as a field for successful farming, if its soil and other natural resources get a chance to be properly used, but, for lack of a proper system of development, the capacity of these resources is apt to be and is being underestimated. Whatever the defects of land settlement in Canada may be, they are not natural defects of the country or its resources, they are not defects of its settlers as a whole, they are not caused by mal-administration, but they are due to the absence of a proper system of planning and development. Being no deeper than that, they are capable of artificial treatment if we are prepared to learn from the mistakes of the past.

Our governments have already used the wisdom that comes from experience to control such natural resources as our water-powers, and have made advances in the direction of guaranteeing the proper utilization and development of our forests. Indiscriminate use of mineral resources in Canada cannot now be made without consideration of the public welfare. Generally in respect of these water-powers, mines and forests great progress has been made in regard to reasonable government control, and in regard to scientific development and efficiency in utilizing the products. It is in respect of the land – the greatest and most valuable of our natural resources – that we are most backward in our system of directing and organizing development.

It might be more profitable for the government of the country, and in any event the matter is worthy of earnest consideration, to adopt the policy which is being pursued in Australia, of purchasing private lands near to railways and re-settling them, in preference to pushing the development of new territory. Corporations like the Southern Alberta Land Company and the Western Canada Land Company, which own large areas of western lands, and are now in liquidation, might be prepared to sell out at a reasonable price. If such lands can be acquired and settled on a profitable basis would it not be better to suspend the free homestead system in remote districts for a time? Homesteads should only he given where there is a certainty that they can be put to profitable use. Abandoned lands should be carefully surveyed, and, where they are forsaken solely for want of capital to improve them, they might first be improved and then re-settled. These questions, together with that of the sizes of holdings for homestead purposes, should be the subject of careful investigation at least; and all such land should be classified and planned to make it adaptable to the best use.

In 1909 the then President Roosevelt of the United States appointed a commission to enquire into the conditions of country life in that country. In the summary of its proposed remedies for the most prominent deficiencies, it made the following as its first recommendation:

"The encouragement of a system of thoroughgoing surveys of all agricultural regions in order to take stock and to collect local facts, with the idea of providing a basis on which to develop a scientifically and economically sound country life."*

A similar thoroughgoing survey is needed in Canada, but it is necessary, if good results are to be secured, that such a survey should not only be prepared with respect to existing conditions, but should be made in respect to all new territory in advance of settlement.

---

* *Report of Commission on Country Life,* page 20.

FEMALE POPULATION

The absence of social attractions in the rural districts helps to encourage the migration of females from these districts – a wholly injurious form of migration, when we consider the need for improving family life in the country, and when we have regard to the valuable part which the woman plays in the economy of the farm and in the building up of a co-operative organization. As Sir Horace Plunkett has so well put it, "Woman is needed in the country to make co-operation successful; home life is impossible without her; social organization needs her." In the older provinces Ontario had the lowest ratio of females to males in rural divisions in 1911, the percentage being 86.73, as against 93.69 for Quebec, and an average of 93.88 for the three Maritime Provinces.*

In the western provinces the deficiency of female population in 1911 was not much greater in the rural than in the urban districts. In the three Prairie Provinces the ratio of females to males in rural and urban divisions in 1911 was 71.9 and 73.9 per cent, respectively. Women are needed in the towns of Western Canada just as much as in the rural districts.

MOVEMENT OF POPULATION

In the census for 1911, it is set forth that the population of Canada was divided into 3,280,964, or 45.5 per cent, urban and 3,925,679, or 54.5 per cent, rural.† These figures, however, are based on a division which includes in the urban population a large number of what are practically small agricultural villages.‡

In 1911 there were 142 towns in Canada with a population of 500 or over which were either not in existence or whose populations were below 500 in 1901. A great many of these will never really be more than rural villages, and in any event they are not at present urban in character. The rural population of the Dominion might very properly be regarded as consisting of the population outside of the cities, towns and villages of 1,500 inhabitants and over. All towns of less than 1,500, which are not immediately adjacent to large cities, are more or less rural in character, and it is not unreasonable to include them in the rural class.

In the United States, all unincorporated and incorporated places of less than 2,500 are classed as rural; the corresponding figures for Ireland and

---

* Table 12, *Canada Year Book*, 1915.
† Table 9, *Canada Year Book*, 1915.
‡ Table 8, *Canada Year Book*, 1915.

Scotland are 2,000 and 1,000; while in England the population of many towns and villages is counted as part of the rural population.

The urban population in cities, towns and villages of Canada, having a population of 1,500 or over, increased from 1,771,435 in 1901 to 2,845,073 in 1911, whereas the rural population outside of these towns increased from 3,599,880 to 4,361,570 in the same period.*

On the basis of these figures the rural population of the Dominion comprises 60.5 of the total, instead of 54.5, the figure usually quoted. The rate of increase of the rural population for the ten years is 21 per cent as against 60.6 per cent for the urban population – the actual increases being 761,690 and 1,073,638 respectively, (Figure 1). This is not a bad showing for a rural population, having regard to the rapid growth of urban manufacturing industries and the lack of organization of rural industries; it practically means that the small towns under about 6,000 in population, together with rural districts, in the ten years had an increase nearly as great as the cities and larger towns. The principal falling off in rural population was in Ontario and Nova Scotia, which, so far as the older provinces were concerned, was largely counterbalanced by a substantial increase in rural Quebec. The increase in Quebec was significant, since it was largely an internal growth, and was apparently, to a great extent, the result of the closer settlement and planning of the land in the lower province.† Much remains to be done in Quebec to raise the standards of sanitation and of building construction (the absence of which has been strikingly illustrated in the disastrous fires in the province) and to remove the causes of the high death rate of 17.02 per 1,000; but in regard to its system of planning land in the past and its highway policy, which is assisted by that system, it has reason to claim better results than the other eastern provinces.‡

The advantage of internal growth of population, as compared with growth from the outside by means of immigration, is being demonstrated during the present war; the sources from which new population is drawn from the outside of the provinces are cut off, while the internal growth continues. More attention should be given than in the past to keeping

---

* *Census of Canada,* Vol. III, Page XV.
† "The closer settlement of the agricultural population (in Quebec), due to the early French system of planning the land, has been one of the factors preventing rural depopulation." — *J.A. Grenier, Deputy Minister of Agriculture, Quebec.*
‡ The growth of Quebec during 1914-15-16 is indicated by the fact, quoted in *The Monetary Times,* that in these years no less than 297 branches and sub-branches of banks were opened in the province as against 72 closed. The totals for all the other provinces were 212 opened and 254 closed.

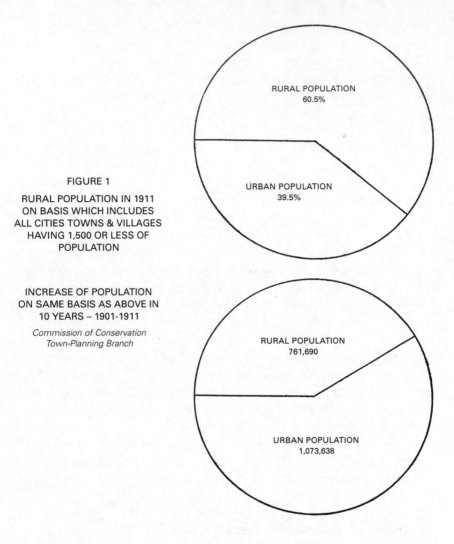

FIGURE 1

RURAL POPULATION IN 1911
ON BASIS WHICH INCLUDES
ALL CITIES TOWNS & VILLAGES
HAVING 1,500 OR LESS OF
POPULATION

INCREASE OF POPULATION
ON SAME BASIS AS ABOVE IN
10 YEARS – 1901-1911

*Commission of Conservation
Town-Planning Branch*

RURAL POPULATION
60.5%

URBAN POPULATION
39.5%

RURAL POPULATION
761,690

URBAN POPULATION
1,073,638

the population on the land that is already settled and encouraging its
healthy growth. Indirectly that will assist the right kind of immigration,
for nothing counts so much as a feature in developing a country as the
health, contentment and prosperity of the citizens already settled in the
country. At the same time the Canadian settlers are, as a rule, better than
immigrants, and we need to pay more attention to the conservation of
our existing population.*

---

* In an investigation made by the Commission of Conservation in the county of Dundas,
  Ontario, the satisfactory condition was found that over 98.7 per cent of 400 farmers
  visited were born in Ontario.

Bad Conditions in Ontario

While it is claimed that the rural decrease has not been so great as it is made to appear in the census figures, *i.e.,* when the agricultural village and small industrial town is included in the rural category, the revised classification does not afford much satisfaction when we come to consider actual conditions in some of the older provinces. Reports have been written with regard to conditions in Ontario, and these are referred to here merely as illustrations and not to show that conditions in Ontario are worse than in other provinces.

Rev. John McDougall, in *Rural Life in Canada,* points out that, while the census of 1911 shows a decrease in the rural population of Ontario of 52,184, or 4.19 per cent, there was, during the decennium, a rural gain of 44,940 in five new districts in that province. Therefore, on the census basis, the rural loss in the remaining territory was 97,124. He also shows that the natural increase of the population of Ontario during the 10 years was 1.5 per cent, which, if it had been retained, would have accounted for an increase of 200,183 in rural population; so that, according to his estimate, the actual decrease in rural Ontario amounted to 373,567, instead of 52,184. In Grenville county, alone, the falling off was from 21,021 to 17,545 between 1901 and 1911.

The effect of this diminution on the educational system is very bad. One school district in Ontario, Mr. McDougall says, had only three children on the roll one year, and during three months only one child was in attendance, although the school register, about 40 years ago, showed an average attendance of 45 children. The average school attendance in the rural schools of Ontario in 1913 was only 22.9, as against 329.1 in the cities.

In one hamlet in Grenville there were seven farms which had once been occupied but were without occupants in 1913, while in the whole county 352, or 9.17 per cent, of the dwelling houses became unoccupied in the ten years prior to 1911.

A report of a Survey of the Trent Watershed, prepared for the Commission of Conservation in 1913, by Dr. B. E. Fernow, Dr. C. D. Howe and Mr. J. H. White, contains some interesting data regarding the social and industrial conditions in the counties of Hastings, Peterborough, Haliburton and Victoria.

The main object of the survey was to deal with forestry conditions, but Dr. Fernow gives as another reason for its prosecution the fact that a portion of the population of the watershed appeared, on preliminary inspection, to be occupying farms unfit for sustaining civilized conditions. "Not only," he says, "have many farms been abandoned by the removal of their occupants to more hopeful conditions, but a considerable number that should be abandoned remain occupied by those who lack the means and energy to move, thus forming a poverty-stricken community. A far-reaching policy for the management of this region must include a plan for the removal of this degenerating population."

This shows that he regards the problem as more serious than is represented by mere figures of depopulation; and he advocates the formation of a broad and far-reaching scheme of development and recuperation. "The waterflow should be safeguarded and industries should be developed to utilize such small resources as are left and to contribute freight to the canal, thus assuring a better future for this area than can be anticipated under the present policy of indifference and neglect."

In the area of 2,100 square miles with which the report deals there are now less than 15,000 people, although it is over 50 years since settlement first took place; hardly 10 per cent of the area of all the 35 townships has been cleared for farm purposes. That this condition is due to the fact that the greater part of the area is not suitable for agriculture is evident by the abandoned farms "which are found throughout the whole region in large numbers, and which are sold from time to time for non-payment of taxes at an average of less than six cents per acre.*

In consequence, during the last decade the decrease in population has been 15 per cent in this area, as against 5 per cent decrease of rural population in the whole province." This is an instance where rural depopulation is a benefit, not an injury, to the country as a whole, although, of course, it is injurious to the people who remain behind in the depleted area. As Dr. Fernow states, "It is to be expected that those who left are elsewhere doing better than merely eking out a precarious existence; the land which they left, being fit for nothing else but forest growth, gradually reforests itself."†

The following is a summary of the facts set out in Part III of the report relating to the economic and industrial conditions of the area:

(1) The geological origin and nature of the soil of the region is for the most part unsuited to agriculture, yet the bulk of the population is engaged in farming.

---

*   A total of 194 farms, comprising 18,085 acres, appeared on the official lists for 1912 to be sold for three years' back taxes, aggregating $3,178.29, or at the rate of less than six cents per acre per year.

†   In another report prepared for the Government of Nova Scotia on "Forest Conditions in Nova Scotia," Dr. Fernow estimates that 80 per cent of the Maritime Province – when not barren – is forest country, and practically destined to remain so.

(2) In two of the townships in the area less than two per cent of the land is cleared, and in the whole area of 1,171,614 acres only about 11.4 per cent was cleared land.

(3) Where land was found to be in possession of considerable settlement, despite the unsuitable character of the soil, this was no doubt owing to accessibility of railway transportation. Specific reference is made to instances of this kind in Hastings and Haliburton counties. At Minden and Monmouth, in the latter county, farming is mostly confined to the vicinity of the railway.

(4) In spite of the difficulties with which the farmers have to contend, it is found heroic efforts are made to build up a system of co-operative dairying, and in each settlement there is a farmers' co-operative cheese factory or creamery.

(5) The prevailing explanation given for farms being abandoned was inability to make a living.

(6) Often the abandoned farms were among the best in the settlement, but their owners could not continue getting a mere subsistence despite their best efforts.

(7) It was usually the more progressive settlers, and the young people who had fewer ties, who were not content to stay.

(8) It is explicitly stated in the report that the settlers throughout were an energetic, hard-working, resourceful people, who had been attracted to the district years ago by the offer of free land, but who are face to face with an impossible proposition. Much of the land was patented for the timber it carried, and not on account of its agricultural suitability.

(9) The economic conditions were associated with a certain amount of social degeneracy, and the low moral tone and mental defects of some communities were traceable to the unsound economic conditions.

(10) The amount of human energy unavailingly expended in this attempt to settle land unsuitable for agriculture represents an incalculable asset lost to the province.

Two significant quotations are given in the report, from reports made in 1855 and 1865, which show that the settlement of unsuitable areas was carried out in spite of advice giving warning of its dangers. The Hon. A. T. Galt, chairman of a Committee of the Legislative Assembly, *e.g.,* reported, in 1855, as follows:

> "It appears from the evidence that settlement has been unreasonably forced in some localities quite unfit to become the permanent residence of an agricultural population . . . Your committee would refer to the evidence, and recommend that the Government should

in all cases ascertain positively the character of the country before
throwing open any tract of land for settlement."

Supplementing the inquiry into the conditions of the Trent Watershed,
Dr. C. D. Howe also made a more detailed investigation of the townships
of Burleigh and Methuen, Peterborough county, in 1913. In this report*
he advocated a classification and segregation of the lands which were
capable of agricultural use from those which should be forever given over
for timber. Much of the land was too poor for successful farming, but
other areas were fertile. At least one quarter was composed of marshes
and swamps suitable for growing hay and raising cattle – and, if drained,
for conversion into market gardens. He claimed that the soil of the marshes
was so rich that 10 acres devoted to garden crops could support a family,
and there were 15,000 acres which might eventually be used for this
purpose in Methuen alone. Co-operative methods of distribution would
however be necessary, as well as large expenditure in drainage and
improvement schemes to make such holdings successful.

The conditions prevailing in parts of Grenville and in the Trent watershed show us that what we have to deplore in certain districts is not that
people are leaving the land but that they have been permitted to go on
the land under such circumstances. When millions of acres of fertile land
are lying uncultivated in Ontario and many more millions in the Dominion
– many thousands of these acres being in the suburbs of our cities and
near to our railways – and when the greatest need of Canada is for more
human energy to cultivate these fertile acres, it is unfortunate, to say
the least, that settlement has been encouraged where failure was inevitable. Although efforts are now being made, in Ontario and other provinces, to stop the settlement of land which is unsuitable for agriculture,†
it is questionable if the organization which is endeavoring to accomplish
this task can do more than touch the fringe of the problem. Having regard
to its seriousness, and to the train of evils which follow as a result of failure
in land settlement, everything possible should be done to safeguard the
country against such consequences. The wasted energy and capital of

---

* *Forest Protection in Canada*, pages 205-206.
† "Having seen the folly of opening for settlement townships which are rough and
   which contain only a small percentage of good land, the Government of Ontario has
   provided that, before a township is opened for settlement, it must be inspected by a
   competent officer to ascertain (a) the percentage of good land in it; (b) the quantity
   and varieties of timber; (c) whether it is chiefly valuable for its mines and minerals."
   — *Hon. Frank Cochrane, Minister of Lands, Forests and Mines of Ontario, in address to
   Commission of Conservation, 1910. First Annual Report, p. 75.*

settlers who break down in a losing fight against natural obstacles is only a small part of the loss to themselves and their country; there is also the physical and moral deterioration which seems to set in, in every poor agricultural district; there is the loss of hope in themselves and their broken faith in the capacity of the land to give them a living. Children who grow up under such conditions are often worse housed, worse cared for and worse educated than children in the city slums. When people reach this condition they warn other people off the land, both by their appearance and by the accounts they give of their hopeless struggles.

Physical and Moral Deterioration

That there is physical and moral deterioration going on in some of the rural districts in Canada appears to be only too well established. This is said to be the case, not only in the old settled parts of the older provinces but also in new regions which are being opened up for settlement. Further evidence regarding Ontario districts is given in a report on conditions existing in a part of the county of Peterborough, prepared at the request of Sir Wm. Mulock, the presiding judge at the assizes held in the city of Peterborough, in February, 1916. In the press report of the remarks made by the presiding judge he is credited with having said:

> "Attention was drawn to the degenerate condition of people in the back townships of this and the county of Hastings. These people were in poverty, living on unproductive land and the children brought up in an immoral atmosphere. The grand jury was asked to make a rec-ommendation as to their opinions in the matter. Jurors, he said, would be more familiar with the conditions than he could gain from hearsay evidence. If the land was rocky and barren would it not be proper for the Government to transport the people to more productive land, and hand the present ground over to the Conservation Commission for forestry production. There was no question that the people were in a wretched condition."

At a subsequent conference the grand jury made its presentment, and stated that the condition of affairs alluded to by the judge was, to some extent, abnormal in the history of the district, that the jury agreed that environment and conditions of living in the sparsely settled and un-productive districts were factors in inducing a relaxation of moral observ-ance and were to be regretted. They also agreed with the assumption of the judge, that the lands in the district alluded to were not suitable to adequately support a population in reasonable comfort nor to afford the

PLATE III   THE BEGINNING

With the exception of patches containing a few square feet, there is no soil on this prospective farm that approaches a loam in texture. It is mostly gravel and sand. Trent Watershed, Ont.

PLATE III   THE END

One of the many abandoned farms in the Trent Watershed.
The amount of human energy expended in attempting to make a living from such areas has been, and still is, enormous. Under proper schemes of development this land would be absolutely closed to settlement.
From Trent Watershed Reports

necessary municipal expenditure to provide what was necessary for the life of the people.

Following the presentment of the grand jury, Chief Justice Mulock adjourned the session until the April following, and asked the jury to make a report to the judge on April 25th. In the report then presented the grand jury stated that they had been unable to make an inspection of the district, on account of the roads and inclement weather, but they submitted a number of opinions of people who were acquainted with the district and expressed the view, as a jury, that there should be a modified system of consolidated schools and improved police patrol of the districts.

The opinions regarding the conditions showed a great diversity of view, but, in the words of the report, showed, conclusively that some action should be taken. The revelations made in the report by some local witnesses were astounding, and, if social crime exists to the extent alleged, drastic steps should be taken at once to arrest the evil. Having regard to the lessons taught by these conditions, the first responsibility of any government and its administrators is to prevent similar conditions where new settlement is taking place. That is the greater responsibility, because, in the first place, the government is directly in control of the new settlement and cannot blame past administrations, and, in the second place, it is always practicable to prevent the beginning of bad conditions, although sometimes almost impracticable to cure them.

Whatever may be the extent of degeneration, or whether or not it exists in any greater measure in Peterborough than in other counties, the serious thing is that such an enquiry should have been necessary at all, and that there is such poverty, as is here indicated, because of the fact that the unoccupied land was incapable of being put to economic use. Poverty itself is not, however, a cause of social crimes, as is proved in the case of the congested rural districts of Ireland and other places; it is when poverty is accompanied, on the one hand, by isolation and the absence of social and religious institutions, or, on the other hand, when it has to be faced in the crowded slum districts of large cities, that it produces the worst evils.

Taken side by side with the report of the Trent watershed, the Peterborough enquiry suggests that there is a serious problem in connection with land development in Canada – in other provinces as well as in Ontario – which requires to be faced without delay. If it be true, as alleged, that similar conditions already exist in territory which has been opened up for settlement during recent years, steps should be taken, even at considerable public expense, to revise the system of land settlement which makes them possible.

Good Conditions in Ontario

Notwithstanding the above evidence regarding bad conditions in certain districts it is necessary to bear in mind that many parts of these districts contain good agricultural land, and that many of the citizens are upright, hard-working and intelligent. It would be a grave injury to these districts, and to the people who live in them, if it were assumed that what might be true of a part were equally true of the whole. The fact that this population is so scattered causes great difficulties in ascertaining the exact condition of affairs and in preventing a few undesirable citizens from giving a bad name to a whole township or district.

We have an indication from these reports of the importance of dealing with causes and the futility of trying to solve such social problems by lessening or removing effects. The causes must be ascertained and removed. It is unfair to assume that any great part of the territory in review would not be suitable for economic use in some form, or that a greater part of the present population could not be comfortably settled in the counties where they are now living, if a thorough investigation of the circumstances were made and a practical remedy devised to re-plan the townships, to classify the land, and to set aside the least fertile portions for purposes of afforestation.

The social investigator is usually employed to make enquiries when something is wrong. As a consequence, reports too often deal with bad conditions with a view to suggesting how to remove them and not with good conditions with a view to showing how to extend them. In a large part of the settled regions in Ontario the land is of the most fertile kind, and farming is being made to pay in a way which can favourably compare with any country. There are still millions of acres of good land unsettled or unimproved. In some of the Ontario counties the area under cultivation and the number of occupiers per square mile is as satisfactory as in the best parts of some older countries. For instance, the district of Essex N. has a population of 158.84 per square mile, and Waterloo N. has 123.06. Out of a total occupied area of 311,754 acres in Waterloo N. and S. it is estimated that no less than 252,253 acres, or 80 per cent, are under cultivation. The corresponding acreage for Dundas is estimated at 75 per cent, for Northumberland 23 per cent, and for Carleton 59 per cent. Even in these districts, however, a large part of the land which is stated to be under cultivation is practically sterile for want of capital and labour to use it. It would be desirable to make a survey of conditions in good counties so as to show a better side to the picture than that which is presented by the investigations which have been made in the poorer counties.

To ascertain causes of failure one must also investigate and ascertain causes of success. Investigation is needed as to why some areas of fertile land in Canada, with good means of communication, have not been so successfully settled as other areas of the same character and location.

A large part of Ontario has all the appearance and features of a highly cultivated English countryside. It possesses these features without having had a rich landlord class to subsidize the development of the land; it possesses them because of good soil, good climatic conditions and good settlers. What has been achieved in the best Ontario counties is practicable on millions of acres of unsettled or partially settled territory in Canada. Perhaps Essex, Waterloo and other counties have succeeded because of circumstances which could not be repeated in other counties, and no doubt different methods will be necessary to secure similar results elsewhere. Greater government stimulus will have to be given in some areas than in others, but with organized effort and careful planning an enormous improvement could be made in many districts. It may be argued that some of the best counties enjoy their prosperity because they include thriving towns within their areas. This condition may indeed be largely responsible for the fact that they have maintained their population while counties like Huron and Wellington have lost as much as 17 per cent in ten years. So far, however, as proximity to cities has conferred any benefit on these counties, it proves the advantage of social attractions as a means of keeping people on the land, and preventing deterioration, and goes to show the need for blending the agricultural and manufacturing population to a greater extent than hitherto in the interests of both classes of industry and population. It also emphasizes the need for some measures being taken to prevent the wholesale subdivision of productive land around cities, where such land is lying idle nearest to the markets.

Conditions in Western Provinces

In the western provinces we do not find much satisfaction from statistics, as the following particulars show:

The scope for filling up the fertile regions of the western provinces is indicated by the following low density of population per square mile in 1911: Manitoba, 6.18; Saskatchewan, 1.95; Alberta, 1.47; British Columbia, 1.09.

The rural percentage fell in Manitoba from 72.4 in 1901 to 56 in 1911 and 44 (estimated) in 1914; in Saskatchewan from 80.7 in 1901 to 73.3 in 1911 and 73 (estimated) in 1914; in Alberta from 71.8 in 1901 to 62.1 in

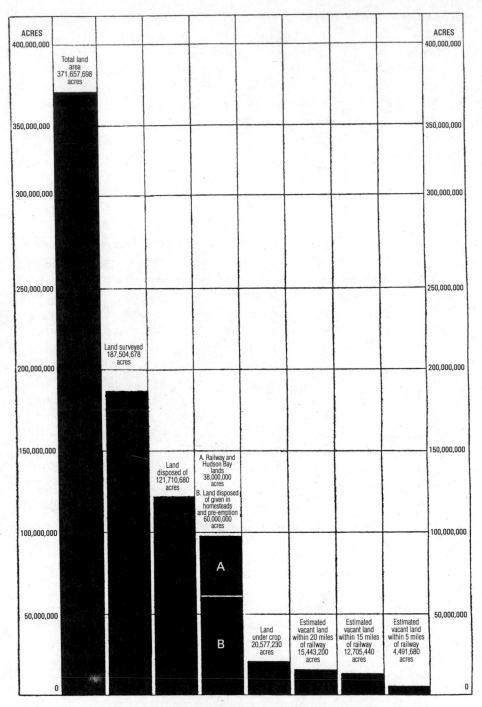

FIGURE 2   LAND CONDITIONS IN PRAIRIE PROVINCES
Note the Comparison between the Land Surveyed or Disposed of and the Land Under Crop.
Commission of Conservation Town-Planning Branch

1911 and 60 (estimated) in 1914; in British Columbia from 49.5 in 1901 to 48.1 in 1911 and 44.6 (estimated) in 1914.*

The land area of the three Prairie Provinces (Manitoba, Saskatchewan and Alberta) is said to comprise 371,658,698 acres. Of this area about 187,504,678 acres have been surveyed and about 121,710,680 acres disposed of, including over 60,000,000 acres given in homesteads and preemptions and about 38,000,000 of railway and Hudson's Bay Company's lands. Of the land disposed of 16.9 per cent being 27 acres in each quarter section, and comprising a total of 20,577,230 acres, are stated to be under crop in the three provinces. It is estimated that there are still vacant and surveyed lands within 20 miles of the railways as follows: Within 20 miles, 15,443,200; within 15 miles, 12,705,440; within 10 miles, 8,914,240; within five miles, 4,491,680. (Figure 2.)

The total extent of land in Canada within about 15 miles of the railways has been estimated to amount to the enormous area of 261,783,000 acres.

The Canadian Pacific Railway Company obtained grants of 28,737,399 acres, of which 23,057,227 acres have been disposed of, and 5,680,171 acres are still unsold.

The total area of land granted to railway companies by Dominion and Provincial governments amounts to 55,740,249 acres, comprising some of the best and most accessible land in the country, a large portion being still unused.

It is unnecessary to go on adding to these figures. They show how great are the areas of land which lie within a short distance of existing means of communication; how deplorable it is that fertile sections of these lands remain unsettled and unproductive for some reason, while settlers are abandoning remote territory because of the social isolation and distance from railways; how wasteful it is that such a great extent of territory is uninhabited where a farm population could thrive and obtain social advantages, and how many and how extensive are the opportunities for preparing a variety of schemes of development which would secure permanent settlement under sound economic conditions.

The soil in the western provinces, of which so much is lying idle in the hands of absentee speculators, has been described by a high authority as worth "more than all the mines and mountains from Alaska to Mexico and more than all the forests from the United States boundary to the Arctic sea ... The worth of the soil and subsoil cannot be measured in

---

* These figures are based on the census classification, and a number of rural villages are excluded from the rural population, although the inhabitants of these villages are engages in rural pursuits.

acres. The measure of its value is the amount of nitrogen, phosphoric acid and potash which it contains; in other words in its producing power." But there are also large areas of poor, stony and muskeg land in the western provinces which are unsuitable for agriculture. A great deal of the land near to the railways is barren and rocky and much of even the prairie land is of poor quality. Care in classifying and planning the vacant land near to the railways is required to enable economic use to be made of it, just as in the case of more remote territory.

DISTRIBUTION OF LAND IN CANADA

Turning to another phase of the subject, the following table regarding distribution of land in Canada will be found to be of interest:

DISTRIBUTION OF LAND IN CANADA IN 1901-1911*

	Total area† in acres	Occupied	Owned	Leased or rented	Improved	Unimproved
1901	988,321,700	63,422,338	57,522,441	5,899,897	30,166,033	33,256,305
1911	977,585,763	106,777,085	98,730,249	11,046,836	48,503,660	61,273,425

The number of farms in 1901 was 544,688, and by 1911 they increased to 711,681. Thus the new farms occupied during the ten years amounted to 166,993 of an average size of 277 acres. The greater part of this increase took place in the western provinces, and there was an actual decrease of 2,427 farms in Nova Scotia.

It will be observed from these figures that, whereas the number of farms increased by 166,993, or about 30 per cent, the acreage of land occupied increased by 46,354,747, or over 73 per cent, indicating a considerable increase in the size of ownerships. Three thousand townships, of 36 square miles (23,040 acres) each, have a total area of 69,120,000 acres, and, allowing for forest, swamp, etc., this area would probably have accommodated the increase of farms. Thus, with the rapid growth between 1901 and 1910, about three hundred townships, or an average of fifty in each of the six largest provinces, would require to be surveyed and settled each year. The number of farms surveyed by the Dominion Government alone

---

* *Canada Year Book,* 1913, p. 146.
† The total areas in the above table do not include the Yukon and Northwest Territories and certain territories in Quebec, Ontario, Manitoba and British Columbia.

in the above period was 401,246, comprising a total area of 64,199,360 acres. It is estimated that an area equal to this has been surveyed in excess of the area in occupation. An effort should be made to limit the surveys to an area approximating to the area likely to be settled each year and to use the surveying staff in making a detailed topographical survey and land classification of the territory as it is opened up.

The changes which have taken place in the ownership of land and the extent of speculation is indicated by the estimate which has been made that out of 129,710,680 acres disposed of about 42,058,400 acres have been cancelled. This figure is the total, and includes lands which have been cancelled more than once.

A more concentrated and detailed survey, and the proper planning of the roads and farm boundaries, would probably involve an increased staff and expenditure, but the advantage to be gained would be enormous.* By this means a valuable topographical map of the areas could be gradually prepared, which would enable government departments to exercise better control over the development of the land, and save large sums in isolated surveys.

Out of the total area of 977,585,513 acres in the nine provinces in 1911,† 109,777,085 acres were occupied as farm land, and 358,162,190 acres was the estimate of possible farm land. These figures indicate how great are the land resources of the Dominion, and give some idea of the scope and need there is for efficient government organization, so as to secure the best conditions of settlement for such vast regions, and how the lack of such organization may lead to great loss.

PROFITS OF FARMING AND VALUES OF FARM PRODUCTS

The most direct cause of rural depopulation in all countries is the fact that farming does not yield enough profit to the farmer to make the industry attractive. Unless a farm yields interest on the capital invested, combined with a satisfactory wage to the farmer, it cannot be regarded as being put to economic use. The farmer is often blamed for this unsatisfactory condition where it exists, but he is to a large extent helpless to improve

---

*   A great many returned soldiers, especially those with engineering experience, could be employed in making topographical surveys with great profit to the country. The valuable ordnance survey maps of Great Britain were prepared from surveys made by military men and no work has been carried out in the Old Country which has been more appreciated or of greater utility in connection with land development.

†   This area was increased to 1,401,316,413 acres in 1912, and the possible farm land is now computed to be 440,951,000 acres.

it. In so far as he has lack of capital and experience the same may be said of many who start industries in the cities and succeed in spite of their deficiencies. Canada has a large population of men who have succeeded as farmers, although possessing little or no experience or capital at the outset. Until better conditions of settlement and improved organization are provided to control and direct land settlement it is not right to blame the farmer for a situation that is due to want of opportunity.

The following comparative table shows values in three leading industries in 1911:*

	Agriculture	Manufactures	Railways (Steam and electric)
Total value of farm property and of capital in manufactures and railways	$4,231,840,636	$1,247,583,609	$1,640,221,548
	Products	Products	Earnings
Total value of products and earnings	(Cereals, etc.) $597,926,000 (Stock) $615,457,833	$1,165,975,639	$209,090,446

Between 1901 and 1911 the total value of farm property other than land more than doubled, indicating a general prosperity which disposes of any suggestion that the industry of agriculture, taken as a whole, has suffered from depression in Canada. The development of the dairy industry has also been satisfactory, the total value of cheese, butter and condensed milk produced being $39,047,840 in 1910, compared with $29,731,922 in 1900. The increase was partly due to advanced prices but to a greater extent to increased production.

That there have been periods during which production has been stationary, and has even fallen off in parts of the country, that there have been good lands abandoned or left unused, and that rural deterioration has taken place, only indicate that there are certain causes at work which prevent us from obtaining the full measure of prosperity which should come to the country. That we do not receive that full measure, even with our available population and capital, is due to the fact that the human

* *Canada Year Book.*

activity and human skill which we possess is not being applied to the best advantage in the conversion of our natural resources to human use.

As an agricultural authority has said, the profits of farming are probably greater than the average farmer thinks they are and less than the city dweller believes them to be. It seems to be taken for granted and is probably true that the earnings of the farmer are less than the earnings in other fields of labour. No accurate figures are available to enable an estimate to be made with regard to farm incomes in Canada, but some information has been collected on this subject in the United States.

Professor G.F. Warren, of Cornell University, found, after investigation, that in the best townships in Jefferson County the farmer and his family, with an average capital of $9,006, made $1,155 above the business expenses of the farm. In addition, they had the use of a house and some farm products. At 5 per cent the use of the capital is worth $450, and unpaid farm work done by members of the family was valued at $96, so that the pay for the farmer's work or his labour income was $609, besides the use of a house and some farm products. He says this is considerably above the average for the States, a statement which is confirmed by Professor W. J. Spillman, of the United States Department of Agriculture. In an article* on the farmer's income the latter gives $640 as the average income obtained in the United States after deducting total expenses from the total receipts. He estimates that at 5 per cent as the rate of interest this should be distributed between interest and labour income, as follows:

Interest on investment	$322
Labour income	318

Another United States authority shows that the average income of 2,090 farmers operating their own farms in eight States was $439.

These figures correspond with rough estimates made in regard to earnings in Canada, and are probably reliable as approximate estimates for one year. But it has to be remembered that the farmer's earnings vary as the seasons vary; also that the unknown factors, including the value of farm products used in the farmer's home, would make a considerable addition to the income, when comparisons are made with those who pay town prices for food and high rents for their dwellings. In any case the general conclusion which may be arrived at in regard to this matter is that the opportunities of the farmer to accumulate wealth are too few, otherwise more men of ability would be attracted to the industry of agriculture.

---

* "The Farmer's Income," in *Selected Readings in Rural Economics.*

PLATE IV   DEMORESTVILLE, ONTARIO
"A large part of Ontario has all the appearance and features of a highly cultivated English country-side."
Photo by courtesy of Immigration Branch, Dept. of Interior

PLATE IV   FIELD OF CELERY ON AN ONTARIO FARM
While this land is producing wealth for the nation and profit for the farmer, there are hundreds of thousands of acres of equally accessible and fertile land lying idle as a result of land speculation and want of proper planning.
Photo by courtesy of Immigration Branch, Dept. of Interior

Whatever we can do by improved methods and organization to increase farm earnings without adding to the cost of the products to the consumer needs to be done in the national interest. Considering the small margin available in the farmer's total income to pay interest on loans, and to meet freight charges on small shipments of produce, it is evidently important that he should have facilities for obtaining cheap capital and improved means of distribution.

RURAL PRODUCTION

In the 1911 Census the following figures are given, showing the capital, earnings and products of manufacturing industries in the urban and rural districts of Canada for 1910 and 1900:

	1910			1900		
	Capital	Earnings	Products	Capital	Earnings	Products
Urban	928,939,482	193,355,373	901,770,217	347,435,241	90,347,067	361,354,833
Rural	318,647,127	47,653,043	264,205,422	99,481,264	22,902,283	119,698,542

We have also seen that the total value of cereals produced in 1911 amounted to $597,926,000. In addition there is the stock on agricultural holdings of Canada of a total value of $615,457,883 – a large portion of which value is converted into cash each year and forms a product from the farm.

We thus see the relatively great importance of production in rural areas and have an indication of close connection between that production and manufacturing in the urban centres. In the United States, 42 per cent of the materials used in manufacture are said to come from the farm, which also contributes 70 per cent of the country's exports. The fact that during the year 1911, Canada imported $72,315,243 in value of agricultural produce and fish is not a matter which can be regarded with complacency, especially in view of the extent of the agricultural areas, on which large sums have been spent for development, still unused, in close proximity to railways and towns. Where there is good land lying idle in the vicinity of existing means of transportation, and in a state of partial improvement, it is unsound either to continue to import what might be produced on such land or to spend money in new equipment to open up remote regions which can be allowed to wait till the equipment already available is put to greater use. This is an additional reason for encouraging greater production and the settlement of more population in the older parts of the provinces near to railways and towns. The fact that most of this territory has been alienated from the Crown presents a difficulty in connection with its more intensive settlement and improvement; but it is not an insuperable difficulty and it should be faced.

If the figures in the above tables regarding production are attainable under present conditions how much greater may production become with proper organization and with the fuller opportunities which are capable of being provided? How much greater might have been the production in past years if the rural population had not been attracted in such large numbers to other lands, and how much greater may it be in future if we make a real effort to conserve our population and to artificially increase the fertility of the soil. As the Chairman of the Commission of Conservation has pointed out, Canada is in need of intelligent application of scientific methods to increase output from the land if it is going to successfully compete with other nations. Even in regard to wheat, which is the staple product of the western lands, we only produced an average of 22.29 bushels per acre in 1914 and 1915, as against 32.25 bushels in Great Britain.

The migration of the farming population has also resulted in the desertion of the rural villages in many countries. In *Rural Life in Canada,* Rev. John McDougall refers to his early experience in the county of Grenville, where, 40 years ago, "each hamlet had its corps of trained and skilled workmen, with sturdily built homes, making the rich contribution to community life that skilled craftsmen bring. The essential industries were everywhere represented. The village had a fairly self sufficing economic life." The re-creation of the rural village in the older counties and the creation of rural villages in the new territory being opened up are needed to give stability to rural life in Canada.

Mining, Lumbering and Fishing Industries

While the greatest volume of production in Canada comes from agriculture and rural manufacturing, and while these industries employ the great majority of workers, there are other important industries which may be classified as rural. These include mining, lumbering and fishing. The workers engaged in agriculture, according to the census of 1911, number 933,735,* and in fishing, hunting, forestry and mining 217,097. Those engaged in manufacture, trade and merchandising amount to 708,886. Of the workers in the building trades (246,201), civil and municipal

---

* Table 26, page 91, *Canada Year Book,* 1915.

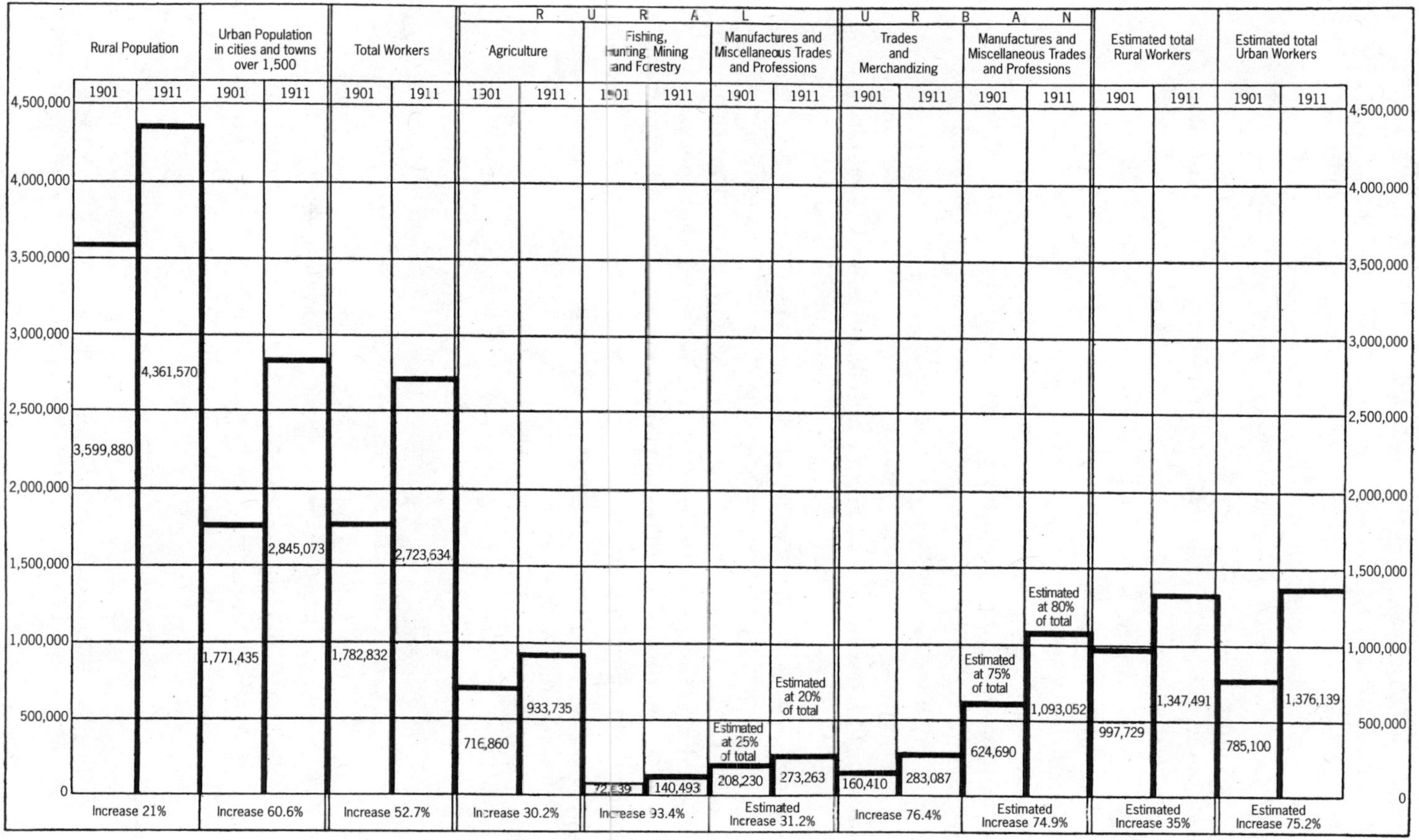

FIGURE 3   WORKERS IN INDUSTRIES IN CANADA 1901-1911

Commission of Conservation Town-Planning Branch

government (76,604), professions (120,616), and transportation (217,544), a considerable proportion belong to the rural population. (Figure 3). It may, therefore, be computed that more than half the workers in Canada in 1911 were directly engaged in rural production and, of the other half, a large proportion were employed as middlemen and distributors for the farmers, the miners, the woodmen and the fishermen. The manufacturers and distributors are better organized than those engaged in producing food and raw materials and no doubt this accounts, in a considerable measure, for the relatively large share which the two former receive in the profits of production. The remedy for this is not to be found in lessening the efficiency and weakening the organization of those engaged in manufacture and distribution, but in improving the efficiency and organization of those engaged in supplying the raw materials.

In so far as the cost of living has been increased as a result of the falling off in production it can only be reduced by increasing production. But increased production can only be obtained as a permanent condition if the profits of the producer provide the stimuli necessary to encourage him to produce. These profits will only be obtained if he is better organized and enjoys the benefit of co-operation and greater convenience for distribution to enable him to lessen the cost of production on the one hand and to secure a larger share of the price paid by the consumer on the other hand.* This applies more to agriculture than to the other rural industries. The industries of mining and lumbering are, for the most part, in the hands of large corporations who can obtain cheap transportation and cheap capital, and organize their own distribution.

The following are the values of the fisheries and minerals produced in Canada in 1915:†

Fisheries	$31,264,631
Minerals	138,513,750

The total value of the forest products in 1915 is given as $172,880,000; the amount exported in 1915 is given as $42,650,683, against which lumber, etc., of a value of $9,613,891 was imported. An unsatisfactory feature is that more minerals are imported than exported, the respective figures being $51,740,989 and $54,171,002. This is due to the fact that the most

---

*   It is usually assumed that excessive profits are made by middlemen, but the lack of co-operative organization and defective methods of distribution probably absorb most of the difference between the price received by the producer and that paid by the consumer.
†   *Canada Year Book,* 1915.

thickly populated parts of Canada rely for fuel on imported coal – this being responsible for no less than $37,063,459 of the amount of mineral imports. How to lessen the reliance of Canada on coal imports, and how to put its great water-powers to more use is one of the great problems to be faced in Canada. Recent events have shown how serious it is and how much more serious it might become.

We thus see that rural development in Canada covers a much wider field than is covered by agriculture and rural manufacturing, and that regard has also to be paid to the important and rapidly growing industries connected with the produce of the mines, the forest and the fisheries.*

New Developments of Rural Industries

Particularly in connection with the mines, enormous developments are likely to take place in the future. New towns are likely to be created and new demands made for more population. In the past, mining operations have been carried on with too little regard to the standard of comfort and living conditions of those engaged in them. The housing conditions at Cobalt, Sudbury, and in the mining valleys of the western provinces have hardly been satisfactory from any point of view. One result of this is that fewer Canadian or British born workers are attracted to mining than to other industries, and reliance has to be placed on a less efficient class of workers than might be obtained if the employers were made responsible for providing better living conditions. Compared with 72 per cent of the workers engaged in agriculture, there are little over 46 per cent of the miners born in Canada. This is both a cause and an effect of bad living conditions. The death rate among miners in Canada is higher than in any other country. A mining population needs more government control than the population of the cities and agricultural districts and they usually suffer from having a low standard of housing and sanitary conditions, and an absence of social facilities which diminishes their producing power

---

* The resources of Canada in soil, in mine, and in forest, have scarcely been scratched. The grasp of Canada upon their responsibilities has hardly been felt. The time is coming, and is near at hand, when the Dominion will experience the onrush of new and powerful energies that only a mighty struggle with self, and a victory over self, could have awakened. — *Christian Science Monitor, Boston, U.S.A.*

† The problem presented to the operator (of mines) is how to obtain labour, and, after obtaining it, make it efficient and keep it contented. One of the great drawbacks to this is due in a great measure to the fact that mining operations are usually carried on in out of the way and unattractive places; again, as the life of the mine is limited, there is little or nothing to encourage the labouring-man to settle down and establish a home. — *W.J. Dick, in the Eighth Annual Report of the Commission of Conservation.*

and moral stability.† The responsibility for securing improvement of these conditions rests partly with the mining corporations, but in a greater degree with the governing authorities who are primarily interested in the public welfare. Where mining is carried on in the neighbourhood of fertile land, such as in the valleys of British Columbia, there are opportunities for creating healthy and permanent towns without much aid from the government or the mining operators; but in more barren regions, where mining is profitable, but where farming cannot be made successful, it is more difficult to secure healthy conditions of settlement, and it is in such areas that the responsibility of the government and the operating companies are greatest. In recent years some mining corporations have recognized the need for improved housing conditions and have laid out and built model villages around their mines.

New developments are also taking place in connection with the lumber industry which seem likely to revive its prosperity on lines which will be productive of permanent settlement. With the growth of the pulp industry and the building of new mills in proximity to the available timber limits, and at points where ample water-power is available, many opportunities are now arising for planning and developing new towns in rural territory. Under the old conditions the workers engaged in this industry lived in temporary lumber camps in the winter and migrated to the saw-mill in the town or worked on the farms in the summer. As is shown in the investigation made into the Trent Watershed regions the forest areas are poorly adapted for successful farming and the combination of lumbering and farming in such areas often produces poverty and degeneration. On the other hand the unsettled and migratory tendencies of the lumber worker who, after having accumulated the savings of a winter's work in the bush, returns to the city, cause him to be more or less of a spendthrift and a less efficient citizen than he would be with more stable and regular employment.

The pulp industry will involve a more elaborate process of manufacturing than the sawmill and will lead to the creation of large village communities with opportunities for creating a healthy social life.

The pulp manufacturers who are developing these new industries are showing an enlightened self-interest in planning and developing the towns around their mills so that healthy and attractive housing conditions will be provided for their employees. One of the reasons for this is, as one of the largest manufacturers has stated, that experience has taught them that the best workers can only be secured if the living conditions are satisfactory. When such industries are established without proper provision being made for housing it has been found that good engineers, chemists and foremen are difficult to obtain even on the offer of higher wages than are available in towns possessing better environment. It is no longer regarded as good business policy to make money out of the sub-division of the land which is required for the homes of the workers, nor to leave the building of these homes and the layout of the towns to the haphazard and greedy methods of land speculators.

Where new mills are being established the planning and regulation of the building development needs to be accompanied by measures to prevent the wholesale destruction of forest growth; and reasonable restriction of the use of water-powers to prevent deterioration of forest floors and agricultural lands.

Improvement of fishing villages presents a difficult problem, but much can be done by more education of the fishermen and better leadership on the part of those who administer public affairs of fishing communities. Greater attention is likely to be given in the future to the creation of small manufacturing industries in fishing villages, particularly in connection with the utilization of fish waste for commercial purposes, and this will result in securing an increase of population and in creating a demand on the part of fishermen for improved facilities for distribution and better social conditions. The betterment of agricultural conditions round fishing centres and the making of good roads will react on these centres and result in their improvement. In any event it is evident that there is need for improved conditions and for more efficient municipal control in such centres.

WATER-POWERS

Extensive developments may be expected in the future in the utilization of the immense reserves of water-power in the Dominion, and in the potentialities which they possess for creating rural industries and new towns. In a report on the *Water-Powers of Canada** published by the Commission of Conservation in 1911, the following is the first of the conclusions summarized in the introductory survey:

> "Water-power is dependent, primarily, upon precipitation. Other interests, such as municipal and domestic water supply, navigation, agriculture and irrigation are likewise dependent upon the same source. The subject of water-powers, therefore, can not be properly considered without making fair allowances for the demands of the other interests that have just claims upon water as a natural resource."

---

* Report on *"Water-Powers of Canada,"* by Leo. G. Denis, B. Sc., E.E., and Arthur V. White, C.E., Commission of Conservation, 1911.

The importance of making an adequate survey and an intelligent classification of the water-powers and of the physical circumstances associated with them is referred to in the above report. The authors point out that it is as unreasonable not to differentiate between water-powers as it would be not to differentiate between timber tracts, mineral lands, etc. This is the same claim that is made by authorities in regard to all natural resources and that is made in this report in regard to land resources.

Underground waters are essential to sustain the forests and the general fertility of the soil for agricultural purposes and no scheme of survey or classification of land would be complete without a study being made of the sources of supply of water and the uses to which the water-power could safely be put. "The water is necessary to the soil and the soil, with its plant growth, is necessary to the economical distribution of the water."

In selecting sites for new towns more regard should be paid to the possibilities of using water-power to generate electricity for industrial purposes.

The great irrigation schemes carried out by the Canadian Pacific Railway and other companies in the western provinces indicate the enormous possibilities of the use of water in promoting successful and more intensive land settlement.

Past Tendencies of Industrial Growth in Small Towns and Rural Areas

Reference has already been made to the desertion of rural villages as a result of agricultural depression in certain districts. The conservation of village life by means of the promotion of rural industries is a matter of great importance.

The question of promoting new and extending existing industries in rural areas will be dealt with in a later chapter, but at this point attention may be drawn to the great developments which have already taken place in Canada in that direction. We have seen that between 1901 and 1911 no less than 142 new towns were created, having a population of 1,500 or less. Many of these new towns are in rich agricultural regions, where distributive and social centres are needed and where they can obtain the needed staying power from the surrounding territory. Others, however, will only succeed in proportion as they have the facilities to enable small manufacturing industries to be promoted, and as they succeed in organizing these industries.

The wealth of old Ontario lies largely in the small industrial town, and while great cities like Toronto are no better from a point of view of public health and convenience than some of the great cities of America and

Europe, the average small town of Ontario is probably superior in regard to the general average prosperity and living conditions of their citizens to any towns of a similar size in other countries. The creation of small towns in rural areas is a much healthier and more stable form of development than the expansion of large cities. Of the towns having a population of from 1,000 to 5,000 in population in 1911, 233 showed increases in the eight mainland provinces between 1901 and 1911, as follows:

Nova Scotia	15	New Brunswick	9
Quebec	81	Ontario	82
Manitoba	9	Saskatchewan	10
Alberta	15	British Columbia	12

In the eight mainland provinces no less than 529 towns or villages having a population of 1,000 or under were either not in existence in 1901, or increased in population between 1901 and 1911. As against 81 of these towns which increased in population in Quebec, only four showed a decrease.

The growth of these towns represented an accumulated development of manufacturing and mining industry in each province of great aggregate volume and importance. A few years prior to 1901 the control of the planning and development of a great many of these towns was vested in rural municipalities and their present condition reflects the good or bad management and direction they received in the initial rural stages of growth. During the next twenty or thirty years new industrial development in rural areas will take place – and should be encouraged to take place to a greater extent than hitherto. The better planning and direction of these new developments by rural municipalities is greatly needed in the interest of increased production and rational development.

In addition to the industrial growth which is taking place within rural areas as a natural outcome of rural development, there is a strong tendency in Canada, as in England and America, for large manufacturers to move from large urban centres to rural and semi-rural districts. The improvement in railway systems in territory surrounding large cities, the development of the hydro-radials, and the making of good roads, together with the increased pressure of taxation in congested centres, are all contributing to a new movement of industries and population from large cities to rural and semi-rural areas. The same tendency in Great Britain has influenced urban and rural development in that country for the past 20 years and was the chief argument used to secure the necessary support to enable the first Garden City to be established in England. In the United States the increase of workers in thirteen large cities was only 40.8 per cent in

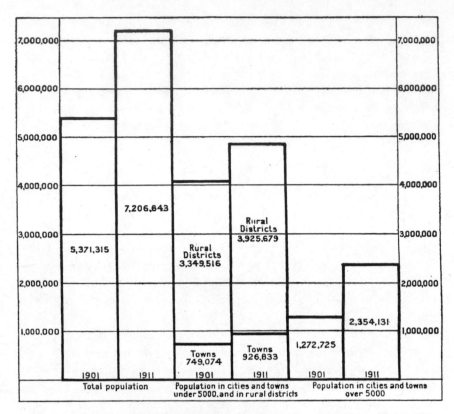

FIGURE 4   GROWTH OF POPULATION IN SMALL CITIES, TOWNS AND RURAL DISTRICTS,
COMPARED WITH GROWTH IN THE LARGER CITIES.
Commission of Conservation Town-Planning Branch

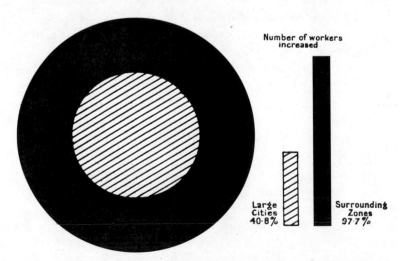

FIGURE 5   INCREASE OF POPULATION IN SUBURBAN ZONES IN THE UNITED STATES
From "Satellite Cities" by Graham Romeyn Taylor

ten years, whereas it was 97.7 per cent in the semi-rural zones surrounding these cities during the same period. Mr. Graham Romeyn Taylor, in *Satellite Cities,* describes this movement as a "sweeping current," which is being accelerated by all that is being done to improve transportation. (Figures 4 and 5.)

In Canada the same movement has begun, and we find satellite towns and industrial villages growing up in the open country around the large cities of Montreal and Toronto, and a more rapid increase of population in the outer than in the nearer suburbs. When the United States Steel Corporation came to Canada, it selected a site and purchased farm land in a purely rural area outside of Windsor, Ontario, to erect its plant and build its own town.

This question of industrial decentralization is of importance from the point of view of rural development. It is a natural and growing tendency, and as such indicates the practicability of artificially promoting industrial village centres and rural industries. Under present conditions decentralization does harm to production around cities, since it is accompanied by the worst and most intensive forms of land speculation, which means that great areas of land are subdivided and exploited for building that should be left in cultivation. It is also harmful from a sanitary point of view, owing to the fact that the rural authorities often look upon these encroachments of urban population with disfavour, as causing them added responsibility and expense. Unfortunately they do not think it necessary to apply other than rural standards of sanitation to the urban conditions thus created. Properly organized, however, the movement should help to increase production by bringing consumer and producer nearer to each other, and if proper planning regulations were made and enforced, unhealthy land speculation and improper sanitary conditions in connection with these new developments would be prevented.

Conclusion

In conclusion it is contended that, notwithstanding the comparatively sound lines on which distribution of population has proceeded in Canada, there is abundant evidence that the settlement of considerable areas of unsuitable or inaccessible land, and the absentee and speculative ownership of large areas of fertile and accessible land, have produced serious social and economic problems which urgently need solution; that while there has been a satisfactory increase of population, production and wealth in Canada, there has been an inadequate appreciation of the importance of conserving and developing human resources, and that the great potentialities of Canada, in respect of natural resources; the tendencies which are at work as a result of improved methods of transportation and the opening up of new industries, and the prospects which these afford for obtaining greatly increased population in the near future make it of vital importance that there should be a national stock-taking of all resources and a sound economic foundation laid on which to build the structure of future development.

RURAL POPULATION AND PRODUCTION IN CANADA

Commentary by Michael Troughton

Thomas Adams introduces his objective of looking critically at the status of and need for the planning of rural development in Canada in Chapter I of *Rural Planning and Development*. He underlines his premise in the last paragraph of that chapter: "Particularly in our rural districts the conditions of well-being of the community have not been sufficiently respected in Canada – and until they are we shall lack the essentials of real progress" (page 16).

Chapter II is wide-ranging and also introductory. It concentrates on what Adams identifies as problems relating to changing rural demographics and production in the context of rural losses and urban gains. He discusses situations that emerged in the early 1900s, many of which have remained critical to considerations of rural Canada, planning, development, and sustainability. Some issues introduced in this chapter that are still being discussed are rural responses vis-à-vis an urbanizing society and economy in relation to both absolute and relative rural decline in peripheral and agricultural hinterland regions, appropriate definitions of *rural* in terms of population numbers and settlement types, and rural sustainability in relation to rural land capability. The underlying goal of the book is to search for answers to the key contemporary question of how to maintain sustainable rural systems.

Adams is a perceptive commentator, but his work is strongly influenced by attitudes of the day that viewed a productive rural economy and viable rural communities in Canada as critical to the country's success and expressed concerns at any signs of weakness. Despite his experience with a vastly more urban situation in the United Kingdom and his recognition of urban growth as an inevitable process, Adams seems to buy into the colonial concerns of his contemporaries. He also echoes some prejudices of the day, including the belief that British settlers were preferable to foreign settlers and that poverty leads to immorality and degradation.

Adams is far seeing, but he was constrained by the time in which he was writing. In the first years of the twentieth century, rural Canada was in flux, and some of the consequences of change were impossible for even a perceptive commentator to assess. Virtually all rural settlement in the nineteenth century had taken place in the five eastern provinces. Peak rural dominance had occurred by the 1880s, and the twin processes of rural rationalization and urbanization were beginning to create changes. By the early 1900s, these developments included both absolute and relative declines to rural population and farm numbers and rising urban activity throughout eastern Canada. Rural depopulation was a major issue and political topic of the day. As was documented in the 1911 census and subsequent *Canada Yearbooks,* these developments peaked between 1900 and 1914. Comparative census statistics, together with contemporary reports, provided evidence of rural decline, which Adams concentrates on in this chapter. What turned out to be temporary circumstances were interpreted by Adams as further evidence of rural weakness. He could not anticipate the postwar renewal of immigration or the emergence of western Canada as the nation's primary agricultural region. Nor could he have foretold the influence of agricultural mechanization, which contributed to successful Prairie agriculture but had profound effects vis-à-vis major reductions to farming in eastern Canada.

Adams' reaction is a little surprising. As an urban planner, he tends to decry urban growth and emphasize its darker side, and despite evidence to the contrary, he tends to be pessimistic about rural Canada. Nevertheless, he does his best to understand rural Canada, despite being caught in the midst of changes whose results would not be fully apparent until several decades later. On the other hand, his perceptions and planning prescriptions provide an important base from which to re-examine the critical period of rural development in the early twentieth century and assess what issues remain at the forefront of planning concerns today.

Adams begins with an examination of rural systems, especially those in eastern Canada affected by urbanization. As a town planner, he is not anti-urban, but he cites instances of urbanization's negative influence on rural Canada and argues that the situation has been exacerbated by the lack of well-planned rural systems. He is particularly troubled by evidence of declining rural populations, farms, and farmland in eastern Canada. He links rural depopulation and poverty to the unwise and unplanned settlement of marginal areas that were unable to sustain viable farm communities. He is most concerned about rural population decline because it reflects wasted human capital, which underscores his pleas for pre-planning, including land classification.

In "Movement of Population," Adams examines the rural and urban components of the 1911 census and identifies and discusses the problem inherent in its definition of *rural populations.* He argues that rural populations are considerably undercounted because the census maintains a low threshold of one thousand people for rural agglomerations and considers all incorporated places urban. Adams reworks the census, using what he argues is a more logical threshold of 1,500 rural dwellers, and demonstrates that his results show a much healthier and "more realistic" rural total. In contrast to the 1911 census, which identified a shift from a declining rural majority (54.5 percent) to an increasingly urban (45.5 percent) population, Adams' revised figures place the rural proportion of the population at 60.5 percent (Figure 1). He even applies a threshold of five thousand rural dwellers to arrive at a rural population of 67 percent in 1911. Even today, the linkages between rural and urban areas make it difficult to categoric- ally define their populations. Place of residence is but one defining characteristic. It is noteworthy that Adams is among the first to recognize the exurban compon- ent, which has engendered so much contemporary debate.

Adams then contrasts bad conditions with good conditions in Ontario, his province of record. Under the heading "Bad Conditions" he uses a mix of census data and reports to document population losses in marginal areas. In particular, he notes significant losses in rural southern Ontario between 1900 and 1910. Interestingly, Adams seems to regard the ongoing settlement of northern Ontario as satisfactory (he expands on this in Chapter VII), whereas Fernow, Howe, and White's prediction of failure came true forty to sixty years later as northern areas in both Ontario and Quebec experienced even more drastic depopulation because of the physical isolation of farms and inadequate farm incomes (Troughton 1987). Adams also notes the significant loss of farms and rural population elsewhere, including the Maritime provinces. Later authors have likewise outlined the prob- lems in these marginal landscapes, including the general failure of colonization roads (Spragge 1957) and the tendency of early township surveys, particularly on the Canadian Shield, to mistake forest growth as an indication of agricultural soils (Maxwell 1966). These problems peaked after the Second World War, giving rise to responses such as the Agricultral and Rural Development Act (ARDA 1964). Adams recognizes the causal factors set out by Fernow, Howe, and White (1913), including the problems of infertile soils, lack of accessibility, and inability to make a living. He emphasizes that the loss of the most energetic settlers leaves a residual group who contribute to "social degeneracy ... low moral tone and mental defects" (page 31).

Assessing "Good Conditions in Ontario," Adams notes that the province gener- ally has better soil and climatic conditions for agriculture and that some of the best farming areas have "the appearance and features of a highly cultivated English countryside" (page 37). However, he is still concerned about evidence of rural decline. To Adams, this key contemporary worry reflected the waste of good settler stock. Recent scholarship has documented a less negative situation. Areas suited to successful farming in lowland southern Ontario were almost completely settled by the late nineteenth century. Farm families were large, but succession was usually of the complete holding to an elder son. Consequently, large numbers of siblings had to find alternative employment elsewhere. Many who wanted to farm joined the westward migration to the Prairies or the United States; others, especially those seeking higher education or a professional career, migrated to the cities. This exodus resulted in numeric declines in the majority of rural mu- nicipalities and led to some loss of activity in the non-farm sector, but it rarely led to weakness in the farming system.

Adams dislikes what the census reveals about conditions in the four western provinces: low population densities, falling rural populations, and a small proportion of land in crops (Figure 2). Low population densities and lack of intensification stemmed from the Prairie's land base, the relatively late arrival of settlers, and the lag between survey, disposal, and improvement. In addition, declining rural population percentages were a direct result of categorizing all incorporated settlements as urban. Adams mentions the problem of categorization but does not recalibrate statistics for the region. A reassessment of the figures shows that, by 1911, large numbers of nucleated places had been established along the railway, but few had populations of a thousand. Throughout the three Prairie provinces, 347 of 381 incorporated towns and villages had fewer than a thousand residents. If these towns are reclassified as rural, the rural population increases to about two hundred thousand, a figure that more than reverses the so-called losses recorded between 1901 and 1911. In retrospect, we know that most of these "wannabe cities" never reached even a thousand inhabitants but remained quintessential rural service locations. On the other hand, their widespread presence, chiefly as grain delivery points, attests to the energy of immigrants and the rapid shift to commercial farming in the newly settled region.

In his broad discussion of demographics, Adams also touches on the issue of gender balance – the low number of females to males – in many settlement areas. At the time, and especially in western Canada, this unbalance reflected a stage in the migration process when males tended to homestead first and then either fetch their families or, if single, marry. The unbalance tended to diminish and was much less marked at the peak of Prairie settlement. However, the issue of gender has been noted, particularly women's critical importance but lack of recognition in farming. Related to this was the shortage of off-farm rural employment, leading to rural to urban migration of young women and/or increased commuting.

Adams' use of the census is a major part of his overall assessment. Although his interpretation sometimes goes awry – for instance, when he interprets low population densities, large farm areas, and low wheat yields in western Canada as problems rather than the consequences of a semi-arid farming environment – he uses statistics to telling effect to demonstrate the perennial problems of low farm incomes and returns to capital. He links the former and the limited returns to farmers to the role of middlemen, who figure in later discussions of the "cost-price squeeze" and today's "treadmill of production" in industrial agriculture

Rural Planning and Development continues to be relevant. Rural communities, particularly those with significant agricultural activity, depend on the quality of their resources. New investment and increasingly industrial approaches to production occur in those areas of the country with the best land and the best climate.

In other areas, agriculture is marginalized. From a planning perspective, distinctive issues relating to land use, agricultural intensification, and environmental health continue to dominate.

REFERENCES

Agricultural Rehabilitation and Development Administration (ARDA). 1964. *Economic and Social Disadvantage in Canada: Some Graphic Indicators of Location and Degree.* Ottawa: Canada Department of Forestry.

Fernow, Bernhard Eduard, Clifton Durant Howe, and James H. White. 1913. *Survey of the Trent Watershed, Report.* Ottawa: Commission of Conservation.

Maxwell, J.M. 1966. "Notes on Land Use and Landscape Evaluation in a Fringe Area of the Canadian Shield." *Geographical Bulletin* 9, 2: 134-50.

McDougall, John. 1913 [1973]. *Rural Life in Canada: Its Trends and Tasks.* Toronto: University of Toronto Press.

Spragge, G.W. 1957. "Colonization Roads in Canada West, 1850-1867." *Ontario History* 49, 1: 1-17.

Troughton, Michael J. 1983. "The Failure of Agricultural Settlement in Northern Ontario." *Nordia* 17, 1: 141-51.

CHAPTER III

Present Systems of Surveying and Planning Land in Rural Areas

Present system of surveying land in rural districts |
Dominion surveys | *Provincial surveys* | *Township planning* |
Fixing road reservations | *Reservation of land adjoining lakes and watercourses* | *Object of surveys* | *Radial plans* | *Proposed scheme for townsite in Northern Ontario* | *Manitoba scheme* | *Practicability of community settlements* | *Diagrams illustrating certain principles of planning rural areas* | *Townsite and building subdivision plans in rural areas* | *Effect of rural on urban planning* | *Ancient rectangular plans* | *The beginnings of urban planning* | *Present control of subdivision surveys* | *Land classification*

Present System of Surveying Land in Rural Districts

As a general rule there has been no proper planning of rural and urban areas in Canada – merely adherence to a rectangular system of survey. Land has been divided according to certain principles laid down by land surveyors, to whom have been assigned greater responsibilities in defining boundaries of municipal areas and land divisions than in older countries. The system originated in the United States. Both in its inception and development it appears to have been designed to promote speculation – both private and public – rather than the economic use of the land.* From the surveyor's point of view it appears to have been influenced in its growth by two main considerations. These were, first, the necessity of mapping out the territory on a geometrical plan, without

---

* The intention of the Government of the United States was not to promote speculation but that was the inevitable result of the system. In 1796 a minimum price of $1 was charged per acre, and was later raised to $2, with the purpose of stopping speculation, but this did not prevent wholesale speculation from being carried on. The Homestead Act was not passed till 1862, but no change was made in the system of survey. Over 250,000,000 acres of land were alienated under that Act. *See also article on "The Settlement of Public Lands in the United States," in Vol. VI, No. 3, of Bulletin issued by Canadian Commissioner of International Institute of Agriculture.*

regard to the physical features of the surface of the land owing to the vastness of the areas to be dealt with, and, second, the need for accuracy and simplicity in defining boundaries of the different units of a geometrical system.

Another influence was of a political rather than of an engineering character. A regular and comprehensive system had to be adopted to enable large areas to be surveyed in advance of settlement for government purposes. Population had to be attracted by the offer of free homesteads or cheap land, without time and thought being given to the planning and classification of the land for economic use and development, or to the distribution of the population to secure successful and permanent settlement. The population thus attracted or anticipated, gave a stimulus to both private and public speculation in the development of natural resources and means of transportation. Everything that contributed to that stimulus was encouraged, and anything that militated against it became an object of criticism as an interference with the free play of natural forces. Having regard to this speculative tendency, and to the need for meeting the competition of other countries in attracting population, the kind of planning or surveying adopted probably served its purpose. But it permitted no discretion or intelligence to be exercised by the surveyor beyond what was required to accurately define and locate the boundaries according to a rigid and inelastic system.

Proper planning should follow no hard and fast rule. It should intelligently dispose the boundaries of at least the smaller divisions of land to suit industrial requirements, to conform to the natural conditions and physical features of the locality, and to provide for the most economical, convenient and healthy development. The American system, adopted in Canada, is unsound, to the extent that it falls short of this standard, even if it could claim to be simple and accurate and to have succeeded for a time in attracting population by speculative means. Of course, it is not claimed that a new country can be developed without speculation, or that properly regulated speculation is injurious.* What is injurious is when speculation is the object of development. Every large railway enterprise is a great speculation, but, if the sole object in constructing a railway is to create and speculate in land values, it may become a social pest instead of an instrument of sound development. A government may be a speculator of an injurious kind if it stimulates immigration and land settlement without proper plans of development, and without proper regard to the social and economic needs of the settlers, although it may receive no actual coin in the process. The proper object of development should be production

---

* See Chapter IV

based on healthy living conditions, and not the mere accretion of numbers. When that is the object of a government it will not unduly facilitate land settlement until the land is properly planned and classified for the purpose, and until steps are taken to prevent injurious speculation.

In Appendix A, a description is given by Mr. H. L. Seymour of the systems which are employed in the different provinces. It will be seen that they all involve the use of the straight line and the right angle right down through the whole series of divisions of the land, including the boundaries of provinces, of counties, of townships, of quarter-sections (homestead subdivisions), and of building subdivisions or lots, and that the duty of the surveyor consists in following a plan prescribed for him.

DOMINION SURVEYS

Under the Dominion Lands Surveys Act of 1908 land is required to be laid out in quadrilateral townships, each containing 36 sections, and each section divided into quarter sections of 160 acres. While, however, this system is adopted for general purposes, the Surveyor General has power, with the authority of his Minister, to depart from the system in respect of certain lands. As Mr. Seymour points out, lands bordering on a river or watercourse can be surveyed or laid out in such manner and with such roads as appear desirable. Under such conditions it is provided that, in the case of settlements already in existence, a road 66 ft. wide has to be laid out across the settlement in the most *convenient* location.

Surveys are now made more accurate and elaborate than formerly, and a good beginning has been made in recent years in collecting information regarding the situation and character of townships. This survey, however, is not sufficient and is too general in character, to provide a basis for classification or a proper system of settlement. A series of reports from surveyors' field books has been published, giving particulars of the nature of the soil, timber, water supplies and powers, climate, etc. It is thus seen that the surveying department of the Dominion Government now recognizes the advantage of obtaining more complete information regarding the character of the land when it is surveyed. The fact that the department reserves to itself and exercises the power to vary the survey for small areas in certain circumstances shows that there would be no difficulty in making a similar variation in respect of larger areas.

PROVINCIAL SURVEYS

Writing, in 1906, with regard to the system in vogue in Ontario, Mr. J. F. Whitson, O.L.S., who is now representative of the Provincial Government in Northern Ontario, stated that one-quarter of the agricultural land in that province was not then surveyed, and "if changed conditions of agriculture within recent years require some change in the system of survey it is not too late for the government to make the change." Referring to the advantages of closer settlement in the clay belt Mr. Whitson said:

> In a wooded country, such as Northern Ontario, while it is a great advantage to the settler to have a liberal frontage to his lot, *it is of greater importance to have concentrated on one line of road two lines of farms as closely situate as practicable,* as clearings are more quickly made. They unite their labour in opening and maintaining the same line of road and combine the more readily in rendering aid to each other when united efforts are required, the population is less scattered, and schools and places of worship can be reached with less inconvenience, *and this is one if not the most important feature in a new settlement.* Many a farmer with a numerous small family is driven from his backwoods home with its many advantages and prospects, for want of schools, or rather because, for nearly half the year, owing to the bad condition of the roads, the children are unable to attend ... The enormous cost of constructing good roads in a new country – between $750 and $1,000 per mile – makes it imperative to have no more road allowance than is absolutely necessary to accommodate the public.

It is unnecessary in this report to go into the merits of the different systems in vogue in Canada. The Quebec system, with its narrow and deep lots, the 1,000-acre system in Ontario, first adopted by the Canada Land Company in 1829 and later by the province, and the revised system now in force in Ontario, seem to possess great advantages over the Dominion square sectional plan as a means of securing closer settlement. For 100-acre farms the 1,000-acre section system seems as good as any stereotyped system can be. The new system adopted in Northern Ontario does not depart in a material degree from the older Ontario systems except in regard to the increase of the size of the township from six to nine square miles. There seems to be no doubt that for purposes of local government the six-square mile township is too small. Townships should be from twice to four times the present area and, as has been proved in some counties, this lessens the cost of administration without any loss of efficiency.

But convenient distribution of the farms and a good road system cannot be obtained with any rigid rectangular lay-out. Nature has provided rivers, lakes, watersheds, swamps, and mixed areas of good and bad land, which should all be allowed to influence municipal and farm boundaries. But even natural boundaries are not always ideal, and any proper system must

PLATE V   BOLTON PASS, BROME COUNTRY, QUEBEC

The character of the topography shown in the above illustrations is typical of a great extent of territory in Canada. Such land should be planned so as to obtain the best use of the fertile valleys and make them accessible to the markets. The roads in the above views are placed in the proper position, but, under a rectangular plan, their probable direction would be across the steep hills and, in the average case, the farm divisions would include only small areas of productive land and much that is entirely useless.

Photos by courtesy of Immigration Branch, Dept. of Interior have regard to employment of intelligence and discretion. In dividing the land for settlement natural boundaries should be used as alternatives to the artificial lines of the surveyor and greater discretion should be employed in determining which boundary to use in the smaller units. It is recognized, however, that there have been certain difficulties to be surmounted in a country where the system of land registration required divisions to be made for large areas for settlement before the land could be surveyed in detail. For county areas, perhaps, the rectangular system could not be greatly improved upon, except by making deviations at the edges of lakes and at river intersections.

TOWNSHIP PLANNING

It is, however, when we get down to the units or sections that lie within the township that greater room for improvement is found. Whatever excuse there may have been in the past for rigid adherence to the rectangular sections, because of the want of men and organization to plan these sections with some regard to physical conditions and future development, there is no longer any excuse for such adherence – although in the case of purely level land, without river intersections, this kind of plan is satisfactory from some points of view.

In territory to be opened up in future a more elastic system of planning should be followed within township boundaries, and regard should be paid to future development, to existing railways, topography, character of soil, and other physical considerations, without any sacrifice of accuracy. The increased cost of making more detailed surveys than at present would be small compared with the saving that could be effected in getting roads in the right place, in lessening the length of roads, and in securing economic distribution of the land; and also compared with the advantages which could be obtained in greater convenience and healthier conditions of development. Moreover, the surveys need not be spread over such large areas and should follow a more concentrated system of land settlement, dealing first with the more fertile lands and with those lying nearest to the means of distribution. It is a fact that, even with the absence of any plan of agricultural areas in older countries like England, the results are better in important respects than in Canada with its rectangular system, because, in the former case, some purpose of using and developing the land has been the primary consideration in its planning, rather than simplicity and accuracy of arrangement to suit a particular mode of placing settlers. There are still enormous areas of new territory in Quebec, Ontario, and in the western provinces where some improvement in system might be adopted.

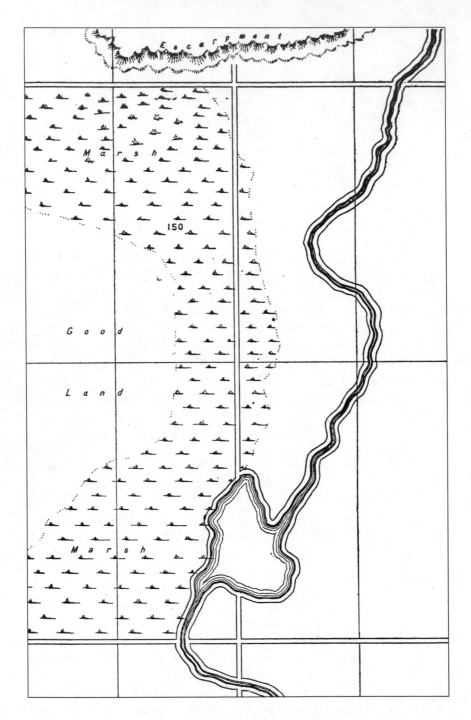

FIGURE 6   ANOMALIES OF RECTANGULAR SYSTEM OF FARM DIVISIONS
Scale 18 chains = 1 inch
Commission of Conservation Town Planning Branch

In parts of organized territory already divided and, to a more or less extent, alienated in homesteads, some readjustment is still possible, and in any event control of future development and of areas where cancellation has taken place can be provided. There are large areas of uncleared and swampy land near to towns and railways which can be rendered fertile at reasonable cost for clearance and drainage, and a thorough survey of such land should be made with a view to securing its improvement and development. But any replanning as distinct from regulation of future growth of such territory raises difficulties which can only be partly and slowly overcome under expert advice. The whole matter should be dealt with by a system so designed as to gradually secure closer settlement, better facilities for making farming more attractive and profitable than is practicable under the present method and for the reduction of the unnecessary lengths of road reservations. Every township boundary could be determined under the present system, but no land should be homesteaded, or boundaries fixed, within the township boundary until a proper plan of development for the whole township was prepared and approved by an efficient director of surveys acting in collaboration with a skilled director of planning in each province. The farms should be laid out with proper regard to the fullest and best use of the land, to convenience and ease of access, to obtaining facilities for water supply, transportation, health, amenity, etc., while the highway system would accord with a provincial plan of main highways.

A sketch showing the effect of one of the present systems, in causing absurd intersections of land, is shown in figure 6. It shows the boundary of farms in which small pieces of land are cut off on one side of an unfordable river, making them entirely useless to the farmers. In such cases the farmers may sell the isolated portions to adjoining farmers, but that does not lessen the absurdity of the plan. It also shows an area of 160 acres of good farm land surrounded by rock and swamp of no agricultural value. This area is divided into for sections, which means that the farms have each only a small acreage of land suitable for cultivation, and even then only accessible across a swamp. Whatever may be the proper kind of division in a case of this kind it is obvious that some system should be adopted which would have regard to the use to which the land was to be put.

Fixing Road Reservations

There are two principal methods employed in fixing road reservations in connection with the surveys. The method employed in the Dominion surveys for western lands fixes the roads as shown on figure D in appendix A without regard to physical or topographical conditions. The other method, which has been used in Quebec and is now the practice in Northern Ontario, is to reserve five per cent of the land for roads, leaving the exact location to be afterwards determined. Neither system permits of the proper planning of the roads, although the latter method is best in allowing discretion to be exercised. But it does not work out satisfactorily in practice, because vested interests are created in the homesteads before the sites of the roads are fixed, and the planning is largely governed by the selfishness and idiosyncrasies of individual farmers, or groups of farmers, who are only interested in securing the location of roads to suit their own separate requirements. In either case roads are usually made to follow the straight lines of the farm boundaries, hills are ignored, and stretches of muskeg or swamp are crossed where good road foundations and satisfactory drainage cannot be obtained.

Reservation of Land Adjoining Lakes and Watercourses

In Ontario and other provinces governments now require that a width of 66 feet of land be reserved round lakes and along the banks of rivers. The effect of this reservation is shown on the division plan illustrated in figure 7. It prevents the encroachment of undesirable erections along the edges of watercourses and provides space for road communication between the farms with water frontage. The principle of reserving these strips of land is a sound one, and in time great public benefit will be derived as a result of its application. But so far as securing protection of the waterfront is concerned little advantage seems to be gained, and inconvenience to owners may be caused by fixing an arbitrary width of 66 feet in all cases. The width reserved should be determined according to the nature and situation of the land. In some cases high rocky cliffs and in others great stretches of swamp surround water areas; such land has no value for private use, and could be retained in public ownership in wide stretches for forest reserves or other purposes. On the other hand the reservation of the strips for road space is frequently of no use owing to the topographical conditions. Even short lengths of road for purely farm purposes cannot be made along steep banks or across swamps. Again when the banks of rivers or lakes consist of hard level land the roads have to wind in and out following every bend and twist of the water area, and there is no latitude for improving the alignment to shorten distances or avoid the tortuous windings.

While, therefore, it is desirable to protect the edges of the water areas and to have roads in many cases running nearly parallel with rivers and around lakes, the roads should be designed as part of a plan and should not follow a meaningless and arbitrary line. As at present laid out they

CLUTE

DISTRICT of SUDBURY

—Scale 40 Chains=1 Inch—

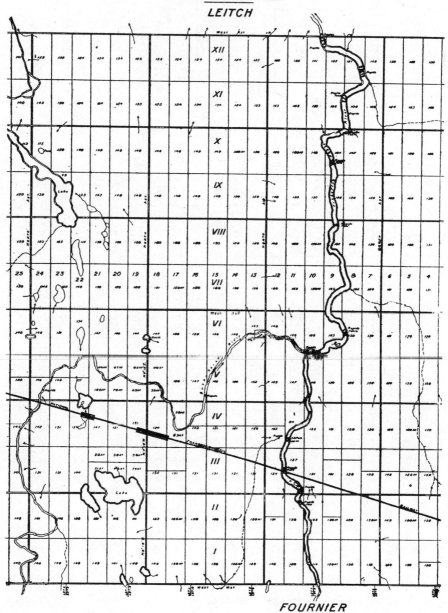

FIGURE 7

Ontario Survey showing Road Reservations, including 66 ft. Reservations along Water Courses.

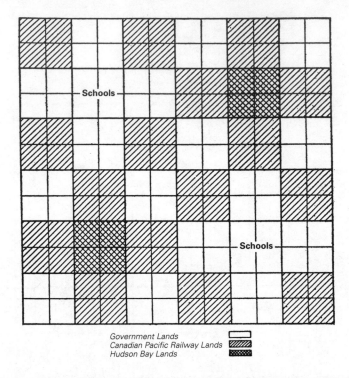

Government Lands
Canadian Pacific Railway Lands
Hudson Bay Lands

FIGURE 8   DIVISION OF TOWNSHIP IN RAILWAY BELT SHOWING ALLOTMENTS
TO RAILWAY COMPANY, HUDSON BAY COMPANY AND SCHOOLS.
Commission of Conservation Town-Planning Branch

are merely an expedient to get over one of the anomalies of the present
system of fixing the farm boundaries. The division of many of the farms
shown on figure 7 leads to great waste of land, to the splitting up of homesteads adjoining water areas in shapes and sizes that cannot be used or
developed, to the placing of roads in the worst positions to secure bridges
over streams, and to cul-de-sac roads running to an end at the water edge
or at the foot of steep hills.

The system of land survey in the railway belts of the western provinces
is not only unsatisfactory, as a system of planning, but the method which
has been adopted, of allocating certain sections to the railway companies
and other sections to the Hudson's Bay Company, interspersed with other
sections retained by the Dominion Government, makes proper planning
impossible – unless by co-operation between the companies and the government before settlement takes place. In this case there is not only a
hard and fast system of subdivision, but also a separate ownership of alternative sections, which adds to the difficulty of applying any discretion

to the planning of the areas. A township allocated according to this system is shown on figure 8.

OBJECT OF SURVEYS

In spite of their defects, however, it is probable that no better series of systems of surveying lands could have been devised when we have regard to the object of making the surveys. That object – important in itself – was to secure accurate measurements and divisions of the land for rapid settlement; and the fact that it did not include a topographical survey, a scheme of classification of the land and planning of the roads was no fault of the surveyor. His duties have been circumscribed within a narrow radius and within that radius he has performed his task with great skill and energy. Under the leadership of Dr. Deville, the Surveyor General, the surveyors of Canada have given able and devoted service to the country, and it is necessary to make it quite clear that what is objected to is not the work or methods of the surveyor, nor the rectangular system as a means to secure accurate measurement, but to the scope of the surveyor's duties having been too limited, and to the rectangular system as a plan for land settlement. The surveyor should not only measure the land, but make a survey of its conditions in the real sense; and *the rectangular survey should not be the plan for settlement, but only provide the basis on which a proper development plan for each township should be prepared.*

Objections have occasionally been made to the system of rectangular survey by those who have noted its defects as a plan of land development; but as it is not a plan of land development at all, and as its geometrical and rigid character make it unsuitable for such a plan, the survey should not be objected to on that ground. The objection should be to the facts that a survey designed for one purpose is used as a plan for another purpose, that it is so used without regard being paid to the soil, topography and future development, and that farms are divided and roads located without any properly conceived development scheme being prepared for the areas in which they are situated.

RADIAL PLANS

As one of the main objects of a proper land development scheme must be to group the population and design the location of the roads so as to secure the greatest efficiency in production, facilities for co-operation, etc., it follows that, other things being equal, a radial system of laying out roads – in which the roads would converge in a direct line to a common

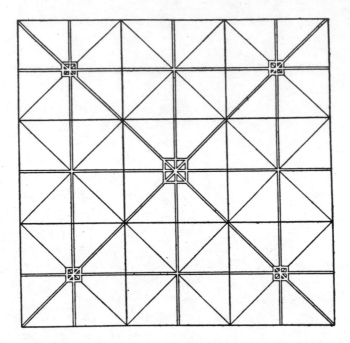

FIGURE 9   SCHEME FOR DIVIDING A TOWNSHIP OF 36 SQ. MILES,
AS PROPOSED BY THE LATE SIR WILLIAM VAN HORNE,
PRESIDENT OF THE CANADIAN PACIFIC RAILWAY CO.

centre in each township or larger area – would best serve these objects.
But there are serious objections to the radial plan when prepared in geometrical form and without regard to the shape of the farms, which in
most radial plans have to be triangular in shape. Farmers prefer to have
square farms and square fields and to that extent they are firm believers
in the square plan. They have to be persuaded that any departure from
the square plan is for a good reason. While not usually opposed to oblong
farms designed to give them access to rivers or to give them fewer and
better roads, they object to the sharp corners of triangular fields. As a
general rule triangular shaped fields should be avoided, but in a properly
conceived design, which included radial lines for the principal highways,
very few triangular fields need be included.

It is unfortunate that farmers seem to imagine that the reservation of
useless road spaces along the boundaries of their farms is of more advantage than securing good roads in the best positions and affording the
most direct access to the railway or village. If a practical experiment could
be carried out on a sufficiently large scale, and the saving and facilities
obtainable under a radial plan could be demonstrated, probably the advantages would be found to outweigh the disadvantages. However that

may be, there is not much to choose between the two kinds of plans, if they are merely geometrical designs, for general application.

Over twenty years ago Sir William Van Horne prepared a radial scheme for a township, but nothing was done to carry it out. This design is illustrated on figure 9, and is taken from a sketch prepared from memory by Dr. Deville. The lengths of roads and fences required to be provided under this scheme did not differ materially from those which are necessary in the rectangular plan. Under this radial scheme, however, the greatest distance which the settler requires to travel is 2.8 miles and for more than half of the settlers, the distance does not exceed two miles. In the typical rectangular plan the settler has to travel as much as five miles to reach the centre of the township.

In a letter addressed to Mr. James A. Smart, of the Department of the Interior, in 1897, Dr. Deville makes the following comment on this scheme:

> The saving in the cost of survey would be considerable.
>
> No reason occurs to me why, in flat prairie, all the advantages claimed for the proposed plan should not be realized. The only serious objection is that, in a rolling country, the central village and the small hamlets might fall in undesirable places. An eligible site may, however, always be found at some section corner which can be taken as the central point and from which the system can be extended in all directions, but this would involve some sacrifice in the general regularity of the plan.
>
> I am inclined to believe that the Governor in Council has the power, under the Dominion Lands Act, to authorize surveys under the new plan. Surveys already made can be changed to the new plan upon requisition of the Lieutenant Governor with the consent of the Governor in Council; no additional survey is needed.

Dr. Deville's objection to the possible location of the central village is one which can be raised to survey plans of whatever pattern which are prepared on a definite system of lines without regard to topography or other local conditions. The location of the village should be one of the first considerations in planning an agricultural area; the village should be placed most conveniently to the railway, or so located as to enable a good road to connect it with the railway, and such questions as those of water and power supplies should be considered. No preconceived plan should prevent these matters being taken into account. When areas are planned to secure efficiency and the economic use and development of the land, it will be found that every district will have to be considered on its merits. Even on flat prairie land there are local considerations, position of railways and rivers, etc., which prevent acceptance of a fixed and general system as a means of making the best use of the land.

Australia also suffers as the result of the adoption of the rectangular system of survey as a basis of land division and subdivision. The need for some change is expressed in a letter addressed to the Premier of Western Australia by Mr. G. M. Nunn, president of the Institution of Surveyors of that state, from which the following quotation is taken:

> When providing for settlement in groups, it would be advisable to abandon our present rectangular chess-board designs for subdivision, and to adopt a system providing for radial centres, where a few village lots could be set out, and where the settlers could live closer together, and thus enjoy a more sociable life. This system would be specifically applicable to the south coast country, where the farms would be small in area. It would give better opportunities for visiting experts to impart advice. It would stimulate the settler to greater effort and would attract tradesmen, storekeepers, etc.

No doubt there would be the same objections to a radial plan as a fixed form of subdivision in Australia as in Canada. As already stated, we should get away from any kind of fixed system – radial or rectangular – which is independent of natural conditions. The directness of route and closer settlement to be obtained by a radial system of roads are only two of the matters to be borne in mind in planning, although, other things being equal, the radial lines are preferable to the zig-zag roads of the right-angled plan.

Mr. W. C. Morham, of New Liskeard, who has farmed for some years in the clay belt of Northern Ontario, and Mr. A. C. Flumerfelt, late Finance Minister of British Columbia, are among those who advocate a radial plan. As a result of experience, both as a farmer and as reeve of his township, Mr. Morham claims that 80 acres is sufficient for a farm, especially for townsmen taking up farming. He writes:

> Such a scheme would make for economy of working and largely solve the problem of the rural school, but no scheme will be successful so long as land is held vacant ... It has taken me some time to arrive at the best plan for laying out the farm communities, and I have adopted the radial system rather than the narrow rectangular lots, with the idea of getting the dwellings close enough together to have a water service to the houses. This, I think, is of immense importance. Wedge shaped farms should not be greatly objected to, as the squarest of farms may be crossed by ravines and creeks, which are a law unto themselves.

PROPOSED VILLAGE SCHEME IN NORTHERN ONTARIO

A plan of a different type is proposed by Mr. William Henderson, who has spent a large portion of the last ten years in Northern Ontario and has travelled many thousands of miles through it. The significance of Mr. Henderson's scheme lies in the fact that he approaches the question from the point of view of the social student, interested primarily in the moral and physical improvement of the rural population, and that, having studied the question from that point of view, he has come to the conclusion that proper planning is the first thing necessary to secure an effective remedy for unsatisfactory social conditions. Whatever the merits or demerits of the details of his scheme, it has unquestionable value as indicating some directions in which improvement is needed and can be found.

A plan of Mr. Henderson's scheme, prepared by H. B. and L. A. Dunnington Grubb of Toronto, is shown on figure 11. This plan has been prepared without regard to the topographical or soil conditions, as it is merely intended for illustration of the principles underlying the scheme. Mr. Henderson gives the following description of his proposal and of the reasons which led him to put it forward:

> The hundreds of deserted homesteads seen everywhere in Northern Ontario, the apparent poverty of a great many of the remaining settlers, and, above all, the dissatisfaction with existing conditions, together with a desire for the amenities of city life, can lead to only one conclusion. If the great clay belt, with its vast potential agricultural wealth is ever to support a thriving population, a policy in regard to land settlement, differing widely to that obtaining in the past, must be put into force.
>
> Until the government and people of Ontario are prepared to face the fact that conditions obtaining one hundred years ago no longer apply, all future schemes for land settlement like those which have been attempted in the past will fail. A day has arrived when intelligent and ambitious young people, with the experience of a past generation before them, will no longer face the privations of pioneer life. The woman will no longer be induced to leave the social amenities of the city for the isolation and slavery of a backwoods farm and, without the woman's help, the man is impotent. The man is unable to see sufficient reward for the years of drudgery and toil held out to him.
>
> When stock farming is not made a specialty, the farmer can operate as efficiently, when living within easy reach of his farm, as he can when living on his farm. In Northern Ontario, the pioneer farmer will be unable to attempt stock farming for many years, except on a very small

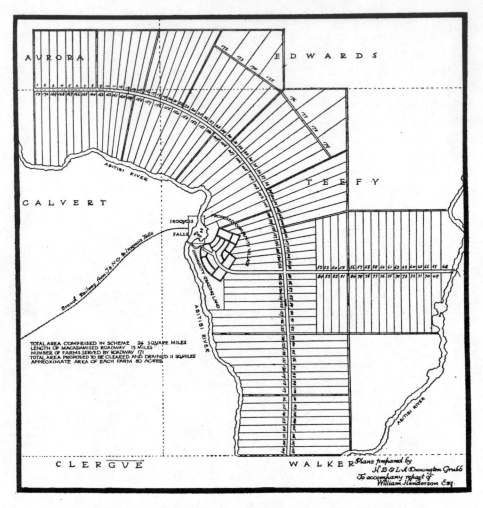

FIGURE 11   PLAN OF COMMUNITY SCHEME IN NORTHERN ONTARIO

scale. If the village were surrounded by community grazing land, the live stock would never need to be taken to the farm at all. All schemes so far proposed for land settlement in Northern Ontario presuppose the construction of a good road for the transportation of farm produce. Given a good road there is no reason why farmers should not live community life in villages with city conveniences, and be taken to and from their farms each day.

In the proposed scheme the cost of building blocks of dwellings and barns in villages would be less than the cost of individual dwellings and barns on each farm. With central heating for the village, water supply, electric light and power, immense economies in the time of the farmer and his family would be effected; with co-operative marketing and supplies, great economies and increased profits could be effected; with a village school within a few minutes' walk of every house, the children would have more time to help, and with half the chores eliminated, the farmers' time for the six winter months would be free and could be employed on lumbering or other industries started in the village.

The scheme calls for the construction of 13 miles of good road, giving direct frontage to 171 farms of 80 acres each. It is proposed that half of each farm, 40 acres, nearest the good road should be allotted to each farmer and sufficient cleared and drained to enable him to make a living. A service of motor trucks traveling at suitable hours along the two main roads would carry the farmer to and from his fields and carry produce. Cheap sheds on the fields, to shelter machinery and horses, would be the only buildings required.

It is proposed that all village property, pasture lands, allotments, etc., should be the property of a joint stock company, with guaranteed bonds and a fixed rate of interest. The plans show two types of house for varying sized families, the rents to include heating and hot and cold water supply. The central heating plant would be run with un-marketable wood as fuel, of which there will be an abundant supply for some years to come. For the benefit of those with large families, or an inclination for the raising of garden produce, half-acre allotments in the immediate vicinity of the village are shown.

The centre of the village would consist of one main street, on which would be built such public buildings as are essential to any community life. (Figure 12.)

MANITOBA SCHEME

As in Northern Ontario so in Western Canada, there are the same allegations of poverty and deterioration, due to social isolation, because of the failure to recognize that social intercourse is one of the necessities of healthy life, and there are the same kinds of proposals being put forward to deal with them, showing the general recognition of the need for better planning as a first step in reform.

Professor A. A. Stoughton, of the University of Manitoba, writes as follows* regarding a settlement scheme, proposed to be carried on in that province:

---

* *Manitoba Free Press*, February, 1917.

The usual homesteading plan of settling families on sections or quarter sections, using only the rectangular system of road allowance, and marking the centre by a promiscuous group of shacks around the railway platform, may have done in the past for our immigrants, but for people whose spirit has been quickened by the thrilling experiences of the past two years, whether in the fighting line or as non-combatants, something more than this is necessary. Otherwise our settlers will become embruited with the loneliness of their isolation and the deadening influence of their surroundings, without alleviation of any socializing agency.

It has been amply proved in the discussions of the recent Social Welfare Congress that if people living on the land are not to degenerate, there must be some sort of community life and the opportunity and the impulse toward a social spirit. There must be an incentive to get together.

It may well be questioned whether any such common activity could be long maintained in the centre of the usual sort, utterly deformed, squalid and ugly, and lacking the barest necessities for the inspiration of a civic spirit. The whole area settled must be properly planned to make the easiest access from the furthest farm to the centre; the centre must be laid out and the building and other features planned with the same sort of care and respect for appearance and the requirements of the situation as is exercised in the civic centres of towns and cities.

To improve this situation, two things are involved. The first concerns the general plan. The deadly rectangle of section lines must be replaced by diagonal or other roads adjusted to the particular conditions, as indicated in the report of the Commission of Conservation, by which distances to travel and the mileage of roads to construct and maintain are greatly reduced, and account must be taken of the topography, streams, woods, or other natural features, in order to make the most convenient and effective plan.

A suitable area should be devoted to community purposes; sites for the school and the community hall; locations for the hotel, the store, the creamery, and all this properly related to the railway station, freight shed, elevator, and other buildings. Around and near the school might be school gardens, through the care of which the children would not only learn about plants and cultivation, but they would cultivate an interest in their parents' chief concern.

The planting of trees along all the roads is very desirable, for shade in summer, a windbreak in winter, and at all seasons for the beauty of the landscape. In places not purely rural, where villages might grow

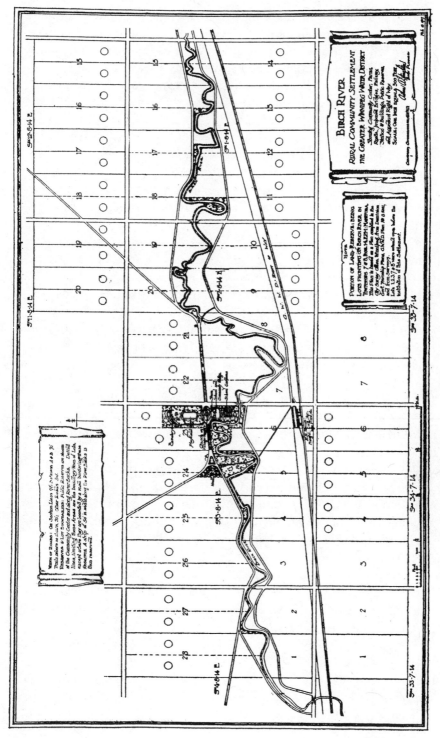

FIGURE 12 BIRCH RIVER RURAL COMMUNITY SETTLEMENT (GREATER WINNIPEG WATER DISTRICT)

up and where small shops or manufacturing plants might be located, a further development of the centre would include the planning of these industrial sites, and possibly a group of houses for the operatives, on the lines of the English garden cities.

The necessity of thus providing the setting must be grasped by someone of sufficient vision to read the signs of the times and appreciate the needs of rural life.

Such a scheme is about to be carried out not far from Winnipeg. (Figure 12.) The Greater Winnipeg Water District is planning a settlement at Mile 79, which will fulfill, as far as the conditions permit, most of the requirements suggested above, and a group of homesteaders are now waiting for the whistle to blow in order to enter upon this promised land.

The Dominion Government gives the land and consents to a certain deviation from the section lines for the roads. The Provincial Government is to make the physical improvements – roads, drainage, etc. The Colonization Department will help in the settling of the men, and will render aid in various ways in starting them in the development of the land, while the Agricultural Department will give them advice as to the best use of the land and instruction in various horticultural processes and methods.

PRACTICABILITY OF COMMUNITY SETTLEMENTS

These isolated schemes are interesting and helpful in their suggestiveness. Theoretically, a great many of the ideas put forward are sound and are based on a right understanding of the root causes of present difficulties. But every system of planning land has its defects, and some which seem to be right in theory do not work out satisfactorily in practice. There is no system which can be put forward as suitable for general application. Moreover, it will probably be found that the "promised land" of the communal schemes will not materialize to anything like the extent anticipated. Difficulties of fitting in the new methods with the old will crop up; prejudiced officialdom will be encountered; individual self-seeking will lead to friction in the co-operative enterprises; some part of the machinery will fail. There is also the danger that in trying new methods the promoters may be too fanciful. They will start schemes that will cost too much, and therefore be condemned at their inception before proper trial; or they will fail to take advantage of the good qualities of the system which has already been tried, and assume too much perfection of the ideas that have not been put to a practical test.

One difficulty that has to be met in connection with these schemes is the misunderstanding which is caused by the wrong use of terms. The words "community" and "colonization" have taken on many meanings, and to a large number of people they are anathema, because they suggest something of an institutional character or something relating to racial or religious community settlement. It should not be necessary to point out that the proper planning of land will not affect the individual freedom of the settler or the members of his family. But because the present system has the presumed merit of representing the extreme of individualism, and because some "communal schemes" have been socialistic in character, it is unfortunately true that this has prejudiced many settlers against departure from the individualistic method of settlement. The right kind of plan and scheme of development will facilitate but not force social intercourse, will permit but not compel co-operation, and will not affect, in the slightest degree, the individual who wishes complete freedom of action.

At a "Closer Community" conference held at Regina, in 1915, a scheme to promote the settlement of agricultural communities was put forward by Mr. J. H. Haslam, of the Regina Board of Trade. The scheme seemed to involve too much paternalism on the part of the government and met with a good deal of criticism, on the ground that the artificial promotion of village communities would not solve the real problem, namely, the unfavourable economic conditions underlying the agricultural industry. It was held by some speakers that the village community tended to attract people of the same nationalities to settle in groups, retarding the process of making the foreign settlers into Canadian citizens with Anglo-Saxon ideals; and that the greatest need was to promote the prosperity and the improvement of social conditions for those already on the land rather than for bringing a greater area under cultivation.

On general principles the advantages of closer settlement were not opposed, but only the artificial promotion of that kind of settlement by means of government subsidies. The creation of an improved organization to further the agricultural interests and to secure better means of raising capital for farming purposes was urged. There seemed to be a general agreement as to the injury caused by speculation, the need for filling up the vacant lands held by absentee owners, the desirability of an investigation being made into the social and economic conditions of Western Canada and the value of co-operation underlying the idea of community settlement. What was objected to were the financial details of the scheme and its paternalistic character. The conference was attended by leaders of public opinion in the western provinces, and, while it revealed the prejudice of some of these leaders to any scheme which savoured of

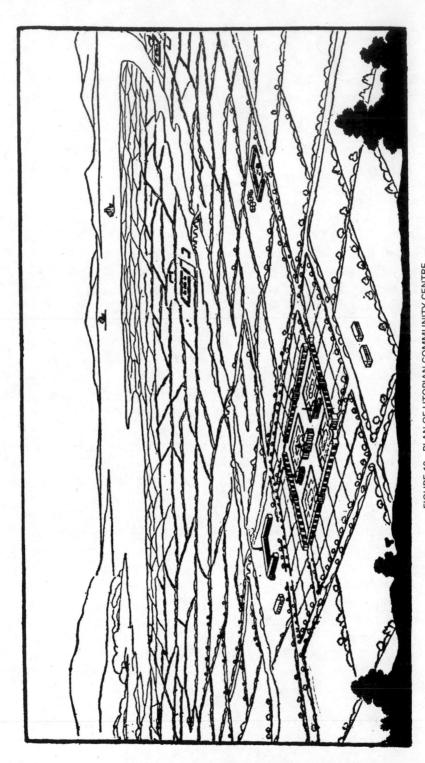

FIGURE 13   PLAN OF UTOPIAN COMMUNITY CENTRE

Robert Owen's scheme for a Model Town "Harmony," from his own Description, Published in 1817. Most schemes of this kind have Ended in Failure.

"socialism," it showed remarkable unanimity regarding the need for improved economic and social conditions, and for filling up vacant lands
and promoting co-operation as a means to obtain that improvement.

The artificial creation of co-operative communities has seldom proved
successful as a means of promoting permanent settlement of the land.*
In certain instances religious ties have held some communities together
for long periods in spite of financial difficulties, but, as a general rule,
they have ended in failure. In any scheme of settlement there must be
full opportunity for the exercise of individual initiative and enterprise
and as little reliance as possible on the paternalism of governments, if
success is to be attained. But, without undue interference with individual
freedom, governments of civilized communities must provide the impulse,
direction and organization necessary to promote the successful enterprise
of the individual citizens. In Canada the governments organize and plan
the settlement of land. If the way in which they do it leads to waste, and
is not economically sound, it will hamper rather than help individual
enterprise. The land can be planned and settled in a businesslike way, so
as to facilitate co-operation and make social intercourse easy, without any
greater restraint on the individual, or anything more artificial in the way
of organization than we have at present. The merit of co-operation is that
it recognizes the individual as an independent unit and leaves unimpaired
his self-reliance and initiative. It may be a harmful thing to create village
communities by an artificial process and with financial aid from governments; it is not a harmful thing to so plan and settle the land that the
village community will grow up in a natural way. In all these things we
want less artificial and stereotyped methods and more room for discretion
and the free play of individual and social forces. *But we must give expert
guidance, and facilities for co-operation, in proportion as we extend individual
freedom.*

DIAGRAMS ILLUSTRATING CERTAIN PRINCIPLES
OF PLANNING RURAL AREAS

In the *Seventh Annual Report of the Commission of Conservation* two diagrams
were shown as illustrations of the report of the Town Planning Branch.
(Figures 14 and 15.)

The diagrams show eight different methods of planning quarter sections
of townships, each method being independent of the others. As stated in

---

* "The deepest impression left on the mind by a review of their history is that co-
operative communities are a failure." (Figure 13.) *Dr. Josiah Strong in Social Service.*

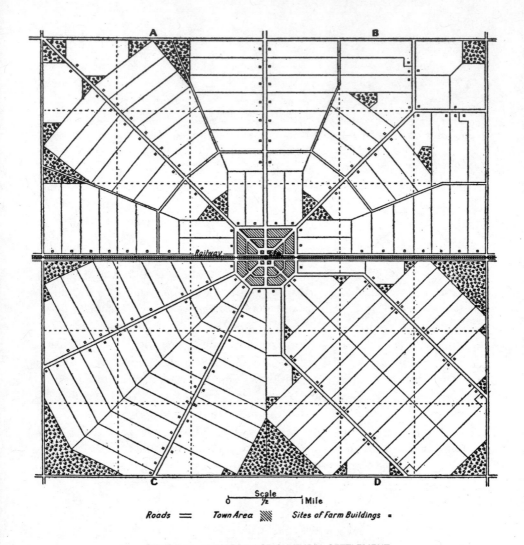

FIGURE 14   PLAN FOR AGRICULTURAL SETTLEMENT

Area, 36 square miles

This and the succeeding diagram show eight different methods of planning quarter sections of townships. Imaginary areas are taken and roads are planned to secure (1) close settlement of the farm buildings, (2) convenience and directness of access to the town area and station, (3) reduction in length of road, (4) use of swampy and rocky land for timber reserves. The buildings are also grouped so as to obtain the best social facilities and economic use of wells for water supply. In the town area it is assumed there would be good facilities for obtaining education, medical advice, and recreation – and an organized co-operative agency under Government auspices to supply farm implements, seeds, etc., to the farmers and to collect and distribute farm produce. On this diagram the total length of road provided to give access to all the farms is 46 miles, of which 11 miles are secondary and not essential. Under an ordinary rectangular division plan the total length of road is 54 miles. In addition to the saving in road construction and maintenance, which would be effected by proper planning, there would be great saving in time and team labour for the farmer, owing to the greater nearness of the farms to the centre. Fewer and more direct roads mean better roads, because it is possible to concentrate a given expenditure on a smaller area.

Commission of Conservation Town Planning Branch

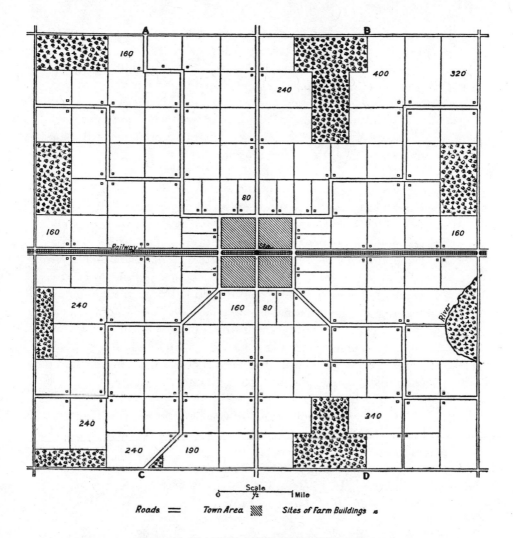

Roads ═══   Town Area ▨   Sites of Farm Buildings ▫

FIGURE 15   PLAN FOR AGRICULTURAL SETTLEMENT
Area, 36 square miles

In this diagram it is assumed that the square form of land division for the separate farms must be adhered to as a condition precedent to the planning of the area. Varieties of size of holding from 80 acres (near the town) to 400 acres (remote from the town) are provided for, but all holdings could be made 160 acres if desired. A different plan is shown for each of the quarter sections, adaptable to the imaginary topography of the land, the only feature common to all the quarter sections being the main roads intersecting the township in two directions – one parallel with the railway and the other at right angles thereto. All the farms are grouped so as to give them convenient access to the town, where the same facilities are presumed to exist as are described in respect of Diagram 1. The total length of road usually provided in a fully developed township is 54 miles. In this plan there are 36½ miles of principal and 3½ miles of secondary road, making a total of 40 miles. Every farm has sufficient road frontage, and the same length of boundary road is allowed for in both the above cases.

The object of these diagrams is not to suggest stereotyped or rigid forms of land division, but to show the desirability of abandoning such forms. Every township should be inspected and planned before settlement.

Commission of Conservation Town Planning Branch

the legend accompanying the diagrams imaginary areas are taken and planned so as to secure the necessary conveniences for traffic and the proper classification of good and bad land. Under any of the proposed systems less road would require to be provided than in an ordinary rectangular division, while in country of average physical conditions less land would be wasted and roads could be shorter in length and therefore could be better constructed. The following comment accompanying the diagrams appears on page 123 of the above report:

> The proposal is not to substitute a new for an old method of stereotyped development, but to substitute an elastic and scientific method for one which is based on no definite principles. Each township should be planned as a unit before settlement, and certain principles followed to enable the best results to be obtained. The diagrams are merely an illustration of some of the principles which require to be considered, and are not to be taken as indicating any particular point of view as regards size of farms or how a particular site should be dealt with. Different circumstances and conditions prevail in different provinces and in different parts of each province, and it is precisely because of these differences that a less rigid form of land division is needed to encourage and facilitate agricultural settlement.

It cannot be too often emphasized that what is required is the departure entirely from any kind of rigid system, except for measurement purposes, so that more discretion may be permitted, and regard paid to topographical and physical conditions. While this is true of areas which are surveyed and laid out for purely agricultural purposes, it is even more true in cases where land is being subdivided for building.

Townsites and Building Subdivision Plans in Rural Areas

We are not concerned in this report with the purely urban aspects of land development, but, in so far as the system of laying out new townsites or suburban land in rural areas is defective, it injures such areas and adds to administrative burdens of rural municipalities. Those who advocate "town planning" are sometimes met with the argument that a city or town grows and that it is not practicable to artificially direct its growth. To anyone who is acquainted with the process of town development on the American continent this argument must sound absurd, since there could be nothing more artificial than the method of laying out and developing cities and towns in the United States and Canada.

Sites for new towns are most frequently selected by the railway companies which, naturally, have regard, in the first place, to the locations most convenient for the area served by the railway, and, in the second place, to what will assist them in selling and developing their own land. The Canadian Pacific Railway Company says its real interest in the settlement of land only begins after the land is sold to the settler, and it has demonstrated this by the way in which it operates demonstration farms and employs expert advice for those who colonize under its system. The business instinct of this and other companies naturally leads them to select the townsites most useful to them – although the selection may not be the best for the public interest as a whole.

In the *Manual of Instructions to Dominion Land Surveyors* the following directions or suggestions have been given to surveyors in regard to the division of townsites:

54. The streets and avenues of a townsite usually cross each other at right angles. The direction of the streets and avenues is made to conform to the natural features of the ground, the avenues following what is expected to be the direction of the main traffic. No street or avenue is less than 66 feet. (Main streets or avenues may be 99 feet).

57. Lots are usually made 66 ft. x 99 ft. or 50 ft. x 150 ft. When lots are laid out less than 66 feet a lane not less than 20 feet wide must be made at the rear of the lots.

While the above appear to be the general rules it is stated that the method may be varied to suit circumstances, and due attention must be given to provincial law. The suggestion that the direction of the streets conform to the natural features need hardly be made, since the surveyor is so prescribed by the right-angled system, and by the width and depth of lots, that he can only consider natural features within very narrow limits.

A townsite plan prepared under the Dominion rules is illustrated in figure 16. These rectangular plans, with their unnecessarily wide streets and lanes, after every allowance is made for their advantages, have not led to good results. The wide streets and lands have not given air space, because the cost of paving and maintaining them is so great that the buildings on the lots have to be congested; and they have not given convenience, because the paving has to be deferred so long, owing to their great superficial area, that they remain great wildernesses of mud or dust, according to the season of the year. In most cases the lanes remain unlighted, unpaved, and a dumping ground for garbage. Indirectly they

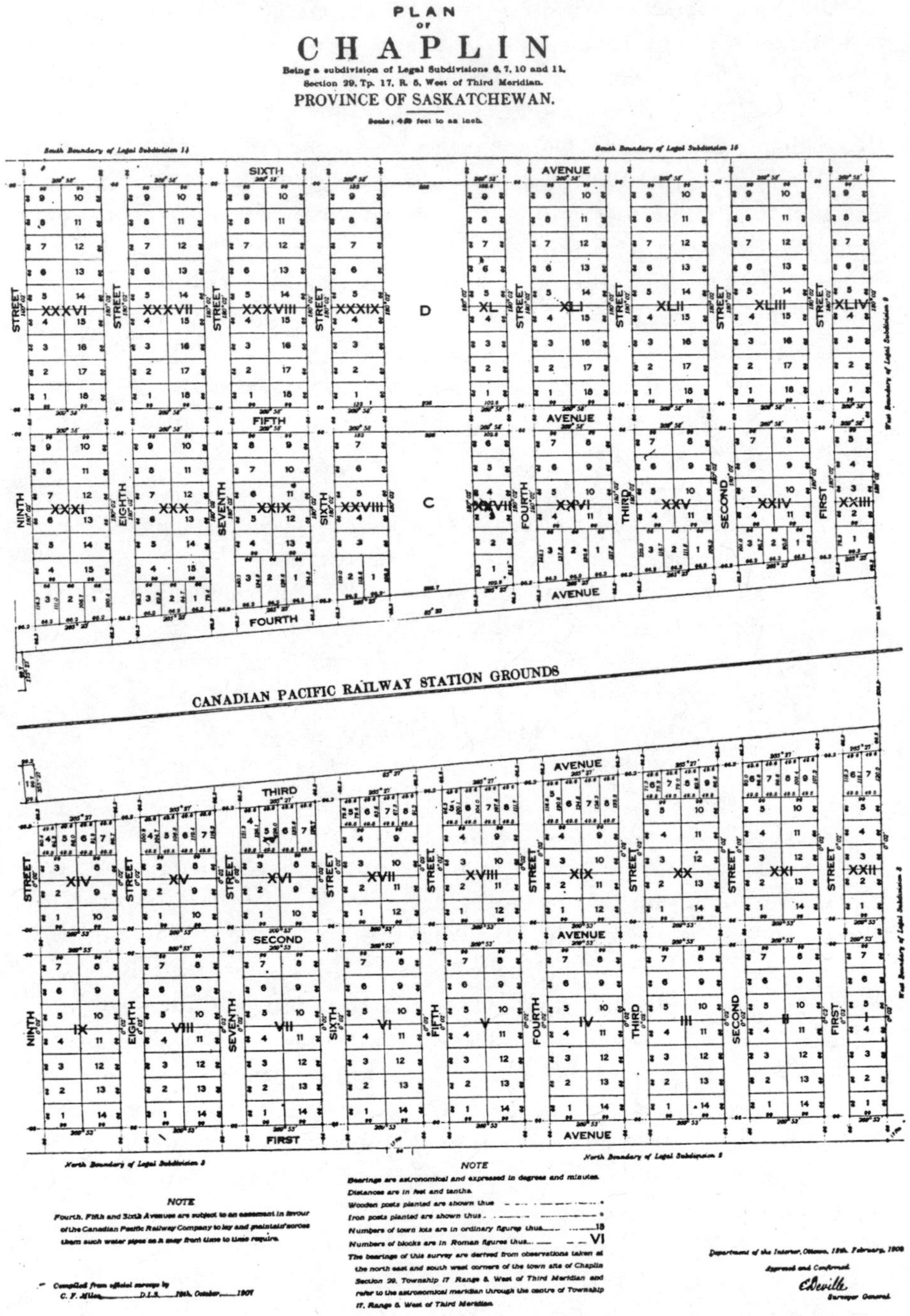

FIGURE 16 PLAN OF CHAPLIN, SASK.

produce bad sanitary conditions, because the cost of the streets reduces the amount available to spend on the dwellings.

The chief advantage of the rectangular plan is, unfortunately, that its uniform lot sizes and dimensions assist speculation in land. It suits the interests of speculating owners, who act without regard to the public welfare. Starting with the unit laid out by the surveyors in the first instance, the city or town is gradually developed in separate pieces, without any one piece having a definite relation to the other pieces.

Effect of Rural on Urban Planning

The influence of the system of laying out land for agricultural purposes on the system of laying out land for building purposes is seen in all countries, but probably the most direct connection between the rural and urban systems of survey is to be found on the American continent. The rectangular system of layout of the city and town in the United States and Canada has been less a matter of choice, by those who laid out the land for building, than a matter of evolution from the square mile section to the right-angled building lot. Some of the critics of the kind of rectangular plan which has prevailed on this continent seem to overlook this fact. The criticism of Mr. H. R. Aldridge,* that the plans of American cities are "little better than block plans of sites, planned grid-iron fashion to facilitate the operations of speculators in real estate," is largely true. But the origin of the plan seems to have been the rectangular system of survey in rural districts, and this was not deliberately designed to facilitate speculation although one of its results was to do so.†

We thus see the important connection between rural planning and city or town planning, and between rural planning and speculation in building lots. The greater part of new development in the future will take place on what is now rural territory under the administration of rural councils. These councils are now laying the foundations of the future extensions of cities. They have the power to prevent most of the bad conditions of development, as by the time the city or town extends its boundaries to include the partially developed areas outside the conditions and planning in these areas are to a large extent fixed.

The city and the town have therefore a direct interest in the planning of the rural districts, and the rural council has a direct responsibility in

---

*   *"The Case for Town Planning,"* page 109.
†   See footnote page 62.

PLATE VI   PLAN OF PHILADELPHIA

The base lines of this plan, as described by Thomas Holme, Surveyor General of Pennsylvania, were the front streets facing each river and High street 100 feet wide running from river to river. On these base lines the city was laid out in "checkerboard" system, in accordance with a rectangular survey of the city area and adjacent townships.

planning the urban developments in these districts. This joint interest and responsibility is recognized in the City and Suburbs Act of Ontario, which gives the large cities of over 50,000 inhabitants a voice in the planning of the lay-out of streets within a radius extending five miles beyond its boundaries, although it falls far short of what is necessary to control suburban development.

Ancient Rectangular Plans

The earliest known plans of cities were mostly rectangular in form, and in these real estate speculation in the American sense must have been unknown. The plan of Kahun in Egypt, founded about 2500 B.C., that of the Greek city of Priene on the Aegean coast, and that of the Roman city of Timgad (A.D. 100) are typical of the chessboard patterns of ancient times. The early city builders carefully selected the sites for their cities, and, owing to their small size, were able to level them when necessary to suit the plan. But neither these plans nor the more irregular plans of the medieval period had any particular relation to the plans of the rural districts adjoining them. Military and other reasons, which have no bearing on planning in the New World, were the dominant influences guiding the design of the rectangular systems in ancient Greece and Rome, on the one hand, and the irregular and crowded city growth which took place within the circular walls and fortifications in the middle ages on the other hand. (Figures 17 and 18.)

The Beginnings of Urban Planning

In modern times the rapid growth of large cities over great stretches of rural territory has introduced a factor unknown in ancient history. In Great Britain, the main roads of the counties and rural districts become the arteries of the cities, as the former are absorbed by the latter. These main roads and the well-made secondary roads have their frontages built up before the city grows out of them and help to pre-determine the lines of development. The boundaries of agricultural estates and also of fields have their influence on the lay-out for building, while the railways and rivers share in fixing the lines of the streets and building plan to a large extent. As the rectangular plan of the farms in Canada lays the foundation of the rectangular plan of the city, so the irregular rural development of the British country side helps to lay the foundation of the irregular city growth. In Germany, the small and narrow farm freeholds around the cities have always influenced the street and building plans. To get over the difficulties and inconvenience caused by these small ownerships, a

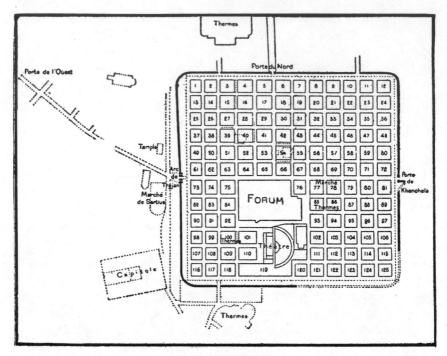

FIGURE 17   TIMGAD
Ancient Rectangular Plan. A.D. 100.

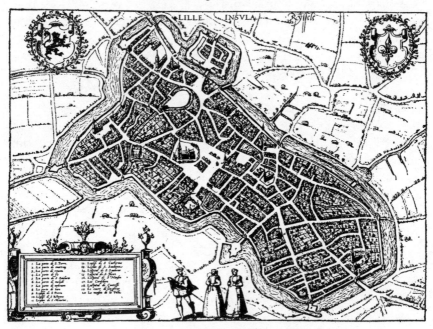

FIGURE 18   LILLE
Irregular Plan of Mediæval Period, A.D. 1550.
Note Irregular Design in City and Surrounding Rural Territory.

law* was passed in Frankfort-on-Main to compulsorily adjust and rearrange the boundaries of the separate parcels of land to fit in with the street plan.

The influence of the rectangular plan of rural territory in the development of the city plan is seen in Penn's plan of Philadelphia, (illustrated on plate VI), which was prepared in 1682. Thomas Holme, the Surveyor General of Pennsylvania, who prepared this plan under Penn's direction, showed that he was probably influenced by the square system of subdividing the farms. The chessboard system is the natural and easiest to follow when the townships and farms form the basis of the town plan, and when it is necessary to consider how to provide for the largest number of building lots with interference to the least number of owners of farms. It will also be seen that the rectangular divisions in the Penn township had no relation to the diagonal roads which formed the means of communication from the city to the surrounding country, and they had still less relation to the physical features of the land.

Although these are urban developments, and will therefore require to be dealt with more fully in the urban report, it has been necessary to refer to them here so as to show that it is while territory is still under the control of the rural municipality that the framework of the plans of cities and towns are determined. In the schemes now being promoted to establish new towns for the workers in new pulp mills, certain choice positions have to be selected, as the mills require to be comparatively close to timber limits, and must have water-power and facilities for transportation. Plans for all such new development should be prepared by competent persons and should be approved by the government authorities. The object of such plans should be to provide healthy conditions for the workers in the factories and mills, together with convenience of arrangement to secure the most efficient methods of carrying on the industry; and not merely blind conformity to meaningless division lines of a rectangular division.

A plan of a new town which is proposed to be developed is illustrated in figure 19, and an alternative plan for the same area, showing the subdivision in conformity with the rectangular system of survey, is shown in figure 20. These two plans prove the point which has been somewhat laboured in this chapter, namely, that no fixed or definite system of planning is desirable and that every plan should vary with the circumstances, conditions and topography. The meaning of this is that planning in all the provinces must be under the control of skilled departments and officials trained to exercise discretion and intelligence in laying out and developing the land. Probably such men could be recruited from the surveying profession, subject to their training being widened to suit them for their new

---

* The "Lex Adickes" passed in 1902.

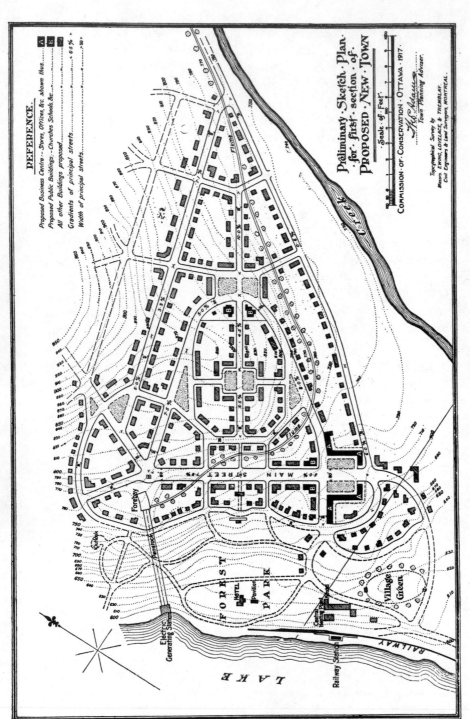

FIGURE 19 PLAN OF PROPOSED NEW TOWN DESIGNED TO SECURE CONVENIENCE OF ACCESS
BETWEEN ITS DIFFERENT PARTS AND ECONOMICAL AND HEALTHY DEVELOPMENT.

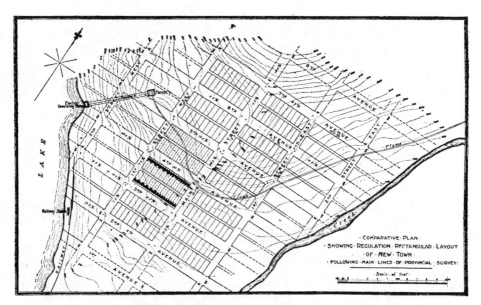

FIGURE 20   RECTANGULAR PLAN OF AREA INCLUDED IN FIGURE 19,
DESIGNED TO SECURE CONFORMITY WITH PROVINCIAL SURVEY,
BUT NO OBJECT OF CONVENIENCE OR ECONOMY OF DEVELOPMENT.

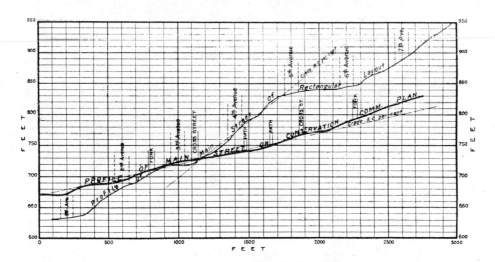

FIGURE 20A   COMPARATIVE PROFILES SHOWING
GRADIENTS OF MAIN STREET OF CONSERVATION COMMISSION PLAN
IN RELATION TO THOSE OF RECTANGULAR LAYOUT

duties; they need not be less accurate in their measurements owing to the fact that they have to take fresh conditions into consideration.

We have seen that the influence of the rural plan on the urban plan is not confined to new countries. But it is mostly in the new countries that the rural plan is rectangular and so completely ignores the topography of the ground. The main roads and the farm and field boundaries of Great Britain have some regard to natural conditions, so that, with all their irregularity, they provide a better and more rational foundation for the urban plan than the rectangular survey plan of rural Canada. Farm land should be planned, first, to secure its best economic use for agricultural purposes, and, second, to adapt itself to the natural features of the countryside. If and when this land became adaptable for building purposes, it could then be replanned to fit in with the general plan of the city or town. The rural plan, being a topographical plan, would then provide the right basis for the city or town plan. (Figures 21 and 22).

Present Control of Subdivision Surveys

Apart from those provinces which have town planning Acts in force, to which reference will be made later, a small amount of government control is exercised over the subdivision of lots, particularly in unorganized territory, and no general system of planning has yet been inaugurated in any province with the exception of the beginning which has been made in Nova Scotia. The requirement in some western provinces that five per cent of all new townsites or subdivisions must be reserved for open space is of great value, but it would be more so if the space was reserved as a part of a proper plan of development.

We have seen that some of the worst results of the present rectangular system, as a basis of development, are shown in the building subdivisions in rural areas lying adjacent to cities and towns. It is there that the plan of the country and the plan of the city influence and control each other; and it is there that the most inconvenient forms of development and some of the worst sanitary conditions are to be found in Canada. The same is true of the outer suburbs of cities in the United States.* The proper planning

---

* Here and there on the outskirts of the village or on the back streets and alleys and even in the open country there can be seen old houses and shacks which exhibit all the characteristics of the worst city slum, as unsanitary and filthy and overcrowded as any building in the North End of Boston or on the East Side of New York. More or less bad housing is to be found in the country all over the United States. — *Elmer S. Forbes, Chairman State Housing Com. Mass. Civic League.*

It is a curious fact in connection with suburban housing that nearly every time we enlarge the boundary of a city we take in an embryo slum. — *Otto W. Davis, Minneapolis.*

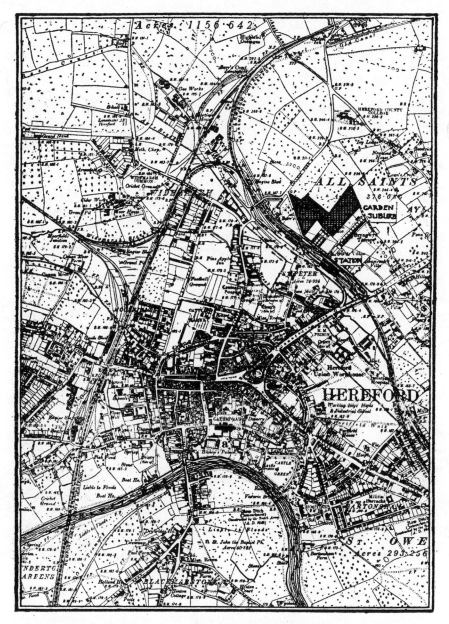

FIGURE 21   MAP OF THE CITY OF HEREFORD, ENGLAND

Showing the influence of the irregular development of the surrounding rural district on the method of growth and the lines of communication of the city. This irregular development, being influenced to a large extent by topographical considerations, affords, in many respects, a more rational basis for development than the rectangular plan, which ignores natural conditions.

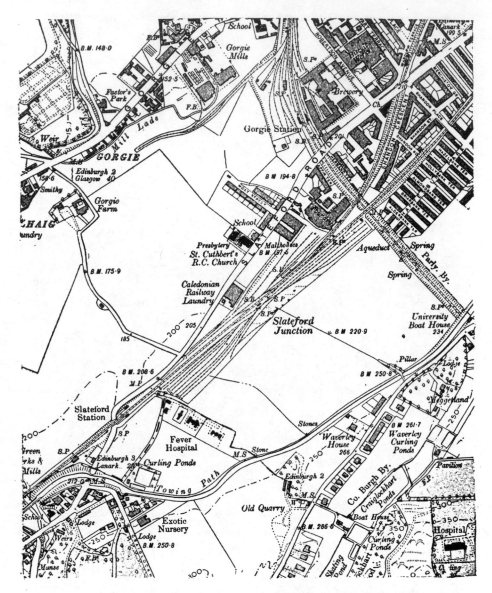

FIGURE 22   SECTION OF ORDNANCE MAP OF EDINBURGH, SCOTLAND

Scale 880 feet to one inch.

This map shows an area of suburban agricultural land within a radius of 2 ¼ miles of the centre of the city of Edinburgh. There are no building subdivisions, as the land is not allotted for building until it is ripe for the purpose. All the land is intensively cultivated and is rented to farmers and nurserymen at from $15 to $25 per acre. It is taxed at half its agricultural value so long as it is used for agriculture. In a large Canadian city this land and thousands of acres further out would be lying practically idle because of speculation in building lots.

The map shows details of buildings, etc., indicated on all small scale maps in Great Britain. Similar maps should be prepared for Canadian cities, a work which would afford a suitable field of employment for many ex-service men.

of these suburban areas is of the utmost importance in connection with the future development of Canadian life. These are the districts which are more in need of control under proper planning and development schemes than any other. At present subdivisions are laid out without regard being paid to the best lines and widths of main lines of communication, to physical conditions or to convenience. (Figures 23 and 24).

But even if we were tied to the rectangular system for township and farm boundaries, that is no reason for not re-planning within these boundaries to suit proper and economic building development as soon as the time arrives for the farm land to be converted into building land. In settled districts we may be compelled to continue to put up with the inconvenience caused by farm roads approaching lakes, hills and escarpments at right angles, and crossing ravines where the maximum of cost is required to be incurred to overcome physical obstacles; but, as soon as building subdivision takes place, a new set of conditions arise and an entire change of plan is needed. Proper planning will give more convenient means of communication between the country and the town, a matter of great importance in connection with cheapening the cost of production and making farming more profitable. This question of communication by road is part of the large problem of transportation and distribution which is dealt with in the succeeding chapter.

Land Classification

Side by side with proper planning for agricultural and building purposes a more extensive system of land classification is needed. A beginning has been made in some of the older provinces to secure the classification and selection of suitable land for farming and the setting aside of unsuitable lands for afforestation, etc. Reference is made on page 32, to the provision adopted some years ago by the Ontario Government to prevent settlement of bad land. If a township contains less than 40 per cent of good land the policy of the Ontario Government is to keep it closed from settlement for the growing of timber. The declared object of the Government is to keep the lands of the Crown for the use for which they are best adapted. Owing, however, to the great area of the province and the scattered nature of the settlement it must be well-nigh impossible to secure adequate inspection. There are 140,000,000 acres in Ontario. In 1910 the Minister of Lands, Forests and Mines announced that 46,000,000 acres in the province had been surveyed and 24,000,000 acres alienated or located. Classification and inspection of such a large area cannot be effectively performed unless preceded by more elaborate and detailed plans of the land than are now prepared.

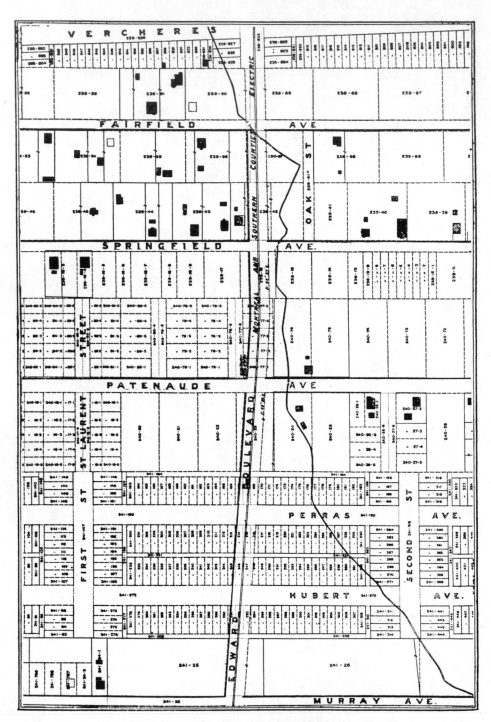

FIGURE 23   PORTION OF PLAN OF GREENFIELD PARK, QUEBEC

Scale, 1 inch = 300 feet

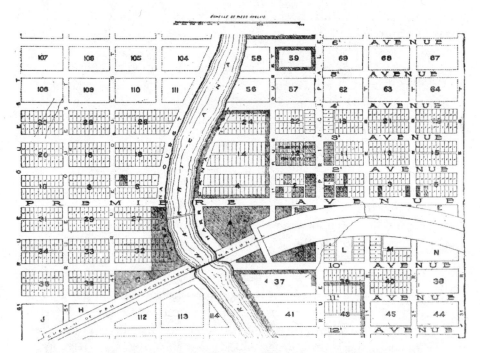

FIGURE 24   AMOS VILLAGE – DALQUIER AND FIGUERY, TIMISCAMING COUNTY

Figures 23 and 24. – These figures illustrate two township plans in Quebec. Greenfield Park in Figure 23 shows the grotesque length to which rectangular planning can go. Formerly subdivided into small market garden holdings it is now being "planned" by each separate owner with numerous cul-de-dacs, absurd variations in street widths, meaningless straight lines and apparent disregard to the public convenience. Streets vary in width from 30 to 66 feet, the narrowest streets being the most important thoroughfares. Edward Boulevard is not a highway and at present there is no means of through communication in one direction across the town for a length of one and a half miles.

Amos village goes to the opposite extreme in having too much road space and too many main thoroughfares. It is characteristic of the more elaborately planned Quebec townsite, made to fit in with the regulation provincial survey, without regard to natural conditions. The streets vary in width from 70 feet to 100 feet, and in all cases there are lanes 20 feet wide. Over 35 per cent of the land is taken up with road space, of which about half would be adequate for traffic needs, if properly planned, and would be as much as the inhabitants of the average town could afford to construct and maintain.

The Immigration and Colonization Branch of the Manitoba Government is now engaged in compiling information with a view to classifying land in the province, and is making efforts to locate settlers on the land best adapted for the class of farming they wish to take up.

In New Brunswick a survey of Crown lands for the purpose of classification was inaugurated in 1916. The object of the survey was to estimate the amount of timber on the land and to delineate the land suitable for agricultural development.* An Act passed in New Brunswick in 1912 created

---

* "The Classification of the Crown Lands in New Brunswick," by P. Z. Caverhill, *Eighth Annual Report, Commission of Conservation.*

a Farm Settlement Board, which is authorized to purchase abandoned farms, improve them and erect buildings thereon, afterwards selling them to *bona fide* settlers.

In British Columbia the need for better classification and better planning was voiced at a meeting of the Advisory Board of the Farmers' Institutes, held recently in Victoria. The board came to the conclusion that the pre-emption system of land now in force in the province was a failure and recommended that:

> Suitable areas of land in different portions of the province be selected by competent agriculturists, the same to be available for homestead entry, and that other agricultural areas not already alienated should be closed for settlement till further lands are needed. It was argued that this would, in addition to assisting the individual farmer, be more economical from the point of view of the administration of moneys, in road and bridge building.
>
> Under the present system, pre-emptors often are isolated altogether or are in small communities, and the government must, if these farmers are to be taken care of, construct roads for them and look after their transportation requirements. This, the board says, in a resolution which was adopted, would be a change for the better all round, would be favourable to social conditions and tend toward the more successful settlement of the farming lands. The board, in this connection, discussed the return of the soldiers and endorsed the co-operation land settlement scheme for them along the lines laid down in the report of the Returned Soldiers' Commission.

The value of the surveys being made for purposes of classifying land will depend on their accuracy. When complete surveys have to be made, and railways, roads, lakes, creeks, swamps, and other physical features have to be correctly delineated, great labour and expense is involved. It will be many years before any province in Canada can face the expense of making a complete survey of all or any considerable part of their territory. *What is more practicable is a partial survey and classification of all the land, with a complete topographical survey of the more valuable and thickly settled areas, and the preparation of development schemes by all municipalities. There is also urgent need for complete surveys of areas within and adjoining cities and towns.*

In the Australian system of surveying land regard is paid to the physical conditions in fixing the sizes and boundaries of the farms, to the purpose for which they are to be used, and to their boundaries. For instance, the Land Acts of Victoria, dealing with the Crown lands, while dividing the colony into arbitrary divisions for purposes of administration, enables the unalienated lands within these divisions to be divided into classes for purposes of agricultural use, such as agricultural or grazing lands, pastoral lands, swamp or reclaimed lands, auriferous lands, state forest, timber and water resources.

In each large district there is a Lands Classification Board, each board consisting of three persons competent to classify the land. Even the tenure under which the land is leased or its suitability for sale varies according to the class under which it comes. The farms range in size from 200 acres of first class agricultural land to 1,280 acres of third class grazing land. There is a limit to the area of land which may be leased by one person, varying from 640 acres of first class land to 1,000 acres of second class land.

The Board of Land and Works of Victoria can also purchase and replan or reclaim areas of good agricultural land, and dispose of it to settlers after improvement. A similar scheme of purchase, of such land as is not being put to adequate or proper use, is needed in Canada. The re-planning of such land would encourage its re-settlement, would enable fewer roads to be set apart and better roads to be made, and would permit of development schemes being prepared to secure the establishment of village centres with marketing and educational facilities.

Those who contend that the fixed system of surveying in Canada, in which the land is divided into sections without regard to its quality and character, is at least suitable for level and unbroken country, do not take into consideration, first, the importance of classifying land and arranging the sizes of the divisions according to its suitability for different kinds of farming; second, the need for linking up the homesteads with the village centres, and, third, the importance of the plan of development as distinct from the surveyor's plan of measurement. (Figure 25).

Another objection to the rectangular system as now carried out is that it forces the subdivision of land and the laying out of streets to follow the cardinal lines of the compass. For purposes of measurement this method ensures accuracy, but it adds to the evils caused by the rigidity of the system, in regard to both farm boundaries and building subdivisions. Lines which run due east and north and have no regard to watersheds and water courses, cause fertile valleys and meadow land to be cut up into awkward shapes and sizes for farming purposes. In regard to building subdivisions it is undesirable for purposes of health that buildings should stand squared by the four cardinal points. Building land should be laid out north-east and south-west and north-west and south-east instead of north-south and east-west, which is the worst disposition in which to place buildings in order to obtain the best distribution of sunlight. (Figure 26).

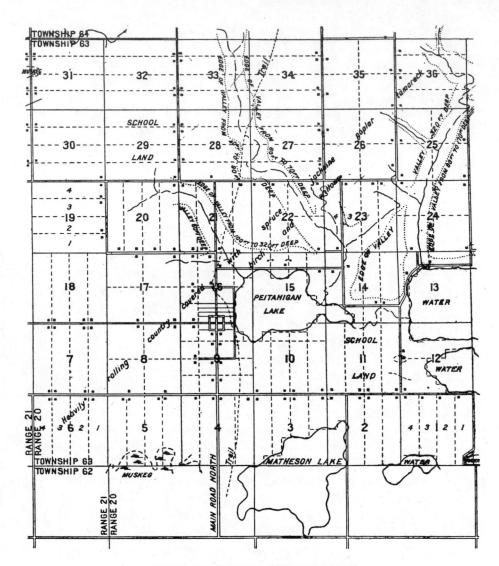

FIGURE 25   TOWNSHIP SETTLEMENT PLAN

Adapted to the Topography of Township 63, Range 20, west of the Third Meridian, Saskatchewan
Scale, 100 chains to an inch.

This plan by W. A. Begg, D. & S.L.S., shows roads and lots designed to suit heavily rolling and much broken country, with adaptability to the existing system of survey. The plan illustrates the second of the three stages which have to be followed to properly plan a township. These are: (1) Survey to index and describe the land; (2) Survey of topography and preliminary planning of roads and lots, and (3) Final planning of proposed development to classify the land and to secure, inter alia, that the roads will avoid steep grades and sudden deflections rather than slight curves, and that the sites of the village and farm buildings will be planned in the most convenient and healthy positions.

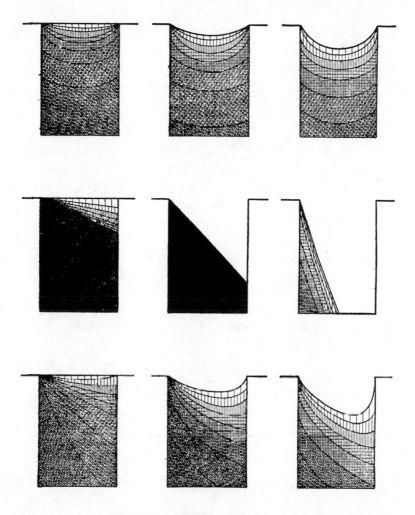

FIGURE 26   SUNLIGHT CURVES IN STREETS

The three upper diagrams are for a street running north and south, the three middle diagrams for a street running east and west, and the three lower diagrams for a street running at an angle of 45 degrees with the meridian. The diagrams of the left-hand column are drawn for the winter solstice; of the centre column for the vernal and autumnal equinox; and of the right-hand column for the summer solstice. The zones between the curves are shaded in a series of tints, the lightest zone being in sunlight between eight and nine hours, and the solid black being without sunlight. The diagrams give the complete series of sunlight curves at typical seasons for streets running north-south, east-west, and at an angle of 45 degrees with the meridian. The height of the buildings is represented as one and one-half times the width of the street. In the north-south street the distribution is symmetrical, the buildings on either side receiving an equal amount. In the east-west street the surface on the street receives no sunlight at all during six months of the year, and the buildings on the south side are in perpetual shadow during the same period. In planning towns the east-west street should be avoided as far as possible and, where unavoidable, the buildings should be of moderate height and built in detached blocks. In the checkerboard plan the best distribution of sunlight is obtained when streets run north-east-southwest and northwest-southeast. — "The Orientation of Buildings," by Wm. Atkinson, Fellow Boston Socy. of Arch.

Owing to the rectangular system in rural districts being the foundation for the checkerboard lay-out of cities and towns it is unfortunate that the direction of streets is fixed according to a rule which has no regard to orientation.

CONCLUSION

The main points of contention in this chapter are: That the present system of surveying land for the purpose of securing accurate boundaries to arbitrary divisions and subdivisions of land, while satisfactory for that purpose, is not a method of planning land, but only a basis on which to prepare planning and development schemes; that no definite or stereotyped system of planning can be satisfactory for general application; that all plans should have regard to the physical and economic conditions of the territory to which they apply and should be made for the general purpose of securing healthy conditions, amenity, convenience and economic use of the land; and that more complete and adequate surveys and a comprehensive classification of land is essential to secure successful and permanent land settlement.

CHAPTER III
PRESENT SYSTEMS OF SURVEYING AND PLANNING LAND
IN RURAL AREAS

Commentary by Hok-Lin Leung

Thomas Adams' *Rural Development and Planning* needs no introduction. It is a timeless classic.

The surveys done in the late nineteenth and early twentieth centuries had one overarching task – to define the boundaries of municipal areas and land divisions for the purpose of opening up the land for settlement and development. "Population had to be attracted by the offer of free homesteads or cheap land" (page 63), and the land had to be surveyed, in a hurry, in advance of the settlement. The surveyors had two concerns: the vastness of the areas to be dealt with and the need for accuracy and simplicity.

Surveyors did their job with gusto, essentially adopting the US system of the six-mile township – six-mile by six-mile squares subdivided into sections, each a square mile, and quarter-sections of 160 acres. A sixty-six foot road allowance (which happened to be the length of a surveyor's chain) passed between the lots. The result was "a checkerboard that was regardless of contours and relentless as fate" (page 369). Granted, not every region suffered this fate, but this rather clinical approach to land division certainly prevailed over much of Canada.

The six-mile township was not, however, the only game in town – there was also a nine-mile township. Likewise, the sixty-six foot road allowance along township and lot boundaries was not the only road scheme – there was also the more flexible 5 percent road allowance scheme. Nor was the right angle the only pattern – there were proposals to lay out townships in radial and hexagonal patterns, which actually represented great savings in overall road length. How did the six-mile township, with its rectangular layout and sixty-six foot rights-of-way, come to be the dominant pattern? Most likely it just happened, but it surely had consequences. Many significant choices are purely historical or accidental.

Take the case of driving on the left-hand side of the road. The story goes something like this. In old England, the highways were infested with highwaymen. Travellers carried swords to defend themselves. Since most people drew with their right hand, they rode on the left side of the road so that they could meet any highwayman with their fighting hand extended in the more advantageous position. The use of the right side of the road by the French came as a result of their use of the four-horse wagon. The lead horse was the foremost horse on the left. To allow for maximum manoeuvrability, the driver would sit on the left side of the wagon, which ran along the right side of the road. As a consequence of these differences, there are now two diametrically opposite systems in the world. Neither system is superior in terms of safety, efficiency, or comfort, but changing from one system to the other would be impossibly costly.

In our case, when administrative and property boundaries are laid out, they are literally cast in stone. The initial choice may seem trivial or even accidental, but subsequent changes are always costly. The moral is: choose carefully and change sparingly.

Much of today's political and business rhetoric glorifies change. We are encouraged to become agents of change. In fact, change has become a value, something good in itself. Constant change is the condition and fulfillment of constant consumption. It is good for the economy, at least the consumption-driven kind. Constant change also opens up avenues for the ambitious to access power. It is good for politics, at least the power-driven kind.

Of course, the status quo is not always satisfactory, and change may be needed. But if change becomes an ideology, we will die of exhaustion. I also notice an interesting cultural divide. The golden rule in Western culture is, "Do unto others as you would have them do unto you." The Oriental (or Confucian) ideal is, "Do not do unto others what you would not have them do to you." This is no simple semantic difference. The former is very much about doing and engaging; the latter is about restraining and coping. It is the difference between being an agent of change or a conserver. They both make choices, but the difference lies in how the choices are made. The litmus test is the assignment of the burden of proof. An agent of change would place the burden on the status quo, requiring a convincing case to be made before maintaining the established order. A conserver would place the burden on change, requiring a convincing case to be made before proceeding with change. When pushed to the extreme, neither position is tenable. I guess we are both agents of change and conservers. Pray that wisdom be our guide when making choices.

Was the survey system adopted "without time and thought," as Adams put it, such a bad choice? One might argue that this simple and relentless survey system probably passed the "so what?" test. After all, it played a significant role in opening up Canada. Although there were spectacular failures because of land speculation, much of the rural areas had done reasonably well, and their decline was due more to the impact of global economic upheaval than to the misuse of land. The sky didn't fall, and cities actually developed out of rural townships.

Humans can cope with a lot of stress, but there is always a price to pay, and there will always be a limit. The production processes and living patterns of the last hundred years were made to fit the rather primitive geometry of the land, even if people were mostly unconscious of it. We filled in the valleys, straightened the paths, and drained the marshes. Human industry and ingenuity have extracted a heavy toll on the environment and seriously disrupted ecological relationships. Next time, when you take off on a plane, look down on the rectangular mesh humans have imposed on the landscape and wonder no more why Nature is not happy. Of course, there are variations within, especially when it comes down to smaller-scale, curvilinear roads and cul-de-sacs. But even they are usually not responses to nature but rather to profit. Man is conquering nature with the straight line and the right angle. Rectangular survey lines dictate ownership patterns, and ownership patterns dictate land use. Nature is put in a strangle hold. But Nature neither accepts Man's dominion nor acknowledges his property rights, let alone the survey lines that stake out his rights. Ecology is about corridors, patches, and islands, none of which are square.

As human society moves from its industrial phase, when economic expansion trumps all, to the more mature ecological phase, when sustainable growth becomes essential, the conflict between individual liberties and the common good becomes more pronounced. Thomas Adams argues that freedom should not be usurped by individual liberty but should represent "the greatest freedom and equality of opportunity for the greatest number" (page 15). This is a prescient acknowledgment of the Brundtland concept of sustainable development – our actions must not deprive our children, and their children, of the opportunity to fully develop their human potential.

Since Adams' time, and especially in the last forty or so years, the purposes of settlement and development have changed. They are less about opening up the nation's vast hinterland than about the accommodation of urban expansion and overspill. Urban expansion eats into the surrounding rural land, changing its configuration forever. Unlike rural land uses, urban land uses are much more comfortable with the survey grid. Indeed, urban transportation is especially fond of the straight line and the right angle, ecological imperatives be damned. Urban overspill is somewhat different. There are urbanites who want to get away from perceived urban ills and return to nature, but they want to do so on their own terms. They greatly romanticize the rural lifestyle and virtues, but they are cross if they are deprived of urban conveniences and services. They want to enjoy the land, but they don't want to work with or on it. One wonders if Adams could have ever dreamed of attracting this crowd, notwithstanding that cities throughout history have always grown at the expense of the rural hinterland and that city dwellers have always sought spiritual refuge outside city walls.

The significant difference in the last forty years, however, has been the scale and scope of this urban to rural invasion. Massive suburbanization continues relentlessly, yet there is a curious perversion of the American dream. Suburbs have become suburbia, a twilight zone of boring houses and bored residents, or at least that's how the urban cultural elite sees them. This elite is the vanguard of the phenomenon of designer suburbs of the Seaside, Florida, type, and it has also spearheaded exurbia living. We don't know if these new ideals of modern living will develop into norms for the urban masses. But one thing is clear. They are no better, though perhaps no worse, on nature than conventional cookie-cutter suburbs.

The rectangular landscape that our ancestors created certainly limits the scope for co-operation between Man and Nature. Over the years, the conflict between human settlement and natural processes has intensified, partly because of increased population pressure and partly because of improved ecological knowledge and monitoring. But Man can be foolhardy, and Nature can be unforgiving. The space for mutual accommodation is ever narrowing.

In a strange way, the rectangular mesh that our ancestors chose to lay out government and property boundaries has made our encounter with ecological reality much more dramatic than if the survey lines had been more natural and organic, as in the old countries, where the tug of war between Nature's needs and Man's desires has been more layered and nuanced. Our survey system brings into sharp relief the overt and uncompromising conflict between artificial boundaries and natural processes. We may yet come to thank the rectangular survey for giving us a much needed wake-up call.

CHAPTER IV

Rural Transportation and Distribution:
Railways and Highways

*Railways | Planning of railways | Highways | Road improvement in
Great Britain | Road construction in Australia | Road improvement in the
United States | Road improvement in Canada | Economic and social value of
good roads | Principle of financing road improvements | The planning of
roads | A concrete illustration of saving due to planning | Planning roads in
Australia | The advantages of planning roads in Canada | Planning of road
widths | The by-law maximum of width | Effect of narrow roads in
Britain | Principle on which roads should be planned | Suburban standards
too high | Cost of roads in relation to housing | Roads and air space around
buildings | Bad roads costly to maintain | Too many roads in
subdivisions | Heavy and light roads | Main arterial
thoroughfares | Incidental problems of road planning*

O NE of the chief objects of planning land is to secure efficiency
and convenience for carrying on industry, and in this connection
we have to consider the means of communication. The means
of communication for distributing the resources of a country consist of
waterways, railways and highways. These are the arteries through which
flow the products of human activity in a constant process of exchange
between producer and consumer, to supply human needs.

RAILWAYS

The development of the railway system in Canada has had a great influence on the geographical distribution of the population and on the
opening up of new fields of production.

Having regard to its population, and the length of time it has been
undergoing development, Canada is in the forefront of civilized countries
as regards its systems of waterways and railways. Admitting that there may
have been extravagance and misdirected effort, everything that a young
country could have done to extend and improve these systems has been

done. It is charged that there has been unnecessary duplication of railway tracks and services, and over-expenditure of public funds in the building up of the railway system. Probably the chief trouble has been due to our common sin of doing things as a nation without forethought, comprehensive planning and preliminary organization; but, be that as it may, the money has been spent, and the railways are there, and the problem is not how can we undo what has been done, but how can we make the best of what we have. About $2,000,000,000 has been invested in the railway system of Canada. There are practically unlimited land resources behind that system which, if put to proper use, would justify all that has been spent, and make men forget any lack of wisdom in the spending. But why are these land resources not being put to proper use, when the country is crying out for cheap food and when the railways are in need of freight traffic to enable them to earn operating expenses and fixed charges? Granting that the trunk lines of railways of Canada are unnecessarily duplicated, that some of the trunk lines have insufficient feeders and terminals, and that a large part of the mileage has been constructed at excessive cost; granting, too, that re-organization and consolidation of the railway companies may be necessary, and that, until more feeders and terminals are provided, probably the greater part of the railway system cannot be successfully operated – granting all this, on the one hand, and on the other hand considering that there are said to be 30,000,000 acres of idle lands in Western Canada alone, a great part contiguous to the railways and of good quality, and that lands in Ontario and Quebec lying within a near radius of the railways are not producing 50 per cent of what they could produce under better conditions, may we not claim that no remedy of the railway situation will be effective which does not include the laying of the foundations of an improved system of land development designed to make the utmost use of the land that lies nearest to the railways?

There are important national problems regarding distribution of freight and transportation which, while affecting the farmer as a producer, do not directly bear on the relationship of the railways to the system of developing the land. But, generally speaking, it is not the railway system that is deficient in the matter of providing facilities for land settlement – it is the system of land settlement that is deficient in respect of being unable to make proper use of the existing means of distribution by rail.

All forms of transportation suffer when population is too congested in some places and too scattered in others. The problems of transportation are most difficult where there are high buildings and tenement dwellings in the cities and a widely diffused population in the country districts. The more evenly we can spread the population, the more efficient and profitable we will make the railways. Decentralization of manufacturing industries will not only bring the producer nearer to the consumer, but will simplify and cheapen transportation. The want of railways in advance of settlement is declared to be a serious drawback in Australia. This need not be so in Canada, except in a very limited degree, if we apply a large portion of our effort for the next ten years to the task of filling up the blank spaces near the existing railways with productive settlers. The railway companies would benefit in the end if the government were to initiate a policy which would, by means of reasonable restrictions, limit the profits which companies could derive from land speculation, and at the same time, place a larger burden of taxation on idle land so as to encourage its use. A cheaper parcel post and lower freights, which might mean temporary loss to the railways and express companies, would ultimately benefit them, because of the fact that it would stimulate greater rural production.

Planning of Railways

Before more railways are built or branch lines are extended land should be planned and the road and railway systems devised so as to fit in with each other.

Railway extensions should be made with the primary object of assisting production and facilitating distribution in the general public interest. The general plan of railway extension should be prepared after and not before a comprehensive survey and classification of land and other resources are made. The initiation of railway enterprises too often rests with railway promoters and too seldom follows any properly conceived plan of development. The railways should be made to serve the needs of the country through which it passes and should be planned for that purpose.

In regard to the detailed planning of railway lines, that is a matter which is safe in the hands of the railway engineers who are entrusted with the work. Whereas, highways are laid out without plan or adequate preliminary survey by government authorities, no railway company has dared to follow a similar haphazard practice in regard to the laying out of railways. No doubt there are many engineering defects in the railway system, but they are not due to want of planning. To some extent they may be due to imperfect judgment or lack of skill on the part of the engineers, but probably they are more due to the influence of ulterior considerations, such as the method of financing railway enterprises.

PLATE VII   UGLY AND DANGEROUS SLUM CONDITIONS ADJOINING A RAILWAY

PLATE VII   BOULEVARD PARALLELING THE RAILWAY

DEVELOPMENT ALONG RAILWAYS

The above illustrations show how two equally good and attractive towns in Canada look from the railway train. Too little attention is paid by the average small town to the railway surroundings. In the above case, one town exposes its worst and the other some of its best development to the passer-by; and each is judged by appearance.

The important questions of planning railway extensions, consolidating railway tracks and terminals, and laying out railway yards and stations in urban areas will be dealt with in the urban report. But there is one aspect of these questions which affects small towns and rural areas, to which attention may be drawn here. Rural municipalities and railway companies require to co-operate to a greater extent in regard to the lay-out and surroundings of country and suburban stations. In many cases municipalities have permitted land to be developed in such a way that dangerous crossings are created over railway tracks; these have to be succeeded in course of time by bridges or subways constructed at great cost by the municipalities and railway companies. Sites for elevators and other buildings are selected without proper consideration of the ultimate effects on surrounding development. Railway companies often develop their own land around stations, with complete disregard of the public interests, of their own future extensions, and of the expenses and inefficiency which is bound to result to all parties in course of time.

The initiation of a proper scheme of development should rest with the local authority, but that authority should have the power to bring the railway company into co-operation in preparing a scheme. Careful consideration should be given in any plan to the prospective development around the railway stations and yards, to the need for adequate and fitting approaches to the station, and to desirability of avoiding extravagant and unnecessary crossings. As a result of careless development and speculation many small towns and villages spread themselves on both sides of a railway line, with consequent danger to life and a burden of expense which is an entire waste, since no object is served by the scattered and severed nature of the development.

To get cheaper transportation, farmers must be able to unite in making their demands on the railway companies for reduced tariff and better services, and must simultaneously be prepared to supply the railways with paying loads. But to achieve these ends farmers must have the means and facilities to enable them to co-operate, and a good roads system is one of the most urgent needs in that connection.

Highways

Because of bad roads, the cost of taking produce from the farm to the railway is often greatly in excess of the cost of shipment over the railway. It is asserted that the traffic at country stations in parts of the United States falls off by about fifty per cent during the season when roads are bad.

The absence of proper road communication is probably the most serious handicap, both to the railways and to those who use the land. It is in regard to highways that Canada suffers most from lack of proper means of distribution. Although, in a country of such wide spaces as Canada, railways are more essential at first than good roads – yet it is also true that the railways can never be put to adequate use without being fed by a system of good roads. With the coming of the motor, the question of road transportation has taken on a new meaning in recent years, and a good road system is essential to successful farm settlement.

One of the reasons for our inability to make better roads is that the road system has not been designed so as to save waste in road space and road construction. Our want of proper planning and our public policies as regards land settlement have encouraged the spreading of the population over too wide a territory. As has been shown in previous chapters, productive land in the older provinces and in the older parts of new provinces is neglected or allowed to be idle, or, where it is being used, too little effort is being made to help in securing its more intensive use on the ground that it has been alienated from the government; meanwhile money is spent, first, to attract population to new areas, and afterwards to provide new facilities to meet demands thus created. In the older settled regions, perhaps ten times the present population is needed to properly use the land as well as the existing equipment in railways, highways, and other facilities. Attractions must continue to be offered to the pioneer who wants to open up new territory, but it should be on a system which would permit good roads to be gradually extended to the new territory, and it should be carried out simultaneously with a policy of encouragement of the industries and resources of the partly improved territory, even where the latter is in private hands.

Road Improvement in Great Britain

Those who say that the good roads in the rural districts of Great Britain are due to the fact that they have been under construction for many hundreds of years, and that some were made by the Romans, are, apparently, not aware that in the eighteenth century the roads in England were hardly passable. For instance, it is reported that in 1703 it took Prince George of Denmark fourteen hours to travel forty miles from Windsor to Petworth. Arthur Young, writing of Suffolk roads in the middle of the eighteenth century, said, "Some of the roads were little more than mere ponds of liquid dirt, with a scattering of loose flints just sufficient to lame every horse that moves across them, with the addition of vile grips cut across the road under the pretense of letting off the water."

On the hillsides in Wales the roads were described as "rocky lanes, full of huge stones and abominable holes." Between 1760 and 1764 it is reported that no fewer than four hundred and fifty two Acts of Parliament were passed for highway improvement, but these affected little change for a long time.

Mr. Herbert Smith, an English expert, in his book on *Principles of Landed Estate Management*, writing of the attitude of the rural population of England to roads in the latter eighteenth and earlier nineteenth century, says:

> So conservative were the masses of the people that the improvement of the roads in many places of Great Britain was strongly opposed and in certain places entailed riot and bloodshed; and even when roads had been made and improved, country people in many districts refused to use them, but their unreasonable conservatism was in the long run powerless to stem the tide of improvement which gradually set in, and brought the roads of the nation to their present admirable state and condition. Thus we see that the history of road making in this country is, to some extent, a record of the progress of its civilization.
>
> There is no greater hindrance to a successful agriculture than the want of good roads. Railways have, of course, conferred immense benefits. They have opened up the country and have generally increased the value of estates through which they have passed, but railways alone are not enough; it is often pointed out that estates, even if lying a long distance from a railway, provided the communication in the shape of roads between the railway and themselves is good, have benefited more than an estate immediately adjacent to a railway but not possessed of adequate means of communicating with it.
>
> Good roads are almost essential to high farming, and farms are increased in value by the existence of them to an extent which it is impossible to overestimate ... There can be no better investment for a landed proprietor than the opening up of his property by the formation of good and substantial roads.

The point of view expressed by Mr. Smith may be said to be also that of the landowners of England who, for the past fifty years at least, have shown their faith in good roads as a means of improving the value of their property. Up till the time when the motor came into general use, British roads were in excellent condition, and were of adequate width to meet the needs of slow-going traffic. But the coming of the motor has made it necessary to improve the surfaces and alignment and in some cases to widen the roads. Bridges and curves, which had previously been safe, became dangerous with fast traffic. To deal with these new conditions, the Road Board was created in 1909. Its chief revenue is derived from motor spirit duties and carriage licenses. In 1915 its road improvement fund amounted to

$8,104,870, and for the five years ending March 31, 1915, it had expended
a total of $23,638,635 in grants and loans. The roads of the country are
divided into first, second and third classes, and the advances are made
according to class – the highest proportion being given to the first class.
As part of its duty, the Road Board compiles statistics of traffic and maintains a laboratory for testing road materials.

The recommendation of a manufacturer or contractor is not a consideration in selecting road materials in Great Britain. Local authorities
have learned that the only way to get good roads at a reasonable price is
by employing competent engineers, who can be trusted to design the
roads, select the best materials, prepare the specifications, and supervise
the work of the contractors. Manufacturers and contractors of road materials in England make sufficient, but not excessive, profits, and they are
strictly the servants of the engineer. County engineers, whose principal
duty is road construction and maintenance, are of the highest standing;
and in most English counties they are paid higher salaries than any provincial deputy minister of roads in Canada. This is found to be the cheapest
and best method, and, indeed, is the only one which is practicable, having
regard to the necessity for good construction and the strictest economy.

Road Construction in Australia

In Victoria, Australia, the report of the Country Roads Board states, that
road construction has never kept abreast of settlement, and that the task
of improving roads has quite outgrown the resources of the shire councils;
therefore some form of state assistance is advocated. The extravagance
of a policy of cheap construction is recognized by the board, and it is
pointed out that many of the old, solidly built roads have stood the traffic
of years, while many roads of comparatively recent construction have
utterly failed. The absence of a systematic policy, as well as a lowered
standard of construction, is given as a reason for the deterioration. Large
sums are being appropriated for road improvement in all the Australian
states.

Road Improvement in the United States

What is being done to improve the road system in the United States is
indicative of what is likely to be done in Canada in a few years. The extent
of improved surfacing of the rural roads of the United States is increasing
at the rate of 16,000 miles a year, and in 1915 about 277,000 miles had

been improved. Half of these improvements have been carried out under the supervision of the highway departments of the separate states, which, up to January 1, 1916, had expended an aggregate of $265,350,825 for road and bridge construction, maintenance and administration.

In the last annual report of the Highway Commission of New York, it is stated that the greatest asset which the state has is its system of improved highways. The appropriation for road improvement in 1914 was about twenty millions. The cost is met in part by taxes levied on the towns and in part by contributions from the state. It is declared that in recent years over 70,000 miles of highway have been widened, shaped and crowned so that travel over them is safe and convenient.

ROAD IMPROVEMENT IN CANADA

Good progress in regard to road improvement is also being made in Canada. The roads in Canada are more important for distribution of produce than in Great Britain, where distances are short and light railways are plentiful. In Canada we have had to start off without any of the advantages possessed by older countries in the matter of old foundations and closely settled populations. We have had to develop motor transportation by road to a greater extent than the more thickly populated countries as a means of feeding the great trunk railways and securing the economical distribution of food.

The respective obligations of the provincial and the local governing bodies in regard to road construction and maintenance have to be considered. Local authorities need to be advised regarding the proper use and value of different kinds of road material, after adequate trial and investigation by expert departments, in order to save hundreds of thousands of dollars spent on unsuitable road material. Better engineering advice has also to be obtained by local authorities. When the enormous amount of money spent on roads and road maintenance, and the great waste raising from the haphazard methods of planning and construction, are considered, it is surprising to find so little effort being made to deal with the matter on more practical and scientific lines.

The Highway Commissioners of Ontario, in their annual report for 1915, draw attention to the need of more co-operation between the cities and the country districts in the matter of road improvement. Ontario has about 50,000 miles of roads, and the Highway Commissioners consider that a sum of $30,000,000 should be spent on these roads during the next 15 years. The following apportionment is suggested:

Province (including revenue from motor fees)	$12,000,000
Counties	12,000,000
Cities	6,000,000
	$30,000,000

To this capital expenditure must be added the cost of maintenance, which may amount to from $300 to $500 per mile.

The amount appropriated in the State of New York is $65,000,000 for 11,000 miles of highways, and about $50,000,000 has already been spent or earmarked. In Great Britain we have seen that one department alone – the Road Board – has raised $32,000,000 for road improvements in four years. Merely for purposes of road improvement Ontario would require to incur an expenditure of about three million dollars annually to bring its current rate of improvement in the settled part of the province up to the British standard. The proposed expenditure of the Ontario Highway Commission, at the rate of two millions annually, would, therefore, appear to represent the minimum, under present conditions.

Under the Ontario Highways Act, the province, the cities and the counties may co-operate to improve main roads in suburban areas. Forty per cent of the cost of construction of such roads is provided by the province, the other sixty per cent being contributed in equal portions by the city and the county; for maintenance, the province gives twenty per cent and the city and county each forty per cent. This arrangement, under which the city contributes towards the cost of construction and maintenance of suburban roads in county areas, is a just one, since the greater part of the traffic passing over such roads is for the benefit of the city; moreover, the average rural municipality cannot afford the preliminary cost of building up a main road system. In Ontario, however, the improvement of highways has to be confined to the principal lines of communication.* As in all the other provinces, there are so many roads in Ontario that only a selected few can be improved. Roads are divided into main roads (between populous centres), market roads and local feeders, and cities are required to contribute to the two former classes in suburban areas outside the city boundaries. In 1914 road surveys were made in certain counties to ascertain the location of roads, the population served by roads, the traffic conditions, alignment, etc. Traffic charts were prepared, illustrating the traffic at certain points in the road system of an Ontario township. These showed that the concentration of traffic took place in a notable degree on certain roads adjacent to shipping points, cities, towns and villages, that certain

---

* Annual Report on Highway Improvement, Ontario, 1915.

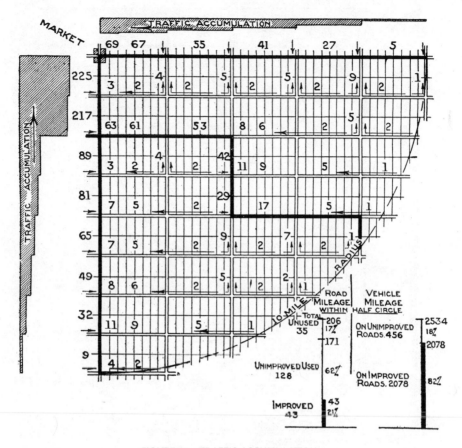

FIGURE 27   TRAFFIC ACCUMULATION
The points to be noted on this chart are:
first, the heavy accumulation of traffic concentrated on the main side-road near to the market centre,
and second, the construction of 21% of the roads serves 82% of the traffic.
Annual Report on Highway Improvement, Ontario, 1915

roads were of little public use, and that the construction of a very limited proportion of the roads, properly selected in relation to traffic, would benefit a large proportion of the total vehicle mileage. In one chart it was shown that 19 per cent of improved roads would carry 80 per cent of the total vehicle mileage – yet the provincial system practically results in making all roads of the same width.

Another chart with a diagonal road showed that the traffic on the diagonal road was more uniformly distributed and had a total vehicle mileage of 2,165 miles, as against 2,535 miles in a road conforming to the rectangular plan. Charts 8 and 9 are given as illustrations of this report. (See figures 27 and 28.) When diagonal roads are included in an original design for laying out of a given area of land, they need not cause greater waste

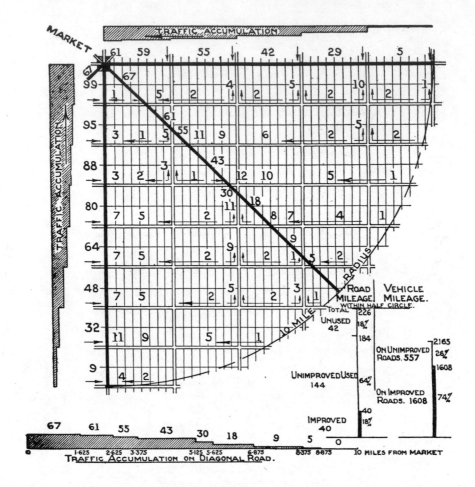

FIGURE 28   TRAFFIC ACCUMULATION

This chart shows the advantages of a radial road in distributing traffic as compared
with the congestion shown in Fig. 27. While the total mileage of road within the half circle
in increased in this chart, the total vehicle mileage is decreased from 2,535 miles to 2,165 miles,
or over 14% of the greater. That is, the designation in this chart cuts off 14%
of the vehicle mileage entirely and carries 74% of the remainder.
Annual Report on Highway Improvement, Ontario, 1915

of land or more inconvenient boundaries of subdivisions than rectangular
roads, but when the diagonal roads are superimposed on a rectangular
system of roads and subdivisions, as is sometimes done, they cause both
waste and inconvenience.

The Quebec Government has adopted an advanced policy in regard to
road improvement. It gives substantial subsidies to rural municipalities,
varying from $100 to over $1,000 – according to the nature of the road
and the kind of municipality – for the purpose of road maintenance. Starting in 1912 with an authority from the legislature to borrow $10,000,000,

it obtained sanction to increase this amount to $15,000,000 in 1915, and to $20,000,000 in 1916. Part of this money was used for purposes of maintenance and part for construction and improvement of trunk roads. In addition to the grants given to municipalities for maintenance, sums of money are loaned to be expended in accordance with schemes approved by the Department of Roads. This money was loaned in 1915 at 2 per cent interest, repayable, with sinking fund, over a period of 41 years. The interest on the additional $5,000,000 borrowed in 1916 has been increased to 3 per cent. In either case the government pays the balance of interest and sinking fund – and it controls the expenditure. The following statement of recent progress is furnished by M. Michaud, Deputy Minister of Roads:

Since 1912, the government has built five provincial roads, namely: the Montreal-Quebec road, the Montreal Rouse's Point road, the Chambly road (from Victoria bridge, Chambly, and then to St. Johns, P.Q.), the Sherbrooke-Derby Line road, and the Levis-Jackman road, covering over 300 miles in all.

Since 1911, there has been built in the province, under the control of the Department of Roads, 1,279 miles of macadam and 568 miles of gravel roads, in all 1,847 miles of improved roads. In these figures are included the 300 miles of trunk roads above referred to.

The Department of Roads owns 57 complete outfits for the construction of macadam. These outfits are loaned or rented to the municipalities. Besides, it owns a certain number of tractors, portable engines, etc., which are employed by the Department of Roads for direct construction.

In addition to the government's outfits, there are about 150 outfits owned by municipalities. They have been paid for with the money allotted by the Government to those municipalities.

The Department of Roads has a well equipped laboratory for the testing of road materials.

For the purpose of this report enough records and figures have been quoted to show the progress in road improvement and the increasing rate of expenditure on roads in Canada and other countries. Details of the progress and expenditure in the other provinces need not be given, as Ontario and Quebec may be taken as typical of the whole country in regard to the growing recognition of the importance of highways. In all the other provinces there is either considerable road development going on or agitation in favour of development. In the western provinces there are progressive and active highway departments and a continuous effort being made to improve administrative machinery.

Economic and Social Value of Good Roads

The value of good roads as a means of improving production is being more and more recognized on this continent. In California, the farmers whose holdings are situated on good roads get higher prices for milk collected by the wholesale dealers than the farmers who have bad approaches by road. Mr. Herbert Quick, of the Federal Farm Reserve Board, whose duty it is to appraise farm values for purposes of loaning money to farmers, has declared that a thoroughly good paved road is a better economic feature than a railroad. In extreme cases, where farms are situated in remote regions, he says that loaning money becomes absolutely safe when good roads are built back into these regions. Loans are made on bottom values, and when new roads are built the farms are worth three, four, five and even ten times the amount of money sought to be obtained on mortgage.

Good surfaces laid on well drained sites and good grades are the two essentials of good roads, and proper planning is necessary to secure both. The following comparative estimate of the cost of transportation by horses and wagons, hauling on different road coverings, is from an article by Joseph H. Pratt, in the *Annals of the American Academy, 1910:*

Pro rata cost of hauling one ton a distance of one mile on level roads:

	Cents.
On asphalt	2.70
Dry stone paving	5.33
Mud-covered stone paving	21.30
Broken-stone road in good order	8.00
Good dry sand-clay road	8.00
Broken stone with ruts and mud	26.00
Earth – dry and hard	18.00
Earth – with ruts and mud	39.00
Loose gravel	51.60
Dry sand	64.00

On level grade, a horse pulls, as a standard, 1,000 pounds. On a rise of

1 ft. in 100 (1 per cent)	900 lbs.
1 ft. in 50 (2 per cent)	810 lbs.
1 ft. in 25 (4 per cent)	540 lbs.
1 ft. in 10 (10 per cent)	250 lbs.

With regard to the general economic value of good roads, an interesting statement has been made by Mr. W. A. McLean, Deputy Minister of

Highways of Ontario, in which he claimed that an adequate road system in Canada would create a profit of $50,000,000 annually. The estimate was based on a computation that 100,000,000 tons passed over the roads in the Dominion, that the average haul was five miles and that good roads would effect a probable saving of ten cents per ton mile. If these figures are an indication of the revenue-producing value of roads, then it would pay Canada to spend $500,000,000 for that purpose; but, if only half of that sum is to be expended in the next twenty years, for the greatly increased traffic that is bound to come, a large sum should first be spent in the work of designing and preparation so as to avoid a possible waste of many millions in construction.

The social value of good roads need not be emphasized. As Prof. John M. Gillette has said, good roads lie at the basis of the social institutions and the associational life of the rural district. Effective co-operation is impossible without them; school consolidation, which is so much needed, cannot be achieved if roads are bad. It is stated that in five bad-road states in America, the average attendance of pupils is 59 per 100, as against 78 per 100 in five good-road states.

Principle of Financing Road Improvements

Before extensive improvements are made in good roads in Canada it is important that a sound financial policy should be adopted. The British practice has been to limit the duration of any loans granted by the Government, or under its advice, according to the actual period during which the improvement is estimated to last. From ten to fifteen years is a proper period during which loans obtained for road construction should be re-paid.

There is danger that Canada may adopt the comfortable theory which prevails in the United States in regard to country roads, namely, that the greater burden of the cost of road improvements should be borne by future generations.

Mr. Nelson P. Lewis, Engineer of the Board of Estimate and Apportionment of New York City, writes* as follows with regard to the practice in the State of New York:

"The State of New York, by the vote of its people, has authorized the expenditure of $100,000,000 for the improvement of the state highways, and this enormous sum is raised by the issue of fifty-year

---

*The Planning of the Modern City, p. 361.

bonds. While a portion of the work to be done is undoubtedly of a permanent character, such as the widening and straightening of the roads, the improvement of grades and provision for drainage by substantial structure of masonry or steel, a very large proportion of the expenditure is for road surfaces, many of which can scarcely be expected to last for more than ten years. Borrowing money for fifty years to pay for ten-year roads is obviously unwise."

The only sound principle in financing road improvements is to pay for all construction over the period during which it lasts, and only to borrow money for any longer period, say up to fifty years, in respect of such portion of the work as is permanent. The planning of the lines of roads, improving the grades, and all other permanent work which is part of the system of planning, can be spread over a long period of years without injustice to posterity. Unfortunately, however, it is this class of permanent work which is usually neglected, and the actual construction of temporary work is paid for by money borrowed for a period much longer than the life of the improvement. This is unsound finance and is improper use of the credit of a province or a municipality.

The Planning of Roads

Up to this point we have only dealt with the relative importance of the road and the railway, the great improvement being made in the construction of roads, the enormously increasing expenditures being incurred to secure this improvement, and the economic and social value of roads. But good roads cannot be obtained unless they are properly planned, as regards position, alignment, directness and width. This is the question with which this report is chiefly concerned, and it is of primary importance. Planning of roads is essential, not only to obtain good roads, but to obtain them in the right and most convenient places and to make them serve the largest possible number of inhabitants. It stands to reason that the shorter the length of road to construct, the better it can be constructed, if the amount of money available out of the taxes for construction and maintenance is limited. *There are too many roads in Canada, because there are more roads than it is possible to make out of the funds likely to be available on the basis of the most liberal estimate of the tax-paying ability of the people.*

Human necessity and the traffic requirements of the whole population should be the guiding principle in laying out a system of roads, and not merely a rigid adherence to an artificial system of straight lines. Considering the enormous expenditures required to be incurred to improve roads, their economic and social value, the importance of directness of

PLATE VIII   SUBURBAN ROADS WITH EASY CURVES

Cheaply constructed and well-graded curved roads in a Baltimore subdivision. The inexpensive development and the care which has been taken to preserve the trees have been great factors in attracting residents to this estate.

PLATE VIII   COUNTRY ROADS WITH EASY CURVES

It is more important to avoid steep grades, bad situations for drainage and sudden deflections than easy curves; in undulating country the curved roads, besides being most practical and best for traffic, are much more pleasant to the eye. No road should be curved except for some useful purpose, but natural conditions in most districts make curves necessary.

Photo by courtesy of Immigration Branch, Dept. of Interior

route, the danger and inconvenience of sharp curves, and the advantage of easy grades, it is an extraordinary fact that the stereotyped rectangular system (which has been fully dealt with in the previous chapter) pays no respect to either of these considerations. The money has to be spent by highway departments which have no voice in their location, for greater lengths of road than are necessary. Directness of route is only possible for short lengths, while sharp corners, collision points, and bad grades are prominent features in the rectangular plan. The absence of radial thoroughfares connecting with village centres creates excessive distances for purposes of co-operation and education. In swampy regions, bad foundations and difficulties of drainage are inevitable, as no choice is open to select the driest positions. In dry locations, where it would be an advantage to fit in the roads with the system of irrigation so as to damp the earth and gravel roads before dragging, this too has to be overlooked so that a fixed system of survey may prevail above all other considerations.

Road planning and engineering is a highly skilled profession, and millions of dollars are wasted in the attempt to save money that should be used to employ good men to design the location and construction of roads.

A Concrete Illustration of Saving Due to Planning

In connection with the construction of a certain road in Cape Cod, Massachusetts, the *Municipal Journal* of America states that the estimates of the cost varied from $14,000 to $36,000. "The layman, without the assistance of the engineer, guessed within 61 per cent of the actual cost. The engineer, without being permitted to make a special examination of the problem, was able to guess within 39 per cent. When permitted to make a proper study of it, the latter was able to arrive at approximately the true cost, and moreover, what is even more important, *was able to reduce the cost by 25 per cent by planning a more economical location.*"

The American Highway Association points out, in a comment on this case, that if construction had been started as soon as the legislative appropriation was available, it would have been impossible to complete the road, and travellers over the completed section would have been led to an almost impassable trail through loose sand and scrub oak barren.

The moral of this is not only that preliminary plans of roads should be made by competent engineers in the interests of economy, but that the engineers should have the power to exercise some discretion as to the location of the road. To fix road locations by the hit and miss method of the rectangular survey plan is to impose upon the community expensive road locations and to prevent them from making proper use of the services of competent engineers.

Planning Roads in Australia

That the importance of proper planning of country roads is realized in Australia is shown by the following statement, taken from the report for 1914 of the Victoria (Australia) Country Roads Board:

> Badly located and badly graded roads are a heavy and constant tax on any community. This is not only because of the fact that the gradient determines the amount of load that can be carried, but because steep gradients cause increased erosion by water and increased wear by traffic. The expensive maintenance is thus greatly increased; so much so that the additional cost each year may exceed the amount of interest on the capital that would have been necessary in securing the better grade in the first instance.

As an illustration, a case is cited where two pieces of road were made of the same material and at the same time, one length being on a grade of 1 in 12, *i.e.,* about 8.3 per cent, the other on the level. While that on the level ground remained in good condition, the portion on the grade had to be reconstructed owing to abrasion and scour. Having regard to these facts, the Board decided, when it was formed, that no expenditure in the way of permanent improvements should be incurred on any road until it was ascertained by investigation that the location and gradients could not be improved at a reasonable cost. It was felt that the labour thus caused in surveys and investigations was worth while.

The Advantages of Planning Roads in Canada

In Canada, good, well planned roads would help to build up manufacturing industries, cheapen production and reduce the cost of living by bringing the farmer nearer to the consumer. They would help to attract settlers to areas that must remain unsettled without them. As new roads are made, farmers are educated to appreciate their proper value and become their most active supporters, but so long as they have five miles of road reservations where one or two miles would serve, they naturally object to face the enormous burden of improving them. Roads cannot be properly classified into different groups, nor an equitable arrangement made for apportioning the cost between the different authorities, unless the system of highways is properly designed in the first place.

Reference has been made in a previous chapter to the good agricultural and industrial conditions prevailing in the county of Waterloo, Ontario. The system of laying out the land and planning the roads to suit the traffic has had something to do with the success of settlement in that region. The lots in Waterloo were laid out by private companies, the dimensions being 80 chains by 56 chains and there were no road allowances. As towns and villages grew up, the settlers made the roads in the most convenient position to give direct access to the market centres. Mr. H. J. Bowman, O.L.S., referring to these roads, in 1906, said he thought they had better roads in the county of Waterloo for less money than any county in the province of Ontario – they were the very best roads all the year round.

Mr. Bowman went on to say that there had been millions of money wasted in Ontario in building roads which were placed in the wrong positions. In his experience, municipal councils preferred to stick to the road allowance rather than make a change, even if the change meant the saving of money. In one case he reported to a council that they could construct a road round a hill for half the money that it would take to cut through the hill, at the same time obtaining an easier gradient; but the council said that the road had always been there and they would go on with cutting. After expending a thousand dollars on the excavation, a railway was constructed through the middle of the cut and it had to be abandoned. "A road," said Mr. Bowman, speaking as an experienced land surveyor, "should be located by an engineer, and not left to the chance of where the township line would come, and the road should be located with a view to getting from one important centre to another in as direct a line as possible, with the easiest gradients and by the most economical method."

Planning of Road Widths

The present unscientific system of fixing the alignment of roads is accompanied by an equally unscientific system of fixing road widths. Most roads are too wide and many are too narrow, and those that are too narrow are restricted in width by reason of the law which requires the others to be too wide. It may be claimed that, both in rural and urban territory, a general average of 66 feet is wide enough for all purposes and that no community, even when comparatively closely settled, can afford to lay out and pave streets of a greater average width. This question may not affect the farmer except in so far as he may have to contribute towards an inconvenient and expensive road system in connection with the urban development in rural territory. It is in this connection that the grievance of bad road planning becomes acute. First, as already shown, the alignment is fixed without regard to contours, and, second, the width is determined on a minimum basis for all roads no matter for what purpose they are to be used.

The minimum standard in Ontario and elsewhere is 66 feet. This standard applies to the main arterial thoroughfare required to carry heavy traffic and to the short residential street required for purely domestic needs of a few houses. In many districts acres of macadam, asphalt and concrete are laid in a few streets and might with advantage be used over twice the length of street now paved. One consequence of this irrational and expensive method is that the cost of focal improvements to the local councils in many localities is so great that money is not available for necessary purposes of public sanitation. Another is that the tax burden on the property owners is so heavy that they are proportionably limited in the capital available for making their houses sanitary and durable in construction, and they are compelled to crowd their land with buildings in order to put it to economic use.

But even at this late day, with all the lessons we have had of waste of land and unnecessary expenditure of capital in providing for too wide roads for purely local traffic – in providing many miles of road space where it is not needed at all, and in thus lessening the ability of provincial and local authorities to obtain the space and provide the means to construct main arterial highways where these are required – there are those who regard any suggestion to make streets narrower than 60 or 66 feet as reactionary. Yet there are few who will deny that it is impracticable, in any community where the density of building is comparatively open, as in Canada, to provide land and make satisfactory roads or streets to a greater average width than 66 feet. What happens is that the land is provided for roads or streets, as the law requires, but that few of the roads or streets are ever properly constructed, the reason being that there is too much road surface for the population, even when the land is closely settled. *Excessively wide streets, instead of securing more air space, cause congestion, e.g., in the erection of apartment houses in towns because without such congestion the frontages could not afford to meet the cost of local improvements.* This has been proved in Germany, Sweden, and other countries where the tenement system prevails, and it is being proved in Canada where the tendency towards the tenement building is being created by the wide street. In the rural districts, although land is plentiful and cheap, it stands to reason that all roads should not be of the same width, and that there should be variation to suit the requirements of traffic.

THE BY-LAW MINIMUM OF WIDTH

What happens in practice is that our by-laws fix a width, not according to scientific theory, nor yet on any practical basis, but simply because of the convenience of making a hard and fast rule in accordance with some custom. The 66 feet width of Ontario seems to have no other justification than the fact that it is the length of a chain. It is about half the width that should be provided for some main arteries, and about twice what is necessary for the short, tributary streets. It is true that, in the absence of proper development schemes, we must have a system of regulations fixing a general standard in these matters – that is the inevitable weakness of the by-law system – but it is quite as absurd to regulate the width of a street according to a fixed by-law standard as it would be to prescribe that all sewers and water-mains should be of the same diameter.

EFFECT OF NARROW ROADS IN BRITAIN

In Great Britain this point has been recognized for some years, but the difficulties of securing variation are not so great as in Canada. The standard width of streets in rural England is from 36 to 45 feet,* and the result is that, while perhaps 75 per cent of the streets are wide enough, the public have to bear a somewhat heavy share of the cost of widening main arteries, which form about 25 per cent, although a great many old highways exist which are much wider than required by the by-laws, and form a sort of trunk system throughout the country.

The narrower widths of roads in Britain, as compared with Canada, is partly responsible for securing a higher standard of road construction and partly for enabling the middle and working classes to secure cheaper housing accommodation in English suburbs and rural districts. In regard to the former matter we are apt to flatter ourselves in Canada that, although our roads are not so good as the British roads, this is because Canada is a new country. We overlook the fact that the high standard applies to all new roads in Britain and not only to old highways, and that it is the new streets and roads which are being made today, rather than the old highways, which set the standard of modern efficiency in street making. When we recognize this fact, it is a proper question to ask why suburban and village roads in Canada should not be as good as suburban and village roads in Britain. A good deal of time must pass, of course, before our rural highways can come up to the standard of those in the older countries, but that does not provide any excuse for the poor roads in many of our newly developed towns and suburbs. *One reason for the difference is due to the fact that in Britain the burden of making new streets is placed on the shoulders of those who directly benefit from the subdivision of land for building purposes, and the roads have to be constructed according to the municipal*

---

* In many cities in the United States the minimum width is 40 feet.

standard before the land is fully used. In some cases buildings cannot be erected until the road is properly made, and this applies to rural as well as to urban subdivisions.

PRINCIPLE ON WHICH ROADS SHOULD BE PLANNED

Roads and streets have to be planned, in all respects, so as to obtain *the maximum of convenience at the minimum of cost.* Even when that principle is acted upon, the tax which industry has to meet to obtain adequate means of communication is as much as it can bear. The comparatively narrow standards of road width in Britain, even when accompanied by having the roads in the position best adapted for cheap construction, and by having only a sufficient number of roads as are necessary, seems to be as much as can be paid for by a reasonable tax on the community.

The ambition on this continent to have over 50 per cent greater width than the British standard, with a more scattered and less wealthy rural population, has meant, in practice, that we have more road space than we need or can properly use, and that, even with the assistance of the provincial governments, only a small proportion can be paved. The absence of planning also results, in many instances, in political influence, rather than the general benefit of the community, being the guiding factor in determining which roads will be improved at the public expense. To say that a 66-ft. minimum is desirable may be true, if it were possible for the community to construct and maintain that minimum. One might also say that it is desirable that every farmer should have a water supply under pressure, a bath room and a motor car, even if they are beyond his means. But should he be compelled to have these things before he is permitted to occupy a farm?

The chief difficulty in getting the public to realize the economic absurdity of a 66-feet minimum is due to the fact that the ultimate cost of making and maintaining a proper surface and other improvements is ignored when the streets are laid out, and that proper expert knowledge is not applied to planning a comprehensive system of highways. Highways should vary from the narrow carriage drive of 24 feet to the wide main thoroughfare of over 100 feet in width, and the character of the development permitted on the land fronting the highway should be controlled so as to secure that the buildings will have proper relation to the character and width of the highway. As already pointed out, air space is a separate matter and should be settled by other means than by fixing widths of the highways. It is erroneous to assume that costly paved streets are needed to provide air space; the required air space round buildings can be more cheaply and effectively provided on the lot by means of building regulations.

At present there are no figures available to enable any estimate to be made of the loss which farmers suffer as a result of the present system so far as purely rural highways are concerned. But it is apparent to everyone that there are more highways and more space in the highways than the farming population can construct and maintain, and that there is incalculable loss due to the want of well-paved roads. It has been shown that the rural system of highways is the basis on which the urban system is developed. The market roads which connect the country with the town usually lead through scattered suburban areas and are often too narrow and badly made.

Suburban Standards Too High

Elsewhere attention has been drawn to the great need for better control of the sanitary condition of subdivided areas in rural districts. It is equally important that the street planning of these areas should be based on sound economic principles. Streets in small towns and suburbs are usually unpaved or too extravagantly paved. There seems to be no adequate appreciation of the necessity for spreading the money spent in local improvements over as much surface as possible, having due regard to the construction being reasonably adequate. We are prone to act in this matter as we do in regard to widths and numbers of roads – we place our standards too high and then, because we find the attainment of that standard too costly, we prefer to do without improvements rather than lower it. We act like a man who is in need of boots and has only five dollars available to purchase them, but who has decided that, unless he can get ten dollar boots, he will continue to use his old ones or go barefooted.

In many suburban areas, where asphalt pavements are laid, an ordinary cheap macadam road would serve the purpose better, and concrete sidewalks are an unnecessary extravagance. The majority of residential streets in excess of 40 feet in width represent so much waste land, pavement, sewer and water connections, etc. Every unnecessary foot adds to the cost of sewerage and sewage disposal, water supply, fire prevention, policing, street transportation, and other public services. It is not too extravagant to estimate that most towns and suburbs cover twice the area they need cover under a proper system of development, and increase the burden of taxation accordingly.

It is no answer to this criticism to argue that land is so plentiful in Canada that we can be indifferent to the amount placed in streets. At Akron, Ohio, the Goodyear Tire Company has developed a model village in which it constructs all the local improvements in advance of building development. Land is comparatively cheap in Akron, as it is in most of

PLATE IX WILSON AVE., ST. THOMAS, ONT.

An inexpensive and attractive street suitable for suburban and semi-rural districts which are served by single-track street cars. The flower beds at the intersections are planted and maintained by the Horticultural Society.

PLATE IX STREET IN ROLAND PARK, BALTIMORE, MD.

In small towns and villages it is a mistake to try and copy the expansive boulevards of the large Canadian city. An even more picturesque result can be obtained by using existing natural conditions, instead of destroying them, and by making simple and inexpensive driveways and sidewalks of the minimum width necessary for traffic needs as is shown in this illustration. This street is only about half the legal width required by the law of Ontario, but it is ample for all practical purposes, and is, for residential purposes, more pleasant than a wide street.

the districts where speculation has not inflated the values. But when land is cheap, it is more than ever necessary to exercise a proper sense of proportion in regard to the extent of land placed in roads and streets. The cheaper the land, the greater the relative cost of development to land value, and the greater the need for avoiding extravagant planning and high costs of construction.

The Goodyear Tire Company has made careful estimates of the cost of the land and the cost of the local improvements. The streets vary from 50 to 70 feet in width. The land costs $75 per lot, and the improvements $500 per lot. It is in respect of the latter cost that economy is most important, for, in proportion as streets are unnecessarily wide, it is this cost which soars up out of all proportion to the advantage gained and beyond the ability of the property owners to pay. No community leaves its streets unpaved and unimproved out of choice, and an adequate conception of the cost of development can only be obtained if we assume that, wherever residences are erected, the streets should be improved sooner or later. The best time to improve them is when the building development takes place, and the chief burden of the improvement should fall on the real estate operators.

It is in the interests of the rural population that they should control building development in rural areas for the purpose of securing healthy and economic conditions. There is nothing more necessary in Canada, in the interests of production and healthy growth, than the further development of the small town, the rural village and the outer suburbs of the large cities. More labour is badly needed in these districts and more consumers of farm produce should be attracted into rural areas to be nearer to the producers. A cheap and efficient system of good roads is needed to encourage more settlement in the urban parts of rural areas, and also to make it practical for the labourer to obtain good and healthy housing accommodation at a reasonable price in the small towns and villages.

COST OF ROADS IN RELATION TO HOUSING

Housing accommodation is cheaper where streets, other than main arteries, are narrower, because the cost of a site for a house consists of three things: (1) The actual site which it occupies, including garden space; (2) the land given up for streets, and (3) the cost of local improvements, consisting of pavement, sidewalk, sewer, water-main, etc., where these are provided. In a country like Canada the cost of the bare land ought not to be a serious matter, and, where it is forced up in value by speculation, as it now is, it ought to be controlled by legislation. The portion of the above cost, however, which seems to require most careful consideration on the part of engineers and administrators is that which is spent on local improvements.

In one English town the cost of the street, including the sewer, works out in an average case at less than $100 for a small workman's dwelling, costing say $1,000 to construct. This includes concrete or stone slab sidewalks and a pavement with a finished surface of bituminous materials. The cost per lineal foot-run for a first class street forty-five feet wide in this town is from $8 to $12.50. As typical houses for labourers occupy only about 15 feet frontage, the cost per house is thus $60 to $93.75. In Canada houses have wider frontages and face wider streets than in England, and for a house with 25 feet frontage on a street 66 feet wide the cost for local improvements when constructed would be from $16 to $24 per lineal foot, or from $200 to $300 per house. By limiting the number of houses that may be erected on each acre to twelve, giving them a frontage of 25 feet on a street 26 feet wide, instead of 36 houses to the acre, with a frontage of 15 feet on a road 45 feet wide, and dispensing with rear alleys, it has been found in England that nearly three times the area round each house can be obtained at no greater cost per house for road construction. *Thus the narrow street enables the house to have more instead of less air space.* The above 26-foot road, consisting of 18 feet pavement and two 4-foot sidewalks, is regarded as adequate for purely domestic streets not required for through traffic, and the buildings have all to be set back 15 feet from the boundary of the street, thus securing a minimum distance of 56 feet between all buildings. This is for a purely working class district.

Having regard to the importance of designing streets on which workmen's dwellings are erected, so as to secure the utmost economy, it would be well for Canadian municipalities to consider whether narrower and better constructed domestic streets, and fewer streets with deeper building lots, *accompanied by regulations limiting the density of buildings and the widths between the building lines,* would not be better than the wildernesses of bare dusty road and the shallow subdivisions that are the result of the present policy. It may be open to question whether roads should in any circumstances be made as narrow as 26 feet, but, as the by-law width in Ontario is 66 feet, as against 45 feet in the above instance, the proportionate reduction in width would be to a minimum 38 feet to secure similar results.

In many small towns and rural districts a cheaper form of street is made than in cities, but in numerous other cases the ambition of the small municipality is to become a pocket edition of the city, and to have the same kind of local improvements. Where the latter is the case the cost of the improvements is as great or sometimes greater than in the city.

The cost of one expensive street 66 feet wide, including a 9-inch sewer, in Ottawa in 1916, was $27.50 per lineal foot. The street pavement consisted of asphalt on concrete foundation 28 feet wide, the sidewalks were in cement, each 5 feet wide; the remaining of 28 feet was left as boulevard in front of the properties. The capital cost of these improvements in respect of lots having 25 feet frontages was thus $343.75. There has to be added to this amount certain costs incurred by the city, and chargeable to the inhabitants at large, including the cost of making the intersections; it would therefore be reasonable to estimate that in a city area it might require $350 to provide local improvements for a 25-foot lot fronting on a 66 foot street. This sum would be much increased if the whole 66 feet were paved and a back lane had to be constructed at the rear of the property, as is required by law in western subdivisions. If the cost of the land is added, it means that from $700 to $900 has to be paid by a working man for a properly improved lot in a city area. The result is that his capital is mostly absorbed in expensive street improvements and in land, leaving a totally inadequate sum for the erection of his home. That is why so many local improvements remain unmade and so many homes have to be left in an unsanitary condition. In England the cost of local improvements and land combined do not usually amount to more than twenty-five per cent of the total cost of the home; on this continent, owing to the combination of inflated land values and costly local improvements, these two things often cost more than the actual house.

The items of expenditure which require to be incurred by a workingman who builds his own home on a typical lot in a medium sized city in Canada and in England, respectively, may be set out as follows:

CANADA		ENGLAND	
Cost of lot 25x100 ft. at $15 per ft. frontage = 2500 ft $375		Cost of lot 16x156¼ ft. at 5 1-3c per ft. = 2500 ft. say $134	
Capital cost of local improvements (66-ft. street) at $8........ 200		Cost of local improvements (36-ft. street) at $4 64	
	$575		$198
Add cost of dwelling, say 1,000		Add cost of dwelling, say 1,377	
	$1,575		$1,575

The question of the difference in cost of labour and value of money does not affect the main point illustrated by the above comparison, namely, that the English workingman has in this case over 50 per cent more than the Canadian workingman to spend on his home; he pays for his sanitary fittings and solid brick construction out of what he saves in cost of land and development. The workingman in Canada has too much to pay for the site of his home and he either pays too much for local improvements or goes without them. In the majority of cases he accepts the latter alternative, and, what he saves by doing so, he pays in extra cost of land due to the inflation of values by speculation. Cheaper housing in Canada cannot be obtained without a more economical and better planned system of streets.

Roads and Air Space Around Buildings

Reference has been made to a principle that has often guided municipalities in determining width of roads, namely, that the road has to be wide in order to secure sufficient air space around the buildings. In some districts it is laid down that roads have to be wide for purposes of air space, and yet the owners of the land are allowed to build up almost every available yard of their site with the buildings, and there is a complete absence of air circulation except in the streets. We have already seen that more air space can be secured around buildings with narrow streets than with wide streets. We have to recognize that provision of air space is entirely separate from the question of street width, and that more air space should be provided by those who erect the buildings. Streets are for the purpose of giving facilities for circulating traffic and for providing access to buildings, and they should be designed for that purpose only.

Heights of buildings should have some relation to the width between buildings, and in rural areas a low standard of height can be fixed with advantage to owners of land. This is needed not only to secure light and air, but to prevent traffic congestion in the suburbs in towns and on rural territory surrounding them. We should determine the question of light and air to buildings by fixing a minimum distance between all buildings on opposite sides of streets without regard to the width of the street itself, by limiting the amount of land in the subdivision which should be occupied by actual building and by requiring a minimum angle of light to all windows. (Figure 26.) Apart from special cases, where the evil of high buildings has already been established, no buildings should be higher than the width of the streets facing them, and rural municipalities at least have power to adopt this standard. Ample justification can be given from every point of view, including that of the interests of real estate, for such a limitation.

Bad Roads Costly to Maintain

In many rural districts and towns in Canada, where the streets have to be 66 feet wide, the only form of construction is the occasional levelling of the soil or the dumping down of loads of cinders. The traffic for the most of the year on these streets follows one line and the pavement area might for that purpose be eight or ten feet instead of, say, thirty feet wide. In a case of this kind, the cost of maintenance is probably greater than it would be if the roads were properly constructed at the outset. There is the mud and the damp of the spring and autumn, and the disease-bearing dust of the summer to contend with. There is the lack of convenience for farmers and manufacturers in teaming their raw and manufactured material and to them it is in many cases a matter of serious loss.

Too Many Roads in Subdivisions

Residential streets, particularly in rural areas, are not only too wide, but they are too many in number, because of our crowded and shallow sub-divisions and because of the absence of a plan. If land is laid out and the streets planned in an economical way, sufficient saving could be effected, in comparison with the system now in vogue, to pay for the extra land required to double the depths of our subdivisions in a suburban or rural area. With a more economical plan of development roads would be better made, gardens would be larger, and more recreation space would be available; the result would be that the public would gain in health and reduced cost of living. (Figures 29 and 30.)

Heavy and Light Roads

The haphazard system, of allowing factories and residences to be mixed together in rural areas as well as in villages and towns, without any dis-crimination, also makes it difficult, on the one hand, to get wide main thoroughfares where they are required, and, on the other hand, to secure a higher standard of road construction, giving access to areas that should be reserved for manufacturing purposes. The heavy trucks and wagons which use the streets in industrial areas require heavy roads, but, because we do not reserve special areas for manufacturing and other areas for residential purposes, we have either to make our roads too light for manu-facturing purposes or too heavy and expensive for residential purposes. Thus in regard to width, length and construction of streets we have to keep up an extravagant standard because we have no proper development plan. It is because of this that the advantage of having wide roads where these are needed for through traffic is often questioned, the plea being that to provide for very wide roads casts too great a burden on the present generation for the benefit of posterity. That plea rests on the erroneous assumption that all roads should be wide and that we do not need to vary

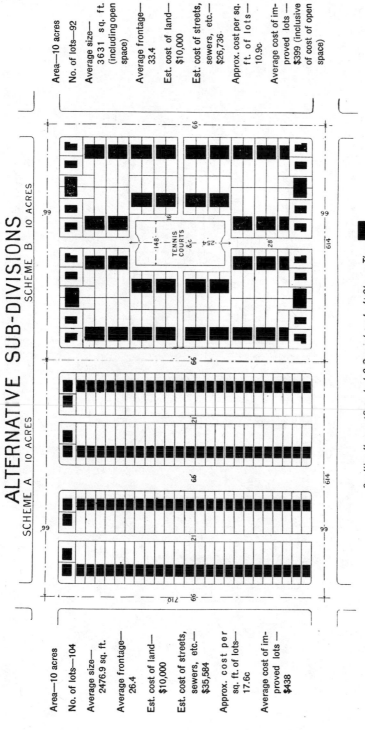

ALTERNATIVE SUB-DIVISIONS

SCHEME A 10 ACRES

SCHEME B 10 ACRES

Scheme A:

Area—10 acres

No. of lots—104

Average size— 2476.9 sq. ft.

Average frontage— 26.4

Est. cost of land— $10,000

Est. cost of streets, sewers, etc.— $35,584

Approx. cost per sq. ft. of lots— 17.6c

Average cost of improved lots — $438

Scheme B:

Area—10 acres

No. of lots—92

Average size— 3631 sq. ft. (including open space)

Average frontage— 33.4

Est. cost of land— $10,000

Est. cost of streets, sewers, etc.— $26,736

Approx. cost per sq. ft. of lots— 10.9c

Average cost of improved lots —$399 (inclusive of cost of open space)

TENNIS COURTS &c

Dwelling Houses (Detached & Semi-detached) Shown Thus

FIGURE 29

The cost of the land is the same in each scheme, A, B, C and D. The differences in the figures is in the cost of the local improvements, due to different systems of planning. Detached houses are shown in Scheme A as being typical of the development in Canadian cities. In the other schemes most of the houses are shown in pairs, which is a more desirable arrangement where practical. Whether the houses are single or in pairs, however, has no bearing on the cost of development of the land.

ALTERNATIVE SUB-DIVISIONS

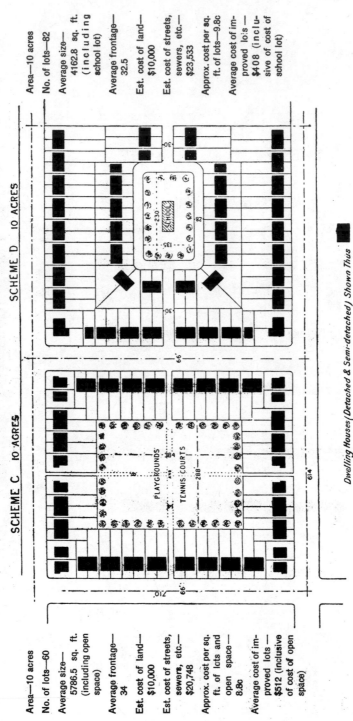

SCHEME C 10 ACRES

SCHEME D 10 ACRES

Area—10 acres

No. of lots—60

Average size— 5786.5 sq. ft. (including open space)

Average frontage— 34

Est. cost of land— $10,000

Est. cost of streets, sewers, etc.— $20,748

Approx. cost per sq. ft. of lots and open space 8.8c

Average cost of improved lots — $512 (inclusive of cost of open space)

Area—10 acres

No. of lots—82

Average size— 4162.8 sq. ft. (including school lot)

Average frontage— 32.5

Est. cost of land— $10,000

Est. cost of streets, sewers, etc.— $23,533

Approx. cost per sq. ft. of lots—9.8c

Average cost of improved lots— $408 (inclusive of cost of school lot)

Dwelling Houses (Detached & Semi-detached) Shown Thus ■

FIGURE 30

The saving in road space in Schemes C and D increases the size of the average lot over what is obtained by mere reduction in the number of lots. Scheme D differs from the other three schemes in that it represents the development of one-half of a 20-acre block and has no street frontage on one side. The interior streets in schemes B and D are deliberately designed to hinder through traffic.

and regulate their width according to the use to which they have to be put. Under a proper scheme roads should not, as a whole, occupy a greater superficial area than they do now, but, complementary to the narrow residential street fringed with deep front gardens or the narrow farm lane, there would be the wide main artery.

Main Arterial Thoroughfares

In laying out main arteries it is cheaper as well as better to make the roads wide enough to meet future needs. This is particularly so where such roads are required for street railways. The expansion of cities into surrounding rural territory is being followed by the extension of street railways into such territory, and there is a growing tendency to construct radial railways parallel with highways through rural districts. Every road which is intended to ultimately carry two streams of ordinary traffic and, in addition, two lines of street railway, should not be less than 100 feet and should, where practicable, be 120 feet wide. The arterial road has to be wide to enable it to be cheaply made. One illustration of the economy to be secured in this connection will suffice. In the suburbs of Liverpool Mr. John Brodie, M. Inst. C. E., the city engineer, has demonstrated that he could widen an existing 40-feet road to 120 feet at a slight extra cost compared to widening to 80 feet, where such a road ran through open country, and was required in part for a street railway. His alternative costs were worked out as follows, for these widths:

Widening to 80 feet (*Tramways Paved*)

Cost of land, 13⅓ yds. at $1.25	$16.66
Street works, per lineal yard	35.62
Tramways (including paving) 1 yard at	33.75
	$86.03

= $151,430 per mile.

The above estimate includes the cost of reconstruction of the old road to suit new levels.

Widening to 120 feet (*Tramways in Grass*)

Land for new road, 13⅓ yds. at $1.25	$16.66
Street works, per lineal yard	23.39
Tramways (in grass) including land, 1 yard at	34.16
	$74.21

= $130,640 per mile.

PLATE X   VIEW OF SUNK BUILDING LOT IN A CITY OF WESTERN CANADA,
SHOWING EXPENSIVE STREET CONSTRUCTION AND SUGGESTING DIFFICULTIES
IN ERECTING BUILDINGS, DRAINAGE, ETC.

PLATE X   VIEW OF STREET CUT THROUGH SOLID ROCK IN A CITY IN WESTERN CANADA.
TO UTILIZE THE LOTS FACING THIS STREET THE ROCK HAS TO BE REMOVED
FROM THE BUILDING SITES AT GREAT EXPENSE.

TOWN PLANNING FOLLOWED BY BAD DEVELOPMENT
Although no expense was spared to secure a proper plan for this city, the fact that part of the town was laid out
in straight lines with rectangular lots prevented the natural difficulties of the site from being overcome to the
extent that would have been possible with a more flexible plan. Whatever advantage the straight lines possess
in such a case are more than counterbalanced by the expensive and inconvenient development.

This estimate does not include for any alteration to the old 40 foot road, nor the extra land required to make the excess of 80 feet in width.

This is a special case, no doubt, as in making the 120-ft. road it is possible to save the cost of reconstructing the existing road; but even apart from that, the wider road would not seriously exceed the cost of the narrower road. The saving of $20,790 in the second case would be nearly sufficient to enable an extra 40 ft. of width of land to be purchased at a price of 10 cents per foot. That price would be sufficient, in view of the greater advantage to the owners of real estate in having the wider road. In any case, if such a road were made in a country district, obviously the 120-ft. road could be made cheaper than the 80-ft., as the cost of the land would be much less and the saving in construction would be the same. The saving in paving alone due to laying the tramways in grass is $15,000 per mile. Another advantage of the cheaper method is that trolleys running on grass are less noisy and do less injury to agricultural and residential land. Alternative road sections are shown on figure 31.

INCIDENTAL PROBLEMS OF ROAD PLANNING

Wearing surfaces of roads have to be adapted to local traffic in agricultural areas, factory areas and residential areas. The complex question of the modern traffic problem requires consideration to be given to the width of main arteries before buildings are erected upon the road frontages, and that is why this question is of particular importance in rural areas. In the financing of roads we have to recognize that everything that is spent on unnecessary width and construction on secondary roads is so much capital withdrawn from use in improving the main arterial system on which the opening up of agricultural territory, and the bringing of the market nearer to the farmer, depends so much.

Improper location of roads not only increases the cost and difficulty of construction, but it adds greatly to the cost of buildings. Owing to building lots being too shallow people who want gardens cannot obtain them unless they have twice the width of lot that is really necessary for the use of a house. Instead of having the land subdivided so as to give them space at the rear of buildings, it is laid out so that they have to acquire frontage areas, with the result that they probably have to pay twice as much for local improvements as is really necessary. In order to get straight streets, when easy curves would be preferable from a traffic point of view, streets are often made in deep cuts or on high embankments with the result that valuable building lots are spoiled. Illustrations of the bad effect of this kind of planning are given on plate X showing building lots in Prince Rupert, B.C.

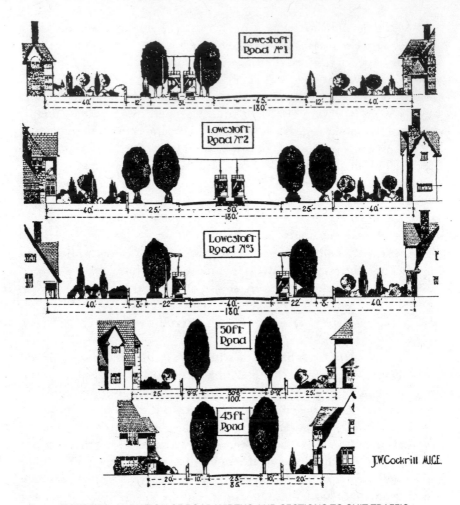

FIGURE 31   VARIATION OF ROAD WIDTHS AND SECTIONS TO SUIT TRAFFIC

The above road sections show the variation in the width of roads proposed to be permitted under a town planning scheme of Great Yarmouth in England. Roads No. 1, No. 2 and No. 3 are each 100 feet wide, and show alternative methods of dealing with a traffic thoroughfare having a street railway track. The building lines in each case are set back 40 feet from the street line, this giving a total of 180 feet between the buildings. Two sections for residential streets are shown. The above 45 feet and 50 feet roads are of ample width for average conditions in residential sections, subject to the 20 feet or 25 feet set-back of the buildings.

When we come to consider bridges and culverts, we have often to face unnecessary difficulties owing to lack of planning of lines of roads. The dust nuisance arises largely from making unnecessary width of street. Who that has studied the enormous cost of maintenance but has been forced to recognize that half of the trouble is in maintaining more surface than the community can find capital to construct properly at the outset?

The issue before the engineers and administrators of this country is not only to have good roads in the sense of having them properly constructed, but to endeavour to foresee and adequately provide for agricultural development and the future expansion of our towns by planning these roads. We want to save cost on unnecessary length and width of minor roads, to lay down main radial roads of adequate width, and of good alignment and grade, and to connect up these radial roads around towns by good ring roads. The question of directness of route cannot be considered in isolated streets or areas, but is largely a provincial, county or city problem. It is not generally practicable to have curved roads in the old settled areas of Canada, owing to our rectangular planning, but curves are often an advantage, subject to a view being maintained of not less distance than 100 yards. It is more important to avoid sudden deflections, steep grades, and collision points than easy curves. Curves are often a physical necessity to avoid the removal of enormous quantities of material. Moreover, we should not be indifferent to the value of giving some aesthetic effect to a road if this can be done without loss of utility. Some regard has to be paid to beauty, to the preservation of trees and to architectural effect and, as it has been stated elsewhere, relief of traffic is not inconsistent with relief to the eye. (Figure 32).

Where wide roads cause development to be scattered and simultaneously cause building congestion on building lots; and where, by reason of their cost to construct and maintain, they lessen the amount that can be spent in securing durable construction of buildings, they have the effect of increasing fire risks. In Canada we pay from two to three dollars per capita for fire insurance and protection more than is paid in some European countries. This excessive burden is borne by the farmer as well as by the townsman.

In a report relating primarily to rural districts, it may seem that too much attention is being given to the question of road planning as it affects the planning of urban areas. *It is in rural areas, however, where the system of planning is adopted which governs all future development, and, to be effective, planning has to precede and not to follow development.* The foregoing considerations apply to three classes of area in rural territory, as follows:

(1) Suburban areas in rural territory which are in course of being used or are likely to be used for building purposes.
(2) Rural areas, especially those which lie near to or between centres of population.
(3) Sites of new towns which are likely to grow up in future.

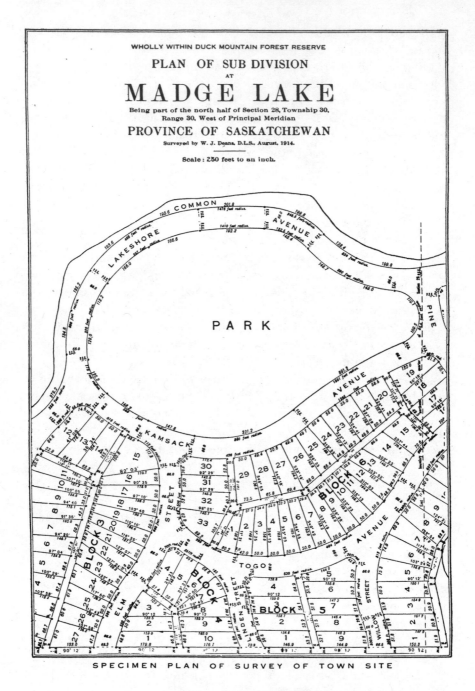

FIGURE 32   PLAN OF SUBDIVISION AT MADGE LAKE

This curved street plan of the townsite of Madge Lake, Saskatchewan, is a specimen of a revised system used by the Topographical Surveys Branch of the Department of the Interior to secure conformity to contours of the land; but as designed it adds to rather than lessens the amount of land given up for streets and lanes in proportion to the area reserved for building lots.

The responsibility for the control of new development and for the planning of roads and streets in these three classes of area rests with rural municipalities.

Conclusion

In this chapter it has been contended *inter alia:* That the closer settlement of fertile land near to railways is needed both in the interest of greater production and improved transportation; that the further extension of the railway system should be directed to secure the profitable development of natural resources rather than profit to railway enterprises, as a first object; that, generally speaking, the highway and street system of Canada has been artificially arranged without regard to any principle of design, economy, natural topography or economic use of the land, although the progress of civilization in Canada, as in all countries, largely depends on the development of good roads; that good roads cannot be obtained at reasonable cost without comprehensive planning; that all roads and streets should be designed for purposes of traffic and access to buildings and not to provide air space, which should be dealt with under building regulations as a separate matter; that it is not practicable to develop a good highway or street system on a basis of a minimum of 66 feet in width within the tax-paying capacity of the people, unless with overcrowded building development on private property; and that a considerable percentage of the cost of making roads and other local improvements should be borne by sub-dividers of land before it is sold for building purposes so that speculation may be hampered, and reasonable access provided to building lots before they are built upon.

CHAPTER IV
RURAL TRANSPORTATION AND DISTRIBUTION:
RAILWAYS AND HIGHWAYS

Commentary by Ian Wight

———

What coloured Adams' thinking when he authored his 1917 opus?[1] How does this colouring hold up in making sense of today's planning world? Adams would be one of the first to hope – fervently – that there has been significant evolution ("improvement," in his terminology) in the intervening decades, now almost a century. It is difficult, however, to avoid the verdict that the present features only more of the same – déjà vu is perhaps the commanding view.

At the time, Adams wrote in response to the increasingly obvious slashing and burning of the young country's precious land resources. He attempted to bring some science-based order to the comparative chaos. Planning, for him, had the "agency of order" quality necessary to better manage the changes besetting the nascent urban-rural "inter-mixings" that were beginning to dominate the emerging Canadian settlement system. His rural focus can therefore be read today as preparation for a more overarching regional approach – an approach that, unfortunately, did not really take root in urban Canada until after the Second World War (Hodge and Robinson 2001).

Based on my own past decade of experience of Manitoba conditions, it is still a challenge today for planners to influence rural elected officials to fully embrace a regional approach: some are only now coming to terms with what Adams would regard as rather basic planning. But the planning is still more intermunicipal than regional and is still narrowly focused on land and its use (rather than on people and how they live and work). Rereading Adams, it is frankly sobering to realize how relevant his advice remains for rural Manitoba. It retains many basic primer qualities. Is it a fundamental trait, or fate, of "compleat" planners – such as Adams – to be decades ahead of their time in their thoughts and advocacy?

Ordered efficiency, underpinned by hard science, dominated Adams' thought and actions in Canada, and it was manifested not only in his historic planning text but also in his efforts to institutionalize both a profession of (town and country) planning and a system of planning legislation and administration, at the provincial level at least. Order, efficiency, and science do not carry the same imperative today; although still very much part of the modern professional planning code (Canadian Institute of Planners 2010), they are being superseded in significance by the new imperatives associated with the postmodernization of planning. Complexity reigns, albeit it conforms to Jane Jacobs' idea of organized complexity. Managing diversity is the challenge. Livability, sustainability, and conviviality compete as macro-missions for planning. Qualitative methods, softer science, and more phenomenological approaches – such as storytelling – are more likely to furnish the cutting edge (Jacobs 1993 [1961]; Sandercock 2003; Eckstein and Throgmorton 2003).

Although regional planning (urban-rural integration) was Adams' overarching ideal in terms of an operating framework, subsequent evolution has cast up even more overarching ideals – environmental and ecological, for example – the seeds of which might be unearthed in Adams' thinking and influences. However, *Rural Planning and Development* suggests that he would have been, at best, a very pragmatic environmentalist and a very utilitarian ecologist. Does this mean his work should be consigned to the archives, to be read for historical perspective only? Not by a long shot! It takes time for great ideals to take hold and for cultural evolution to catch up. As is illustrated in the uncommon sense and logic on display in this chapter on transportation and distribution, Canada would probably be much better off today if it simply embodied the comparatively simple planning ideals espoused by Adams in his day.

Many planners today, in their often uphill struggles, voice complaints that echo Adams: "Probably the chief trouble has been due to our common sin of doing things as a nation [or province, city, region, district] without forethought, comprehensive planning and preliminary organization" (page 114).

Adams could also have been talking about Manitoba's capital region today, and probably many more Canadian city-regions, when he wrote the following statements: "Our want of proper planning and our public policies as regards land settlement have encouraged the spreading of population over too wide a territory" (page 118); "All forms of transportation suffer when population is too congested in some places and too scattered in others" (page 114); "The absence of planning also results, in many instances, in political influence, rather than the general benefit of the community, being the guiding factor in determining which roads will be improved at public expense" (page 135); and "It is in rural areas, however, where the system of planning is adopted which governs all future development, and, to be effective, planning has to precede and not follow development" (page 149).

Adams was much exercised by the lack of planning in advance of major infrastructure expenditures. He anticipated sentiments that might be associated with the federal auditor general today: "When the enormous amount of money spent on roads and road maintenance, and the great waste [arising] from the haphazard methods of planning and construction, are considered, it is surprising to find so little effort being made to deal with the matter on more practical and scientific lines" (page 121). He always argued for some upfront investment in planning: "A large sum should first be spent in the work of designing and preparation so as to avoid a possible waste of many millions in construction" (page 127). "Good roads cannot be obtained unless they are properly planned, as regards position, alignment, directness and width. This is the question with which this report is chiefly concerned, and it is of primary importance. Planning of roads is essential, not only to obtain good roads, but to obtain them in the right and most convenient places and to make them serve the largest possible number of inhabitants" (page 128).

As is still often the case, proper planning, to use Adams' terms, tended to be subordinated to rough-and-ready regulating (or crude township-and-range surveying). Much of his exasperation-filled critique centred on road alignments and widths: "The present unscientific system of fixing the alignment of roads is accompanied by an equally unscientific system of fixing road widths. Most roads are too wide and many are too narrow, and those that are too narrow are restricted in width by reason of the law which requires the others to be too wide" (page 132). "What happens in practice is that our bylaws fix a width, not according to scientific theory, nor yet on any practical basis, but simply because of the convenience of making a hard and fast rule in accordance with some custom ... the length of a chain. It is about half the width that should be provided for some main arteries, and about twice what is necessary for the short tributary streets" (pages 133-34). Out of these frustrations, Adams produced this enduring maxim: "Roads and streets have to be planned, in all respects, so as to obtain *the maximum of convenience at the minimum of cost*" (page 135).

Planning is a future-oriented, intervention-informing endeavour. It responds to an inherently speculative line of questioning (What could be? What might be? What should be?) that is always open to interpretation. It could benefit from more mainstream academic lines of questioning (What was? What is?) and research by the scientific method, but it must ultimately target an unknown and unknowable future, subject to the vagaries of individual preferences and desires. The best planning today will contribute to the meaning-making that makes collective action for the greater good possible. Planning today is an explicitly political and, ideally, democratic act; it is much more than a merely technical or technocratic procedure. Adams was spared concern for the public participation requirements that are now so much a part of planning. Would he relish or revile this aspect of contemporary planning?

As this chapter certainly shows, Adams was very much at home number crunching and marshalling facts from a range of authoritative sources, a skill set that is still essential for planners, especially those who prefer to "say it with numbers". But it makes one wonder if Adams would also have been up for the storytelling that is edging its way into postmodern planning. He seems to have been partial to the odd anecdote, where it suited his purpose, so perhaps he would have been open to a more explicit valuing of stories, and "the truth about stories," especially if they could help him connect with a wider audience (King 2003).

In *Cities of Tomorrow,* Peter Hall considers alternative visions, and visionaries, of the good city, which, for our purposes, can be interpreted as the good city-region or regional city, an entity that intrinsically embraces both urban and rural (a testimony and testament to Adams, among others): "Much if not most of what has happened – for good or for ill – [since 1945] can be traced back to the ideas of a few visionaries who lived and wrote long ago, often almost ignored and largely rejected by their contemporaries. They have had their posthumous vindication in the world of practical affairs; even, some might say, their revenge on it" (Hall 1996, 2).

Although Hall does not include Thomas Adams in his "pantheon of the planning movement," as the commentaries in this book attest, his inclusion would have been a no brainer, especially in the Canadian context. And Hall's (1996, 3) observations can also be applied to Adams' influence and effect: "Most of them were visionaries, but for many of them their visions long lay fallow, because the time was not ripe ... When at last the visions were discovered and resuscitated, their implementation came often in very different places, in very different circumstances, and often through very different mechanisms, from those their inventors had originally envisaged. Transplanted as they were in time and space and socio-political environments, it is small wonder that the results were often bizarre, sometimes catastrophic." Is this a valid epitaph for Thomas Adams? He was visionary, but was he a visionary? His vision seems to have been eminently practical and, as a consequence, in no way utopian, bizarre, or catastrophic. He respected and revered much of the status quo and could not be regarded as radical. He worked within the system, trying to change – rather than transform – it.

The more sophisticated and technologically advanced slashing and burning that is now being experienced on an unprecedented global scale suggests that we need more postmodern versions of Thomas Adams to institutionalize a type of planning to span the scales – from the local to the global. Would he be up to the task? Or would he be forced to the conclusion that planning, as he saw and envisaged it, would continue to languish until it entered the culture, so to speak, until societies had literally and figuratively become acculturated to planning? Could it be that planning's time has yet to come? If so, Adams' vision is the road we should travel, to better position ourselves to transport planning to higher and wider levels of public consciousness.

NOTE

1 The reference to colouring is spurred, in part, by my interest in applying an emerging
   perspective, termed spiral dynamics, to better locate the context for Adams' thinking in
   contrast to more modern contexts. Spiral dynamics is an application of the developmental
   psychology of Clare Graves, popularized by Don Beck and Chris Cowan. See http://www.
   spiraldynamics.org/Graves/colors.htm. The application of the theory uses various colours
   as shorthand for major stages in cultural evolution. Using this perspective, I hypothesize
   that Adams responded to red (characterized by slashing and burning) by proposing more
   blue (order and stability, represented by Adams' advocacy of planning legislation and
   institutions) en route to pioneering orange (harnessing planning in an entrepreneurial
   manner to the ideals of industrialists operating on ever-larger scales – a feature of the
   later Adams, especially in his work in the New York region). Today's planning challenge is
   to integrate all these earlier influences with a strong green influence (best manifested in
   the environmental movement), while pushing up and out to what is sometimes referred
   to as a second tier of more integral thinking and acting, coloured yellow and turquoise.
   For more on the integral perspective, see http://www.integralinstitute.org. This is probably
   the postmodern planning frontier for today's successors to Thomas Adams.

REFERENCES

Canadian Institute of Planners. 2010. "Planning Is ..." http://www.cip-icu.ca/.
Eckstein, Barbara, and James A. Throgmorton, eds. 2003. *Story and Sustainability: Planning,
   Practice and Possibility for American Cities.* Cambridge, MA: MIT Press.
Hall, Peter. 1996. *Cities of Tomorrow: An Intellectual History of Urban Planning and Design
   in the Twentieth Century.* Malden, MA: Blackwell Publishers.
Hodge, Gerald, and Ira Robinson. 2001. *Planning Canadian Regions.* Vancouver: UBC Press.
Jacobs, Jane. 1993 [1961]. *The Death and Life of Great American Cities.* New York: Vintage
   Books.
King, Thomas. 2003. *The Truth about Stories: A Native Narrative.* Toronto: CBC/Anansi.
Sandercock, Leonie. 2003. *Cosmopolis II: Mongrel Cities of the Twenty-First Century.* London:
   Continuum.

CHAPTER V

Rural Problems that Arise in Connection with Land Development

Land speculation in rural areas | Absentee ownership | The spirit of gambling | Speculation in western lands | Speculation worst in fertile areas | Why farmers have been indifferent | Speculation in other countries | Building subdivision problems of rural areas | New settlers and speculation | Does speculation pay? | Taxation and assessment | Taxation of agricultural land in urban areas | Increment value tax of Great Britain | Proposals for common ownership of land | Other systems of taxing land values | Some conclusions regarding land taxation | Defects of rural sanitation | Keeping young people on the farm | Sanitary problems in fishing and mining villages | Mining villages in Great Britain | Water supplies and sewerage in small towns | Economic loss from sickness | By-law administration | Lack of co-operation between municipal authorities | Fire prevention in rural areas | Forest fires | Fire safeguards and regulations | Development schemes and fire prevention | Problem of high cost of living | Unemployment and land development

LAND SPECULATION IN RURAL AREAS

I N a new country a certain amount of speculation is inevitable, and is not an unmixed evil. It draws out and stimulates energy and enterprise that might otherwise lie dormant; it accompanies a spirit of optimism that is needed to blaze trails into new regions and overcome the obstacles that confront pioneers. Canada has been largely developed by speculators of the right type. Men have left the comforts of refined homes in older civilizations and have gone into the prairie and the bush to endure hardship in the hope of earning big rewards in return for their sacrifices. They have gone forth to conquer nature and have expected the homage and the dues which are usually rendered to the conqueror. But, when the pioneer stage is over and the building up of the social life of a new community begins, speculation takes on new and injurious forms. Socially created values are inflated and exploited and monopolies in natural resources are established. It is in this latter form that speculation in Canada in recent years has produced deplorable moral and financial results, in rural as well as in urban areas.

Farmers, whose land is contiguous to urban areas, have occasionally enjoyed large profits from inflated speculative values, but, probably in more cases, they have suffered serious injuries from the effects of speculation. In any event it is not open to question that the speculation in suburban lots has been an unmixed evil to agriculture in the neighborhood of towns. The planning of the suburban areas of cities and towns, and proper regulation of building development under statutory development schemes, could have prevented this evil. But there has also been excessive speculation in farm lands, as such, and this has been the chief factor in causing absentee ownership and other evils which are threatening to undermine the prosperity of great parts of the agricultural territory of the Dominion. The great achievements of the Federal and Provincial Governments in building up the population of the country during the past twelve years have in large part been rendered nugatory by the speculation which has followed the settlement and arrested the development of the land.

ABSENTEE OWNERSHIP

The form of the absentee ownership in Canada makes it much more injurious to the country than a similar degree of absentee ownership in old land-owning countries like England. In the latter case the absentee owner has usually a social or family interest in his property; if he has the means to maintain it in good condition he does so, and, as he depends to a large extend for a livelihood on the income he derives from it, he makes sure that a deputy is left in charge to maintain good relations with the tenants and keep the farm premises and improvements in repair. In any circumstances there is always the tenant to cultivate the land and to keep on producing from it. In Canada there are few cases in which family traditions form a link between the owner and the land, and the absence of any general system of tenancy often means that when the land is owned by an absentee it is not cultivated at all. The idle lands held by speculators greatly increase the inconvenience and the lack of opportunities which are so effective in causing the settler to leave the land. The taxing of wild lands has not, so far, proved sufficient to arrest the evil.

The holding up of large areas of idle lands for speculative purposes also results in inflating the values of improved farms within easy reach of transportation facilities, owing to the idle territory forming a buffer area between the improved land and areas available for new settlement. Because of speculation improved farms in good districts in the United States and

Canada are often too dear to enable purchasers to make an adequate profit after allowing reasonable interest on the capital cost.

When the price of land is high the mortgage and interest charges have also to be high. Farmers should co-operate, not only to secure improved credit facilities from their governments, but to eliminate speculative values of farm lands which prevent adequate security being given to private investors. When excessive prices are paid for land it means that there is so much capital withdrawn from productive use. One of the greatest causes of farming being unprofitable is that the average farmer has not sufficient working capital; and when he has to borrow money he has to pay too high a rate of interest. Private ownership of land requires to be buttressed with cheap capital to enable improvements to be carried out for the purpose of making economic use of the land; but cheap capital can only be attracted on a sound basis of land valuation.

The Spirit of Gambling

There are forms of speculation which are not directly connected with farming itself, but which pursue the farmer and take his hard-earned savings to bolster up some crazy financial enterprise. Monseigneur Choquette, in a paper read at the seventh annual meeting of the Commission of Conservation, strongly condemned the allurements which were permitted to follow the farmer into the most distant parts of the rural districts, and which resulted in the farmers bartering their farms "for a scrap of paper which guaranteed them the ownership neither of an inch of land nor an ounce of silver." That is an aspect of the problem of speculation which is rather outside the scope of this report, but it shows the wide ramification of the spirit of gambling which is doing so much injury to agriculture and from which the farmer wants to be saved by legislation.

Speculation in Western Lands

In an address delivered in Winnipeg on December 18, 1916, Sir James Aikins, Lieutenant-Governor of Manitoba, stated that out of about 100,000,000 acres of arable land, granted to homesteaders, railway corporations, the Hudson's Bay Company, and other private interests, only one-third was being used for productive purposes. The following part of the address is quoted* as an excellent presentation of facts relating to this problem and their bearing on speculation:

---

* *The Credit Men's Journal,* February, 1917.

"Let me give you a few figures:

"As at Sept. 30, 1916. Total area granted in homesteads is 51,012,550 acres. Military homesteads, pre-emptions and purchased homesteads increased this to 62,775,510. The following statement shows estimate of areas under crop in the three Prairie Provinces in 1916, according to the *Census and Statistics Monthly*, of the Department of Trade and Commerce:

July, 1916:	Acres
Wheat	10,493,200
Oats	6,283,000
Barley	936,000
Other grains	487,290
Total acreage	18,199,490

"In proper farming a portion of the cultivated land should be rested; allow then one-third more for fallow, making a total of 24,265,000. Add one-third more of last mentioned acreage for pasturage making a total of 32,354,000 acres.*

"Can you estimate the loss to the Prairie Provinces by reason of the non-use of over 30,000,000 acres of the very best land specifically granted to persons for residence and cultivation? That is not all of this mistaken policy, for the Crown has alienated other lands:

	Acres
Railways, Hudson's Bay Company, school lands sales	36,647,996
Sales, special and halfbreed grants	7,129,066
Mining lands sold	101,701
Mounted Police, etc.	33,078
	43,911,841
Less H.B. Co. mining land	6,881,601
	37,030,240

"Total, without Hudson's Bay Company mining lands, 99,805,750 acres. Of this arable land in the three provinces granted in freehold, only about 32,354,000 acres are used for farming – less than one-third of the granted land.

"Manitoba and all its citizens should recognize the fact that the useful occupation of the land is the chief of all its economic questions.

---

* See also figure 2.

"The same damage results from speculators securing possession of our other natural resources – for example, our water-powers, coal fields, minerals, fishing rights, and the like. Surely these natural resources were intended for the benefit of the people of Manitoba, and not for people residing elsewhere or for speculators. If single individuals have not the capital to develop them under government control, the government, representing the people, has the capital and will have the support of the people in owning and using for our advantage. I am not urging that the western provinces give up their Dominion subsidies granted in lieu of natural resources, but may not the government acquire those found useful, on a basis similar to that on which private enterprise does or speculators do, and so keep and administer them for the people. The people on our farms need cheap coal, cheap power for farm purposes and cheap fish. These would contribute not only to comfort but profit on the farm."

In commenting on the above statement the *Toronto Mail and Empire* advocates the increase of the idle land tax in the western provinces, and concludes as follows:

"The old idea held in the west about growing rich by selling lands is gone. Capital that merely comes to keep lands out of production is a loss, not a gain, for production only is what counts now. Courage and fidelity to the larger good of the country as a whole are needed to deal with the larger land questions."

Speculation Worst in Fertile Areas

Most frequently it is the good land lying closest to the railways that is held by speculators, causing the land users to pay excessive prices or to go on the poorer land in more remote districts, and producing the kind of evils that did so much injury to Ireland before the Lands Purchase Acts came into operation. The kind of speculation in farm land which has been so injurious in the western provinces has blighted all the most fertile areas in Canada. Wherever land has proved to be most productive and has been best adapted for putting man's energy and enterprise to the best use, there the paralyzing fever of speculation has left its deepest marks. The rich fruit-bearing lands of Ontario, British Columbia and Nova Scotia*

---

* "We cannot live on land speculation. The profits from this are vanishing and visionary. We must get down to actual realities and utilize our wealth for right purposes. Of all our natural resources, land is the most prolific, and yet the least looked after. Our land problem is at the present time the poorest organized of all our problems." — *Report of the Secretary of Industries and Immigration, Nova Scotia, 1915.*

have suffered, as well as the wheat belt of the west. Sale prices have been magnified far above real values and large profits have been made at the expense of the agricultural industry. A large share of these profits has been put into the pockets of men who have left the country or have gone into the towns, and those who have suffered most are the producers who have remained on the land. These are left to pay interest on an excessive capitalization and taxes on an excessive assessment.

No country can prosper which permits high land values to be created by speculative means. When the value of land is increased as a result of expenditure of capital on improvements, that increase is a form of wealth, but when it is increased by "boosting" and speculation it is a tax upon industry. The real value given to land by improvements, *e.g.,* by the making of roads, may be much greater than the cost of the improvements – yet the land-owner who makes the improvements is entitled to the full increase thus given to the value of the land, and not merely to the return of his money. He is not only entitled to it, but, if and when he sells the land at the full value and leaves the district, he does not take away more than he has produced. Up to that point individual enterprise and speculation produce wealth. When beyond that point land is increased in price by gambling the increase is fictitious and represents a tax on industry – whether it be agriculture or manufacture.

WHY FARMERS HAVE BEEN INDIFFERENT

The fact that most farmers own the land has made it difficult for them to see the folly of speculation. Indeed, as speculation causes the value of land to rise, it seems, on the surface, to help the farmer by giving a higher selling value to his property. Then there are many cases where considerable gains have been made by farmers as a result of land speculation. These are known and widely advertised. What is not so well known and is scarcely ever advertised is the irreparable injury suffered by the industry of agriculture as a whole. Whether farmers be owners or tenants they have to debit their holding with the cost of the capital invested in it. If a farmer is owner of his farm he has to pay interest on the mortgage, or he has to credit his own capital with interest in lieu of the rent paid by a tenant. In an economic sense there is "rent" even if the owner and the user of the land be the same person. *High land values mean increased "rent" to the farmer or user, whether he be owner or tenant.*

Speculative land values also impair the security of land for investment, and, by raising the assessment, increase the burden of taxation. These and other evils are now beginning to be recognized by farmers, as is shown by the policies being advocated by their organizations in regard to taxation and control of land and other natural resources.

SPECULATION IN OTHER COUNTRIES

In other new countries land speculation is producing similar results to those in Canada. There are the same complaints in Australia and the United States regarding idle lands near railways, the absence of close settlement, and absentee ownership. The president of the Land Surveyors' Association of Australia, in a public memorial, says that there are many large areas of good country privately held and adjacent to existing railway lines which could be acquired by the State, and which are eminently suited for close settlement. He condemns the policy which has brought about the holding of these large areas of land which are not used to the best advantage, and which has resulted in isolated patches of cultivation with huge intervening areas of untilled land.

It is well known that speculation in farm land and the holding of large areas of idle lands by private corporations is causing serious evils in the United States. The value of farms in the United States in 1910 was put at $32.40 per acre, as compared with $15.75 per acre in 1900.* Mr. Ethelbert Stewart, Chief Statistician of the Bureau of Labor Statistics, Department of Labor, in giving evidence before a Committee on Labour in June, 1916, said:

> In my own state, for instance, they are charging $12 and $14 an acre rental. Land that was bought of the government by the present owners for $1.25 per acre now rents for $10 per acre. The land which sold there a few years ago – it seems a few years to me; it was 35 years ago – land which sold there for $50 an acre is now being held at $240 an acre, and with all the work I could put on that land at $50, I could not raise the mortgage. You cannot expect men to go back to the land under the present conditions, and you cannot expect them to stay there with the present conditions existing."

The growth of absentee ownership which accompanies speculation is shown by the increase of tenancies. According to the census figures, there were 37 tenant-operated farms in each 100 farms in the United States in 1910 as compared with 28 in 1890.

---

* *Monthly Crop Report,* United States Dept. of Agriculture, April 15, 1916.

The kind of tenancy created under the United States system appears to be socially and economically unsound. The United States Commissioner on Industrial Relations reported in 1915:

"Badly housed, ill-nourished, uneducated and hopeless, these tenants continue year after year to eke out a bare living, moving frequently from one farm to another in the hope that something will turn up."

Here we have the curious anomaly of increasing poverty among farmers side by side with increasing values of farms. There is much to be said in favour of tenancy when the tenant holds under a system of leasehold directly from the Crown, but tenancy under a speculative and absentee landlord system is indefensible.

In the suburbs of cities in the United States most unhealthy conditions are resulting from the system of speculation in suburban subdivisions and the absence of proper control over development.

Mr. Nelson P. Lewis, Chief Engineer of the Board of Estimate and Apportionment of New York City, writes of the unsightly approaches to American cities in his book on "The Planning of the Modern City." He says:

"Cheap and hideous groups of houses are much in evidence in their suburbs. This is in marked contrast with the manner in which towns in Continental Europe move solidly outward into the surrounding country, one block at a time The building stops abruptly and beyond the last developed block is the open country, so that the cities appear more compact."

Mr. Lewis might have added that the open lands immediately adjacent to the developed blocks are, as a rule in Europe, intensively cultivated – in contrast to the idle vacant lots in American suburbs.

The methods by which public lands have been disposed of in the United States have been largely responsible for injurious speculation. Referring to the disposition of the public lands in the United States, Mr. Albert B. Hart writes:*

"The land-grabber is, in most cases, simply taking advantage of the chances which a defective system has cast in the way of shrewd and forehanded or unscrupulous men. The difficulty is certainly not in

---

* *Quarterly Journal of Economics,* Vol. 1, pp. 169-251.

PLATE XI   BAD SUBURBAN CONDITIONS

Unhealthy conditions in a rural district outside Ottawa where there are hundreds of acres
of fertile land lying idle because of injurious speculation. Much of the land is adaptable, with drainage,
for intensive culture, but quite unsuitable for dwellings.

PLATE XI   GOOD SUBURBAN CONDITIONS

A more satisfactory form of development is seen in this illustration showing compact groups of buildings
and intensively cultivated land immediately outside Woodstock, N.B.
Photo by courtesy of Immigration Branch, Dept. of Interior

the Land Office, which, in the midst of perplexing complications, has striven hard to protect our lands. The fault lies at the door of the Congress of the United States, which has the power, but not the will, to correct notorious defects in our system. Still further back, the fault is with the free citizens of the republic, who have been too busy to insist that there should be a comprehensive land policy, providing for the equitable disposition of all classes of the public lands."

The land policy of Canada has largely followed the "defective system" of the United States, with the same injurious results.

The mistaken policy of granting large areas of the public domain in the United States to railway companies is causing consideration to be given to the question of how parts of these areas can be restored for public use. The Secretary of Labour, in his annual report, says:

"By a recent decision of the Supreme Court, Congress is soon to have power, and to be under an obligation, to treat with land-grant railroads regarding the terms on which large areas of that domain heretofore granted away may be restored."

Building Subdivision Problems in Rural Areas

The bad sanitary conditions in the suburbs of towns, and in rural territory adjoining them, which are typical of American and Canadian cities, are largely the result of speculation in suburban subdivisions.

The subdivision of land for building purposes during periods of boom extends into rural areas round cities up to a radius of from three to ten miles or more outside the city boundaries. A diagram of Ottawa and Hull shown on Map I* illustrates the extent of such subdivision round two cities having 123,000 inhabitants. It shows that the present cities would occupy five square miles if the density were forty people to the acre. On a liberal estimate the population of these cities will increase to 350,000 in 50 or more years, and a total area of fifteen square miles will provide for this ultimate population, with a density of 40 people to the acre. But the subdivided area indicated on the diagram consists of 65 square miles of territory, only a small part of which is likely to be required for building in a gradual way after 50 years. A great part of the area of 65 square miles (41,600 acres) is lying idle and uncultivated, because it is subdivided into small lots and held by absentee owners, whose sole interest is in securing

---

* See also drawing No. 20 in the Report of the Ottawa Federal Plan Commission, 1915.

the profits of speculation, which, in the circumstances, are not likely to be realized. Even that part of the subdivided area which is still held by farmers is not being properly cultivated owing to the erroneous expectation that it will be used for building in the near future, notwithstanding that there are 50 out of 65 square miles that are not likely to be wanted for that purpose. This land lies near to the market and a large portion of it is excellent farm land. Meanwhile city fertilizers are going to waste, prices of food have greatly increased and ordinary farm produce is almost beyond the means of the poor. The case of Ottawa is typical of every large city in Canada. For this condition a solution is sought by trying to artificially control distribution and cultivate a few acres of vacant lots.

Plate XI shows illustrations of two portions of land around Ottawa and Woodstock, one showing idle land with scattered buildings and the other showing land put to use as a market garden. The latter condition is the exception, whereas it ought to be the rule. Plate XII shows land which is subdivided ten miles from Toronto, in the midst of open country.* Whole farms in this neighborhood have been destroyed and the owners of the scattered shack dwellings are struggling to pay off the installments due on their holdings.

In consequence of such conditions as these great areas of land nearest to our large cities are withheld from production, farms are made useless by being broken up into small lots, either occupied by occasional small shacks or held by unknown owners; sanitary arrangements cannot be provided because the buildings are too widely scattered, the township authorities lose rather than gain in revenue, the workingmen who build have to travel long distances to their work, children are too far from school, thousands of vacant lots nearer to the city are unoccupied, and in some cases there is general paralysis of the whole neighbourhood.

In three cities in western Canada there is an average of less than three people to each acre within the city boundaries. A healthy and economical density of population would be ten or even fifteen times that number, but even with the three to the acre there is overcrowding in spots. In the same cities the number of vacant lots is estimated at an average of 84 per cent of those subdivided. At the rate of 40 persons to the acre these cities would occupy a combined area of 4,500 acres for their aggregate population. This being one-sixth of the total area subdivided, and partially improved, we have 21,500 acres in these three cities alone, largely withdrawn from agriculture, in immediate proximity to the market, paying taxes on a building value they do not possess, and creating a burden on all the

---

* See Map II (pp. 178-79).

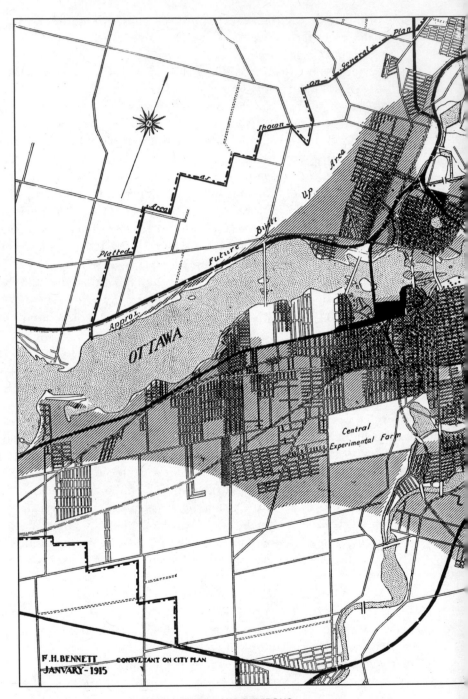

MAP I   OTTAWA AND ENVIRONS

Map of Ottawa Showing present built-up area, and probably extension of built-up area;
also parts of platted area comprising 65 square miles. The general plan referred to in the
legend is Drawing No. 21 in the Report of the Federal Plan Commission.

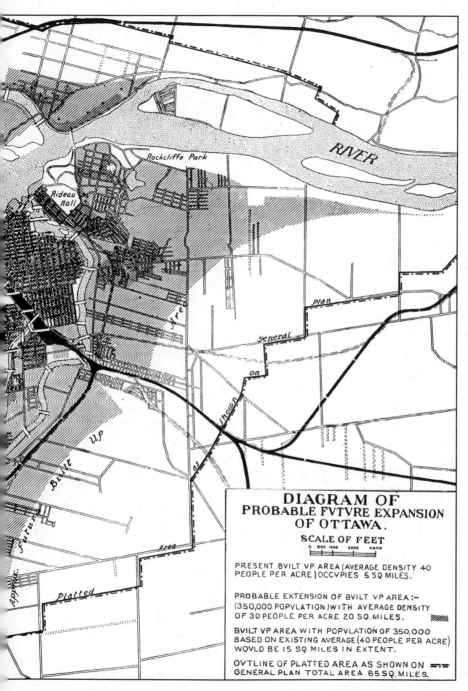

RIVER

Rockcliffe Park

Rideau Hall

fire

General

plan

on

nwon

of

Up

Built

Suburbs

Aylmer

Area

Platted

DIAGRAM OF
PROBABLE FVTVRE EXPANSION
OF OTTAWA.

SCALE OF FEET
0   800 1600   3200   4800

PRESENT BVILT VP AREA (AVERAGE DENSITY 40
PEOPLE PER ACRE) OCCVPIES 5 SQ. MILES.

PROBABLE EXTENSION OF BVILT VP AREA :-
(350,000 POPVLATION) WITH AVERAGE DENSITY
OF 30 PEOPLE PER ACRE 20 SQ. MILES.

BVILT VP AREA WITH POPVLATION OF 350,000
BASED ON EXISTING AVERAGE (40 PEOPLE PER ACRE)
WOVLD BE 15 SQ. MILES IN EXTENT.

OVTLINE OF PLATTED AREA AS SHOWN ON
GENERAL PLAN TOTAL AREA 65 SQ. MILES.

Adapted from drawing No. 20 – Report of Federal Plan Commission surrounding resident population. In addition to the 21,500 acres, there is from twice to three times* as great an area of farm land within and immediately adjacent to the city boundaries, which is not being properly farmed because of the expectations of the farmers that they will be able to dispose of their lands for building subdivisions. There are serious effects arising from this condition of affairs on the cities themselves which will be dealt with in the urban report, but there are also the deplorable effects in reducing production in respect of the areas which could be put to economic use as agricultural land.

NEW SETTLERS AND SPECULATION

Land speculation stimulates the kind of tendencies which we want most to suppress in a new population. The average immigrant needs to be helped to become a permanent citizen – to be made to look upon Canada as his adopted country and not as a place of temporary residence. He may come with the idea of making money and then returning to his native land, or he may come with the intention to remain; but, in either case, the influence of his environment and not his original ideas or intentions, will most likely determine his future action. In recent years the fever of land speculation has been the first influence to grip him in his social life; his natural inclination to be migratory and unsettled in disposition is encouraged. He finds land speculators apparently making money without effort and farmers struggling to make ends meet, notwithstanding the natural advantages of the soil and climate. If he takes a farm near a town he finds himself severed from the market by large areas of land which has produced profit to the speculator without effort and is lying idle and unused. He is cut off from social intercourse, and facilities for co-operation and education, largely because of speculation. In that kind of environment can we expect a man to settle down and become an industrious producer and a contented citizen?

DOES SPECULATION PAY?

But it is a mistake to assume that the average speculator really makes money. What he makes in times of boom he usually loses in times of depression – unless in the few exceptionally lucky cases. The loss in real estate operations, due to the expensive methods necessarily employed to *force* more land on the market than is required, to accumulation of

---

* The actual areas of the cities referred to is over 74,000 acres.

compound interest charges on the capital invested, to loss of deposits and waste in local improvements, to payment on borrowed money, etc., must, in many cases, absorb all the profits realized – although these may appear substantial when one side of the balance sheet only is considered. Thus we have the great monetary losses of those of the general public who have bought lots, the loss in production due to idle land, and, as a rule, no benefit to the speculator. Happily this fact is being realized by large corporations like the railway companies in Canada, and by leading men in the real estate exchanges of America, and there is a growing tendency to promote planning and development schemes so as to stop injurious forms of speculation. *In Canada, more than in the United States, we are in need of outside capital, and, if we are to obtain it, we must re-establish confidence in real estate investment, and in the economic soundness of our methods.*

Taxation and Assessment

The questions of land taxation and land assessment in Canada would require a special report to deal with them, and only brief reference can be made to them here.

Important problems of taxation arise in connection with the subdivision of rural lands to accommodate, what is to a large extent, a forced overflow of urban population into rural territory to suit speculative schemes. In Britain, land is taxed at 50 per cent of its net annual value for agricultural purposes as against a tax on 100 per cent of its net annual value if used for private residences. It is held that the land used by the farmer is just as much a part of his stock-in-trade as his cattle and implements and that he should not be required to pay as heavy a tax on a farm worth say $500 per annum – when his income is probably no more than $500 – as the man who occupies a house worth $500 per annum and whose income may therefore be reckoned at ten times as much. One may reasonably ask why the farmer, earning perhaps $500 per annum net income should pay as much in property taxes as the suburban resident earning $5,000 a year – even though their properties are of the same value? Whatever the merits or demerits of the British system, under a system of tenancy, it shows an attempt to adjust taxation so as to help the producer.

In valuing land in Canada more regard should be paid to the revenue producing capacity of the land and less to its so called "prospective" value, which, in the majority of cases, never materializes. When money is worth six per cent, the average farm is only worth 16½ years' purchase of the annual rental value, *e.g.*, if a farm is worth $10 per acre per annum and if the current rate of interest for an investment with good security is six per cent, it would be safe to pay 16½ years' purchase of the rental of $10,

PLATE XII   RESULTS OF INJURIOUS SPECULATION

Scattered shacks on a subdivided farm ten miles outside Toronto; most of the surrounding land
is lying idle. Between this farm and the city the greater portion of the land served by roads has suffered
from injurious building speculation. (See also Map II, pp 178-79).

PLATE XII

Carpenter's "home" on the same farm. Unhealthy isolation is not confined to poor farming districts,
and is here the direct product of injurious land speculation.

namely $165 per acre, for the farm; just as when a farm is bought for, say, $165 an acre it should be worth a net rental of about $10 per acre to a tenant.

In the same way, when a house and lot is purchased, the price paid should be based on the revenue-producing character of the investment, and, in an average case, when the land is put to full use, should not exceed twenty years' purchase of the net rental of about $10 per acre to a tenant.

In the same way, when a house and lot is purchased, the price paid should be based on the revenue-producing character of the investment, and, in an average case, when the land is put to full use, should not exceed twenty years' purchase of the net rental; this rental being arrived at after deducting the whole of the outgoings (taxes, etc.), together with a sum for repairs equal to from ten to fifteen per cent from the gross rental.

Difficult as it may appear to be to reduce values in Canada to a revenue-producing basis it is only wild speculation and wrong theories of assessing land values that have caused it to become difficult. When assessments are made by competent valuers on a scientific basis both vendors and purchasers of real estate will obtain much needed guidance in their transactions. In places where land is assessed with some definite relation to its revenue-producing value, having regard to the purpose for which it is best adapted, arrears of taxes are practically unknown, investments in real estate become as secure as investments in city bonds, the chief sources of cheap capital are no longer cut off from owners of land, vacant suburban lands are cultivated and taxes are paid on the basis of ability to pay. In normal times a purchaser of an improved lot in England can borrow two-thirds, and in some cases a greater proportion, of the actual price he pays for the land and improvements at from 4 to 4½ per cent. Such land can usually be purchased at a figure approximating to its real value as a revenue-producing investment, and the local assessment is based on the annual rental value.

Where speculation occurs it should be the subject of a high increment tax at the time when any land is transferred; a tax which would act both as a deterrent against speculation and as a means of obtaining for the community as much as possible of the value which is socially created. Ordinary revenue should be obtained from taxes levied on the actual value of the land as a revenue-producing investment, and an assessment roll prepared on this basis would be a guide to purchasers and mortgagees.

Under present conditions the revenue obtained from local taxation is probably no greater than would be obtained on the above basis, since a large proportion of real estate value is now escaping taxation. A tax based on inflated values helps to sustain these values, is costly to collect and is uncertain.

The inequalities which result from the present system are illustrated by the following table giving assessed and actual values in certain county areas in Ontario, the assessed values being taken from the assessment roll, and the market values being less than the price at which the land has been purchased or is available for purchase:

	Total assessed value of Land	Assessed value per acre	Approximate market value per acre	Approximate percentage of market value assessed
(1) 212 acres, farm land	$8,810	$41.50	$1,000	4.1%
(2) 15 acres, building land	16,500	1,100.00	1,100	100%
(3) 10 acres	2,000	200.00	2,000	10%
(4) 3,300 square feet	450	5,940.00	5,940	100%
(5) 5,000 square feet	500	4,356.00	4,356	100%
(6) 19 acres	5,500	289.40	5,000	5.7%

In one of the above cases a property is valued at $5,000 for one purpose and $78,000 for another purpose. If, on the basis of the lower valuation, taxes were placed entirely on land values it would make no difference to the tax, since the market value of the land alone is much greater than the present assessed value of the whole property. The farmers of the counties in which the above properties are situated are not only getting no relief in taxation, in comparison with the owner of residential property, but they are probably paying taxes on 100 per cent of the value of their farms, while some residential owners and real estate operators in the districts are paying on less than five per cent of their real values.

A change in the system of assessment is needed, including standardization, in each province. The appointment of competent and trained valuers, who understand the principles of land valuation, with tribunals of experts to determine appeals, is required to precede any reform in taxation and are necessary as a means to assist agriculture and arrest injurious speculation. Real estate operators are not good valuers, and their experience is hurtful rather than helpful to sound judgment, while legal tribunals are incompetent to decide appeals on purely economic questions requiring scientific training in the principles of valuation. It takes about ten years of special training in the principles and practice of land valuation to make a land valuer in Britain, although the system of taxation in that country has not hitherto been based on the capital values of land to any great extent. The land valuer in Canada should be trained and protected in the same way as the land surveyor; indeed, the proper method would be for the surveyor to be the valuer, after receiving special training in valuation.

People who buy land for use should be safeguarded against their own natural ignorance of a matter requiring great skill and much experience to determine, and also against misrepresentation. This safeguard should be in the form of an assessment roll prepared by qualified persons.

The whole system of taxation for local purposes in Ontario, and generally throughout Canada, is based on the present system of valuation which, as has been shown, is so absurd that land in some districts is valued for assessment for one purpose at from fifteen to twenty times its declared value for another purpose – both values being sworn by the assessors to be the market value of the land.

The system of public valuation encourages land gambling, whereas it should hamper it by providing a basis on which to arrive at real values. In so far as land values are high from the following causes they are injurious to the community:

(1) Speculation and improper assessment.
(2) Overcrowding of buildings on lots and high buildings.
(3) Owners not being compelled to finance their own improvements and provide proper sanitary arrangements in advance of building.
(4) Too costly system of developing land, due to want of planning and excessive widths and lengths of road.

If, under proper development schemes, these matters were regulated in the interests of the community, it would go far toward solving the problem of taxation of land.

Taxation of Agricultural Land in Urban Areas

At present, the farmer who owns land within the boundaries of a city, has to pay taxes on its building value, which makes it impossible for him to farm at a profit. This land, when of good quality, is best suited for intensive culture. Much good land near to the markets is sold for building lots many years before it is wanted, because it does not pay to farm it. Any change in the incidence of taxation should be designed to relieve the *bona fide* user of the land of that burden and not to increase it, unless the object is to stultify agriculture in the districts where it can be made most successful.

Ample safeguards against the user making excessive profits out of converting his farm or garden land into building subdivisions can be provided by an increment tax, to be collected when the conversion is made.

There are large areas of highly cultivated farm and garden lands within the boundaries of the British cities, where the system of taxation is designed to encourage the best and most appropriate agricultural use of the land as well as to secure a fair proportion of the "unearned increment" when such land is utilized for building purposes. The rents paid for such farms are much higher than those in the districts more remote from the market. There are comparatively few cases in which farms are subdivided before the land is actually required for building, and, even then, only small parts of the farms are appropriated for building purposes, as and when they become quite ripe for development.

As already stated, there are large areas of agricultural land within the boundaries of western cities. When these areas are subdivided they become liable to be taxed on their presumed value for building purposes; but a great many of them never had, and do not now have, any real building value. At the close of periods of excessive speculation, in such cases, taxes become an unreasonable burden to the owners. As showing the need for tax classification, according to use, some cities have obtained power to grant temporary relief of taxation in respect of some parts of their areas where, *in the judgment of the city assessor,* they are suitable only for agricultural purposes. Such relief, amounting to 25 per cent, was given in Calgary during the years 1915 and 1916. An effort has been made to permit this relief to be given permanently. The assessor is to be judge as to whether the lands are used for agricultural purposes, and, if so used, he may, at his discretion, assess them at agricultural value. That an expedient such as this is resorted to shows the extremities to which the present system of taxation may lead. To give an assessor discretion of the above kind is to open the door for the worst sort of abuses. Moreover, as soon as the present period of depression is over many areas which have enjoyed relief will be placed on the market for building purposes in competition with areas which have had no relief. The whole system of assessment needs revision, and any attempts to bolster up the present system by methods such as those referred to, will make the remedy worse than the disease, and cause serious injustice. The city assessor of Calgary is reported to have stated that claims would be made to bring no less than 20,000 acres of land under the heading of "lands used for agricultural purposes" in 1917.

The time has come, not only for municipalities in Canada to cease to be bankers for real estate operators, but for the municipalities to make it obligatory that the local improvements necessary to provide certain minimum standards of sanitation and convenience of access should be provided before lots are put on the market for building purposes. In Cincinnati and a few other American cities, where most local improvements are made by the real estate men before building takes place, development is stimulated rather than hampered by the practice.

If the temporary speculating owners of real estate were compelled to provide their own local improvements in advance of development, they would contribute, in doing so, more to the public revenue than they would be likely to contribute by a tax on the land, and would, at the same time, ensure healthy and economic development. The cost of such preliminary improvements might amount to from $1,000 to $2,500 per acre. It would be paid by the developer, and only a portion of it, based on the demand for the land, would be recoverable from the purchaser on whom the subsequent taxes fall. If it had to be paid by the developer he would not, as a rule, put land on the market till it was ripe for building, and the public would thus get rid of one of the chief causes of speculation. It is true that some speculators have lost large sums of money as a result of making expensive improvements out of private capital, in order to force land on the market before its time; but for every speculator who will take this undue risk with his own capital there must be many who will take it with capital provided by a local authority.

The important connection between taxation and land speculation is shown by the large areas of lands that are being sold every year for non-payment of taxes. Railway companies, private corporations and even governments have taken part in the booming and selling of thousands of lots which had no building value at the time they were subdivided; and had no prospect of ever having a building value. Many thousands of families have lost all they invested in these wildcat schemes, while those who engineered them have been permitted to enjoy the profits of transactions which should never have been permitted by law.

In 1916 the county of Simcoe offered 300 lots at its annual tax sale, the large majority of which were lands in the village of Port McNicoll. At the time of the sale it was stated that "Port McNicoll was exploited as the coming inland lake port of Canada, a town that would be unrivalled as a railway shipping centre. Farms were surveyed into lots, streets laid out and cement walks built. The probability is that much of the land will go back into farms."

Port McNicoll is typical of scores of instances that could be quoted – and which, in the aggregate, have resulted in an enormous waste of wealth, of human effort and of natural resources in the Dominion. These material losses are serious enough, but the bad moral effects are still more injurious to the national life.

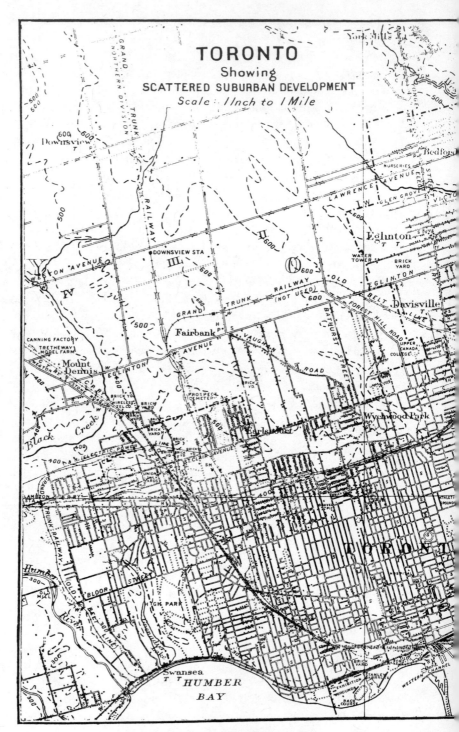

MAP II   TORONTO AND ENVIRONS

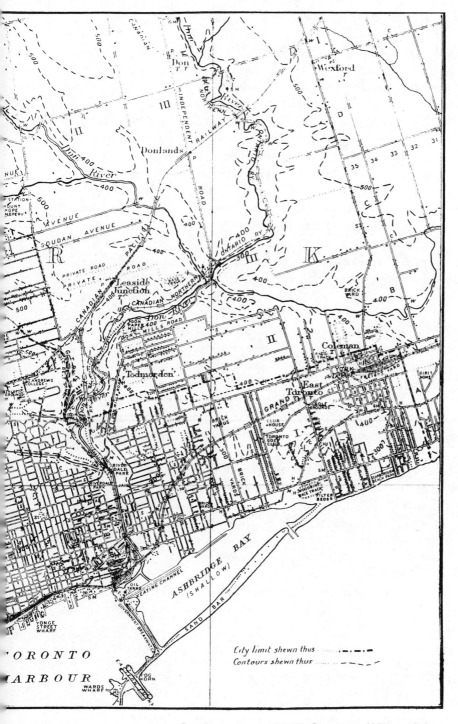

City limit shewn thus .... ---- --- ----
Contours shewn thus .... ---- ----

From Toronto sheet published by Department of Militia and Defence

Increment Value Tax of Great Britain

When Mr. Lloyd George was Chancellor of the Exchequer of Great Britain, in 1909, he was responsible for the passage of the Finance Act of that year. This Act introduced entirely new principles in the system of land taxation in England, and aimed at securing for the community a portion of the increase of future values created by the community. It followed the principle advocated by John Stuart Mill, rather than that of Henry George, in that it was designed to avoid the confiscation of any values created in the past. Under the Act the duties or taxes levied on the capital of freehold land were two in number, one called the increment value duty, and the other, the undeveloped land duty. The increment value duty is charged at the rate of $5.00 for every full $25.00 of the increment value (profit) accrued in respect of any land, *on the occasion of any transfer or sale of the land,* or grant of lease of a certain length or on the occasion of death. The increment value represents the difference between the value of land at the time the valuation is made and the sale value of the same land when it is sold, the former being called the original site value. This site value is determined apart from buildings, good will, matters personal to occupier or owner, occupier's or owner's improvements, etc. From it is also deducted the amount which is due solely to its value for agricultural purposes.

The undeveloped land duty is charged at the rate of one cent for every $5.00 of the original site value of undeveloped land, *i.e.,* one-fifth of one per cent. This tax is only levied on land which is not built upon or is not used, *bona fide,* for any business, trade or industry other than agriculture; and it is not levied in respect of agricultural land where the value does not exceed $250 per acre. The intention and the effect of these duties are to tax profits made in selling land for building purposes. Agricultural land is expressly exempted where it does not possess a building value. The increment tax is only payable on the transfer of land, that is to say, when the profit is realized by the vendor. In this way there is a certainty of the collection of the tax. It may be regarded as a tax on the speculator and not on the user of the land. Some of the proposals for taxing land in Canada are such that the speculator would entirely escape from the tax, and the burden would have to be borne by the person who buys the land to retain and use it.*

---

*   It is just the successful speculator who suffers least of all from any annual tax upon land. The really successful speculator, as evidenced in the remarkable history of land speculation in western Canadian towns and cities during the past few years, holds his land for so short a period and makes such phenomenal gains on his sales, that no annual tax on his land can do more than take the merest fragment of his profits." Dr. Adam Shortt.

Proposals for Common Ownership of Land

It is advocated by a group of reformers that the system of private ownership in land should be changed, by gradual confiscation of the rent under
a system of single tax, to a system of common ownership, as advocated by
Henry George. Even if such a great change is ultimately made, it will still
remain true that the proper planning and development of the land will
always be essential, and that a sound and equitable method of assessing
the value of land and improvements should be employed. The character
of the remedy proposed by Henry George, namely, "to substitute for the
individual ownership of land a common ownership,"* has caused many
who oppose that remedy to ignore or overlook the wisdom and insight
showed by Henry George in his analysis of social problems. He clearly
showed the evils of speculation and high land values and their effects, in
causing good land to remain unused and to produce tramps on virgin
acres and breed paupers on half-tilled soils. He demonstrated that speculation in producing high land values checked production and lessened
the returns due to labour and capital. As a remedy, he said, "We must
make land common property,"† and, as a method, he proposed the appropriation of all rent, by abolishing "all taxation save that upon land
values." While not enquiring into the merit of applying that remedy as a
cure for the social evils produced by the present system of ownership, or
perhaps, to be more correct, we should say produced by the absence of
proper regulation of that system, we may venture to doubt the practicability of applying it in a country where the great majority of the citizens
are private owners. In any case, having regard to that fact, we may anticipate
a long delay before any such radical departure is inaugurated, even with
such modifications as may remove all elements of confiscation from any
process by which the result is to be secured.

So long as we have private ownership, the urgent necessity is to control
it in the public interest – to properly regulate the use of privately owned
lands and to determine their correct value in relation to improvements.
A large portion of the land of Canada is still public domain, and the
process of alienation to private owners continues. This land is granted as
homesteads, on the assumption that it possesses practically no value except
that which may be given to it by the enterprise and energy of the settler.
If, in process of time, the land so alienated should increase in value, owing
to the presence of population in its neighbourhood, it would be possible

---

* *Progress and Poverty*, Book IV, Chapter II – The True Remedy.
† *Progress and Poverty*, Book VI, Chapter II – The True Remedy.

to tax that increased value, and, indeed, to obtain the greater portion of the increment for the benefit of the community. But, so long as the government recognizes private ownership by granting homesteads or selling land, it cannot equitably seize the rental value of land previously alienated as a means of converting such land to common ownership. If common ownership is best, the first step to secure it should be the retention by the government of the land now held by the Crown. But while the government continues its present policy it may be asked whether anything can be gained in advocating the social injustice of confiscation of rent by taxation of land values.

Henry George did not deny that there might be "improvements which, in time, might become indistinguishable from the land itself." Whether admitted or not, such improvements as streets, sewers, sidewalks, etc., do come within this category, as, owing to our complicated system of paying for those improvements, in part by the owner of the land and in part by the inhabitants at large, it would probably be impossible to distinguish between the public and private expenditure in any system of valuing land apart from improvements.

Moreover we have seen that any method of valuation may be subject to abuse, and destroy the object of any system of taxation. To avoid the confusion of distinguishing between public and private expenditure, it is claimed that "the individual right is lost in the common right," thus showing that, in confiscating rent, a certain amount of confiscation of improvements would almost be inevitable.

But whatever practical difficulties there might be in applying the theories of Henry George, they could be overcome by any people willing to allow land to revert to common ownership. That is the simple and straightforward proposal of Henry George, who claimed that "if chattel slavery be unjust, then is private property in land unjust."

OTHER SYSTEMS OF TAXING LAND VALUES

Numerous hybrid systems of taxing land values are advocated which have little in common with the system propounded in *Progress and Poverty*. So far as these systems are designed to secure for the community that which belongs to the community, and for the private owner that which he has created or produced by his labour and enterprise, few people are likely to object to the proposal. But, before that end can be obtained there must be a just and scientific system of valuation on which to base taxation, and there must be recognition of the fact that land has different values for different uses and should be valued with some regard to these uses, no matter where it is situated.

If agricultural land within or near a city is taxed at its value for building land then, as already pointed out, the owner cannot farm it at a profit; and yet it may be in the interest of the whole community that he should farm it. On the other hand, it is not desirable that he should be permitted to hold it up for inflated building values without having to contribute a large portion of the "unearned increment" to the community which, by its presence and expenditure, has created that increment.

If a man has a nursery in the city, which provides a desirable open space and is put to full productive use for horticultural purposes, is it desirable that he should be taxed out of existence as a nurseryman because the land has a potential building value? On the other hand, is he to enjoy a low tax, which he can bear as a nurseryman, when it is known that he has the power to sell his land for building purposes at perhaps twenty times the nursery value? These are the kind of issues which have to be considered in connection with any systems of taxation. As a matter of fact, taxation of land values prevails almost universally in Canada today. Land is taxed, or is intended to be taxed, on its prospective value for building, whatever its revenue-producing value may be, while, as already stated, land in Britain is generally taxed for local purposes, according to the revenue-producing capacity at the time each assessment is made and according to the use to which the land is put at that time.

It has been claimed, and justly so, that the system of taxing site values only, as applied in some western cities, cannot be regarded as a fair test of the single tax proposals of Henry George. The western system was not designed to bring land into common ownership by confiscating rental values, but in practice it went much further than even Henry George ever contemplated, *because it resulted in confiscating more than the rental values in a great many cases.* A great deal of the land is not only taxed on a building value it never can possess, but the tax amounts to more than can be derived from the land in the form of rent for any use to which it can be put. Some single taxers claim that the failure was due to the tax not going far enough. This might be the case in regard to some valuable building lots near to the centres of the city, but, in the case of remote subdivisions, the tax is actually greater than the rental value and the owners have to pay more in taxes for the privilege of holding the land than they are able to earn from it, after making allowance for any prospective increase of value. So long as private ownership in land is permitted by law this is economically un-sound and is a social injustice.

The large amounts of arrears of taxes in western cities have brought home to the taxpayers the fact that a sound system of taxation must have regard to the ability of the taxpayer to pay the tax out of the earning power of his property. In referring to the problem of taxation of site values in the city of Winnipeg the *Manitoba Free Press* says:

> "That problem is involved in the conflict between the principle of taxation of unearned increment of value of land, reduced to an annual basis, and that of ability to pay as gauged by the income or earnings of the individual taxpayer ... Much injustice is done by taxing the landowner upon the basis of year to year growth of value from natural causes, there being no necessary connection between that growth and earning power or ability to meet the rising tax bills; change of ownership, however, implies that ability."

But the injustice goes further than is here indicated because, in the present system of assessing the value of the land, practically little, if any, regard is paid to its earning power, and the discount which is allowed, in fixing the assessment, in respect of the loss of compound interest while the land is being held is, as a rule, totally inadequate. When the basis of assessment of land is the sale price of other land in the same neighbourhood that price should be discounted by the number of years which the land is likely to be held in expectation of being sold – making allowance for the owner being willing to sell. Land which is worth $500 in five years is not likely to be worth more than half that sum today, having regard to the loss of compound interest on the investment and the taxes which will have to be paid.

Commissioner Yorath, of Saskatoon, in a recent report to the city council, quoted in the *Canadian Municipal Journal,* reports unfavourably regarding the system of taxation which has been in operation in western cities. He argues that the basis of taxation should be broadened so that taxes are distributed according to ability to pay, that the land taxes, under present conditions, create a burden which is becoming almost unbearable upon owners of vacant property, and that they do not compel an owner to improve his property.

On the other hand, the system of single tax appears to be successful in its operation in the rural districts of Alberta. The Deputy Minister of Municipal Affairs of Alberta says that limiting taxation to land values has worked out satisfactorily in the rural part of the province and any attempt to change it would be resented.

Other proposals of taxing land are made, such as that advocated by the United Farmers of Ontario, namely, the application of a direct tax on improved land values, including all land resources.

Some Conclusions Regarding Land Taxation

The variety, complexity and number of the proposals for land taxation reform which are discussed from time to time show that the public mind is dissatisfied with existing conditions. An effort has been made to summarize the nature of some of the proposals, without attempting to arrive at any definite conclusions on their merits.

But it is held that:

(1) Until the system of assessment is rectified no system of taxation can be sound or achieve its object;

(2) The operator in real estate, who holds land in temporary occupation for purposes of speculation, rather than the permanent holder or user, needs most to be taxed on excessive profits;

(3) No system should be adopted which will sterilize, or force the subdivision of, agricultural or nursery land within or adjacent to city boundaries;

(4) If real estate operators were to be made to carry out their own local improvements before development, they would be making a larger contribution to the public purse than they would under some systems of taxing land values, and, at the same time, would be hampered in forcing land on the market before it is ripe for development; and

(5) The planning of the land for right use and development should precede any taxation reform, so that the tax would have some relation to the use to which the land was to be put in the same district; whether, for instance, it would be used for building skyscrapers or workmen's dwellings, or for growing fruit or vegetables.

With regard to the last of these matters, it has to be noted that a development scheme could permanently define areas for specific purposes – some for business premises, some for residential purposes and some for market gardening or farming, so as to afford an equitable basis for taxation. In the case of cultivated areas, a practical arrangement can be included in a scheme either to delimit the land for purposes of cultivation, subject to relief of taxation and the saving of expenditure on local improvements; or to give the relief during occupation as a farm or garden, subject to a heavy increment tax on its transfer for building purposes. Much land, even in cities, cannot be drained or served with water under adequate pressure, except at prohibitive cost, and in many cases it would pay the owner of such land to have its use restricted for purposes of cultivation, if he were taxed on the basis of that use and not on an inflated building value which he was never likely to realize.

Finally, in regard to taxation as in regard to restrictions on speculation, the aim should be to secure healthy living conditions for the people, to prevent large profits being reaped without being earned, and to secure the application of capital to forms of real development.

Defects of Rural Sanitation

Land speculation is one of the contributory causes of bad sanitation in rural suburbs of cities, and, both in these suburbs and in rural districts in general, sanitary conditions need great improvement. There are those who are of the opinion that improvement in sanitation will only come through the education of the individual, and, to a large extent, that is true; but sanitary improvement in all countries has required government leadership and initiative. In Canada we possess useful and progressive Boards of Health in the provinces and municipalities which are doing splendid work for the improvement of sanitation, but they are necessarily limited in their opportunities, owing to the facts that they have no control over the method of planning and laying out the land; that they are not competent to exercise that control if they had it; that they are largely absorbed in the task of correcting evils that have been allowed to become established because of the want of that control; and that building and real estate regulations are so defective and lacking in uniformity. Schemes adaptable to different kinds of rural areas should be prepared, and some lead given and standards created which would lay the foundation, at least, for better sanitation.

The death rate in rural districts is not so high as in urban districts, but it is still far higher than it should be. The vital statistics of the provinces that have grown in population as a result of immigration cannot be relied upon as a guide to health conditions for obvious reasons. The whole question of vital and municipal statistics in Canada requires serious consideration, with a view to securing improvement. The statistics of the older provinces are, however, of some value as a guide, and show that Canada is still behind older countries in regard to health conditions. In 1914 the death rate of Quebec was 17.02, the worst in the Dominion. The death rate in the rural districts of Nova Scotia was 13.7 per 1,000, as against 18.4 in the urban communities. The death rate for the whole of England for the same year was 14 per 1,000, and for the rural districts of England was 12.63.* In the Garden City of Letchworth for 1912 the death rate was only 6.1 per 1,000.† Bad sanitary conditions are, of course, only one of the causes which lead to a high death rate, but it may fairly be claimed that it is these conditions which are chiefly responsible for any inferiority of Canadian as compared with English conditions. Great improvement of the sanitary conditions in England began with the administration of the Public Health Acts in 1875, and until we in Canada similarly improve the standards of our sanitation we are not likely to make much progress in lessening the death rate or in securing the amelioration of health conditions in the rural areas. In the last forty years the death rate has fallen about eight per thousand in England and Wales.

The difficulty of obtaining good water supplies in schools and of equipping them with proper sanitary arrangements, adequate surface drainage, dry playgrounds, etc., is largely due to the want of resources caused by the scattered situation of the schools and of the dwellings from which the children come. In too many cases, the farmer has his farm in a situation where he cannot get a good water supply or cannot co-operate with his neighbours in obtaining it from a distance. In numerous cases his well is in porous ground, at a lower level than his barn, his pigsties, and his manure heaps, and his privy is constructed without proper sanitary precautions. Education is necessary to secure much improvement in conditions which must necessarily remain under the direct control of the individual, but education itself would be easier and more likely to lead to results if farms were situated nearer to each other and hygiene was practised in the village communities.

It is stated by federal authorities who have been engaged in the examination of water from farm wells, that about seventy per cent of farm wells are contaminated and the water unfit for use. As against the difficulties of meeting the expense of making proper sanitary arrangements in villages and on farms, there is the advantage of space and the latitude of choice of situation for buildings which does not pertain in urban communities.

KEEPING YOUNG PEOPLE ON THE FARMS

One of the essential factors in encouraging the young people to remain on the farm is the provision of good sanitation in rural homes. A drainage inspector in a Canadian province once visited a certain farmer and found

---

* *77th Annual Report, Registrar General,* "Births, Deaths and Marriages in England and Wales, 1914."
† *Town Planning Review,* Vol. IV., page 247.

him not only in possession of a good house, with modern sanitary equipment, but he and his family were enjoying the occupation of the best rooms in the house. On being asked why he did not live in the kitchen like his neighbours, and why he looked so much after the comforts of his home, he replied that he wanted to keep his boy on the farm, and that he could not expect to do so if he did not provide him with home comforts equal to those enjoyed by people of equal means and rank of life in the city. There is more sound philosophy in the method of that farmer than is found between the covers of many text books on rural depopulation.

The average farmer has learned to appreciate the value of giving his children a good education but, in too many cases, he does not appreciate the fact that this education kindles desires and awakens sensibilities which he may not have experienced. The boy and girl goes to the high school in the city, and visits the homes of scholars whose parents are no better off than their own, but whose home comforts are superior. Can it be wondered at that the children of the farmer are ambitious to enjoy these comforts and do not realize that they are available on the farm? Whereas the tradesman and professional man in the city use their best rooms, have a bath-room and other conveniences, the farmer lives too frequently in the kitchen, and regards a bath-room as a luxury – even when he has had the ambition to build a good house or run a motor car. Motor cars and telephones will help to revolutionize rural conditions for the better, but they will do so more effectively and rapidly if good roads are made, good sanitary conditions are provided in the home, and some facilities for social intercourse and educational development are provided in the country districts. Failing these requisites, the motor car and telephone may only help to make it easier for the young people to drift to the city, and increase their appetite for the comforts of the city home, and for the social and educational facilities they cannot secure within easy access of the farm.

Sanitary Problems in Fishing and Mining Villages

Special sanitary problems arise in connection with fishing villages, where the absence of drainage and the presence of decomposed offal cause most unhealthy conditions. The material which is the chief cause of trouble might be put to economic use and converted into animal food or fertilizer; thus a valuable element in production would be obtained and an evil remedied, with little cost, if not with actual gain, to the community. A fishing community is not usually alive to its opportunities in this respect, partly because it does not contain a sufficient number of residents to appreciate the importance of good sanitation. It is also at a disadvantage for want of ability to promote the union of forces, or co-operation, necessary to create a paying fertilizer plant. In such a case provincial initiative and help would be most valuable.

No more effective educational campaign can be conducted than one which carries with it an object lesson in showing how the material prosperity of a community will be increased by the means which are necessary to improve its health and moral conditions.

Reference has been made in a previous chapter to the importance of co-operation between the mine operators and their employees, in regard to improving the environment in mining districts. One important and specific direction in which this co-operation is most needed is in improving housing and sanitary conditions in mining villages. We are familiar with the records of the deplorable consequences of sanitary neglect in Cobalt and other mining centres, resulting in serious loss of life from preventable disease.

We see, on the one hand, balance sheets of mining corporations that bulge with big dividends, and, on the other hand, the dreary, disorderly and unhealthy shack towns in which the miners are forced to live, unredeemed by any public-spirited effort to improve them by those who conduct the operations. Canada is only following the lead of other countries in that respect.

MINING VILLAGES IN GREAT BRITAIN

Britain, which has attained a high standard in public health during the last 30 years, has failed to deal satisfactorily with the problem of mining villages. Within the past ten years new mining areas have been developed in England and Scotland and some of the worst housing and sanitary conditions in these countries have accompanied these developments.

During the years 1911 to 1914, the writer investigated the housing and sanitary conditions of the great mining field in the Doncaster area of Yorkshire, comprising about 300 square miles, for the Local Government Board of England and Wales. In 1913, no fewer than nineteen new pits were projected in that area. A large amount of building development had taken place during the few years prior to 1913. Numerous towns and villages, which, in 1901, had a population varying from 400 to about 3,000, had increased to from 3,000 to 7,000, and urban districts adjacent to Doncaster had nearly doubled in population. The problem in this district in regard to development was very similar to what exists in the mining districts of Canada. When the population in one parish increased from 250 to 4,897 in ten years, it was almost impossible to provide adequate sanitary arrangements to cope with the rapid growth.

The principal obstacle to the provision of up-to-date methods of drainage and sanitation was the inability of the rural districts to borrow money for the purpose of providing the necessary facilities in advance of development. It was apparent that the only solution of the problem was for the government to help to finance improvement schemes in such districts, placing part of the burden for providing such improvements upon the large colliery companies which were responsible for causing the development. In these areas, crowded rows of houses were being built right up to the boundaries of existing narrow highways; roads, which had been adequate for agricultural purposes, were being rendered impassable by the traffic of the collieries; houses were cracked owing to subsidence; and, in many cases, miners were housed in temporary wooden shacks, similar to those which are found in the early stages of development in a Canadian mining village. But, in spite of all the effects of the mining development taking place in Doncaster district, nearly every one of the large colliery proprietors was engaged in carrying out, or in considering, schemes for creating model villages and for securing proper housing and sanitary conditions for the workers.

The late Sir A. B. Markham laid out a model village called Woodlands (Figure 33) in which he provided dwellings of a modern sanitary type and having pleasant rural surroundings. In spite of certain defects, Woodlands represented a great advance in regard to housing in mining districts, but it has not been followed up to any large extent. This was partly due to some practical defects in the scheme, and the reaction which consequently followed towards the rows of houses to which the miners had previously been accustomed. Improvement of conditions must proceed slowly, and the people for whom they are being improved must be consulted as to their wishes and educated to appreciate good environment.

The two outstanding features in the Doncaster situation were, first, the enormous difficulty of making proper sanitary provision in a rapidly growing mining district and, second, the responsibility assumed by some of the great mining magnates in trying to overcome these difficulties and erecting good housing accommodation for their workers. What the late Sir A. B. Markham and the other great mine owners have done indicates what the English government might have done with the co-operation of these owners, and what the mine-owners in Canada might do with the help and co-operation of the governments of Canada (Figure 34).

But the situation must be dealt with by comprehensive treatment of the whole problem. Of course, there can be no finality in an artificially promoted scheme, dependent, as it is, for a full measure of success on the slow process of education. But if the beginning is made in Canada, as it has been in England, the goal of improved standards of comfort, efficiency

FIGURE 33   WOODLANDS

Plan of Colliery Village, in Yorkshire, England, by Percy Houfton. A great part of the buildings as shown in solid black, have been erected. The plan has suffered in execution, partly owing to the excessive width of streets.

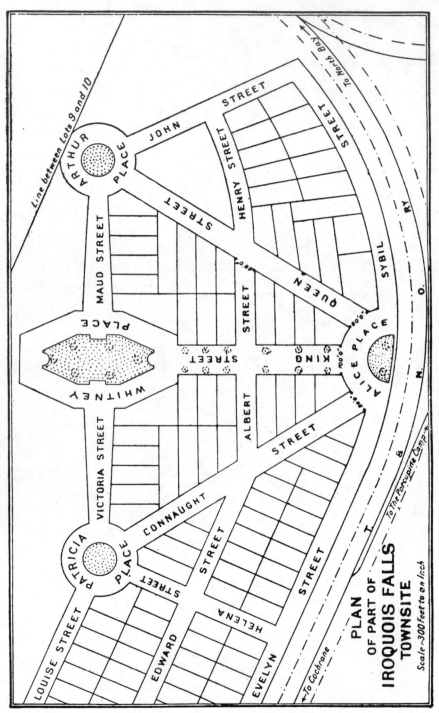

FIGURE 34   PLAN OF IROQUOIS FALLS TOWNSITE

This plan of a townsite in a mining region of North Ontario shows that attention is being given to the planning of new sites by the Timiskaming and Northern Ontario Railway. The plan is excellent from the point of view of street direction, but as about twice as much street area as is necessary or as can be constructed on an economic basis.

and social amelioration will be reached in time, whereas the longer the beginning is deferred, the difficulties of achieving the goal will increase.

There is urgent need for improvement of living conditions in mining areas, from the point of view of conserving the social stability of the country and preventing conflicts between capital and labour. Mr. Thomas Richards, M.P., general secretary of the South Wales Miners' Federation, referring to this aspect of the question, says:

"In South Wales and Monmouthshire socialism and syndicalism and other advanced schools of thought have made progress because the workers deeply resent the degrading system under which they work, and the sordidness and monotony of their housing conditions and home surroundings. There can be no doubt that the unwholesome environment of mining towns and villages has much to do with the creation of industrial unrest."

WATER SUPPLIES AND SEWERAGE IN SMALL TOWNS

Polluted water supplies and lack of sanitary and efficient sewerage systems are only too common in the small towns and rural districts of Canada. The comparatively small resources of such towns and districts make the problem one of peculiar difficulty from an economic point of view. In one small town in Ontario bad sanitary conditions, resulting in diarrhea and enteritis (under 2 years), have been the chief cause of an average death rate of 11 per cent of the reported births, with the death rate in exceptional years running as high as 22.9 percent of reported births. The *Report of the Provincial Board of Health* states that – "Conditions such as these are intolerable, and some method of financing the needed improvements must be arranged for."

Many municipalities in Canada, having water and sewerage systems, have imperfect means of distributing water and large parts of their areas are unsewered. Others, which are dependent on private wells for their supplies of water, show great carelessness in the construction of cesspools and closets, with resultant contamination and outbreaks of typhoid. Statements are frequently made that sanitary inspectors are prevented from doing their duty because of unjustifiable pressure exerted upon them by members of councils. Surely this should be prevented by law, in view of the essential importance of conserving life and health.

But, in spite of the backwardness of councils in appreciating the advantages of better conditions, considerable improvement has been made in recent years, and a more enlightened public opinion is being formed.

Conditions are so widely different that no general rule can be applied, and, as with all other matters of land development, questions relating to sanitation must be considered on their merits in each district, with due regard to the ability of the district to bear the cost of any particular scheme or mode of treatment. In many towns which can afford to have engineering advice, the advantage of employing an engineer is not appreciated, but the saving effected by the neglect to do so is lost in other directions. The Provincial Governments, through their Boards of Health, are doing much to improve matters by inspection and education, but more might be accomplished if this work was supplemented by means of financial assistance from the Provincial Governments in needy cases.

Economic Loss from Sickness

The improvement of sanitation is most important, from the point of view of conservation of human life. It has been stated that the deaths in Canada from preventable diseases alone, amount to no fewer than 40,000 per annum, or about one person in every 200.

Dr. C. J. Hastings, medical officer of the city of Toronto, has stated that the total number of deaths in the Canadian Expeditionary Force during the first two and one-quarter years of the war was 15,755, while during the same time there were 17,350 deaths in the Dominion from typhoid fever and tuberculosis, which two diseases – both preventable – took their greatest toll among those of military age.

The economic loss caused by this wastage of human life cannot be estimated in figures, but it must be enormous. There is not only the actual loss of life to be measured, but also the loss of productive power which occurs during the period of sickness that precedes death. Added to that, there is the fact that a large proportion of these deaths occur from contagious and infectious diseases which affects the health of those who come in contact with the diseased. Moreover, for every person who dies of sickness there are many others who are left wounded and crippled, to become less efficient as producers or a charge on the nation. Some idea of the economic loss in a community of 218,149 inhabitants can be gauged from the sickness survey of Rochester, New York, which was carried out by the Metropolitan Life Insurance Co. of New York in 1916. Although the instance given is with respect to a city area, the lesson it conveys applies to any kind of community. The report of this survey contains the following paragraph:

"The estimated male population of Rochester, 15 years of age and over, for the year 1915, is 92,552. On the basis of the above sickness rates, we may conclude that there are, throughout the year, at least 2,147 males constantly sick. This means approximately 644,000 days of disability for males alone, for we may count 300 working days per year per individual. At an average daily wage of $2, the wage loss alone for a year in a city like Rochester would be $1,288,000, and this figure, we have observed, is a minimum. It does not include cost of medical care, drugs, nursing, etc., nor for the loss sustained through disability of 2,400 females by sickness in the same city."

A few years ago, Sir Thomas Oliver, professor of the practice of medicine in the University of Durham, made an enquiry into the causes of death of the Boilermakers' Society in England. The society has a membership of upwards of 66,000. The percentage of deaths from pneumonia was 9.51, and from tuberculosis 11.75, a total of over 21 per cent. He reported that the mortality from pneumonia was unusually high between 40 and 60, and that tuberculosis claimed its victims at an early age. "At 23, tuberculosis is asserting itself; the mortality rate continues to be high till over 50 years of age, that is, it lasts through all the best period of a man's working life."

There is a heavy death rate from these causes in rural districts in Canada among comparatively young people, and a large proportion of the mortality from respiratory diseases is undoubtedly due to defective sanitation and want of proper ventilation. In Ontario, the total number of deaths from tuberculosis in 1915 was 2,466, of which no less than 1,707, or 69 per cent, occurred between the ages of 20 and 59. It is stated that one-third of all the deaths on the American continent, occurring between the ages of 15 and 60 years, are from tuberculosis.

By-Law Administration

In many rural districts in Canada there are no building or sanitary by-laws, and, even when they exist, they are not administered in a satisfactory way. It is one of the defects of our municipal system in Canada that we rely on local by-laws – where we have them at all – to regulate sanitary conditions and building development. Matters requiring the exercise of the best skilled advice – which can only be dealt with equitably under a system based on continuity of policy and management – are administered by men whose terms of office are too short to enable them to learn even the rudiments of municipal government. Whatever discretion they are permitted to exercise they are prone to use as a means of barter with private interests and, frequently, under the force of political pressure. It is not suggested that the criticism of some people, that municipal rulers in

Canada are more open to corrupt practices, or are less efficient, than the rulers of European countries, is a just criticism. The average council of a rural district in Canada is as honest and efficient as that in a rural district in England. On the whole, both endeavour to be just, and both have the kind of ability best suited for the work. But in England the local administrator is not a legislator – he is elected to carry on the executive duties of local government, under a system based on the best principles that can be devised by the expert advisers of the central government of the country. By-laws, both in England and in Canada, have the defect that they have to be specific in their character and general in their application. They can make no allowance for special cases. What is good for one party and condition must, according to a by-law, be good for another party and condition. Some more elastic and discriminating method is needed to control development, and there should be more co-operation and interdependence between the provincial government, with expert municipal administrators, and the local council.

LACK OF CO-OPERATION BETWEEN MUNICIPAL AUTHORITIES

Lack of co-operation between rural and urban municipalities, in the interests of health, is another cause of bad suburban development. Urban authorities often refuse to give facilities for extending their public services into adjacent rural areas, even when suitable financial arrangements can be made. The natural desire of the urban authority to conserve its population and prevent its overflow into rural territory is largely responsible for this attitude. The general experience, as may be seen around Montreal, Toronto, Ottawa, Winnipeg, Vancouver and other large cities, is that this desire does not prevent the overflow, but that it injures both the migrating population and, indirectly, the city from which it comes. In a paper read before the conference of Medical Officers of Health of Nova Scotia, Dr. A. C. Jost, the Medical Officer of Health for Guysboro, N.S., refers as follows to a case of lack of co-operation of a kind that is altogether too common in rural communities in all the provinces:

"I have in mind a community in my own municipality. Along its entire waterfront the land is owned by a corporation. Above this, on the steep hillside, are rows of lots, several tiers in depth, separated by streets which parallel the waterfront. The owners of the properties facing the lands owned by the corporation are prevented from draining their land through or on the corporation-owned lands. The rear of their own lots, separated by a narrow street from their immediate neighbours in the next higher tier, is liable to contamination, and, not from their neighbours alone, but from all the properties above them on the hillside. The accumulated refuse of all is washed down the hill during the progress of a rainstorm or a spring freshet, over-flowing the property on the waterfront, after endangering every immediate holding in its passage ... What must be the condition of the water derived from wells in a community such as this, where the houses have been huddled together on the hillside and where settle-ment took place some score of years ago?"

Dr. Jost naturally asks how this condition is to be remedied, and states he considers the laws unsatisfactory to deal with it. So far as future develop-ment is concerned, however, there is adequate power under the Nova Scotia Town Planning Act to effectively control the situation if the Act is properly administered.

There is also the necessity for preventing owners of lands, which form the natural drainage areas of districts, from withholding easements for the proper drainage of areas belonging to adjoining owners, even when such adjoining owners are willing to make adequate compensation. Power is also required to deal with the frequent cases in which the public suffers owing to roads and streets being blocked in subdivided areas by reason of the conflicting interests of adjoining owners. Expensive and wasteful plans are often the result of subdivisions being made of separately owned properties, without any co-ordination and, often, at such intervals of time, that no one can foresee when one plan is submitted how contiguous areas will be affected.

Fire Prevention in Rural Areas

The preparation of development schemes designed to eliminate the most injurious forms of speculation on the one hand, and to secure uniform by-law administration of sanitation and building construction on the other hand, would do much to remove the principal causes of loss of life and money due to fire.

The per capita loss from fire in Canada is one of the highest in the world and is increasing. During the last 50 years the fire losses have amounted to $350,000,000; in 1890 they were $5,500,000 and in 1914 they were $21,500,000, an increase of 290 per cent as against an increase of only 67 per cent in the population. The value of buildings erected in 1914 was $91,000,000 and of this amount $21,500,000 was spent to repair fire losses. The total cost of fires and fire protection in 1914 was $45,000,000.*

---

* Address of Sir Clifford Sifton, *Eighth Annual Report Commission of Conservation.*

The loss in Canada which is due to fire is a tax on all classes of industry, and is severely felt in rural districts and small towns. The burden of the loss has to be borne directly or indirectly by every citizen. In proportion as the risk of fire is greater, the cost of insurance has to be increased. Although buildings are more scattered in country districts, they are, for that very reason, less satisfactorily provided with water supply under pressure. The consequence is that high insurance has to be paid upon them, and the risk of loss in rural suburbs and in connection with large rural institutions is sometimes much greater even than in the comparatively crowded city. One of the most frequent causes of great conflagrations is the starting of forest fires, sometimes for agricultural purposes, and at other times as a result of mere carelessness.

Forest Fires

In 1908, forest fires raging in the Kootenay Valley district completely destroyed the towns of Fernie and Michel. About 80 lives were lost and 3,000 homeless refugees were forced to seek shelter in other towns. The loss of agricultural property is said to have amounted to about $4,000,000.

The fires in Northern Ontario in 1911 and 1916 caused severe losses of life and property. The first fire is reported to have resulted in a death roll of over 100 and an estimated property loss of $1,450,000. Several towns and villages were wiped out by the fire in 1916, with the result that about 200 lives were lost and the property loss is alleged to have exceeded $2,000,000. Following the fire at Cochrane the town council drew up a by-law defining fire limits and the class of building therein.

A missionary, who has spent many years working among the people of Northern Ontario, writes as follows, in March, 1917:

> "Here at Jacksonboro (North Ontario), the American company that is colonizing the land is putting in 40 new families this spring. Many of these have left homesteads elsewhere, and are buying the land at $3.00 an acre in 75 acre lots from this company, making a small payment down.
>
> "The reason for this is that the company gives the men regular employment summer and winter. To fulfill government conditions they erect a small shack on their lot, which lot is but a mass of cut brush ready for the fire, and leave their wives and children there, while they work either in camps in the winter or at the sawmill in the village in the summer.

PLATE XIII   FIRE AND DISEASE TRAP, ENDANGERING BOTH LIFE AND PROPERTY
This class of development should be rooted out under proper sanitary and building laws.

PLATE XIII   REMAINS OF SETTLER'S HOME
After forest fire in the "Clay Belt" of Northern Ontario, 1916.

"Finding there was one English-speaking settler, I called on him on a Sunday afternoon. His little one-roomed shack seemed so neat and clean, that my first remark was, 'This is a nice little shack you have.' His reply was, 'Well, it is good enough to be burnt up, as it is sure to be the first dry summer we have.' I said, 'Well, what about the wife and baby?' He replied, 'Oh, the river is only a quarter of a mile away and is deep enough to protect them.' She said, 'Indeed, I am not going to take any chances, but will go into town when the dry spell comes.'

"The young doctor of the settlement remarked, 'It seems almost criminal for the government to allow these people to settle in these conditions,' and my reply was, 'I consider it not "almost" but *quite* criminal.' Worse horrors than last summer's fire are surely ahead, if this sort of thing goes on."

Scattered and badly regulated settlement makes it difficult to control forest fires or to establish a system of inspection to enforce regulations in respect of fire-guards. Where land is covered with forest, or is of muskeg formation, special steps should be taken to guard against indiscriminate selection of homesteads by settlers. Settlement should be started from a railway centre and gradually extended outwards, one good road at least being provided as expansion takes place. Several townships should be opened up at one time, but it should be required that a considerable percentage of these be in occupation before others are placed on offer.

The chief dangers of fires occur in regions where settlement goes on in the immediate wake of logging operations. The carelessness of the settler and the absence of roads are among the chief causes.

These awful fire risks are not confined to British Columbia and Ontario. The editor of *Canadian Finance* points out that most of the new emigration to the Prairie Provinces is taking up lands in the northern timbered areas, thereby duplicating the forest fire hazard of the Ontario clay-belt. There is no need for these hazards being permitted in any serious degree. Burning permits should be enforced and land should be planned and developed in such a way as to secure less scattered and more continuous settlement.

Fire Safeguards and Regulations

Two safeguards are essential in dealing with fire, first, the prevention of the starting of fires, and, second, the regulation of building construction and land development so as to minimize the possibility of conflagration following a fire.

It was noticeable in connection with the fire in Northern Ontario, that the fire worked around cultivated land, leaving it almost untouched. It was a muskeg rather than a forest fire, and some effort should be made to remove the danger by assisting in bringing more land into cultivation as settlement proceeds. The building of good roads, simultaneously with land settlement, and the provision of village centres with local organizations, etc., are necessary to facilitate fire-fighting and to lessen danger to human life.

The question of proper control of buildings by regulation, for the purpose of fire prevention, must be taken up in Canada, in view of the tremendous burden which has to be borne on account of the present haphazard and wasteful system. Whatever regulations are necessary to reduce fire risks and to control construction for purposes of fire prevention are at the same time effective in improving sanitary conditions. What is called the "moral hazard" in rural districts is caused, in a large measure, by the temporary and fleeting interest of the so-called "settler" on his property, because – notwithstanding the fact of his ownership – the conditions of settlement, the temporary character of his buildings, and the difficulty of making ends meet render him careless and indifferent.

The restriction of the proportion of a lot that can be built upon in suburban areas, of the height of buildings, or of the character of the material used in towns or villages, have all a bearing on the question of fire as well as on that of sanitation.

Apartment houses, hotels, and other buildings of that class are erected in rural districts without being required to have fireproof construction or to have sufficient space surrounding them to provide adequate light, air, and means of protection from fire. Paving of yards is neglected, and wooden buildings are permitted to be erected in close proximity to one another. Factories and residences are indiscriminately erected in the same districts, with the result that the residences adjoining factories have to meet excessive rates for fire insurance.

New towns and villages are laid out and developed without provision for cleared areas between them and forest areas. The system of developing land and encouraging speculation prevents proper restrictions being placed on the location and construction of buildings to prevent fires. By more effective control of land speculation, fire risks could be reduced in areas being developed for building purposes. It should be a rule that no dwelling should be occupied till a water supply was provided, and that, where several buildings were erected in close proximity, the supply should be in a water main under pressure. If less money were paid for bare land there would be more capital available for securing proper construction and sanitary conditions.

Development Schemes and Fire Prevention

With respect to the question of preparing development schemes to assist in securing better control of fires, the following advantages may be pointed out:

(1) The closer settlement, by better planning, will enable the population to deal more effectively with fires by co-operative means and to effect a larger amount of clearance of forest areas.

(2) The development of land in a more gradual way, and the improvement of the road system simultaneously with, or in advance of settlement, will remove one of the chief causes of forest fires.

(3) As land is put to more economic use under a proper system of development, regulations may be imposed requiring a standard of building which could not be secured under present conditions.

(4) With improved social conditions, better roads and buildings, more co-operation, and good systems of water supply, farmers and householders will become settlers in a more permanent sense and with a greater respect for their property, thus reducing the moral hazard which accompanies the temporary nature of land-holding and cheap construction.

(5) In building subdivisions there should be a requirement that dwellings could not be inhabited until provided with a satisfactory supply of water and with good access by road. The total cost of a dwelling under these conditions need not be much greater than the cost where no such regulation existed, since the outlay in better construction and sanitation would be mostly saved in the cost of the site. It is the speculator, and not the builder or user, who gets most of the pecuniary benefit of the absence of proper building regulations. In countries where land is less plentiful than in Canada, it is cheaper, because the purchaser is not free to use it for unhealthy dwellings or without making adequate protection against fire.

(6) In new towns and suburbs, zones should be fixed for different purposes, one zone for manufacturing and business, another for residences, with proper regulations regarding the character of construction of the buildings and the distances between them, according to the use to which they were to be put.

Problem of High Cost of Living

The inhabitants of rural districts are injured by the high cost of living partly as consumers, but also – in so far as they do not enjoy the benefit of the increased prices – as producers. It seems to be an admitted fact that the profits of the farmer have not materially advanced, in spite of the largely increased cost of farm produce to the ultimate consumers. If, as a result of this increased cost, the agricultural industry had been made substantially prosperous, and more people had been attracted to the land, the problem would soon have righted itself, but there is no evidence that the high cost of living is making farming sufficiently profitable to attract the residents of the cities to go back to the country districts.

As far as Canada is concerned this problem has not been created, although it has been intensified, by the war. It had become so acute in 1913-14, before the war started, that in 1914 a special Commission of Inquiry was set up to study it. In the report of that inquiry some conclusions are set forth which have a bearing on the subject of this report. These may be summarized as follows:

(1) The main factors in restricting supply and enhancing cost are depopulation of rural districts, concentration of population in towns and cities and uneconomic methods of distribution.

(2) The means of securing improvement are greater attention to mixed farming, increased production, standardization and improvement of quality of farm products, co-operation in distribution, extension of parcels post system, making of good roads, cheaper working capital, improved system of education, vocational training, and improved conditions of living.

In a statistical examination of economic causes of the high cost of living laid before the Commission of Inquiry by the Department of Labour, it is pointed out that the remedial lines which the inquiry indicates are the encouragement of food production and the removal of every possible economic weight in the distribution process. Sir George Paish is quoted as saying that it is of the greatest possible importance that the work, of directly increasing the productive power of Canada by placing a larger proportion of the population upon the land and in the mines, should be carried out with the least possible delay.

While the stimulation of agricultural production is suggested in the above conclusions as the principal means to counteract the high cost of living, it must be borne in mind that we have to avoid overproduction as well as underproduction of raw materials; indeed, Sir Robert Giffen has pointed out that new countries like Canada are apt to suffer in bad times more than manufacturing countries, owing to the greater liability of the latter to produce raw materials in excess.

The important things to aim at are to secure a satisfactory and stable equilibrium between town and country, to encourage the dispersal of manufacturing industries over the whole country instead of concentrating them too much in large cities, and to so plan and develop the land as to enable the facilities for improving distribution, education and living conditions to be provided. The main factors, which are shown by the above report to cause the high cost of living, are products of an unscientific system of land development, and the means of securing improved conditions can only be attained by re-laying the foundations on which that system is built up.

UNEMPLOYMENT AND LAND DEVELOPMENT

During the same period that witnessed an increased cost of living in Canada before the war, there was much suffering due to want of employment in the cities. Whatever may have been the main causes of this parallel condition there is no doubt that the condition was largely artificial and that, having regard to the need for the application of human resources to develop the natural resources of the country, there was no necessity for there being any serious lack of employment, had it not been that the cities had been over-developed in proportion to the development of the rural districts. Nor could it be expected that the orgy of land speculation, and the investment of large sums of borrowed money in railway enterprises prior to 1913, would leave no traces of unsettlement and disorganization of labour behind them, after the speculation and railway development practically ceased. The issue of the exhaustive *Report of the Ontario Commission of Unemployment* (1916) makes it unnecessary to do more in this report than to briefly refer to the conclusions arrived at by that commission.

One of the proposals outlined by the commission is as follows:

> "A vigorous policy of community and assisted land settlement would develop natural resources and assist in restoring industrial activity. Training schools for agricultural labourers, in connection with provincial farms, are desirable as a means of lessening unemployment and training for employment. Greater access to the land by means of cheap and rapid transit would prove of great advantage to urban workers, especially in periods of unemployment. An improvement in methods of taxation, by which speculation in land would be made unprofitable, would assist in making this possible, and is equally desirable for other reasons."

The policy here outlined cannot be achieved without better organization of land settlement itself. It is fundamental to any satisfactory system of settlement, and to any scheme for restoring industrial activity, improving rural education and means of communication, and rendering speculation unprofitable, that a sound scheme of development, so designed as to accomplish these objects, is formulated in the first place. To attain the conditions of success outlined in Section IV of the above report, such as the transfer into new settlements of the occupations and variations of older communities, the improvement of marketing and facilities for cooperation, the withdrawal of Crown lands open for settlement after careful study of these lands and the greater mobility of labour, it is first necessary to prepare a scheme of organization and development.

The taxation of vacant lands recommended by the Commission so that the evils ensuing from speculation in land, which contributed to the recent industrial depression and makes more difficult any satisfactory dealing with unemployment in industrial centres, is both just and desirable if the taxation is based on a sound basis of valuation and has regard to the need for encouraging the best economic use of the land. Such a policy requires, however, as has already been contended, first that there shall be no loose and indiscriminate application of any system of taxation in the expectation that that system can, by itself, remove all social evils; second that safeguards will be provided to prevent the tax from increasing instead of lessening the burden on production; and third that it will be complementary to a system of laying out and regulating land development.

CONCLUSION

The facts and considerations set out in this chapter lead to the general conclusions – That there has been a large amount of injurious speculation in land in rural and suburban areas in Canada, causing absentee landlordism, idleness of fertile and accessible areas, inflated land values representing a tax upon industry – and unhealthy living conditions; that injurious speculation, accompanied by improper assessment and taxation of land, has impaired real estate as an investment, caused serious financial difficulties and injustice to the taxpayers, and prevented productive land within and near cities from being used; that land in Canada has been valued for taxation with too little regard to its earning power, its economic use and its real value; that, to be sound and achieve its object, a system of taxation should be based on an equitable system of assessment, should secure a large share of the increment of land value on the occasion of transfer or sale, should encourage agricultural use of land within and near cities, and should have regard to ability to pay; that mining, fishing and other rural villages are in urgent need of improvement in regard to sanitation and living conditions; that fire risks cannot be successfully combated without adequate regulations and control of land settlement and erection of buildings; that the causes of high cost of living and of unemployment largely arise from the want of more scientific methods of land colonization; and, finally, that improvement of all those conditions cannot be achieved unless on the basis of a well organized, carefully planned and economically sound system of land development.

CHAPTER V
RURAL PROBLEMS THAT ARISE IN CONNECTION
WITH LAND DEVELOPMENT

Commentary by Len Gertler

The really interesting thing about *Rural Planning and Development,* and this chapter on land development, is the mindset and scope of its author. For a man who was invited to Canada (as Sir Clifford Sifton, chairman of the Commission of Conservation, Canada, explained in 1914) because he was a specialist in a particular field, "one of the foremost and ablest authorities" on the "science of town planning," he had a remarkably broad view of his mission. Coming from the traditions of turn-of-the-century Britain, directly influenced by Patrick Geddes and Ebenezer Howard, and involved in the Garden City movement, his concept of planning encompassed, comfortably, both town and country (Armstrong 1959, 23). He had a holistic perspective. Urban and rural were related and interdependent spheres that equally required a conscientious stewardship to sustain healthy living conditions. And for that we have reason, in Canada, to be grateful. So I do not understand the basis for the entry in *The Canadian Encyclopedia* that states that "recent assessments have diminished his contribution to Canadian Urban and Regional Planning" (Saarinen 1985, 8).

This substantial chapter of about forty pages addresses three main subjects:

1 Land speculation in the rural and suburban areas of Canada and its "injurious effects."
2 The defects of the system of land assessment and taxation and necessary principles of reform.
3 The issue of living conditions in mining, fishing, and rural villages (marked by poor sanitation, fire risks, high cost of living, and erratic employment), which are in critical need of improvement.

Issues raised by all of these points have some resonance today, but the second and third points, about the system of land assessment and taxation and about rural natural resource–based communities, are very much defined by circumstances of time and place.

Adams' introductory observations on land speculation show his capacity to be, at once, historical and contemporary. He writes:

In a *new country* a certain amount of *speculation* is inevitable, and is not an unmixed evil. It draws out and *stimulates energy and enterprise* that might otherwise lie dormant; it accompanies a spirit of optimism that is needed to *blaze trails* into new regions and *overcome the obstacles* that confront pioneers. Canada has been largely developed by speculators of the right type ... But, *when the pioneer stage is over* and the building up of the social life of a new community begins, speculation takes on *injurious forms*. Socially created values are inflated and exploited and monopolies in natural resources are established. It is in this latter form that speculation in Canada in recent years has produced *deplorable moral and financial results*, in *rural* as well as in *urban* areas. (Pages 157-58, emphasis added)

Adams then proceeds to provide examples of the injurious effects of land specu-lation, concentrating on the interface between rural and urban land uses. His account of the experience in the Ottawa-Hull area bears a strong resemblance to what we in the twenty-first century would call urban shadow effects – the spread of urban-related land use features into the countryside far beyond any realistic provision of land for future development needs (Gertler 1972, 34-38). "The subdivision of land for building purposes during periods of boom," he wrote, "extends into rural areas round cities up to a radius of from three to ten miles or more outside the city boundaries." He cites information for the capital region to establish that a population increase from 123,000 in 1917 to an expected 350,000 in 1967 would require, at a density of 40 people to the acre (about 99 per hectare), 15 square miles (about 22 square kilometres) – 23 percent of the 65-square-mile area (about 96 square kilometres) already subdivided but not built upon at that time (Adams 1917, 166).

This phenomenon of premature and excessive subdivision of rural land for urban development, Adams notes, was common throughout the country. He gives as examples the Toronto area and cities in western Canada. In his dissection of three western cities, he makes an important distinction between (1) land withdrawn from agriculture in the form of subdivided but vacant lots and (2) an area of farm land twice or three times as great "within and immediately adjacent to city boundaries, which is not being properly farmed because of the expecta-tions of the farmers that they will be able to dispose of their lands for building subdivisions." In addition to deploring the negative impact of this "condition of affairs" on agriculture and rural communities, he observes that "there are serious effects ... on the cities themselves which will be dealt with in the urban report" (page 170). Although that study, unfortunately, never saw the light of day, we can surmise from Adams' own catalogue of consequences, and a little hindsight, the nature of his concerns.

The adverse effects on Adams' list were as follows:

- Great areas of land around large cities are withheld from production – farms are rendered useless by being broken up into small lots and occupied by occasional small shacks or held by absentee owners.
- Sanitary arrangements cannot be provided because the buildings are too widely scattered.
- The townships lose rather than gain revenue.
- Construction labourers must travel long distances from home to work.
- Children are too far from school.
- Thousands of lots, close to the city, are unoccupied.
- In "some cases, there is a general paralysis of the whole neighbourhood" (page 167).

Writing from an early twenty-first-century perspective, it is sobering to report, and a little sad, that similar land development forces and effects continue to prevail in the environs of our cities. Around 1960, the concept of urban shadow came into focus, reflecting the notion that the influence of the city on land use extended deeply into the enveloping countryside. In that year – when I was appointed coordinator of regional development for the "Resources for Tomorrow" conference (in some respects, a descendant of the Commission of Conservation) – I took the opportunity to explore the concept empirically. With the help of researcher Joan Hind Smith and the support of the Conservation Council of Ontario (whose executive director, Gavin Henderson, became a co-coordinator of regional development), I undertook a pilot study of four places: Lindsay (population 12,500), Stratford (22,000), Kingston (61,000), and London (175,000). The idea was to assess the direct and indirect effect of urban development on land in a set of areas that approximated (apart from Toronto and Ottawa-Hull) a cross-section of the type and size of Ontario communities, ranging from rural service centres to metropolises.

In each place, we documented (A) the land used for every urban purpose and (B) land indirectly affected as defined by (1) undeveloped subdivisions, (2) non-farm ownership of rural land, (3) farmland for sale for urban purposes, and (4) above "normal" assessed values of rural land. The ratio of B to A provided an index of the urban shadow, which was, in order of population size, as follows: 1.25, 1.6, 5, and 2. The conspicuously higher 5 to 1 ratio in the Kingston area might have been due to the proximity of the Canadian Shield landscape – at once attractive as a recreation area and relatively unproductive as farmland. Concerning the spatial spread of the shadow, we found that the distance of its outer boundaries from built-up limits increased with an increase in the size of the centre – Lindsay, approximately 1.6 kilometres; Stratford, 6 to 11; Kingston, 19; and London, 32 kilometres (Gertler and Hind-Smith 1962, 155-80). Our findings corresponded closely to what Adams discovered, as reported above, in the rural-urban fringe of western Canadian cities.

The persistence of the outward thrust of land development forces in Canada's largest urban area has been revealed recently by a study, prepared for the Neptis Foundation in 2004, of urban pressures on Simcoe County, north of Toronto, situated between Lake Simcoe on the east and Nottawasaga Bay on the west. The authors, three graduates of the University of Toronto Planning Program, made a telling discovery. Notwithstanding that there is enough land south of the Oak Ridges Moraine (part of the southern boundary of Simcoe County) to accommodate Toronto-generated development at current residential densities until the year 2031, there is now a push for major urban uses north of the moraine. Current plans and proposals include a town of 114,000 residents on 2,500 acres of prime agricultural land in the Bradford West Gwillimbury area, precariously close to the highly productive market garden area (about 2,900 hectares) known as the Holland Marsh.

The study reflects on the implications of this kind of exurban development. In essence, the concern is that, given the key location of Simcoe County, the acceptance of such a large outlying development (and the Bradford-related proposal is only one of several) would mean that the form of growth would be determined by default, without due consideration of critical regional factors (Birnbaum et al. 2004, 30-32, 44, 52-54, 74). As the authors express it:

> In the absence of a region-scaled growth strategy defined by the Province for how the Toronto-related region should grow, developers have established the dominant development pattern by exploiting marketing opportunities and building according to industry norms ... The final plan will have as its base motivation profitability for the developer, not the creation of the most rational growth pattern for the area in the context of the Toronto-related region ... The challenge in Simcoe is not merely of a technical nature. It is fundamentally political, and political challenges require political solutions. (Ibid., 55, 56)

The double-edged nature of the effect of cities on the countryside, of their effect on both rural and urban development, did not escape the authors. "The city creates the urban shadow," I wrote earlier, "And the urban shadow shapes the city" (Gertler 1972, 40). This matters because of the form and extent of the shadow, which has repercussions on rural society, environment, and development patterns that extend far beyond urban limits and the reasonable needs of urban growth. Reflecting on the public policy implications of these features, I was naturally led to invoke regional planning – a strategy for managing growth – as a way to minimize the uncertainty, the ubiquitous expectations that feed land speculation and the spread of urban shadow (ibid., 45).

Which brings me back to Thomas Adams. His prescriptions were, of course, shaped by his times. He saw the issue of speculation and land development, in suburban and rural areas, as part and parcel of the way in which the public sector managed the opening up of lands to new settlement. He therefore writes, forcefully, that improvement in conditions "cannot be achieved unless on the basis of a well-organized, carefully planned and economically sound system of land development" (page 206). That was ninety-four years ago. Anybody listening?

REFERENCES

Armstrong, A.H. 1959. "Thomas Adams and the Commission of Conservation." *Plan Canada* 1, 1: 14-32.

Birnbaum, Leah, Lorenzo Nicolet, and Zachary Taylor, 2004. *Simcoe County: The New Growth Frontier*. Toronto: Neptis Foundation.

Gertler, Leonard O. 1972. *Regional Planning in Canada*. Montreal: Harvest House.

Gertler, Leonard O., and J. Hind-Smith. 1962. "The Impact of Urban Growth on Agricultural Land." *Resources for Tomorrow Background Papers, Supplementary Volume,* 155-80. Ottawa: Queen's Printer.

Saarinen, O.W. 1985. "Adams, Thomas." *Canadian Encyclopedia.* Vol. 1. Edmonton: Hurtig Publishers.

CHAPTER VI

Organization of Rural Life and Rural Industries

*The social structure of rural life | Rural co-operation in Canada |
Co-operation in other countries | Difficulties of obtaining capital and rural
credit | Rural credit in Canada | Education and scientific training |
Proportion of cost of education between urban and rural districts | Education
and rural industries | More comprehensive educational system needed |
Scientific and industrial research | Proposed national organization |
The organization of rural manufactures | Domestic industries |
The example of France | Development of artistic skill | Organizing new
industrial centres | The promotion of industrial decentralization |
The Garden City form of development | Industrial, social and civic welfare*

THE SOCIAL STRUCTURE OF RURAL LIFE

THE matters which have been dealt with in previous chapters of this
report relate to the foundation which has to be laid before a sound
structure of rural life and rural industry can be built up. But, in
laying the foundation, by proper planning and by the regulation of development, we must of necessity have regard to the kind of social structure
we desire to create. That structure must be economically sound as well as
the foundation on which it stands. In addition to a proper plan of development, and efficient control of resources, we need a social organization of
rural life and rural industries which will yield us the best possible results
in the volume of production, in the efficiency of distribution, and in the
character and stability of our citizenship.

That organization will only be successful if there is greater co-operation
in the future than in the past between those engaged in rural industries,
if rural manufacturing is encouraged to a greater extent than hitherto, if
there are increased opportunities for social intercourse and scientific
training in rural districts and if capital is made available at cheaper rates
of interest than at present for purposes of rural development. All these
matters are receiving attention in Canada; legislation is being passed and
administrative and research bodies are being created to advance the interests of agriculture and the social organization of the rural districts.

Commendable activity is being shown by the Federal and Provincial Departments of Agriculture to promote education and to encourage production by improved organization. It is not a purpose of the present report to deal with these questions in any comprehensive way but we have to consider them in outline so as to judge how far the success of the efforts being made are hampered by want of proper planning and development of the land; we have to consider whether, if the governments had originally exercised their proper functions in preventing forced, haphazard and speculative settlement of land, their present efforts to promote rural organization and increase rural production would have been less necessary, or, alternatively, would have yielded better results.

In recent years, at least, it has not been for want of government aid or direction, nor for want of inclination and ability on the part of the farmers themselves, in any serious degree, that difficulties have arisen in providing social and educational facilities in rural districts and in securing co-operative action on the part of farmers. The main causes of these difficulties have been the scattered nature of the settlement, the using up of capital in speculation which should have been devoted to production, the placing of men on unsuitable land, and the inadequate means of communication. *The primary and most important duty of governments which control the disposal of the public domain, is to so plan and dispose of it that the resultant social development will largely take care of itself: in so far as this primary duty may be neglected the governments have to artificially promote the social development to make up for the neglect, or else to witness consequent failure and decay.*

RURAL CO-OPERATION IN CANADA

Co-operation is essential to the success of modern industry in any form; indeed, it is open to argument that, in so far as the city has grown at the expense of the country, the chief reason has been that co-operative organization has developed in the city more rapidly than in the country. But that defect is being gradually removed, either as a result of greater enlightenment or the awakening of the sense of self-preservation on the part of the farmers.

Some of the most successful farming enterprises in the Dominion have achieved their success as the result of co-operation. A notable example is the successful organization of the Grain Growers Association. The successes of the co-operative elevators, the Government creameries and the rural telephone system in Saskatchewan are due to co-operative organization.

We also find the greatest private corporations of the country founded on co-operative principles – the Canadian Pacific Railway Company, the Manufacturers' Association, the Fire Underwriters' Associations, and the great industrial combinations, are all great co-operative trusts. Co-operation in small industries and organizations is often criticized by the very men whose successes in life are due to co-operation in a large capitalistic corporation. Of course, business principles underlie success in co-operative as in individualistic enterprises – and, under proper conditions, initiative and self-reliance are promoted and not stifled by co-operation.

Considering that Canada is a new country, we have already made satisfactory progress in rural co-operation under the leadership of our Ministers of Agriculture. A large amount of educational work in regard to agricultural co-operation is carried on by the Department of Agriculture of the Dominion, and the extent of co-operative effort in the provinces is greater than seems to be generally realized.

There are 175 co-operative agricultural societies in Quebec, the most important of which is the Cheesemakers' Society, which transacted a business of a value of $3,600,000 in 1916. This society has 3,500 members. Several of the societies own creameries and cheese factories. Under the guidance and stimulus of the Quebec Department of Agriculture, co-operation is steadily advancing in the province.

According to Mr. F. C. Hart, of the Ontario Department of Agriculture, there are in Ontario 160 creameries and 1,000 cheese factories. Most of these are joint stock companies. The dairy branch of the department has a corps of instructors visiting all of these factories regularly. Writing in the *Agricultural Gazette,* Mr. Hart says:

> "Milk producers all over the province are organized into Milk Producers' Associations. These do not handle milk, but are used as a means by which the producers can deal with the trade in the matter of contracts, etc. At one centre only there is a producers' organization which collects the milk of its members and distributes retail with very apparent and growing success.
>
> In their initial stages co-operative associations are not equipped to take over all the functions of middlemen and deal directly with consumers. Their trade is largely with the wholesale houses and their operations so far have been too limited to largely affect the price of such farm products to consumers.
>
> In practically every instance, however, the quality of the output has been increased and there has been less waste caused by marketing of unsuitable food products. For instance, the egg circles have almost wholly eliminated their share of the 17% of bad eggs which are estimated to come to market; the result being that the producer has received a slight advance for his product – (one to three cents per

dozen average for the year) – and the consumer, although paying a
larger price for circle eggs receives much better value. This seems to
be the tendency in all these producers' organizations. The advance
of co-operation in the province certainly points to the fact that, the
growth of these producers' organizations, and the elimination of these
wastes (and the standardization of the product through organization)
must inevitably lessen the cost of marketing; a gain that should be
shared by both producer and consumer."

The total number of agricultural societies, women's institutes, farmers'
clubs, and other co-operative organizations in Ontario is about 3,500, of
which over 1,300 are engaged in marketing farm products. Many of the
latter both buy and sell. There are about 20 District Breeders' Associations,
and a number of the Farmers' Clubs carry on co-operative shipping of
live stock.

The co-operative agricultural societies of Ontario were quoted by an
English writer as an example, as far back as 1898, when it was stated that
"1,164 cheese factories in that province exported 110,000,000 lbs. of cheese
and 4,500,000 lbs. of butter."

In New Brunswick there are 121 agricultural societies which co-operate
in the purchasing of live stock, seed and commercial fertilizers.

Legislation is being promoted in the western provinces to facilitate and
encourage the formation of co-operative societies. In 1915 there were 261
co-operative societies in Saskatchewan, as compared with 113 in 1914. Of
these, 173 were Grain Growers' Associations, with 5,537 shareholders.
Creameries only increased in number from 4 to 15, but their output increased from 66,246 lbs. in 1907 to 2,012,402 lbs. in 1915. The policy in
Saskatchewan is to discourage building of creameries unless there is good
reason to anticipate success.

It has been proved that co-operation helps the public to get what they
want – namely, good articles of uniform quality at a reasonable price and
regularly supplied.

Co-operation in Other Countries

Co-operation amongst Irish farmers, under the able guidance of Sir
Horace Plunkett, has greatly increased production and stayed emigration.
Mr. G. W. Russell, the president of the Board of Agriculture of Ireland,
has stated that co-operation has done more for the betterment of conditions among the rural peasantry of Ireland than all the efforts of the
politicians – "with more economic business methods, with cheapening
of purchase, combination of sale, science in the farm and dairy, with

expensive machinery co-operatively owned, and with complete control of their own industry – farmers could create and retain a commercial wealth, which could purchase for them some of the comforts and luxuries of civilization."

Herschel has said that the people must have the stimulus of increased comforts and elevated desires to create the wide demand for manufactured articles that alone can lead to great and rapid improvements. The increase of land settlement on a permanent footing will create an increase in the demand for manufactured articles, and co-operation on business principles will enable us to secure rapid improvement of our social condition. What the Hon. Walter Scott said of the farmers of Saskatchewan is true of the farmers of the Dominion:

> "Co-operation in mutual liability engenders mutual trust. Wherever there is constant give and take – wherever the prosperity of the individual depends directly and obviously upon the prosperity of the community about him – there the social order tends to produce the fine type of character with a devotion to public ideals and public duties ... The plain lesson is that the farmers of Saskatchewan, who have to count themselves at present among the victims, should no longer remain divided, but should band themselves together by the principle of co-operation."

Co-operation in rural areas, for productive and distributive purposes, tends to increase co-operation in public affairs and increases the interest of the farmer in local government. He thereby becomes a more responsible citizen and is given an incentive to become a more permanent settler. The realization of his power to make or unmake provincial and national governments is already growing, and, whether this power be exercised for good or ill, will depend on the extent to which better facilities for co-operation and education are provided.

A significant movement of the farmers in the western United States to use their power is seen in the recent achievement of the Farmers' League of North Dakota, which succeeded in electing the Governor and officials of that state. In France and Denmark, farmers have much more influence over the legislatures and over government administration than in America generally. Sir Horace Plunkett points out that the absence of the parcels post, the domination of the express companies, and the bad state of the country roads on this continent are proof of this. He also claims, in regard to the effect of co-operation on education, that the natural education of the countryman is better than that of the townsman and that co-operation will help in the organization and practical working of education.

The business men of the city may consider that they are best fitted to control the politics of their provinces as well as the machinery of distribution, but they cannot be regarded as being free from the temptation of using both in their own interests. An increase of weight on the rural side would only be equitable and proper, but it will only be expedient in the public interest if it is accompanied by improved education and the spirit engendered by co-operation.

Denmark is one of the best examples of a country which has successfully developed its agriculture under co-operation, although it has always to be borne in mind that Denmark is essentially a dairying country, and that there is a comparatively small area of land used for grain growing. Between 1890 and 1901, the agricultural population of Denmark more than doubled. From 27.1 per cent it increased to 48.2 per cent.* The farmers of Denmark co-operate to select the best farms and to improve stock and husbandry, as well as to organize collection and distribution of farm products.

Irish co-operation was started in 1829, during a period of depression. There are now about 1,000 co-operative societies at work, with a membership of 100,000. Co-operation in Ireland, as in Denmark, has been stimulated by land ownership and the two together have greatly assisted in increasing production.

Mr. Vernon E. Fox, in an article in the *Farmers' Advocate,* says the European system would not be satisfactory in Canada, because farmers' homesteads are too scattered; the farmer does not held his land for life – he is ready to sell; and he is opposed to long term mortgages. The first difficulty can be largely overcome by reducing isolation and the others by lessening the tendencies to land speculation and making farming more profitable and attractive. But in Ireland, in Denmark and in Flanders, co-operation succeeds all the more because of the fact that facilities for obtaining rural credit and for carrying on rural industries are provided, and successful co-operation in Canada will never be attained unless we can simultaneously provide means to obtain cheap money and to build up rural industries as part of our co-operative organization.

DIFFICULTIES OF OBTAINING CAPITAL AND RURAL CREDIT

The farmer must have more capital and means of obtaining more ready money. Capital at the lowest possible rate of interest, to assist agricultural development, must be provided by any government in a country which is being opened up for settlement. Gradually the increase of capital will come

---

* In 1911 the town population of Denmark was 1,109,726 while the rural population was 1,647,350. — *Statesman's Year Book, 1913.*

with increased production, the only sound way of securing that increase. But as Adam Smith has said, "to obtain increased production we must provide means to incite the natural efforts of the producer." In Great Britain one obstacle in the way of increasing production is the lack of security of tenure; in Canada it is primarily the lack of proper planning for industrial efficiency and convenience, and of efficient organization to enable advantage to be taken of the security of tenure which is given. In both cases it is an absence of opportunity – different in character but equally restrictive in degree. Settlers must be able to enjoy a greater share of the fruits of their industry before they will exert themselves in increasing production.

The Hon. Walter Scott, late Premier of Saskatchewan, in an address delivered before the Legislative Assembly of Saskatchewan in 1913, on the subject of "cheaper money for agricultural development," stated that there were four acute agricultural problems in his province. These were: (1) The excessive cost of loans, (2) lack of any profitable market for the savings of the people, (3) the excessive cost of supplies, and (4) the depressed prices of farm products.

He stated that the farmers of Saskatchewan were paying 8 per cent for loans in 1913, and that, after adding 2 to 2½ per cent as the cost of commissions, etc., on obtaining and renewing the loans, the actual cost to the farmers was 10 to 10½ per cent, which he declared to be an excessive cost. On the other hand, the depositor of savings received from 3 to 3½ per cent. In North Dakota, government reports show that the amount of money loaned to the farmers in that state was $100,364,000, at an average rate of 8.7 per cent. In Russia, before the war, the agricultural investor received 3½ per cent from co-operative credit societies and borrowed on farm loans at 4 per cent.

With regard to the returns obtained by the farmer for his products, Mr. Scott quoted an article by Mr. B. F. Yoakum in *World's Work*, wherein the calculation was made that the farmers of the United States received six billions of dollars for products that cost the ultimate consumer thirteen billions of dollars. The following table shows the distribution of cost of the thirteen billions of dollars paid in 1911:

	Amount	Per Cent
Received by the farmers	$6,000,000,000	46.1
Received by railroads	495,000,000	3.8
Legitimate expense of selling	1,200,000,000	9.2
Waste in selling	1,560,000,000	12.0
Dealers' and retailers' profits	3,745,000,000	28.9
	$13,000,000,000	100

The value of the field crops alone in Canada in 1910 was $597,926,000, but the proportion of this production that reached the consumer would probably cost twice as much.

In Germany, farmers obtain cheap loans by pooling their credit. They obtained money before the war up to two-thirds the value of their security at from 3½ to 4½ per cent. In France, money was then obtained from the Credit Foncier at 4.3 per cent. Financial aid is also rendered to the settlers in all Australian states at cheap rates. In evidence given by the late Mr. A. F. Mantle, Deputy Minister of Agriculture for Saskatchewan, before the Standing Committee on Agriculture and Municipal Law of the Legislature in Saskatchewan, he pointed out that the great disparity between the rates paid in continental Europe and in western Canada could not be regarded as inevitable or unavoidable. Money for loans was provided through too many different sources in Canada, it was indiscriminate and ill-regulated, it was too static, *i.e.*, it was borrowed on mortgage to meet current expenses. "Were the farmers," he adds, "banded together in suitable organizations for the purpose, they could obtain all the money they required."

Next to the question of increasing production comes this question of reducing the cost of production so that the farmers of Canada may survive the test of bad times. It is during bad times that loans are most wanted.

The term "rural credit" is generally used to denote some government or co-operative scheme for lending money to those engaged in rural industries – particularly agriculture. In considering the importance of providing cheap capital to the farmer, too little regard is paid to what may be called the "credit" side of the transaction, namely, the capacity of the industry, to pay interest upon the capital involved in its development. There must be security for the investment of capital, and, owing to its mobility, capital is one of the most sensitive of economic instruments.

In order that capital may be obtained for those engaged in small detached industries, or for farmers whose trading transactions spread over long periods, it is essential that there should be co-operation in order that the security to attract capital can be mobilized to the best advantage.

Speculation in farm lands has had a tendency to destroy the real values on which any sound system of credit must be established. Moreover, homesteads have been arbitrarily fixed at sizes which cannot be justified by the amount of capital which the new settler has available to improve and develop them. It requires from $1,000 to $2,500 capital to work a farm of 160 acres to advantage, and some authorities advise that the settler should have a minimum of $1,000, plus credit of $500 to $1,000, to "make good."* Unfortunately, the average settler has too little capital, and the man who has been successful in making money in the city does not usually go on the land. The want of sufficient capital, when land is taken up, is one of the most prolific causes of failure in farming.

One weakness of rural credit legislation is that the whole value of it may be lost by land speculation. Unless accompanied by a proper system of organized colonization, the lending of money at low interest may help to increase the selling price of land and therefore, give to the seller the whole advantage intended to be given to the purchaser. Thus a man who wants to go on the land may have to pay more for it in proportion as he can obtain cheap money to buy it.

Rural Credit in Canada

During the past few years there has been no subject which has been more widely ventilated in Canada than that of rural credit.

A joint committee of commerce and agriculture, composed of representatives of the business interests of the western provinces and representatives of the organized farmers' associations, has been meeting in conference during the past year and discussing problems affecting the mutual welfare of the agricultural, manufacturing and general business interests. The object of the organization has been to bring the different rural and urban interests together and to endeavour to find a basis of agreement on public questions, on which to take joint action towards a solution. At its numerous conferences the joint committee has devoted most of its attention to the question of finance, especially with that aspect of finance which relates to what is known as rural credit.

Bills are now before some of the provincial legislatures for the purpose of legalizing the formation of rural credit societies and the co-operation of the provincial and municipal governments in giving financial assistance to such societies.

The British Columbia Act, passed in March, 1915, providing for the incorporation and regulation of agricultural associations and making provision for agricultural credits, is an example of what is being done in this direction. This Act authorized the borrowing of $15,000,000, to be administered by a commission – the debentures to be guaranteed by the government.

---

*   "On the whole we would not feel warranted in advising any man to buy a farm unless he had a minimum capital of $1,000. Even then he will need our assistance. Without it, $1,500 to $2,000 is little enough. The same holds good even in homesteading on government land where the land costs nothing." — *Mr. G. L. Robinson in Report of the Jewish Immigration and Industrial Aid Society, New York.*

The specific purposes for which loans may be made include the acquiring of land for agricultural purposes; clearing, draining, dyking, waterstorage and irrigation works; the erection of farm buildings; the purchase of live and dead stock, machinery and fertilizers; discharging liabilities incurred for improvements; and any purpose which, in the opinion of the commission, will increase the productiveness of the land.

The Hon. Mr. Manson, superintendent of the commission appointed under the Act, recently stated that it was already proving of advantage in securing the improvement of farms and the assistance of agricultural production. A total of 1,041 applications for loans, amounting to an average of $1,554 and a total of $2,175,445, had been received up to October 25, 1916. The loans granted up to that date amounted to a total of $234,430,* and were 144 in number. The individual loan given varied from $250 to $8,000 and the average $1,628.

The Act deals with the formation of agricultural associations, having for their object the holding of exhibitions, the purchase of seeds, plants, etc., or for carrying on any co-operative industry; also for the formation of a Farmers' Central Institute for the whole province, and of incorporated associations for the purposes of the manufacture of dairy and fruit products, dealing in all classes of farm produce, fertilizers, farm implements, the erection of buildings, cold storage plants, etc. The dividend payable in the share capital is limited to 6 per cent. Associations may join together in district exchanges for the purpose of developing and improving the industries of agriculture and horticulture.

Legislation is being promoted in Manitoba and other provinces to grant rural credit, and the Federal Government is also reported to be giving consideration to a scheme for advancing money at cheap rates to farmers.

It is questionable whether sufficient attention is being given in any of the above schemes to the importance of limiting the use of cheap money to productive purposes and not permitting the advantage of it to be conferred upon the vendor of real estate. *Speculation must first be restricted, if any scheme to advance money at a lower rate of interest than is prevalent in the open market is to succeed in achieving the object in view.*

EDUCATION AND SCIENTIFIC TRAINING

We have not been slow in Canada in promoting scientific training, and in some cases we seem to have expected too much from it. An experienced

---

* In a statement dated February 9th, 1917, it is stated that about $1,000,000 has been advanced in British Columbia under the Agricultural Credits Act.

man can often succeed where one with a good scientific training would fail. In older countries farmers hesitate to place much reliance on theory, because they recognize that skill in cultivating the land can only be acquired slowly by long experience – and often by a process of drudgery which is not congenial to the educated man. A well known English surveyor* says that farm practice in Great Britain has not altered much in the last fifty years, in spite of numerous scientific discoveries, if we omit the advances made in regard to machinery, artificial manure, etc. In defense of the farmer he says the people of the city are too apt to assume that the farmer is very conservative in his ideas and unbusinesslike in his methods. He points out the futility of sending young inexperienced lecturers with plenty of scientific knowledge but no personal experience to teach old experienced farmers about agriculture. A man who acts as a teacher should have practical experience as well as theoretical training. This is a matter which should be borne in mind in connection with technical education.

But while regard must be paid to the importance of practical experience in farming, there is no question as to the need for more industrial training and education in connection with agriculture and other rural industries. This has been recognized in Canada for many years, and, in 1910, the Federal Government appointed a royal commission to report on the subject. The importance of protecting and preserving health was the first consideration put forward by the commission. It advocated more vocational training, conservation of the interests of the rural population by education suitable to their needs, training of the girls and women in the elements of the domestic science and arts, and more participation by citizens in local administration. It pointed out the importance of encouraging local initiative and quoted Sir John Struthers, secretary of the Scottish Education Department, who said that his department "would rather have a thousand men and women in Scotland thinking and planning and striving to make the courses of study and the education meet the needs of their own communities than have 10,000 implicitly doing what the department directed."

The commissioners stated that, elsewhere, "experience showed that it was an advantage to leave the initiative, the control and administration of the general work of the school, largely in the hands of the local authority. The central authority should co-operate by putting at the service of the local body the full information which it alone could possess and the benefit of inspection, counsel and advice by experts."

---

* Mr. H. Herbert Smith in *The Principles of Landed Estate Management.*

PROPORTION OF COST OF EDUCATION BETWEEN URBAN AND RURAL DISTRICTS

The commission expressed the following opinion regarding the cost of education:

> "The cities derive the most immediate benefit from the maintenance of industrial training and technical education, and are financially better able to support it than the small communities in towns and villages and in rural districts. For both reasons a larger proportion of the cost of industrial training and technical education might and should be borne by cities than by smaller towns and rural communities."*

The above would probably be true in any country, but is especially true in Canada, where the rural population is so scattered and the production of the rural territory so necessary for the prosperity of the cities.

EDUCATION AND RURAL INDUSTRIES

The commission recommended that in smaller towns the provision at first should be in the nature of courses in industrial science, drawing and calculation, with opportunities for constructive work in wood, metals, textiles, foods or other materials appropriate to the larger industries of the neighbourhood. Out of such classes would grow classes or courses specifically appropriate for the workers in the various industries.

In the view of the commission one reason why the farmers were leaving the rural districts was to obtain a better education for their children, and it pointed out that in all progressive countries education was being adjusted to meet the needs of the children of the rural population, to interest them in rural life and to qualify them to follow it with advantage. Keen attention was also being directed in these countries to means for the instruction and guidance of the adult population. It also concluded that it was high time for Canada to recognize the difference between the primitive conditions of the undeveloped country and the complexities of advanced rural life in a democratic civilization. The way to satisfaction and success in rural life was by pooling the intelligence, the business ability and the social spirit of the neighbourhood.

Rural high schools and schools for fishermen and navigation were recommended.

---

* *Report of Royal Commission on Industrial Training and Technical Education, 1913.*

The above commission was appointed in 1910 and reported in 1913. It visited 100 places and took evidence from 1,470 persons in Canada, and it also investigated conditions abroad. It made enquiry into the needs of existing industry in respect of labour and the requirements of such labour in industrial training and education. No action has been taken on the commission's report, but no doubt this, in part, has been due to the war.

MORE COMPREHENSIVE EDUCATIONAL SYSTEM NEEDED

The great value of the educational work now being carried out in the splendidly equipped and organized agricultural colleges of Canada, of which the Macdonald College, Quebec, and the Ontario Agricultural College at Guelph, Ontario, are two outstanding examples, must not be overlooked. But this work, even when coupled with the object lessons and propaganda of the boards of agriculture, does not reach the majority of farmers and their children, and for want of social organization in the rural districts much of the value of education is lost. Some more comprehensive system is needed, and the consolidation of the rural school must be an essential part of any plan. The problems of development, as well as the science of successful cultivation, need to be discussed by the older people; and teaching in the arts of rural life, and in manual and vocational training, must be given to the children in rural districts. It has to be remembered that knowledge cannot be cultivated or enjoyed in any adequate sense by few people or by any people living in sparsely populated territory. In proportion as education is improved, the facilities for cultivating and enjoying it in rural districts must be provided, or the emigration to the towns of the best young people must continue.

As the farmer advances in knowledge, and in business efficiency as a result of that knowledge, as his revenue increases and he thereby receives a stimulus to acquire a higher measure of comfort, he will thereby become a better customer for the manufacturer.

More education and scientific training of farmers and their children is therefore needed. But how can it be given when farms are so scattered and village centres in agricultural districts are so few? How can the farm be brought nearer to the school, and the school taken nearer to the farm? Why should the potentialities of the picture house as an educational institute be so little developed in rural districts? These are no idle questions, for the solution of the land problem lies very largely in finding an effective answer to them.

SCIENTIFIC AND INDUSTRIAL RESEARCH

Under the chairmanship of Dr. A. B. McCallum, of the University of Toronto, an advisory council of experts has been appointed by the Federal Government to enquire into scientific and industrial research work in Canada and, *inter alia,* to make a study of commonly used resources, the waste and by-products of farms, forests, fisheries, and industries, with a view to their utilization in new or subsidiary processes of manufacture. In announcing the appointment of the advisory council the Government expresses the hope that it will thereby render valuable assistance to a movement the "expansion of which is not only vital to the proper develop-ment of our rich resources, but which is absolutely necessary in order to enable us to compete with progressive countries in the great race of na-tional expansion."

PROPOSED NATIONAL ORGANIZATION

In a memorandum on "Industrial Preparedness," submitted to the Prime Minister of Canada by a committee of well-known engineers, it was argued that a concerted effort should be made to determine our requirements for domestic and foreign trade and to investigate the results from an economic standpoint. "Rapid increase of population and urban concen-tration demand the creation and development of new mechanisms to provide food, clothing and habitations. Industrial enterprises must be created to support the population." A national organization is advocated, in which regard would be paid to the following:

"(a) The gathering of statistics of the products of the country as regards both quality and quantity, the conditions of production and growth, the cost of production and the cost of marketing.

"(b) An investigation as to the possibility of the economic produc-tion of any article of commercial importance not now manufactured, mined, or grown in Canada.

"(c) The most profitable methods of manufacture or growth of present or future products and the increase of output. This involves provision for research, trade schools and the intimate personal training of the farming community by means of model farms and otherwise."

The memorandum very properly emphasizes that greater use should be made of the engineer and chemist, in whose hands is the material development of modern civilization.

The Organization of Rural Manufactures

There are three kinds of development in connection with manufacture which may be organized and stimulated in rural areas. Firstly, there are the domestic or petty industries, which can be carried on in the homes of the people and consist to a large extent of the making of small articles for domestic use, souvenirs, etc. This class of industry has been successful in building up the rural districts of France and Belgium, where a large variety of manufactured articles are made in the homes of the peasant farmers. Secondly, there is the kind of development which consists of the establishment of new factories in rural territory where the existence of natural resources, including water-power and raw material for manufacture, may enable a small town or village to be extended into a large industrial centre, or may result in an entirely new town being created. Thirdly, there is the class of development which is taking place in suburban and rural areas near large cities and towns as the result of the growing tendency among manufacturers to move out from the big crowded centres in order to escape high taxation and to get room for expansion.

Some reference has already been made* to the last two movements, showing that they are natural developments only requiring to be properly organized to enable them to yield results of great national importance in connection with the distribution of population and the utilization of the resources of the country.

Domestic Industries

In regard to domestic industries carried on in the homes of the people comparatively little has been done to promote them on this continent and, no doubt, they will be very difficult to establish in a country which has such a scattered, cosmopolitan and restless population as that of rural Canada. In France and Belgium the people have been long trained to make small articles in their homes during the periods of the year when they are not engaged in cultivating their farms. They are firmly rooted in their respective localities and accustomed to practice small economies, thus being restful and contented with their simple surroundings and small, but steady, incomes. In Canada the rural population is more independent and enterprising, and less tied by family traditions and personal associations to the localities in which they live. Farms in Canada are larger than those in the European countries where domestic industries have succeeded,

---

* See pages 51-52.

and, although the economic conditions are such that a great part of the winter would seem to be suitable only for indoor occupations, it is said that farmers, as a rule, have plenty to do in the winter in connection with the work of the farm.

No doubt there is less idleness on the farm in the winter than some people seem to believe and probably there is not the same need for domestic industries in Canada as in countries where small agricultural holdings exist and the people live closer together and enjoy good facilities for distributing the products of their labour. But everything that can be done to bring agriculture and manufacture closer together and to develop, on the part of the farmer and his family, the skill and social interest which can be developed in connection with domestic industries, will be of considerable value to the country. Agriculture is the parent of manufacture and the closer identification of the two classes of industry is necessary in the interests of economic production. The farmer and his family also need the ready money which domestic manufacture would bring them, particularly in lean years and during slack seasons. More young people could be kept on the farm if there was suitable occupation for them of a kind which would develop their artistic faculties and give them a greater interest in creative work. With more intensive cultivation and increased occupation for the young people on the farms and in rural villages we would thereby be able to improve the social conditions and the co-operative facilities which can only come with increased rural population. In proportion as we could successfully develop domestic industries we would be able to eliminate the cost of distribution and waste which results from conveying small manufactured articles over long distances and we would be reducing the distances which at present separate the farmers and the manufacturers.

THE EXAMPLE OF FRANCE

Some light on the methods which are necessary to achieve success in domestic industries is thrown on the problem by what has been accomplished in France. Petty industries and intensive farming are carried on side by side in the most populous and richest parts of France, and on land less fertile than that of Canada. Referring to the social conditions and activities of France, Erik Givskov wrote in 1904 thus: "No one can travel through the French villages and hamlets without being struck by the comfort and cleanliness generally prevailing. Almost every house lies half hidden behind a thicket of fruit and rose trees, and behind the flower pots in the large windows or sitting on the threshold, as the case may be, one sees the whole family in busy activity turning out ribbons, laces, brushes, combs, knives, baskets, or whatever may be the special industry of the district." Mr. Givskov added," It is man, not land, that produces – draws forth – wealth." But satisfactory social conditions are as essential for production as ownership of the land. In Canada we need to provide the social and business organization which is as essential to secure success as the fertility and ownership of the soil.

But even the combination of good soil, ownership, agreeable social conditions, and the creation of small domestic industries are not sufficient in themselves, as has been proved in parts of Europe where these things are available. There must be co-operation and modern industrial equipment as well. Competition of small manufacturing industries with the great factories is always difficult, but proper organization and the use of water-power to produce electric energy in the villages can do a great deal to overcome that difficulty. Then there are industries in which constant change of process, individuality and artistic skill count for so much that these industries can be successfully manipulated on a small scale.

In the part of Northern France devastated by war are areas where successful small industries have been carried on by the peasant population, and where before 1914 the French peasant prospered by uniting agriculture and manufacture. Between St. Quentin and Cambrai, which, at the moment of writing, are within the zone of one of the greatest battles of history, and at Le Cateau, Caudry and Solesmes, to the south of Lille, shawls, curtains and tulle used to be woven before the war. The work was mostly done in the winter between the seasons suitable for working on the land.

Near Caudry no less than 36,000 people were said to be living on 30,000 acres of land, with the result that fine crops of sugar beet and grain were being produced from poor soil. At Sedan, in the valley of the Moselle, hand-weaving was carried on extensively, and each of 3,500 weavers owned their own house and field; earning from two to three francs per day from weaving. Bolts and nuts were also made by the men, and brushes by the women. The intelligence of the peasantry was improved as a result of being engaged in skilled industry, and they enjoyed seeming comfort and prosperity. Round Nancy and Mirecourt, in the Vosges, the women engaged in hand-embroidery and the making of lace and straw hats from imported plait, while the men made stringed instruments.

Pictured as before the war, Amiens, behind the present British lines, is a great centre for the manufacture of parts of umbrellas, shoes and ironmongery. At Escarbotin, in the northwest of Amiens, a large amount of ironmongery – padlocks, screws, safes, etc. – is made. Although this town and its environs contain only about 1,200 people, it is the centre of a population of over 40,000, distributed in small villages, and living in comfortable houses situated in large productive orchards. Each family has its cow and pig. Even here, however, is found the drift towards the towns, for there is that lack of co-operation and modern methods of manufacture which is necessary to make these small industries successful.

Between Amiens and Paris, the towns of Beauvais, Mouy and Noailles are centres of a great brush-making industry, employing about 15,000 persons. Some of the peasants live on their holdings, and work in factories in the town – one factory employs 3,000 workers and has an annual output valued at 5,000,000 francs. Boots, shoes, and hair and tooth brushes are also made in this district. The handles of the brushes are made in the homes of the workers, with the aid of electrical power obtained from the river Thérain. It is said that in this district and in Neuilly, near Paris, nearly every peasant carries on some petty industry. In the department of the Oise, in which Beauvais is situated, the value of the vegetable crops in some years has amounted to over 1,000,000 francs. At Meru, in this department, paper knives, napkin rings and shoehorns are made, and the famous French fan industry – which alone yields France about 10,000,000 francs per annum – is carried on.

At Nogent-le-roi, to the south of Chaumont, on the Marne, the peasantry make all sorts of cutlery, each peasant having his small holding and making penknives, scissors or surgical instruments in his home.

Development of Artistic Skill

The artistic skill and taste of these peasants, in providing so many varieties of useful articles from bone, ivory, horn or mother-of-pearl, is wonderful. It may be thought that it would be difficult to develop similar skill among the settlers in Canada – and so it would for a time – but, with government assistance and proper organization any difficulty could surely be overcome, and the work would be well worth while. It is only by hard work that the French peasantry have acquired their artistic qualities, but, so far as these might be a special attribute of the French race, Canada has a sufficiently large French population to make it to her interest to cultivate the taste and skill which have contributed so much to the prosperity of France. As for the Anglo-Saxon race, Mr. Erik Givskov rightly pointed out that in America and elsewhere they "have given abundant proof that under favourable conditions they are able to turn out artistic work of the highest quality and of the most exquisite taste and beauty." But for the fact that during times of peace we neglected such small industries as those carried on in France, and allowed them to become the monopoly of other countries, we should not have had to pay such high prices for many manufactured articles today and would have had healthier agricultural conditions.

Of course, industries which are successful in France may not be adaptable at all to Canada, but, on general principles, there can be no question that the combination of village industries with agriculture would be a valuable thing to promote. As to its practicability, it may be that until it is tried out, it is not wise to assume too much on that count. But allowing for intelligent adaptation of the system to our conditions, and not for mere blind imitation; considering our climatic conditions, which make it difficult for the farmer's family, even if not for the farmer, to do outside work for much of the winter; considering the opportunities there are for making useful articles out of our native materials, and the innumerable sources of water-power available to create electric energy, is it too much to say that there must be many domestic industries which could be developed? It is true that there are examples in France where the peasant farmer is earning a starvation wage from his village industry because of lack of co-operation; just as there are others where, by co-operation, the same industry produces excellent results. This only proves the need for proper business methods after the foundation of ownership and technical skill has been laid. In the basket-making industry the earnings of those who work under firms of osier planters, without co-operation, is from one-fifth to one-ninth of the earnings of those who work through their own co-operative association.

Canada is peculiarly rich in native woods, but we have not yet attempted to convert them into manufactured articles to any extent. There is nothing which illustrates the strength of petty industries in France to a greater extent than the use to which the peasants put the native woods. Great quantities of fans, paperknives, brushes, spoons, saltboxes, scales, flutes, spindles, funnels and boxes are turned out by the peasant workers in such places as Fresnaye, near Alençon. Wood is obtained from adjacent forests, each peasant having his own lathe, which he works when not engaged in cultivating his garden or his field. Carvers and makers of furniture and souvenirs are to be found in the rural districts all over France – other articles which are made are bellows, tapestry, pottery, metal work, telescopes, watches, etc. In the case of watches, which is one of the most important small industries, particularly around Lyons, it is interesting to find that, although these are largely made in the homes of the people, yet hardly any single man can turn out a complete watch – showing that even in these small industries the advantage of the division of labour is recognized. At Cluse electric power is transmitted to the homes of the watchmakers from a power station adjoining the river – and the yield of the industry in this district alone is 3,000,000 francs annually. Schools for training watchmakers have been established at Besançon, which is the great watch-making centre of France. There is no machinery used, but labour is well organized and subdivided. About 8,000 workers in Besançon produce from 400,000 to 500,000 watches every year.

These industries are all carried on in conjunction with farming, and it is this that has helped to give to France her strength of manhood, her intelligent citizenship and her enormous wealth. The present war has revealed to many how great France really is; it is no new-found strength, but the product of a combination of intelligent application to skilled industry and healthy life in the open country. As much as $240 per acre per annum is made from land cultivated by the peasant workers in some districts, so that their skill in gardening or farming does not suffer from their ability to manufacture. There must be many groups of people of different races in Canada who have had experience of some class of domestic industry while in their native countries. Under proper direction and with government stimulus and organization such people might be encouraged to start the manufacture of useful articles. A large amount of skill must be lying unused and dormant because of the absence of opportunity, thus causing an economic loss to the country.

Probably, however, the difficulties of organizing domestic industries in the homes of the people would be too great to be overcome, except in rare instances until after a period of well organized education. Perhaps the proper duty of the governments would be to organized that education rather than to artificially stimulate the starting of the industries themselves. There is no question as to the desirability of encouraging rural manufactures and, while it may not be feasible to make a beginning with domestic industries under present conditions, it is both feasible and desirable that the educational process needed to encourage rural industry and make it economically successful should be set in motion at once. The initiative in this direction must come from the governments as part of the administrative machinery directed to bring into play all the kinds of forces, facilities and organization necessary to build up a healthy social life in the country.

ORGANIZING NEW INDUSTRIAL CENTRES

While the promotion of domestic industries would be largely an artificial process, the development of small factories, groups of factories and large mills, in country districts is a natural movement which has already begun. A number of new industries are being established in Canada in rural districts remote from large centres of population. This is particularly so in connection with pulp mills, which are being located in the rural districts of New Brunswick, Quebec, Ontario and Manitoba. New towns are growing up around these mills and in some cases existing towns are being extended as a result of similar classes of development. Reference has already been made to the need for planning these new towns and the extensions of existing towns which result from the growth of new industries. The value of this industrial penetration of rural territory in helping to build up the social organization of the country cannot be overestimated and everything should be done to encourage those industries which are being developed at present and to promote other industries which would be likely to succeed. A great many minerals in Canada are capable of being converted into manufactured articles and only need the organization to enable them to be produced under sound economic conditions. A careful survey of the whole situation in regard to rural industries is urgently needed, not only to enable the government to appreciate the nature and extent of industrial tendencies, but also to enable them to forecast those directions in which successful new developments are likely to be promoted.

Opportunities for creating new industrial towns and extending existing towns is not confined to the eastern provinces. In a memorandum prepared by Dr. W. W. Andrews on behalf of the Regina Board of Trade, which was prepared for the Dominion's Royal Commission, on the subject of "The Scientific Development of the Natural Resources of Saskatchewan," reference is made to the great opportunities of the western provinces in regard to industrial development in rural areas in the future. Dr. Andrews points out that the laboratory experiments and analyses in Saskatchewan show that they have clays from which can be produced the finest of egg-shell chinaware, porcelaines, pottery, glasses, brick and tiles, which only need cheap fuel to enable them to be manufactured on a commercial basis. He advocates that in the case of pottery a beginning could be made in the manufacture of souvenir pottery in some of the towns, a line of manufacture which might go far to meet a deficiency that is always apparent to visitors to Canada, namely, the absence of any choice in home-made materials which are distinctive of the country and suitable for souvenirs. In many countries an enormous trade is done in small manufactures of this kind.

Dr. Andrews draws attention to the remarkable developments in the great extension of the use of liquid fuel in automobile and other engines. In Canada we used 15 million gallons of gasoline in 1915. The present alcohol output of Canada, if reduced to concentrated motor spirit, would equal five million gallons, and if all the alcohol factories were used to manufacture motor spirits, they would only provide a third of the liquid fuels required. The present high cost of gasoline is having a serious effect upon many industries; e.g. Dr. Andrews claims that at least fifteen hundred of the six thousand tractors on the farms of Western Canada were idle last spring because it was not profitable to run them. According to his estimate, this represented a loss of 1,800,000 bushels of wheat.

It is known that alcohol may be profitably used as a fuel in automobiles and if, by its manufacture, we can secure a reduction in the cost of liquid fuel and, at the same time, the utilization of by-products of our industries, the matter is one which requires urgent attention on the part of a research commission. Sawdust, straw, potatoes, artichokes, injured wheat, etc., can all be employed for the purpose of manufacturing commercial alcohol for motive power. From the potato we can also get meal, dextrin, glucose, pure albumen and valuable cattle feed. When we consider the enormous yields of potatoes which can be obtained under intensive culture in nearly all the provinces, we have an indication of the important connection between agriculture and what may prove to be one of the largest of the new industries of the country. The matter has only been incidentally referred to here, because of the opportunities which this and other forms of industrial expansion will provide for developing new towns and generally decentralizing manufacturing industries. The matter of the manufacture of alcohol from farm produce as a means of helping agriculture and checking the excessive growth of cities has been referred to in a memorandum prepared by the Assistant to Chairman of the Commission of Conservation. It was shown in that memorandum that, as a result of the German policy, the consumption of industrial alcohol rose from 18,976,500 gallons in 1895 to over 39,000,000 gallons in 1906. It is claimed that this laid the foundation for the chemical and industrial supremacy of Germany in many lines of manufacture and gave a great impetus to agriculture.

With regard to other new forms of industry in the western provinces, Dr. Andrews points out the need for textile fibres for binder twine, sacking and linen paper. Attention has been drawn by Messrs. Arthur Little & Co., on behalf of the Canadian Pacific Railway Company, to the value of flax for making paper and fuel.

The Promotion of Industrial Decentralization

The tendency of manufacturers to erect factories and mills in rural territory is not, however, confined to those who want to be close to their raw material and in touch with water-powers. As stated in Chapter II of this report, the decentralization of manufacturing industries is taking place on a large scale around existing cities. This movement requires to be stimulated and organized. Perhaps the largest development of this kind which is taking place in the United States and Canada is in connection with the great steel mills of the United States Steel Corporation. When this large company contemplates the erection of new mills they usually acquire a site in rural territory, within easy reach of some large centre. They not only purchase land to build their mills but sufficient to erect a town for the accommodation of their workers, as well as for the population likely to be attracted to supply the social needs of the new town. New towns have been created in this way by the Steel Corporation at Gary, Ind., and in the suburbs of Duluth, Minn.

In Canada the Corporation has acquired a large area of land adjoining the towns of Windsor and Sandwich, in southwestern Ontario. They propose to erect their works on this site, lay out a model town, and provide the whole of the public services, local improvements and social organization needed for the building up of a healthy community. Before any building took place the area was incorporated as the town of Ojibway. These movements of the Steel Corporation, and other large concerns, form part of the modern tendency of manufacturers and population to disperse over wider areas. Unfortunately, it is accompanied by speculation of the worst kind on the areas immediately adjacent to the town sites acquired by these corporations. All round the towns of Gary and Ojibway land has been subdivided on a large scale and real estate subdivision has been carried out in such a way as to largely nullify the good effects of the efficient control exercised by the Steel Corporation over its own estates. The absence of proper regulations over these suburban excrescences of new industrial towns leads to disorderly and unhealthy development of the worst kind. The responsibility for this condition rests with the provincial or state governments and rural municipalities, who alone have the power to regulate it. The granting of a charter by the Ontario Government to Ojibway should have been accompanied by some measure to regulate adjacent development and to prevent haphazard, unsightly and unhealthy conditions being created round its boundaries. This was a case in which no money had to be expended to remodel or reconstruct built upon areas, but only common sense exercised in preventing bad conditions being established. Unfortunately nothing has been done and unbridled speculation in subdivisions has been proceeding all round Ojibway. Every advance made in subdividing the land is adding to the difficulties that will have to be encountered to secure proper sanitary conditions and the prevention of slum property being erected. Land will be built upon which cannot be drained or served with water and in the course of time the general community will be called upon to remedy at great cost a set of evils that are the product of neglect and indifference in the initial stages of development.

The Ontario Government has been appealed to by numerous municipal representatives and associations to pass a planning and development act which will provide for the effective control of these new developments, but the matter is still in abeyance.

In England the movement on the part of the manufacturers to emigrate from crowded centres to rural districts has been a strongly developed one for over thirty years. Many large works formerly located in London and other large cities, have been moved out in that period, and industrial villages created to accommodate the workers. The two best known cases of this kind are the developments which have taken place as a result of the building of the new factories of Messrs. Cadbury at Bournville and Messrs. Lever at Port Sunlight. Messrs. Cadbury moved out from the city of Birmingham and acquired a site large enough to build a new village as well as their factory. The result has been one of the healthiest and most efficient industrial developments in England. The village has been established on a paying basis and there is freedom from undue paternalism – hence its great success. The Port Sunlight scheme is architecturally superior to Bournville, but is more paternalistic in its management. The benefit of these schemes is not only the great advantage conferred on the workers and their families by their improved environment, but the financial gain they have been to the manufacturers, by giving them more efficient and healthy employees, and, by providing them with adequate space to erect healthy and roomy factories and to permit of extension, as required, to meet the growing needs of the industries. But these villages have been surrounded by undesirable building development on the land not owned by the manufacturers. Government authorities in both England and Canada have so far failed to secure the same standard of public health and amenity under public regulations that some private corporations have obtained and have been prepared to pay for, as a business proposition.

As a result of the realization of the need for greater agricultural production, and for lessening the cost of distribution in England new advocates are now coming forward in favour of a greater stimulus being provided to this movement. Those who, only a few years ago, saw the rapid growth of this industrial tendency, and appreciated the great opportunities it provided for improving health and securing greater efficiency, had to encounter much indifference and even considerable opposition from people having conservative or ultra radical ideas in regard to land development. Among the earliest and most active advocates of decentralization and co-operation in industry in England was Earl Grey, before he became Governor General of Canada, and the Right Hon. A. J. Balfour, both of whom lent their support to the movement for industrial dispersal at the Bournville conference in 1901. But there has been slow progress in England in giving any government stimulus or leadership to

PLATE XIV   WOODSTOCK, N.B.

The healthiest and most prosperous conditions in Canada exist in the large number of small industrial towns situated in the midst of good farming country, where the lands adjacent to the towns have not been destroyed for productive use by injurious speculation in building subdivisions.

Photo by courtesy of Immigration Branch, Dept. of Interior

the movement which, if it had been more actively encouraged, would have resulted in enormous benefit to the country at the present time. Nevertheless it has to be acknowledged, that the achievements of England in regard to the healthy distribution of its industries, and the regulation of their surroundings in town and country, have probably been greater than in any other country in Europe or America.

Among the latest advocates of the industrial penetration of rural districts in England is Mr. Theodore G. Chambers, F.S.I., who read a paper before the Surveyors' Institution, England, in January 1917, advocating the movement as a means of solving the problem of rural depopulation. He argued that the tendency to purchase supplies of food in foreign markets could be considerably reduced by dispersing the industrial population over wider areas and taking the market to the producer. The significance of this contribution to the subject is that it is apparently put forward by one who has not been in touch with the organized movement for industrial decentralization which has been a more or less active force in England since 1901, and has succeeded to a greater extent than Mr. Chambers appears to realize. What he calls "the industrial penetration of rural districts" can only be successfully attained by the creation of what are known in England as "garden cities." The garden city movement in England is an organized attempt initiated by Mr. Ebenezer Howard, in 1898, to establish new industries in rural territory and to move industries from crowded centres to rural and semi-rural districts. That movement has achieved a great measure of success in spite of the fact that it has been hampered by want of capital and of the government aid which it should have commanded.

The creation of single industry towns or suburbs has serious defects and, as a rule, either leads to paternalistic control in order to secure health and efficiency or, alternatively, to the kind of disorder and haphazard development which follows from unhampered speculation. Many new towns with adequate capital behind them have been a complete or partial failure because of one of these weaknesses. In some cases, like that of Pullman, failure has been caused by excessive zeal of the promoters in attempting to control the social welfare of the workers and, in other cases, the failure has been due to the tendency to go to the opposite extreme and leave the workers at the mercy of their own ignorance and of speculators in real estate.

THE GARDEN CITY FORM OF DEVELOPMENT

The garden city form of development has the advantage of avoiding the evils incidental to single-industry towns and of providing for the intermingling of both urban and rural life. Most of the other model villages and garden suburbs are purely urban developments, but a distinguishing feature of the one garden city at Letchworth is that a definite part of the estate which has been acquired for the scheme is set apart for agricultural purposes. The general objects of the scheme are as follows:

(1) The purchase of a large agricultural estate, on which to establish an industrial and residential town, principally by securing a concerted movement of manufacturers from crowded centres.

(2) *The restriction of the area set apart for urban development and the permanent retention of the greater portion of the estate for agricultural purposes.*

(3) The planning of the whole area, in order to secure health, amenity, convenience and efficiency.

(4) The limiting of the dividend to shareholders to 5 per cent per annum; the balance of the profits to be used for the benefit of the town and its inhabitants.

In a previous work of the writer* it is stated that the scheme, among other things, will have the effect of promoting the agricultural industry in the district in which it is established by bringing the market to the door of the farmers, providing security of tenure, establishing small holdings, promoting co-operation and giving the rural labourer accessibility to the social attractions of the town. It is pointed out that the lack of public control over the building of towns and the scarcity and dearness of urban land, due to the system of land tenure, and the natural selfishness of the land owner, are among the chief causes of overcrowding; and that the wider distribution of urban populations should be encouraged.

Large cities entail huge expenses for distribution, and even in England, with its closely settled population, and good means of communication the producer does not receive an adequate proportion of the price paid by the consumer. Among the causes of rural depopulation in England have been absentee landlordism, isolation of the farm land from the market, intensified by high railway rates and undue growth of cities; absence of co-operation among farmers, and national neglect of agriculture in matters of education. In Canada these impediments are further aggravated by the speculation that has taken place and the necessarily scattered nature of the rural population.

The aim of the garden city movement, as set out in the above objects, may be described as the marriage of town and country. The scheme has

---

* *Garden City and Agriculture*, 1905.

now been in operation since 1903, and has made substantial progress. It has suffered, however, from the lack of sufficient capital, without which an experiment of this kind cannot be made a rapid and pronounced success. For the purpose of starting the scheme a number of properties were purchased in the county of Hertford, making up a total area of 3,818 acres; an additional area of 750 acres has since been acquired. When purchased by the Garden City Company in 1903 the estate comprised fourteen separate agricultural holdings. About 1,300 acres, or approximately one-third, were set apart for the building of the town and for open spaces, and the remaining 2,500 acres (now about 3,300 acres) were definitely reserved for agricultural purposes for all time. (Figure 35).

Including legal and other expenses the Letchworth Estate cost about $225 per acre. This was not only for bare land but included valuable buildings and timber of a gross insurance value of about $125 per acre. In 1905 it was estimated that the part of the estate reserved for the townsite should be calculated as having cost $325 per acre and the agricultural estate $175 per acre, both figures being subject to a reduction of about $62.50 per acre, as being a fair allowance for the capital value of improvements. Thus the cost of the bare building land might be put at $262.50, and the agricultural land at $112.50. It was presumed that an average rental of about $7.50 per acre per annum for land and buildings and $5 per annum for land without buildings would be fair to the farmers and provide a satisfactory return to the Garden City Company.

The situation of the estate was 33 miles from London, with no large city intervening. At the time of purchase there was approximately a population of 450 people – all engaged in agriculture – and no railway station on the property. The population now numbers about 13,000, and there is a splendid new station in the centre of the town. The company has, in addition to existing county roads, made 10 miles of new roads and provided 20 miles of water mains, 15 miles of gas mains and 14 miles of sewers. The ground rents created up to 30th September, 1915, amounted to over $38,000 per annum, equivalent to a capital value of about $760,000. The net profit in 1915 was $28,600, showing that the experiment has begun to pay its way, although it is well known that in connection with land development it is essential that capital should be sunk for a considerable period before yielding a profit, unless in the case of a purely speculative enterprise. The number of inhabited houses, factories and workshops is about 2,500. There are some 30 industries established in the town, engaged in engineering, printing, embroidery, book-binding, pottery, weaving, motor engineering, metal works, organ building, implement and scientific instrument making, etc.

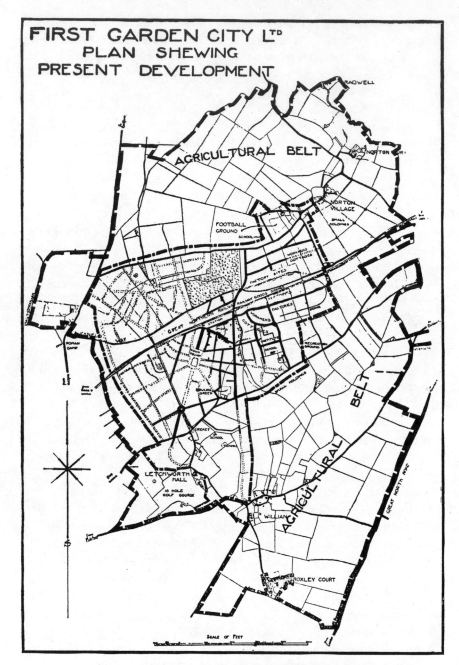

FIGURE 35   LETCHWORTH GARDEN CITY

The town area is shown within the boundaries of the broken line. Streets already made are in
solid black, the proposed streets being in dotted lines. The agricultural belt is reserved permanently
for agricultural purposes. All the factories are concentrated in one part of the town.

Not more than twelve houses are permitted to be erected on any one acre, and the average is approximately about half that number. All new buildings which have been erected are connected with sewers and water mains.

When the town is completed the population will number about 35,000. The city will not be permitted to expand beyond the area delimited for urban development, unless as a result of the process of jumping over the agricultural belt and forming new urban developments beyond the rural area. Thus there can be no separation of the urban and rural parts of the scheme, which affords an example of a kind which is unique in the world.

Another scheme, which may be referred to as an example of the extent to which the garden city movement has influenced the development of private estates, is that of Knebworth, belonging to the Earl of Lytton. The new town, which was planned in 1908, will be practically in the centre of the Knebworth estate, of which the greater part will be reserved for agriculture. This scheme is, of course, not a social experiment, but merely has the advantage of proper planning and building regulations imposed by the owner. (Figure 36).

These movements indicate the importance which is attached in England in recent years to the linking up of urban and rural classes of development and the intermingling of agriculture and manufacture. The greatest success achieved by the garden city so far has been in demonstrating to the British people the value of organization, proper planning and healthy conditions of life for those engaged in industry. Education by means of such an object lesson is convincing and effective. In Canada we are greatly in need of an object lesson as a means of educating our people on the subject of the right kind of development. In spite of the rapid progress that has been made in removing prejudices against any control by governments over development of land and the erection of buildings, and in spite of the gradual realization that unhealthy housing conditions, the separation of town and country and the congestion of industries, do not pay, there is need for a practical demonstration of the value of good development so as to convince the man in the street.

Probably the garden city movement points the way to the soundest kind of scheme that could be developed for the purpose of dealing with the problem of the returned soldiers, which is alluded to later.* There should be no difficulty in starting a garden city in Canada as an experiment, but such a scheme could only succeed if there was adequate capital available and if the main objects of the Garden City Association were adhered to.

---

* *Chapter VIII.*

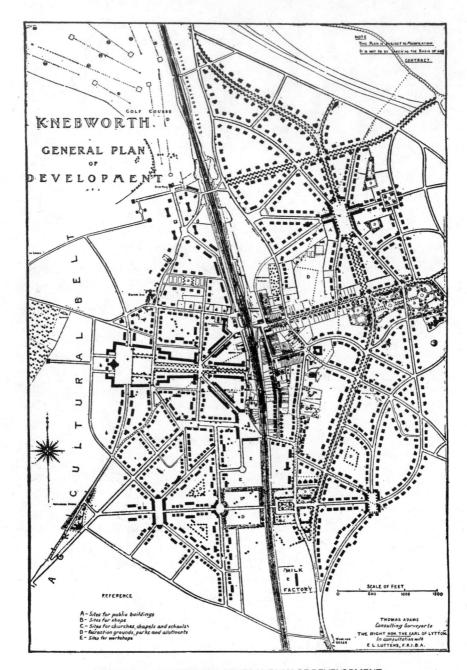

FIGURE 36   KNEBWORTH GENERAL PLAN OF DEVELOPMENT

Plan of a new town on a country estate with agricultural surroundings. The small lots near the railway were laid out and sold before the plan was prepared and this greatly hampered the subsequent development.

The lack of capital has prevented the English Garden City from becoming as quickly successful as it would otherwise have been, and if the company had had two or three million dollars to start with, instead of about $500,000, there can be no question that much better results would have been achieved. On the other hand, any temporizing with the objects in order to serve some speculative purpose, would inevitably end in failure.

The town of Walkerville, Ontario, or at least the portion of it which has been developed under the guidance of Messrs. Hiram Walker & Sons, has important features in common with the garden city type of development. The grouping, arrangement and durability of the buildings, the paving of the streets and the preservation and development of natural features, in this town, make it compare favourably with the model village of Bournville and Port Sunlight in England.

Started as a one-industry town, it is gradually losing that character, to the injury of its amenities, although possibly to the advantage of the community in other respects. What has been accomplished by Messrs. Walker is only feasible where land speculation is prevented and where there is adequate control over development. The contrast between the well-balanced and orderly development on the Walkerville estate with the scattered and disorderly development outside its boundaries indicates how far short government regulation is of attaining the best business standards of a private company in the matter of land development.

But the peculiar distinction of Walkerville, as compared with other model communities, is that it affords us an example of that combination of manufacture and agriculture which is a leading feature in the Letchworth scheme. Immediately surrounding the town of Walkerville, and lying largely in the adjacent township areas, are large farms comprising thousands of acres which are controlled and worked by Messrs. Walker as part of their business.

A large dairy industry has been established on these farms and, in addition, there are 2,400 head of feeding cattle. These animals use up the by-products of the distillery, and, by this means, great waste or loss is avoided and the soil of the surrounding territory is much improved in fertility. What is practicable for a private firm in such a case should not be beyond the power of governments. Such limitations as a private scheme may have can be removed in public schemes without lessening the economic soundness of the method. It is by having a more definite link between manufacture and agriculture that we may expect to achieve the best results in the way of stimulating production in Canada as Prince Kropotkin has said, "both these industries are inseparable and the combination and integration of both brings about the best results." It is by this means that the welfare of rural and urban industries can be promoted and that the economic distribution of the people can be secured, instead of having them crowded in large cities on the one hand or doomed to unhealthy isolation on the other hand.

INDUSTRIAL, SOCIAL AND CIVIC WELFARE

It is a mistake to assume that it is only in the rural districts that there is need for means of social intercourse for the great body of industrial workers. Social life is best stimulated and social intercourse is most easy in the comparatively small town. Most of our small towns, however, are deplorably backward in regard to the planning and development of their streets and public spaces, and the control of building construction. Towns and villages should be more than a collection of houses, stores and factories; they should be places in which the residents can take a pride, where the beauties of nature are protected and unsightly billboards are prohibited. One of the reasons why factories are being moved out from large cities into country districts is due to the desire on the part of the manufacturers to obtain better recreation facilities for those whom they employ. In this matter they are not entirely selfish; but, however much they may be actuated by altruistic motives, their main object arises from enlightened self-interest. They know that it pays to have good environment for their work people, and that they cannot acquire good sites for the dwellings and plenty of recreation space in the crowded cities. If these things pay the manufacturer, how much more will they pay the communities which are desirous of attracting manufacturers or of keeping existing factories in their localities? Manufacturers would rather have good facilities and pleasant surroundings provided for their work people than have to take the trouble and invest the capital necessary to obtain these things for themselves. It is only because they are dissatisfied with existing methods of development by urban and rural councils that they enter into the business of town development themselves, although they would prefer to confine their attention to their own particular business.

In the city of Cleveland, there is an Industrial Welfare Department of the Chamber of Commerce, and in several factories in Canada there are social welfare secretaries who are giving their whole attention to the work of providing social opportunities for the employees. This kind of organization of industrial life should not be left to the manufacturers. The employees have always a suspicion of the paternalistic employer. The duty of promoting industrial welfare outside the factory in connection with the homes of the people, the provision for recreation for the children, etc., should be dealt with by the community as a whole. Such matters are

PLATE XV   A CANADIAN FARM

Farmers are in such close contact with nature that they are perhaps less appreciative of natural beauty than those whose lives are spent in the drab city, but it is not true that farmers prefer ugliness to beauty.

Photo by courtesy of Immigration Branch, Dept. of Interior

usually best managed by voluntary associations, such as a civic or village improvement association, formed for the purpose of promoting community welfare. The council of a municipality, is necessarily absorbed in the task of managing the business affairs of the community, and it is usually found that the care of amenity, and the work of making a town or district more pleasing and beautiful, protecting rivers from pollution, caring for rural cemeteries, and organizing village or town festivals, can be best promoted through a democratic but voluntary organization. Village improvement associations have been successful in many parts of the United States and have done much to improve community life and to advance the welfare of industries. They should be a feature of every town and village. In Canada a Dominion Civic Improvement League has been formed, for the purpose of promoting the welfare of the citizens by the study and advancement of the best principles and methods of civic improvement and development, and by securing a more effective public interest in municipal affairs. One of the objects of this League is that it should be a link between civic improvement associations in all the cities, towns, villages and rural municipalities in Canada. Local associations should be formed in all urban and rural districts and should devote themselves to the conservation of their industrial and physical resources, the preservation of beauty, the securing of increased production from the soil and the development of a healthy community and national life.

Whatever may be done by governments to promote the right foundations for healthy development, it is essential that the people themselves, who have to live in the rural districts, should organize for the purpose of improving their social conditions. No doubt the chief hindrance to this being done in the past has been the defective character of the original development that has taken place and the lack of proper facilities for intercommunication. Improvement in these things, however, must be accompanied by an increased desire on the part of the people to benefit from them. The self-seeking individualist must be taught to realize that real prosperity cannot come without co-operative effort, and that co-operative effort involves that the people shall have the spirit of co-operation and also regard for promoting the social life of the community.

One of the most hopeful signs of the times is the growing interest of farmers in the amenity of the farm – in the making of farm homes more healthy and attractive to live in and the surroundings of farm buildings more orderly and pleasant. In Quebec and other provinces the farmers are being encouraged by the Board of Agriculture to improve their environment by means of competitive awards, with excellent results of a far-reaching kind.

Every step which a farmer takes to make his homestead more pleasant helps to make him a more useful citizen and a more permanent settler. The pride which he takes in his crops is a seasonal pride; it comes and goes with the crops and the only permanent impression it leaves behind is a possible balance in the bank account; but when, from year to year, he sees his soil becoming more clean and fertile, his fences more tidy, and his buildings more trim and substantial than before; when the trees he has planted grow up to be both useful and beautiful, and when the community of which he is a member is benefiting from his example, he begins to enjoy that sense of pride that comes to all men who create permanent things. He becomes more closely wedded to his farm, makes it more interesting for his family to remain upon it, and develops his own citizenship.

Farmers are in such close contact with nature that they are perhaps less appreciative of natural beauty than those whose lives are spent in the drab city, but it is not true that farmers prefer ugliness to beauty or are vandals at heart.

There are some farmers, as there are some city dwellers, who scorn beauty, rather because of a habit of mind that counts only the material value of things and not because of any lack of taste. That habit usually dwindles as settlements grow older – it is stronger in the new west than in the older east – but it is a real pity that it exists, as much of the difficulty in keeping healthy-minded people on the land is due to the disorder and ugliness of village settlements. Failure more often than success accompanies ugliness and disorder.

The work now being done by the Federal Government in helping with tree planting in the western provinces will one day be appraised as one of the most valuable contributions to the social welfare of the west. Already thirty-one million trees have been given free from the nursery station of the Department of the Interior at Indian Head to establish 31,000 plantations on the prairies, and another five million will be given this spring. That the farmers appreciate this work is shown by the fact that up to this year it has been extremely difficult to keep up with the demand. Trees cool the air in summer and provide shelter in winter; they add to the value of property and purify the atmosphere in towns.

There are other directions in which the improvement of social life in the village and rural districts is urgently needed. One is in making the surroundings of the schools more pleasant and in providing ample and well furnished recreation places for the children. In New Westminster, British Columbia, good work is being done to make school surroundings attractive and interesting. Progress is also being made in different parts of the country in the organization of boys' and girls' clubs, school gardening, etc. Perhaps to achieve real success in these directions in rural areas, schools will have to be consolidated to a large extent, but a great deal can be accomplished by planning the land in such a way as to improve the means of communication between the farms and the schools.

The development of more village centres in the country would also enable provision to be made for the establishment of picture houses as a means of entertainment and public education. Some kind of co-operative organization is necessary for this purpose as, under present conditions, picture houses cannot be made to pay even in towns of two or three thousand inhabitants isolated from large centres. The absence of more accessible medical aid for the women and children of the country districts, and of many other advantages which the town possesses as compared with the rural districts, are the result of the present scattered and unsatisfactory method of development. The need for these advantages will continue and will have to be dealt with by organization, no matter how we plan. But, for the most part, the organization of rural life and rural industry must begin with the laying of a proper foundation by those who have the power to plan and develop the land. If once this foundation is properly laid, and the rural population have the facilities provided to enable them to organize and develop their social life, they will do so as successfully as is done in any other country. The opportunities must be provided and the conditions of settlement properly organized under government leadership, after which the more that is left to the people to do for themselves, the better it will be for the country. This statement is of course subject to the qualification that government initiative must continue to be exercised and extended in the direction of improving education. Just as one of the deplorable effects of the present haphazard land system is that it hampers educational progress so one of the most beneficial effects of a properly conceived and scientific system would be that it would give facilities for carrying on a more aggressive and comprehensive educational policy. The better training of the Canadian citizen, simultaneously with the better training of the immigrant before he is permitted to settle on the land, is of vital importance in connection with the building up of a sound organization of rural life and in promoting industrial and social welfare.

CONCLUSION

The contentions in this chapter may be briefly summarized as follows: That the character of the social structure it is desired to build should be kept in mind in laying the foundation by means of proper plans of development; that the improvement of agriculture and rural conditions generally cannot be effectively attained without the extension of co-operation, and of facilities for obtaining cheap capital, education and scientific training, as part of the organization of rural life; that good progress is being made in Canada with the aid of the Federal and Provincial Governments in extending co-operation, rural credit and education, but that this extension is inadequate to arrest depopulation, to improve living conditions and to increase production owing to the original defects of the system of land settlement; that the existing tendencies of manufacturing industries to move out to, or become established in, rural areas indi-' cates the direction in which government stimulus should be provided to secure a closer combination of manufacture and agriculture, to bring the producer nearer to the consumer, and to provide opportunities for education and social intercourse in rural territory; that the establishment of garden cities and the promotion of domestic industries in rural areas should be encouraged as the best means to promote a healthy and economically sound system of development; and that national and local progress in the future will largely depend on the extent to which we promote education and industrial and civic welfare in the small towns and rural districts.

CHAPTER VI

ORGANIZATION OF RURAL LIFE AND RURAL INDUSTRIES

Commentary by Tony Fuller

Thomas Adams was a visionary planner. He held strong views on agriculture and industry at the turn of the twentieth century, and these views matured into thoughtful planning advocacy by the time of the First World War. He combined a planner's view of the problems in rural life, especially the conditions that prevailed in agriculture, with an imaginative set of suggestions for their improvement. This discourse forms the core of Chapter VI, in which Adams deals with the organization of rural life and industry. Adams was well read, conversant with European opinion, and full of ideas about how to apply external experience to Canadian issues. Most importantly, he presented a clear record of agriculture and rural life in the first ten years of the twentieth century.

Most rural histories are of great interest, at first, because of what they convey to us about the past and because they show, in many ways, how certain issues and conditions prevail today. In this respect, historical treatises are like mirrors, for they reflect the origins of our current dilemmas and give us food for thought about the way issues have emerged and been dealt with. It is always surprising how many features, issues, and ideas in the social and political landscape of the past have prevailed today. This adds the second layer of interest: the sorting out of the subtleties of what has changed in substance and what has essentially remained the same. The work of Thomas Adams is a wonderful example of both levels of interest for those concerned about rural issues in Canada, today or yesterday.

In Chapter VI, Adams does not follow one theme. Through general international comparisons, Adams shows that access to capital, the promotion of domestic industry, central planning, better rural-urban relations, and the reorganization of rural schooling would all greatly improve the rural economy. Significantly, all of these subjects are found in the rural development discourse today and can be used as organizational headings to review contemporary conditions in rural Canada.

The imperative of co-operation – a central thesis in Adams' work – refers to co-operation among farmers, the value of co-operative societies, and the prospect of co-operation among rural industries. Adams viewed co-operation as a nation-building activity. When he wrote, the co-operative movement had become international in scope, and it was appropriate to consider how co-operation could be promoted in rural Canada to spur rural industry, consolidate agriculture, and develop ideas of community. These themes were also present in the rural discourse of the United States (Williams 1926).

It is evident that Adams saw co-operation as an organizing principle for many aspects of economic and social life. He observes that "co-operation in mutual liability engenders mutual trust," and notes that the co-operative movement in Canada is strongest in Saskatchewan and Quebec. These are the centres of vibrant co-operative associations even today. Although new generation co-operatives such as those associated with housing, food, and bicycle sharing are more urban-focused, the co-operative movement is still alive and active in rural areas across Canada. Other long-lasting highlights of the Canadian co-operative movement are Antigonish in Nova Scotia and Evangeline in Prince Edward Island.

The story of agricultural co-ops since the time of Adams is one of great success. The massive wheat pools, the insurance association known as the Co-operators, and the credit unions have all prospered in rural Canada, to the point where many of them resemble corporate operations rather than co-operative associations. New generation co-ops tend to be small and are especially important for helping fledgling groups reach a size that enables them to do business effectively, whether accessing low-cost supplies or marketing their products. Many new generation co-ops are service-oriented and in the future may provide an alternative solution to service provision in rural and remote parts of Canada. Community-based wind energy generation may well be the next venture in which farmers and rural citizens alike engage in under the co-operative banner.

Agriculture was in poor shape in the first decade of the twentieth century. Adams saw mainly structural problems and "attitudinal" problems among farmers. He noted that Canadian farmers had small-scale operations and felt that this inhibited the progressive farming he had witnessed in Europe. In *Rural Planning and Development,* he laments the lack of enterprise and invokes the ideas of Adam Smith to point to a lack of individualism among Canadian farmers. His observations seem, however, to contradict his assumptions about the value of co-operation as the overall organizing mode of development. He points to the two models of organization – the collective and the individualistic – current at the time. The two models today are less in contention, but collective action and resistance to change are still issues among farm organizations throughout Canada. In retrospect, Adams seems to have been lamenting the lack of intensive farm enterprise that characterized European farming at a time when much of Canadian farming was already destined to be more extensive and market dependent (Fuller 1984).

One of the main causes of problems in agriculture, according to Adams, was the lack of access to capital. He recognized the absence of a central borrowing service, the reluctance of the private sector to invest in agriculture, and the lack of initiative by farmers themselves. This situation has changed appreciably in the intervening period. A centralized agency, Farm Credit Canada (formerly the Canadian Farm Credit Corporation) has been servicing farm debt for several decades and, together with the central banks, has made credit more available. In the early 1980s, it could have been argued that there was too much credit available to those who suffered financial ruin at a time when annual interest rates rose above 20 percent. There is little doubt, however, that the massive capitalization of farming, particularly in the period after the Second World War, was fuelled by greater access to capital in the agricultural industry in general. And access to capital is still an issue today.

Adams felt that increased education and training opportunities would help farmers to develop more industrial practices. He suggested that the agricultural colleges at Sainte-Anne-de-Bellevue, Guelph, and Truro, although doing good work, were not sufficient to meet the needs of a progressive industry. Interestingly, the extensive college system that grew up to do exactly what Adams suggested is now shrinking as demand by the farm community declines in the face of a changing industry and alternative job opportunities for farm youth. The state has also relinquished its role as promoter of this type of nation building. Most agricultural advisory services have now been abandoned to the private sector. Today, public education and training programs, such as the Community Futures program, are directed more explicitly to community economic development (Fuller, Larsson, and Pletch 2010).

In contrast to education and training, research investments in the agriculture and food industry have steadily increased in the past and represent a major investment by the public and private sectors. Research is focused on the food chain, and food health and food safety are the main areas of concentration. Biotechnology absorbs the other major share of research investment. State intervention, a central theme in the work of Thomas Adams, is now more subtle. Today, the federal state is geared toward managing the terms and conditions of international trade, providing safety nets, and investing in research to develop the knowledge economy. At the provincial level, the state is increasingly concerned with regulating land use and the environmental conditions of the agricultural industry. It is significant that the environment was not a consideration for Thomas Adams or for any of his contemporaries.

The most advanced form of advocacy put forward by Thomas Adams was based on his analysis of the opportunities for industrial development in rural areas. He wanted to see, throughout rural Canada, industrial development in the form of factories and associated businesses. He saw opportunities in rural areas close to existing cities, where he felt cheap land and abundant labour supplies were comparative advantages for industrial growth. Adams felt that industrial growth was a key component of the "great race of national development" (page 225).

Adams saw three opportunities for industrial development: (1) home industry, (2) factories in new towns close to the supply of raw materials (single-industry towns), and (3) suburban industries. One of the most interesting ideas that Adams promotes in this book and other work was the concept of home industry: adding value to farm products and using artisanal skills to produce crafts and goods of local and regional value. Such activities could be carried out on the farmstead as the job of farming continued. Adams argues that home industry would engage underemployed labour in the farm household and counter the seasonality of grain and crop farming. He illustrates the value of this practice by referring to the European model, which he saw as highly diversified and resourceful.

The domestic industry model described by Adams never took hold in Canada. He was an advocate for the very thing that many settlers felt they had escaped by coming to the New World, where specialization beckoned as a means to earn a good living and contribute to the "feeding the world." The Canadian family farm industry adopted the full-time farming model and rejected the pluriactive farm household model that is prevalent in Europe today (Brun and Fuller 1991). It is curious, however, that over 60 percent of Canadian farm households derive more than 50 percent of their income from non-farm sources (Fuller and Bollman 1992). The dominant image of farming as a full-time occupation in Canada may explain why the idea of multifunctionality – farmers receiving payment for their farm products from the market while receiving a payment from the state for providing public goods and services – is not well received in Canada. Looking to Europe for new ideas, models, and incentives was not popular in Adams' time, and it is not part of the farming modus operandi today.

Single-industry towns became the main focus of rural growth after most of the accessible farmland had been settled in Canada. Early versions of single-industry towns were company towns, in which almost all the economic and social needs of the labour force were supplied by the mining company exploiting the natural resource in the area. Such towns, made up of company houses and a company store, often suffered boom and bust cycles and housed highly transitory populations. Today, the labour force for new mines and natural resource operations is flown in and housed on a temporary basis. New towns with attractive living conditions for families, such as Tumbler Ridge, British Columbia, are probably a feature of the past (Sullivan and Halseth 2004).

Suburban growth is an important phenomenon today and promises to be the main form of development in the early twenty-first century. Suburban areas today house more Canadians than central cities, in direct contrast to Adams' time, when fully two-thirds of Canadians lived in rural areas (Ehrensaft, Gertler, and Fuller 1990).

Although rural populations and economies in periurban areas benefit from suburban growth, it is hardly a development model for rural Canada as a whole.

There are only three metropolitan areas in the country, and it would be a sad response to Thomas Adams' hopes for a vibrant rural Canada if growth occurred only in these three zones. It remains to be seen if the same suburbanization phenomenon will take place in medium-sized or second cities, a development that would certainly extend some of the benefits to rural Canada. Yet there will continue to be rural and remote areas that need the attention more. Whether suburban growth will draw immigrants from overseas or migrants from remote and other rural areas in Canada remains to be seen.

Certainly, Adams' vision of factory-led, capital-intensive suburbanization is now being realized. Many of the types of industry that Adams believed would be important are also part of the new growth paradigm today. Adams viewed energy as a future problem and was an advocate for experimentation with bio-fuels by the end of the First World War. Although the materials for biofuels are produced in rural areas, value-added processing facilities are generally located in suburban areas adjacent to metropolitan centres.

The negative consequence of suburbanization, however, is commuting. Various means of transportation make it possible to live in one community and work in another, with implications for local development and community and social cohesion. Almost all of the problems faced in rural Canada today are mentioned by Adams.

Clearly, when Adams called for the "organization of industrial centres" in rural areas, he did not envisage the suburban-industrial model and its consequences, especially as driven by the conditions of the new economy and the pre-eminence of the distribution economy. Distribution of consumer goods and services requires massive transportation industries, good roads, and all the attendant services that make a distribution economy efficient and effective. Many of the economic benefits accrue to rural communities – for example, truck ownership and trans-portation services are growth sectors in many parts of rural Canada. This example, however, suggests the dilemma of rural planning: should the benefits of growth come at the expense of the social or physical environment?

Has Thomas Adams' dream of an integrated agricultural and industrial economy been realized, at least in southern Ontario? It has come at a price. But then what profound change has not? Many changes recommended by Adams – municipal amalgamation, health care reform, and school consolidation – have occurred in the past twenty-five years. Whether activated by the unseen hand of capitalism or as accidents of an unplanned economy, elements of Adams' vision have come true, at least in the southern and suburban parts of rural Canada. Thomas Adams' vision of a strong Canada was a rural vision built upon the mainstay of industry. In large part, his vision has come to fruition, but not with the same ethical out-comes that Adams anticipated. The continued internationalization of trade in agriculture has given different signals to the research and education community, for example. Is there really a global food crisis or merely a food distribution problem? Industrialization, on the other hand, has slowly become a reality in several different forms, from single-industry towns to suburbanization. Thomas Adams would have had mixed feelings about the state of rural Canada today and would no doubt call for renewed efforts to stimulate more co-operation and invention to overcome the apparent problems. A renewed effort in rural planning would have certainly been at the top of his list.

REFERENCES

Brun, Andre, and Anthony M. Fuller. 1991. *Farm Family Pluriactivity in Western Europe.* Streatley, UK: Arkleton Trust.

Ehrensaft, Philip, Michael Gertler, and Tony Fuller. 1990. "Sustainable Rural Communities in Canada: Issues and Prospects." In *Proceedings of Rural Policy Seminar 1,* ed. Michael Gertler and Harold Baker, 1-41. Saskatoon: Agriculture and Rural Restructuring Group.

Fuller, A.M. (Tony), and Ray D. Bollman. 1992. "Farm Family Linkages to the Non-Farm Sector: The Role of Off-Farm Income of Farm Families." In *Rural and Small Town Canada,* ed. Ray D. Bollman, 245-68. Toronto: Thompson.

Fuller, Tony. 1984. *Farming and the Rural Community in Ontario.* Toronto: University of Toronto Press.

Fuller, Tony, Lars Larsson, and Carolyn Pletsch. 2010. *An Evaluation of the Community Futures Program in Canada and the LEADER Program in Europe.* Sudbury, ON: Industry Canada.

Sullivan, Lana, and Greg Halseth. 2004. "Responses of Volunteer Groups in Rural Canada to Changing Funding and Services Needs: Mackenzie and Tumbler Ridge, British Columbia." In *Building for Success: Exploration of Rural Community and Rural Development,* ed. Greg Halseth and Regine Halseth, 310-37. Brandon, MB: Rural Development Institute/University of Northern British Columbia/Canadian Rural Restructuring Foundation.

Williams, James Mickel. 1926. *The Expansion of Rural Life: The Social Psychology of Rural Life.* New York: Knopf.

CHAPTER VII

Government Policies and Land Development

*The functions of government in connection with land development |
An Imperial land settlement scheme | Canada a great business
enterprise | Devolution of power to permanent officials | Federal methods
and administration | Proposals for a new federal department | National
development in other countries | Provincial organization of land
settlement | Unorganized territory | Organized territory: Provincial
administration of local government | Cost of local government | Government
stimulus to rural manufactures and mining | Improvement of highways
and control of railway development | Government policies and land
speculation | Colonization by railway companies | Need of a constructive
policy in regard to scientific training and research and industrial housing*

THE FUNCTIONS OF GOVERNMENT IN CONNECTION WITH LAND DEVELOPMENT

THE functions of government in a civilized society are exercised by two main groups of governing authorities – national and local. In Canada our national government is apportioned between a federal and nine provincial legislatures, and our local or municipal government is carried on by councils of county, city, town, village, township or rural municipalities, the latter differing in name according to the terminology used in the different provinces. Outside of the machinery of government, as thus defined, we have commissions, boards and other chartered bodies with definite duties assigned to them by the elected authorities. The policies of all these groups of governors are indirectly controlled by the electors, to whom they are severally responsible.

All classes of government are concerned, *inter alia,* in the duty of securing that land will be planned and developed so as to promote the best economic uses of the resources of the country and healthy conditions of life for its citizens. Under the British North America Act the Federal Government has no direct control of local and municipal affairs – this being the function of the provincial governments. But the Federal Government, as owner of large areas of land in the western provinces; as the authority which has the greatest responsibility in connection with immigration and with the settlement of a great part of the new population, and as the body which deals with the principal means of distribution by waterway, by railway and by mail, has the greatest power in the Dominion and, therefore, the largest responsibility, in connection with questions of land settlement.

We have seen that when land is not properly planned social evils arise in connection with its development which are costly to remedy. Governments have to apply remedies to secure the removal of these evils at immensely greater expenditure than would have been necessary to prevent them in the early stages of development, with the result that they simply lessen effects without removing the causes which are responsible. In a country like Canada, where civilization is only in the formative period and where we are only at the beginning of development, it is absurd to argue that it is too late to start to remodel our system of land settlement in the light of the experience we have gained. Nor need our efforts to correct the mistakes of the past be diminished because we use the lessons they teach us to prevent the recurrence of similar mistakes in the future, in respect to the areas that are still undeveloped or are in course of development.

To diagnose social evils and interpret causes with any degree of accuracy we must first take the trouble to ascertain such facts as are available, and we must get out of the ruts of the theoretical extremists who have persuaded themselves that any one solution will meet the needs of our complex social problems.

Governments may do more harm than good by tampering with the natural tendencies of social development after the first stages are past, and by attempting to influence its later stages in the direction of what is called socialism or individualism. Some good may come from efforts to subsidize development of resources or any particular form of industry, but it is just as easy for these efforts to produce harm – for industry may suffer deterioration as a result of coddling, as well as individuals; and social life may be stimulated at too great an expense to individual life. When we have to deal with human society there must be compromise between social and individual ideals. *If we would only apply sound social principles to the early stages of our individualistic system of developing land, we would be less in need of applying socialistic remedies of doubtful value in the later stages.*

Governments should lay the foundations correctly and provide the skeleton plan for the building up of the social system; after that the strength and beauty of the structure will be the greater in proportion as the citizens themselves have been able to do the building without government aid, but subject, of course, to government protection of personal rights and constraint of personal wrong-doing.

The first object in rural development should be to make rural life healthy and rural industries profitable. The user of the land should be encouraged to secure for himself the full benefit of his enterprise and energy, subject only to the discharge of his social responsibilities and obligations.

An Imperial Land Settlement Scheme

The vague proposal which has emanated from a group of public men in England, and which, as it is described in the press of Canada, has for its object the "liquidation of the war debt" of the Empire by the development of the untapped resources of Canada, is evidence of the fact that some men of high business attainments view the question of land development from an entirely wrong standpoint. Canada needs more capital, and, if the British Treasury will provide any such sum as $200,000,000, as is suggested, to develop the western lands, it will benefit both Great Britain and Canada. But no profit from the expenditure could be expected other than a reasonable interest on the money invested, together with a gradual return of the capital, otherwise the scheme would be economically unsound for Canada. It would simply be a repetition on a large scale of the blunder of the speculator who has tried to grow rich out of selling lands, and found that his chief success lay in keeping lands out of production. Real wealth can only be produced by the user of the land and, in proportion as the profits of rural production are absorbed by governments, corporations or individual speculators, beyond what is necessary to pay a reasonable interest on capital, or to give a return for value received, the source of wealth is cut off by making the industry of land cultivation unprofitable.

Canada a Great Business Enterprise

New countries like Canada have more to do with the work of directing the growth of their social organizations than older countries, which are in a more settled condition and have comparatively few natural resources to develop. The governments of Canada are engaged not merely in administering the law and regulating public conduct; they are jointly engaged in one of the most stupendous business enterprises in the world. In the performance of such a task it is of the highest importance that the business side of the undertaking should be in skilled hands, that the control of all beginnings of development and of the utilization of resources should be under the direction of the highly qualified administrators – responsible to political heads but with discretionary power to act within certain limits prescribed for them by the governments. The objection that is sometimes made that the placing of more reliance on skilled administration will lead to bureaucratic control is usually voiced either by men who are interested in conserving power in their own hands or by those who fear the effect of more efficient management in curtailing their profits from vested interests. The successful democracy entails two kinds of trust – trust in the people by their rulers and trust by the people and the rulers in their public servants – both forms of trust, in the words of an eminent statesman, being qualified by prudence.

DEVOLUTION OF POWER TO PERMANENT OFFICIALS

According to Sir George Murray, the present system of transacting public business in Canada imposes an intolerable burden on ministers; the growth of government business can only be met by the division of labour and the devolution of power, unless it is permitted to become less efficient or to break down. In any sound system of departmental organization it is necessary, in his view, that the minister shall confine his attention to laying down a line of policy to be adopted by his department, leaving the administration to his subordinates.* In his investigations into the public service of Canada Sir George confined himself to the Federal service, but had he made similar investigations in the provinces and the municipalities he would probably have found that one of the weaknesses of Canadian government, in all its ramifications, as compared with government in older countries, was the condition under which elected rulers were required to take upon their shoulders too many of the burdens of administration. The sound system to which he referred prevails in English government, where the executive details in the national and local governments are left to departmental heads, leaving the elected superiors time to deal adequately with questions of policy. One result of this system is that an efficient permanent staff of expert administrators has grown up in the old country, in all classes of government, and matters of technical detail are dealt with more largely by experts. The tendency in Canada in administration has been to adopt the American system of mixing up legislative and administrative functions in such a way that there is no clear line of demarcation between them. This has been an effect in preventing land

---

* *Report on Organization of the Public Service of Canada,* by Sir George Murray, 1912.

development to be controlled as efficiently and economically as it could have been under a sounder system of national and particularly of local administration.

FEDERAL METHODS AND ADMINISTRATION

Whatever methods and administrative machinery may exist or be adopted by the Federal Government for planning and developing the territory over which it exercises direct jurisdiction as owner, or in connection with the planning and development of lands held by private owners – over which it exercises the supreme powers which are vested in a national government – these methods are certain to have a great influence on those adopted by lesser authorities, corporations, and individuals. Moreover, whatever action the Federal Government may take in extending or in restricting the means of distribution, or in controlling and directing immigration, may have the effect of stimulating either good or bad conditions of land settlement. The results of Federal methods and action in the past have been more or less satisfactory and criticism of them should be tempered with recognition of the difficulties which have had to be surmounted.

The building up of a new country in any other part of the civilized world has probably not been carried out with fewer mistakes or with less political corruption than is the case in Canada. But even if we could claim that the methods and action of past governments were the best that could have been devised, that is no reason why they should not be made the subject of reform if, as a result of the practical experience we have gained, and in consequence of new conditions that have arisen, we are now able to detect the imperfections of the system we have hitherto pursued. "The science of government," says Macaulay, "is an experimental science and, like all other experimental sciences, it is generally in a state of progression." Referring to political progress in England he said: "The very considerations which lead us to look forward with sanguine hope to the future prevent us from looking back with contempt for the past. We do not flatter ourselves with the notion that we have attained perfection and that no more truth remains to be found."

Progress involves change in matters of government and in matters of administration as in other things; and when proposing changes for the future we may be showing more respect for the past than if we blindly assume infallibility for any system that happens to prevail at the moment, even when it has attained a measure of success.

The form of surveying and planning which has existed in this country since it was borrowed from the United States has had its day, and whatever merit it may possess has been fully exploited. Now we are face to face with

certain facts and conditions that show the need for modification or extension of that system. To carry out effective reforms may require some addi-
tions to administrative machinery – in the Federal as well as in the
Provincial Governments.

As already stated, the Federal Government is not only a government in
the ordinary acceptation of that term: it is the owner of vast possessions
in real estate and national resources. Towards that estate and these resources it has a double responsibility; first, that of managing and planning
them to the best advantage as an owner and, second, that of controlling
their development and use in the interests of the people as a whole. Is
the character and efficiency of the organization we now possess adequate
to enable the Federal Government to control and influence that development to the best advantage? To fully answer that question would involve
going into details of the administrative methods and machinery now
existing, a task which is outside the scope and purpose of this report. What
may be done is to repeat the contention that there does not appear to be
any national task so important, so complex, and requiring such skilled
organization, in Canada, at the present time, as that of the proper management and development of the human and land resources of the
country. Further, we may make the suggestion that to adequately perform
that task, in respect of land and other resources, and in respect of immigration, probably means that one department of the Federal Government, with the assistance of such provincial and municipal boards or
commissions as may be needed to deal with such vast areas, should concentrate entire attention upon it. Only after such a department – or a
branch connected with the existing Department of the Interior – was at
work for some years could the ground work be prepared to secure a proper
system of planning, settling and developing land.

While it is perhaps beyond the power of any one to promulgate the
details of the kind of system to be followed, with the information now
available, that does not mean that there are no obvious steps which cannot
be taken at once to make experiments along lines that experience has
shown to be sounder than those that have hitherto been in operation; it
does not mean that every effort should not now be made to direct such
system as we have, or can employ, so that the final purpose of securing
conservation and development of human resources will be kept more
prominently in view.

Proposals for New Federal Department

From other quarters suggestions have been made as to the need for setting
up a new Federal department to deal with settlement and immigration.

In order to obtain uniformity throughout the Dominion, and get over the difficulties created by dual Federal and Provincial control in the different provinces, it has been proposed that a consultative or land settlement board, representative of the Dominion and each of the provinces, should be appointed to act as an advisory council to the proposed new department or commission. Mr. C. A. Magrath, Chairman of the International Joint Commission, suggests that such a commission should comprise three members and be non-political in its personnel. A feature of some of the proposals is that a Director-General of Emigration, with headquarters in London, should be attached to the department to direct emigration from Europe. The need for attention being given to this question of government organization is undoubtedly pressing and of vital importance to the country. Social and economic questions in Canada are only now coming to the front; after the war they are certain to be forced upon the attention of every statesman and party.

It has been declared that the Federal immigration policy has failed to secure appreciable results to fill up vacant lands which are owned by speculators.* Obviously, however, it is no easy task to formulate a policy which will be practicable, equitable to owners, and of certain public benefit. That an inventory and classification of such lands should be made goes without saying and that some policy of purchasing, subdividing and re-selling vacant lands should be adopted as a matter requiring careful consideration after the inventory and classification is completed. But between the two stages of making the inventory and re-selling the land the most important duty of re-planning them under expert advice, so as to make settlement permanent and stable, should not be neglected. The variety and complexity of the problems to be dealt with during all these stages have been indicated throughout this report.

Sir George Murray, in the report already alluded to, referred to the wealth of the natural resources of the country and expressed the doubt whether adequate steps were being taken to preserve and develop these resources. His advice was that in dealing with the question of great complexity which would arise in laying down a policy in such matters, it would be necessary to treat them from a comprehensive point of view and with the assistance of the highest technical and professional skill. In this connection he referred to the appointment of the Commission of Conservation as a first step towards the comprehensive treatment of the important question of the development of natural resources, and suggested that the Commission should be a thinking, planning, advising and training body, with no executive functions, and should examine and report on every

---

* *Regina Leader,* April 12, 1917.

scheme affecting natural resources, whether promoted by the government or by private parties, before it is sanctioned by Parliament.* The Commission cannot direct its attention to any task of greater importance than that of suggesting plans for the future development of the natural resources, including land in town and country.

NATURAL DEVELOPMENT IN OTHER COUNTRIES

The creation of the Development Commission in Great Britain in 1909, to act in co-operation with the British Boards of Agriculture, in promoting the resources of the old country, is evidence of the need, even where land conditions are more fully developed than in Canada, for some special organization to concentrate on problems of development. The Development Commission was formed and provided with a large grant of money to aid and develop agriculture and rural industries by promoting scientific research, methods and practice of agriculture, co-operation, marketing, forestry, reclamation and drainage; and to improve rural transport, harbours and fisheries. Under Part II of the same Act a Road Board was formed for the purpose of improving the facilities for road traffic.

The United States Congress discussed a National Colonization Bill in February, 1916, to develop the welfare of wage-earners in the United States, and create new opportunities for permanent and profitable employment. The bill provided for the creation of a Colonization Board to examine, survey and classify lands. After selection of areas the bill proposed that the board has to make or cause to be made a detailed plan of development and colonization. In the words of the bill:

> "Such plan shall, in each case, provide for the necessary clearing of the land, for the construction, maintenance and operation of the roads, ditches and other reclamation works necessary to make the land accessible and cultivatable, for developing and supplying timber, coal, power, telephone and other services to settlers for their domestic use, for organizing facilities for purchasing, marketing and other co-operative activities, and for securing any other improvement or services necessary for the efficient organization and development of any community to be colonized on the location."

---

* The Dominions Royal Commission on the Natural Resources, Trade and Legislation, seems to take a different view, and to approve the co-ordination of executive and advisory functions in the administrative departments of the Government. — *Fifth Interim Report of the Commission*, p. 51, par. 186.

The project had to offer a reasonable presumption that the soil and other physical conditions, and the markets and other economic conditions, would permit of immediate, continuous, permanent and profitable employment for the settlers. A colonization fund of $50,000,000 was proposed for the purpose. The Hon. Robert Crosser, in evidence before the committee on the bill, referred to the "dog's life" of the western settler without any community co-operation. The land under the scheme would remain government property, and tenants would pay interest on the land value and improvements.

The administrative functions of most of the land departments of the Australian states are to some extent decentralized, by a division of states into districts, in each of which there is a land office under the management of a land officer. Under this decentralization scheme it is possible to properly classify the lands according to situation, character of soil, etc. In all the states Acts have been passed to facilitate the purchase of alienated lands for the purpose of improving and re-settling them. Under the closer settlement acts of the Australian states, 2,717,463 acres of land in the Commonwealth have been acquired at a cost of $51,553,145, and of these 2,223,808 have been allotted in farms. The settlement of village communities is provided for, but comparatively little has been done in this respect. Proposals have been put forward during the past year to appoint district surveyors to prepare more detailed surveys and plans in advance of settlement, as has been advocated in this report.

In New Zealand there is an interesting village settlement system, designed to enable labourers to acquire small holdings varying from 1 to 100 acres, on which to erect their homes near to their work, but there has not been much advance made in extending this system.

In South American states community settlement under government control and assisted by government organization has met with some success. The general land law of Argentina (1903) relates to the founding of colonies and towns and provides that land has to be surveyed, classified and planned, and that the government executive *"shall reserve such tracts as may be found appropriate for the founding of towns and the establishing of agricultural and pastoral colonies."* The work of directing settlement in Brazil comes under the Board of Immigration and Colonization. Before lots are colonized a field survey has to be made and a general plan drawn up. Where building development is likely to occur a proper town plan has to be prepared. The government of Brazil recognizes the importance of selecting land with a view to securing its full economic use and the health of the settlers. Colonies are established on the most fertile lands, with facilities for water supply and means of communication and occupying *"an economical location."* Among other forms of aid rendered by the government is the giving of free food, free medical care, free seed, etc., during periods of varied length. Homesteads vary in size according to character and location. Those near a railway do not exceed 61.78 acres and in other cases the size is 123.6 acres. In 1914 the Board had established twenty colonies, which are reported to be very satisfactory.

Experience in colonization in all the new countries referred to has apparently led them to devote a large amount of government attention and effort in recent years to secure closer settlement, and to plan and select land that can be put to profitable use. The point that seems to have been originally overlooked in all new countries – and still is, to a large extent – has been that land settlement was a great business requiring scientific organization and the guidance and direction of experts, just as much as any other great enterprise. The anxiety to get settlers was greater than the anxiety to get land properly settled; it was easy to hand out titles to homesteads and to select rectangular areas on paper plans; and what happened to the settlers afterwards was regarded as the business of the settlers themselves, so long as they fulfilled their paper obligations. All these countries are beginning to learn that different methods are needed to secure prosperous settlement. They are realizing that the evils produced by the easy-going methods of the past, are trifling compared to what they will be in the future. National competition is going to be keener in the coming years and the nations which will prosper most will be those which, having adequate natural resources, will use science and skill to manipulate them to the best advantage. Science and skill coupled with sound business organization needs first to be applied to the seemingly simple, but really difficult and complex, problems of land settlement.

The development of our rural civilization in Canada requires that one of the most urgent duties of the governments is to assist to a greater extent than hitherto in making the business of agriculture more successful, and to do so on sound economic lines. *But before the business of agriculture can be made generally successful it is first necessary to intelligently carry out the business of land settlement in accordance with proper schemes of development.*

PROVINCIAL ORGANIZATION OF LAND SETTLEMENT

What has been said regarding Federal administration of land settlement and other matters, applies generally to provincial administration. It is unfortunate that there is no uniform system of controlling immigration and settlement in force in all parts of the Dominion. There is inter-locking of interests and overlapping between Federal and provincial institutions, which has been the chief cause of many defects in connection with the development of land and the system of government, although the latter, in most other respects, is admitted to be sound in principle. It is not suggested that this lack of uniformity and overlapping can be avoided, but an endeavour should be made to minimize their effects as far as possible by co-operative means.

A leading highway engineer and land surveyor in Saskatchewan writes as follows, in April, 1917, with regard to the overlapping of Federal and provincial administration of land settlement and highways:

"The difficulty of securing any action in the way of improvement, as far as Saskatchewan is concerned, lies in the division of authority, the Federal Government having control of the Crown lands and the provincial authorities being concerned with the roads. There are too many absurdities in the present system, and the chief one would seem to be that a branch of the Dominion Government should make the survey of the township, including the road allowances with which the government is not concerned, and the provinces must accept the roads so laid out and make the best of what, in the northern and surveyed parts, is a very difficult situation.

"It has been chiefly due to their connection with the problem of amending the badly located road allowances that the surveyors have come to realize the faults of the system. In my own experience, gained in six years' work on highway location and improvement in practically every part of Saskatchewan, I have found that, in hilly and rough country, *the road allowances are not only useless for miles at a stretch but, by their very existence, are a detriment to the location of roads in the natural and most economical position.* Local opinion is always strongly against any departure from the system of road allowances other than is absolutely needful in order to avoid some insurmountable difficulty."

All governments derive their power from the people, and what are the most efficient methods to apply that power within legal limits should be adopted, as far as possible, even where it means the strengthening of one branch of government at the expense of another. In those provinces in which the Federal Government is not responsible for the administration of Crown lands there are still vast areas of land available for colonization. More co-ordination would appear to be desirable between the colonization, highway and municipal departments of these provinces, so as to secure more efficient and scientific land development. In the first place, no definite line can be drawn between colonization and highway administration if the planning of the province as a whole is properly undertaken; and in the second place, the fact that unorganized territory has in course of time to become organized suggests that the municipal department of each province should have a definite policy, and the power to give effect to it in regard to the system of land development, so that the system will provide the right conditions for municipal organization. Provincial and municipal governments are primarily responsible for the control of land development after the possession of the land has passed into private hands. They have the control of the use of the land so far as that use may affect the health of the people or influence taxation. The evils which arise from private property in land are too frequently of a kind which are produced by no other form of private ownership; and take the form of the owners being permitted to enjoy possession of their rights without having demanded from them the obligations which these rights entail.

It may be claimed that no province has properly safeguarded its future which fails not only to keep an up-to-date plan of its system of transportation by waterway, railway and highway, but also to maintain an expert staff continuously at work preparing schemes for the extension and improvement of that system, and acting in co-operation with the municipalities in controlling land development.

In defining the highway system of a province different methods have to be pursued, according to whether territory is organized or unorganized, but whatever steps are taken to administer these different classes of territory there should be a director of surveys co-operating with a director of planning, responsible for the complete scheme of development for the province. The skilled department should be in a position to prepare the plan of main arterial highways, to properly plan the area so as to secure the best agricultural development, and to approve or disapprove all plans for the subdivision of such territory and all schemes for the laying out of new townsites.

The regulations respecting the subdivision of land in Saskatchewan indicate the kind of powers already being exercised outside of comprehensive planning and development legislation. The regulations are issued under Section 7 (a) of the Public Works Act, and not only apply to new towns and cities, but to the subdivision of all land outside the corporate limits of towns and cities. It is required that a preliminary plan shall be made of the subdivision and presented to the Director of Surveys for his approval. Such plan shall show the location and dimensions of all streets, lanes, public reservations, etc., and contour lines showing every difference of five feet in the elevation of the land. The Director of Surveys has power to approve or disapprove of the plan. As a condition of his approval the plan must show a part of land, which must be at least five per cent of the total area being registered, and in no case less than two acres, for the purpose of dedication to the public for schools or other purposes. An extravagant rule is laid down that no street shall be less than 66 feet wide

PLATE XVI   FRUIT RANCH, VERNON, B.C.
Photo by courtesy of Immigration Branch, Dept. of Interior

PLATE XVI   MAITLAND DAIRY FARM, ANTIGONISH, N.S.
Typical views of different kinds of farming land in Canada. Land should be classified and planned according
to character and economic use.
Photo by courtesy of Immigration Branch, Dept. of Interior

and no lane less than 20 feet wide, and every lot having a frontage of 55 feet must be provided with a lane. The Director of Surveys may draw up a street plan for any area to be subdivided and when the preliminary plan of the owner is submitted for approval the Director may require the plan of subdivision to conform to the plan so prepared by him. He may also alter the street plan from time to time where the acquisition of public land in parks, railways, etc., makes a change desirable, or may make amendments on consideration of requests from the owners. While these regulations are satisfactory in general principle, they are defective in detail, since they insist upon too high a standard of width of streets and a waste of space in laying out the towns, which would involve any ordinary community in more expenditure for local improvements than it is possible for them to meet.

For purposes of provincial government territory may be considered under the two main heads of unorganized and organized territory.

Unorganized Territory

In unorganized territory the control of local administration is vested directly in the Provincial Government. This being so, the successful development of such territory should be an easy matter, since there is supreme power in the hands of one authority.

In such territory classification of land, the direction of settlers to the most fertile and accessible districts, the adequate planning of the land for economic use, the construction of the necessary drainage and roads before settlement in accordance with topographical surveys, the provision of proper water supplies and the securing of close settlement are all matters which simply depend upon the kind of management in force and not on any lack of legislative powers. On every hand these things are admitted to be desirable in the interests of proper development and stable social conditions. Representative bodies are constantly passing resolutions in provincial centres favouring improved facilities for better planning, co-operation, marketing of products, good roads and rural credit. As we have seen, commissions appointed to study education, unemployment and the cost of living have come to the conclusion that rural problems cannot be effectively solved without improved rural organization. But one point which is usually overlooked is that improved rural organization cannot be provided in any comprehensive way under our present system of land development, and, in the absence of a scientifically arranged system of highways. The tendency has been to approve of the need of comprehensive co-operative organization but to ignore it until after settlement has taken place, when it is too late to get the advantages to be derived from it. In the past the organization which has preceded settlement has usually been confined to that which is sufficient to attract people to the land, and to secure accurate measurement of the areas. In some cases this is being added to by efforts to train the settlers, to give them some means of communication, and to assist them financially. But, with all these advantages, success cannot be achieved because of the original handicap that sufficient skill has not been applied to the laying out and classification of the land.

Dr. B. E. Fernow, in his report on the *Conditions in the Clay Belt of New Ontario,* expresses the opinion that the experience of the less prosperous parts of Ontario will be repeated in the clay belt unless efforts are made to control development and to classify land for farming purposes. He gives extracts from the reports of the township surveyors of one hundred townships to show that 20 per cent are poor and not fit for farming purposes, 40 per cent are of medium quality, and 40 per cent are deemed first class.*

This clay belt comprises about 16,000,000 acres of land which, in the opinion of the Provincial Department of Lands, Forests and Mines, is estimated to be suitable for farming, and in *Bulletin No. 11,* published by the Timiskaming and Northern Ontario Railway Commission, it is stated that there is no place in Ontario where bigger crops of hay, roots, barley, peas and wheat can be grown. On pages 5 and 6 of the bulletin it is stated that the best quality of settlers are being attracted to this territory, 90 per cent being English speaking. "The greater part of them are from Old Ontario, and there are a great many of them from the United States as well, and the greatest part of the remainder are the pick of the immigrants from England, Scotland and Germany."

We thus see that the soil of Northern Ontario and the character of the settlers are all that can be desired, while the Ontario Government appears to be willing to spend large sums in making roads and other improvements. But the results, in spite of all these advantages, do not appear to be satisfactory.† This is probably due to the fact that sufficient money is not spent before settlement, that the land is not properly planned and classified, and that a stereotyped system of surveying is permitted to take the place of a series of proper development schemes. The provincial governments have greater power to make or mar the future of unorganized territory than the municipal governments which follow them. Most of the evils of

---

*   *Conditions in the Clay Belt of New Ontario,* Commission of Conservation, 1913, Appendix 2.
†   See pages 77 and 198-200.

bad development are created in the initial stages, when nothing but proper organization and planning are needed to prevent them.

The suggestion was made by the Ontario Commission on Unemployment that, to make closer settlement plans effective in Ontario, it might be desirable for the government to withdraw Crown lands now open for settlement and to re-open other districts best suited for intensive cultivation. This might be a desirable course to pursue in all the provinces, and certainly there is need for consideration being given to the improvement of all old settled areas already equipped with railways and roads. Small expenditure in these areas, in reclaiming swampy land and in improving roads, would probably yield more permanent results than the same expenditure in new areas. The whole matter requires thorough investigation and a complete survey of conditions.

As evidence of the want of efficient administration of Crown lands in some provinces, we have such an admission as was made in the report of the Crown Land Department of New Brunswick for 1915; wherein the Hon. George J. Clarke, Minister of Lands and Mines, stated:

> "At present there is no information in this department bearing on the extent of our Crown lands, nor have we any data as to the value of the forests. Producing as they do the largest revenue return of the province, more up-to-date methods should be taken in the management of the Crown lands."

In some western provinces there are local government areas called "local improvement districts," with an organization of a simple character, which seems to be suitable for more general adoption in Canada, to secure a more gradual building up of the local organization. In the future more reliance should be placed on local machinery, but this should be accompanied by more and not less activity by the province in supervising municipal affairs, with the assistance of a skilled department.

There are two classes of development in unorganized territory which have to be dealt with. One is the agricultural settlement, which is directed either by the Federal or a Provincial government or by railway or land companies to whom grants of land are given. The second is the development of towns and villages and the laying out of townsites on land which has been alienated from the Crown. With regard to the former, there does not appear to be any doubt that the greatest need in new territory is to concentrate development on as small an area as possible and within easy reach of existing means of transportation. Only in very special circumstances should settlement be permitted in isolated districts remote from railway communication. Comprehensive plans should be prepared of portions of each province, for the purpose of showing the topography, classifying the land, and determining the order in which different parts of it should be opened for settlement. The principles on which such land should be settled will probably vary in different parts of the country because of the different local conditions. It should be one of the main objects, however, to secure that homesteads should not be granted in more than one township in the same district until two-thirds or three-fourths of that township was taken up for settlement, and that the townships opened up first should be those nearest existing centres of population and railways. Instead of giving so much land away the government should make the farms smaller and devote more capital to making good roads and assisting with the clearing of a larger percentage of each farm. A plan of each township should be prepared, with special regard to its topography and at least one good connecting road made in accordance with the plan, between the farms and the village centre or railway depot. To prevent squatters from settling upon unplanned and isolated land, thereby becoming a menace to the community owing to the danger of fire, and causing difficulties in organizing consecutive development, it should be punishable for anyone to occupy land without government authority, except in such locations as the government may determine.

In many districts settlement has to be encouraged at a distance from the railways and village centres because there are often large areas of marshy, rocky and unfertile soil adjacent to these railways and centres. But a great deal of this land could be made suitable for cultivation after the expenditure of a comparatively small sum for drainage or some other kind of improvement. But it requires less organization, less skill and less expenditure to deal with the land that is naturally adaptable for agriculture than that which requires artificial improvement. Because of the unwillingness to meet the cost of such improvement the settlement is permitted to be scattered and "buffer" areas of intervening land are created between the settlers and their marketing facilities. More effort should be made to secure settlement on some of the crown lands near railways which can be converted into good farming land at a reasonable cost for drainage.

The question of draining land is not only important in the above connection, but is also of great importance in connection with the improvement of large areas already settled. There are many farms which are just drained enough by natural means to make them workable, but more drainage is needed to improve their fertility to the point of making them really profitable to their owners. In some of the older parts of organized territory large areas of land which are close to markets and good means of communication have long remained sparsely settled because of the proportion of these areas which is water-logged or marshy in character.

Much of this land is of the most fertile kind, but, for lack of government policy to promote its improvement, it has to remain in what is practically an idle condition. Private capital is not available to improve it on any large scale. Such land should either be purchased by governments, as is done in Australia and other countries, and sold for re-settlement, after being improved; or government aid on liberal terms should be given to owners to make the improvements, subject to re-payment of principal and interest over a period of years. Large sections of the best land in England, which is today producing the finest market garden crops, especially in the fens of Lincolnshire and Cambridgeshire, have been reclaimed by drainage. The cost of drainage of such land is less on the average than the irrigation of dry land, and probably more permanent results can be obtained.

It has been demonstrated in the farm work of the Dominion Board of Agriculture that seeding should be completed as early as possible in the spring in order that good crops may be obtained and, owing to the climatic conditions in Canada good drainage is essential to permit of early seeding.

In regard to the subdivision of land for building purposes in unorganized territory, there has been great laxity of proper regulation in the past in Canada. Land and railway corporations have been left too much to themselves as to the method of locating and laying out townsites. Legislation, in the form of planning and development acts, as hereinafter described, is needed to enable the provincial governments to deal with this matter in a uniform way in both organized and unorganized territory.

ORGANIZED TERRITORY:
PROVINCIAL ADMINISTRATION OF LOCAL GOVERNMENT

In organized territory, where the machinery of municipal government has been set up, the objects to be achieved, in regard to land open for new settlement, or land which is in such a condition that it is desirable that it should be re-settled, are precisely the same as in unorganized territory. But the methods have to be different, because two governing authorities have jurisdiction instead of one. A municipality has no control over Crown lands and, being the creature of the province, it is circumscribed in its legislative power; but in Canada it has very wide local powers, both as a legislative and administrative body.

In each of the provinces there is some kind of provincial machinery to deal with local government. In some cases the administration of local affairs is spread over a number of departments, but in one or two provinces attempts have been made to obtain concentration and uniformity of administration. There are departments of municipal affairs in three provinces and a local government board in Saskatchewan. It cannot be said, however, that any province in Canada has a fully equipped municipal or local government department in the sense that prevails, for instance, in Great Britain. The need for such a department has often been urged as a means of securing greater uniformity and improved administration of municipal finance.* It is equally needed as a means of enabling more effective control to be exercised over the planning and development of land.

Although the systems of local government in most provinces of Canada were originally founded on the British system, the two countries have been drifting apart during the last forty years, in this respect. In Canada local government has been subject to a powerful influence of United States precedents, although conditions in the United States are constitutionally quite different from those in Canada, and municipal government has not been a uniform success in the former country. In Britain the whole municipal system has been overhauled during the past forty years and, since the formation of the Local Government Boards in England, Scotland and Ireland (the first in 1871) municipal government in Great Britain has developed to a state of remarkable efficiency. A close study of the British municipal institutions should be made before any large measure of reform is introduced in Canada. It will be found to be not only efficient but economical and democratic. Its defects in the past have been chiefly due to its neglect of the problem of land development, but an effort is now being made to remedy this defect under town planning legislation. As an American writer has said, however, nowhere else is municipal government more successfully administered than in England.

The British Local Government Board is the great loan sanctioning authority; part of its function is to specialize in the kind of knowledge and experience which enables it to prevent serious local mistakes and wasteful expenditure; it is the supreme authority in connection with the planning and development of land; its experts hold public hearings in relation to most proposals affecting expenditure by local authorities; it is the head of an extensive and uniform audit of municipal accounts; it is

---

* The following resolution was passed at the First National Conference of the Civic Improvement League of Canada, held in Ottawa in January, 1916; and numerous other organizations in Canada, including the Associated Boards of Trade, have adopted similar resolutions:

"It is hereby resolved to recommend each provincial government to create a department of Municipal Affairs, whereby the best expert advice will be placed at the disposal of the municipalities and proper control will be secured over municipal finance, and in view of the great need for uniformity in sanitary and town planning administration and the exercise of economy in regard to municipal business, we urge the desirability of early steps being taken to have such a Department created in each province."

the administrative body under the public health acts and drafts all by-laws relating to streets, buildings, fire prevention, etc.; it secures comparative uniformity of administration or local improvements; it examines all private bills relating to municipal affairs and saves Parliament a great deal of time; it deals with unemployment, old age pensions, the census, the fixing of administrative areas of municipalities, etc., etc.*

In England and Wales one department does the work for over 40,000,000 people; in some Canadian provinces, with a population of a city, the same work is spread over a number of departments, with resultant loss of efficiency.

Reference is made to this central department because it is believed that one of the great needs in Canada, to secure the proper planning and development of land, is that municipalities should have greater assistance given to them by expert municipal departments of the provincial governments and that there should be greater co-operation between the provincial and municipal authorities. The central department in Britain is primarily responsible for securing the freedom from dishonest dealing and uniform efficiency which are sometimes wrongly ascribed to the personnel of the municipal councils in Britain as compared with that of councils in Canada. The result has been that, although the system appears on the surface to be more bureaucratic than the Canadian system, it has led, in its practical results, to municipalities being entrusted with greater responsibilities than would be possible without having a central administrative body in supreme control. Among these responsibilities is that of preparing schemes for the planning and development of land under the British Housing, Town Planning, etc., Act of 1909.

Municipal legislation in Canada has grown up in a more or less piecemeal fashion. It should be remodelled on a definite system, and some attempt made to secure as much uniformity as possible between the different provinces. More reliance on expert advice needs to be given in regard to the financial and engineering aspect of local undertakings. The imperfect and sometimes unfair method of controlling building construction and planning of land by local by-laws should be revised.

One great difficulty in Canada is due to a fact already referred to, namely, that there is too much overlapping between legislative and administrative functions. In municipal matters this overlapping is particularly unfortunate, as it leads to the elected rulers, whose term of office is frequently limited to one year, having to give attention to executive details which can only be dealt with efficiently by permanent and expert officers.

---

* See also "Local Government in Great Britain and Canada," by Thomas Adams, *Report of Ontario Commission on Unemployment, Appendix D.*

In the rural districts and small towns, there is a tendency to try and manage the complicated and highly technical questions relating to township and town development by men without adequate knowledge or training for the task. Real economy is only possible where a full advantage is taken of skill and experience in carrying out constructive improvements and the work of developing land. It seems to be assumed that municipal affairs can be managed by lawyers, tailors, grocers, and others who, whatever their expert knowledge in their own business, have not – as a rule – the kind of experience and capacity necessary for municipal administration. A tailor, who very naturally would not accept the advice of an engineer to cut cloth for a suit of clothes, will act as chairman of a public works committee of a town or village and direct complicated engineering construction requiring many years of special training to understand even its general details. With all its advantages, even the British system has not been able to overcome this difficulty in small towns and rural districts. Where new developments take place in Britain, as in mining areas, there is a lack of efficiency, but that is not due to any defect in the system, but rather to wrong administration. We cannot entirely overcome this defect in Canada, any more than in Britain, but we may do much by change of system to lessen its evils.

This question of municipal government is intimately bound up with that of the proper control of the development of land in all organized districts. A municipality is a corporate body of citizens looking after the social and industrial interests of the community. The greater part of the expenditure by municipalities is incurred directly or indirectly in connection with the development of real estate – whether it be rural or urban in character. In view of the enormous expenditure on municipal development it seems extraordinary that there is so little effort made to avoid the waste which results from lack of co-operation and from want of the knowledge which can only be derived from wide experience. Small municipalities, with scattered populations and few resources, have not the means to employ men of adequate skill and are compelled to undertake highly technical work without knowledge of mistakes or successes made by other municipalities. It is no excuse that these small and poor municipalities have inadequate means to employ experts or obtain knowledge; in so far as this lack of means exists the need should be met by the aid of the provincial governments. In view of the great issues and large expenditure involved it is of urgent importance to Canada that each province should have a well-organized municipal department with expert advisers on all kinds of municipal affairs. One of the special tasks of such a department would be to advise and assist small municipalities.

PLATE XVII "CENTRAL BUILDING" ON LOT 25 FEET WIDE IN A SMALL WESTERN CITY

As will be seen from the following plan of the lot there are two stores facing the street and five houses facing either side of the alley which runs down the middle. Adjoining is a bakery.

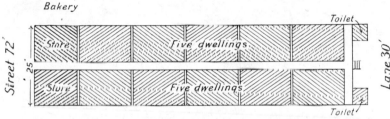

PLATE XVII REAR VIEW OF THE SAME LOT FACING BACK LANE

Note ten dwellings (five on each side) facing 3 foot alley and two unsanitary toilets on extreme right and left, the only toilet accommodation for twelve buildings.
Lack of provincial and municipal control and employment of expert supervision over development, and not want of planning, is responsible for such bad conditions as those here illustrated.

Cost of Local Government

Some idea of the cost of municipal government in Canada as a whole may be gathered from the figures which are published by the Ontario Bureau of Industries. In the *Municipal Bulletin No. 10* of the Bureau it is shown that the total population in the towns, villages and townships in Ontario in 1916 was 1,560,625, as against 1,019,627 in the cities, and that the former increased in three years ending 1916 by 21,834 as against 19,553 in the case of the latter. The total assessment of the towns, villages and townships was $941,507,541, as against $1,033,117,544 for cities, in 1915 the increase in the first case from 1913 to 1915 being $48,996,054 as against an increase of $208,585,743 in the second case. The municipal taxes collected (not including school taxes) in the towns, villages and townships in 1915 amounted to $7.73 per capita as against $20 per capita in the cities, the percentage of increase of taxes between 1913 and 1915 being 26 and 50 respectively. The total debenture debt in the counties, towns, villages and townships in 1915 amounted to only $38,754,681 as against $148,684,937 in the cities, being, respectively, $24.8 and $145.8 per capita.

We thus see how much more economically the small towns and the rural districts are managed as compared with the cities, although it is no doubt true that the rural expenditure is too small and should be increased in order to secure a greater measure of efficiency. On the whole, however, apart from road improvements, the small towns and rural districts have apparently as healthy conditions as the cities.

The above figures may be taken as evidence of the probable extent of municipal indebtedness and the cost of municipal management in Canada. If we assume that the urban population in cities and towns of over 1,500 population spend $20 and those having less than 1,500 spend $7.73 per capita per annum and that their respective per capita indebtedness is $145.8 and $24.8, the annual municipal expenditure and indebtedness in the Dominion would be as follows:

		Debt	Annual Expenditure
Rural population	4,361,570	$108,166,936	$33,741,936
Urban population	2,845,073	414,868,544	56,901,460
		$523,035,480	$90,616,396

The amount of the municipal indebtedness and the high annual cost of government is due in a large measure to land speculation, to the extravagant methods of developing land, and to our municipal system of assessment and taxation which have been dealt with in this report. In large cities in England the cost of local government per capita is about half what it is in Canada and the United States, largely because of the absence of injurious speculation in land. Difficult as it may be to arrest speculation and revise present methods of development and taxation in large cities and towns, it is comparatively easy to alter conditions in small towns and rural areas so as to secure more healthy and economic growth in the future. Particular attention needs to be directed to the removal of the evils of bad sanitation and unhealthy housing in suburban and rural districts.

Government Stimulus to Rural Manufactures and Mining

If the conditions of land settlement are improved for purposes of agriculture and to assist in lessening the cost of government, one of the effects will be to promote rural manufactures and domestic industries. This should, however, be encouraged directly as well as indirectly. The tendencies to build factories in small towns, and to develop entirely new towns near to raw materials and sources of power supply, have been shown in this report to be growing tendencies, and they would be still further accelerated if land was laid out on more scientific principles and better means of communication were provided. Reasons have been given in previous pages as to the desirability of this movement being encouraged. Its special value in enabling Canada to utilize its water-powers and to develop its minerals is of particular interest and importance to governments at this time. Sir Clifford Sifton, in his annual address to the Commission of Conservation, emphasized the importance of the position regarding electrical energy. He quoted Dr. George Otis Smith, Director of the United States Geological Survey, as follows:

"It is only through abundant and well-distributed power that the other material resources of the country can be put to their highest use and made to count most in the nation's development. The people's interest in water-power is greatest in its promise of future social progress and such an interest is well worth protecting."

In view of the enormous potentialities of the water-powers of the Dominion, government aid should be given in the future to help in the creation of new industries in rural areas where these powers are available. In some industrial processes the greatest factor is cheap electric power.

Were agriculture and some existing forms of industry to be subsidized beyond a certain point, until overproduction brought down prices below a subsistence level for the producer, and were large quantities of manufactured goods imported simultaneously, which goods might have been produced at home at a profit, it would be harmful to the country. Many new industries which can be made profitable cannot be started without the research, initiative and financial assistance being rendered by the government. Attention needs to be given to the opportunities for producing gasoline, ammonia, and other materials for which there is a growing demand, and in respect of which we rely entirely, and without any real necessity, on imports. The refining of metals and the promotion of electro-chemical and electro-metallurgical industries so as to give our own people the maximum of employment in connection with the manipulation of our own natural resources is also a matter requiring even more attention than is now being given to it.*

The need for organizing and encouraging the mining and rural manufacturing industries of Canada is desirable, both in the interests of agriculture and of transportation. An additional fact may be added to those already mentioned to show the importance of mining in regard to transportation. It is not commonly known that mining furnishes most of the traffic on railroads. Mr. Arthur A. Cole, president of the Mining Institute, in an address given before the Montreal Canadian Club, stated:

> "In the report for the fiscal year 1913, the Department of Railways and Canals published figures from which the following are pertinent: For the year 1913 the products of agriculture handled by Canadian railways formed 16 per cent of the total, and during the same period the products of mines was 38 per cent of the total, or more than twice as much; and these percentages were practically the same for six years previous. The manufacturer need not think that he makes a better showing than that, for manufactures come 1.2 per cent less than agriculture (14.8)."

He also showed that the mining industry had been responsible for 47 per cent of the total freight revenue of the Timiskaming and Northern Ontario Railway, as against 13 per cent for agriculture, although that road was built for the purpose of agricultural colonization. He added that the

---

* "Canada is destined to secure the principal electro-chemical and electro-metallurgical industries of eastern North America" — W. J. Dick, mining engineer of the Commission of Conservation, in a paper read before the Canadian Mining Institute, March, 1917.

products of agriculture were responsible for 9 per cent, while the products of mines formed 53 per cent of the freight traffic of the United States railways over a two year period.

The great mineral resources of Canada, alluded to in Chapter II, and its immense coal, asbestos, nickel, talc, feldspar, mica, graphite, silver, gold, cobalt and tar-sand deposits, have enormous potentialities for future development. Capital, brains and planning are needed to secure and direct that development to the best advantage. Better housing and social conditions are needed for those whose labour is largely responsible for the increasing mining wealth and the traffic which it produces in the Dominion.

As Mr. Cole points out, there has been a lack of organization and co-operation in regard to mineral production in the past, and the great need is to make this production the basis of manufacturing industries at home. These would be primarily rural industries, helping the farmer with markets as well as increasing the country's wealth. Why should most of the $7,000,000 which it costs to run the Cobalt mines be largely spent in the great cities? By making life in mining centres more attractive, much can be done to keep the wealth of these centres where it is produced. Why should the men who, with their labour, produce the $20,000,000 in gold and silver in Northern Ontario be so poorly housed, to the injury of themselves and the nation and to the advantage of the agitator for indus-trial unrest? Much is being done to improve conditions, but not enough by means of government guidance, and the Cobalts and Porcupines of the future will thrive all the more if the social organization and planning of the new centres of industry receive adequate attention of government authorities. This matter may come more directly under the jurisdiction of provincial governments, but the lead of the Federal Government, and the provision by it of financial aid to stimulate rural manufacturing, subject to proper schemes of development, will be of great value in promoting the industrial welfare of the country.

While the organization of community settlements by special pressure and artificial means hardly ever leads to permanent success, everything points to the conclusion that efforts given to artificially promote rural industries, which are established to develop natural resources and are economically sound, can produce successful results.

The education and training of inhabitants of rural districts in handicrafts similar to those which have been so successful in Europe in developing artistic skill and in preventing rural depopulation, and the stimulation of domestic industries in the homes of farmers and villagers, is another important direction in which governments can assist to build up a more stable rural organization.

Improvement of Highways and Control
of Railway Development

Federal aid to highway development should be given in co-operation with and not independent of the provinces. If this matter is taken up by the Federal Government the precedent of the British Government, in placing the administration of road improvement under an expert board instead of under a department of the government, is one which it would probably be safe to follow. There is no matter in regard to which there can be greater waste in construction than in a highway system which is badly planned. Only after a well-defined system of highways fitted into detailed schemes of development has been prepared by the provincial governments should national assistance be given. The construction of a national highway should not be undertaken until a proper plan is prepared showing the tributary systems of the provinces through which it would pass. The design of the location of feeders and terminals is as important in highway as in railway development. When new arterial thoroughfares are made at public expense sufficient width of land should be acquired for the purpose to enable the government to obtain the increment of value created by its own improvements. In proportion as private lands may be increased in value as a result of public expenditure in road improvements, provision should be made for making special assessments on such property to meet a portion of the cost. A sound financial system should be adopted, under which money borrowed for road construction should be repaid with interest during the life of any improvement. Public land should not be alienated until after access by good roads is provided.

The extension of railways so as to distribute the population with more regard, than hitherto, to successful industrial settlement, and the linking up with the railways of a good roads system designed to facilitate rapid motor transportation in rural areas, also need consideration by the governments with a view to helping and advising provincial and municipal authorities. *Our governments have to recognize that it is of more importance to the farmer to have the land economically planned and developed in advance of settlement, than to get land cheap, or for nothing, or to get the benefit of rural organization under conditions which make such organization expensive and largely ineffective.*

Good roads to facilitate motor transportation and a cheaper parcel post organized in co-operation with the railway companies could be of great advantage to the farmer and help him in distributing small articles direct to the consumer at reasonable cost. One of the merits of an improvement in this direction would be that it could be taken advantage of by every producer, as it would be of general and not of limited local application.

In many cases the railway lands which have been alienated are being administered with as great an efficiency as they could be under a government department, but the railway companies, like all private owners, are necessarily influenced by considerations of profit to themselves rather than the public advantage.

COLONIZATION BY RAILWAY COMPANIES

The Canadian Pacific Railway Company has pursued a business-like policy in regard to the settlement of its agricultural lands, although, like other railway corporations, it has been hampered in the past by its failure to recognize the folly of uncontrolled speculation in building subdivisions. In Appendix B particulars are given of the schemes which have been inaugurated in the western provinces by the company. The company has shown its appreciation of the fact that successful settlement of rural territory cannot be secured without the combination of co-operation, financial aid to the settler, good facilities for transportation, social intercourse and education. When all these factors are present, and land is properly planned in the first place, and when a careful and economical organization is behind any scheme, success seems to be achieved – even if it sometimes is delayed in its consummation.

But a railway company is a traffic authority and the less it is mixed up in real estate manipulation the better. The interests of real estate and traffic often conflict and many of the difficulties and the bad planning of railway terminals and stations are due to the influence which the real estate departments of railways have had over the traffic departments.

The action of the United States government in securing the restoration of railway lands to the public shows that in that country it has been realized that the policy of making railroad grants is not to the national advantage where it can be avoided. It is true in a sense that what is to the advantage of railway enterprise may be for the general good, but the responsibilities of a railway company to its shareholders prevents it from being a disinterested public servant. There is undoubtedly an extent of vacant land near to railways which requires to be classified in order to ascertain what government action is necessary to limit speculation and to impose an adequate tax on the holders of idle land. We have also to recognize that all the capital invested in railways, and not merely the portion which has been guaranteed or subscribed by governments, has to be paid for by the public and that every effort should be made to secure that that investment will be reasonably remunerative so far as it has been properly made.

GOVERNMENT POLICIES AND LAND SPECULATION

If the government confines its attention to assisting settlers with capital, to subsidizing railways, to affording facilities for the farmer to borrow cheap capital and to promoting co-operation, the effect may be to help the speculator rather than the farmer. When an owner of land spends money on its development before he sells it he is able to provide conditions suitable for the efficient working of the land and to recover for himself some of the benefit of his expenditure. If, however, he first sells the land and then starts to spend money in improving the roads, and in organization, all the profit derived from his expenditure will go to those who have purchased the land from him. What applies in the case of the individual owner applies in the case of governments. When a government sells the land without having it properly planned, without constructing adequate means for transportation in advance, without having first provided facilities for rural credit and means of obtaining financial aid in other forms, it must find, when it comes to provide these things after it has sold the land that it is merely conferring a benefit on the land owners. If these owners be land speculators and not producers the public expenditure and organization may help in retarding instead of increasing production. *The more the government can do to improve its own territory before it disposes of it the sounder will be its investment in the end.* The more it can do to plan the land and to develop it for efficient use the more it can restrict speculation and the less it will have to do to incur unremunerative expenditure in development after land is alienated. The government policy in these matters should be directed to help the farmer to make his business more profitable rather than to help to increase land values.

The present effect of homesteading, as shown in this report, has been to encourage speculation, and that may also be the effect of any government policy to promote co-operation and rural credit, and to subsidize the improvement of homesteaded land, which has not been properly planned at the outset.

Experiments have been made with various systems of land colonization, including the free homestead, homestead purchase, the provincial free land grants, provincial sales, C.P.R. and Hudson's Bay Co. systems. The time has come to make careful investigation of the results of these systems and, in view of their variety in different provinces, this investigation should be made by the Federal Government. The Australian and other overseas systems require to be studied, especially with regard to conditional purchase schemes, granting of leases, classification of land and administrative machinery. While there are objections to the leasehold system, it possesses

PLATE XVIII   PRAIRIE GARDENS, INDIAN HEAD, SASK.

By the provision of trees and shrubs and the encouragement of improved environment round the farms the Federal and Provincial Governments have done much to make farm life more attractive in recent years.

the great advantage of restraining injurious speculation and of leaving the farmer's capital free for farming operations. The latter is no small advantage, especially in view of the fact that one of the reasons for failure in farming is due to lack of sufficient capital. If land were planned and more improvements were made than at present, before settlement, it would be easy to get settlers to take up leaseholds.

Need of Constructive Policy in Regard to Scientific Training and Research and Industrial Housing

An enlightened policy of investigation is now being pursued by the Federal Government in regard to scientific training and research, but the benefit to be derived from this work will depend on the extent to which actual steps are taken to apply any measures that may be recommended. So far the important proposals of the Royal Commission on Technical Education have not led to the formulation of any constructive policy to promote improvement in conditions, notwithstanding the vital need of improvement. In this connection, as well as in connection with the importance of conserving and developing human skill, and of providing healthy living conditions for industrial workers, a forceful and significant address was delivered by Col. Carnegie before the Ottawa Branch of the Canadian Society of Civil Engineers, of which an extract is printed as Appendix C.

Some of the worst and most unsanitary housing conditions in Canada have recently occurred in semi-rural districts, where the manufacture of munitions and other materials of warfare have caused concentration of population. This is a national problem, because the Imperial and Federal Governments are responsible for the growth of the industries in certain districts and because efficiency in production cannot be maintained unless the shelter provided for the workers in these industries is adequate and healthy. New arsenals are erected and new works established without proper provision being made to provide suitable dwellings for the workers. In Germany it has long been an established policy to organize the development of healthy and attractive village communities for munition workers, as at Essen, because of the fact that the chief raw material of a skilled industry is the skilled worker, and in proportion as his health suffers from unhealthy environment he is less efficient as a producer. Since the Ministry of Munitions was established in England great care and vigilance has been exercised in securing that the physical capacity of those employed in munition factories would not suffer from bad environment and lack of provision to protect public health. Experts are engaged in building houses and developing garden villages in neighbourhoods where

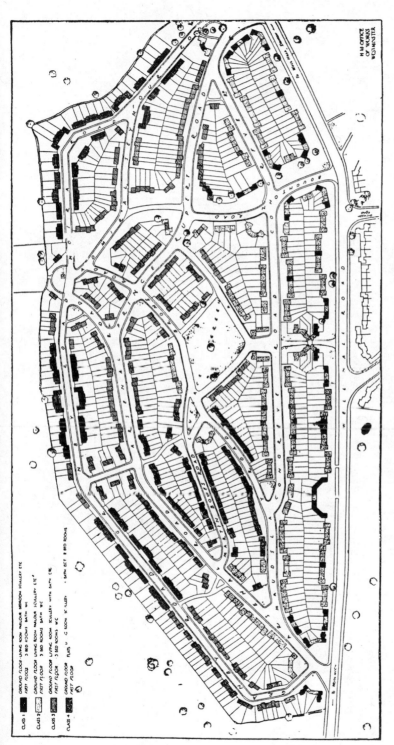

FIGURE 37   WOOLWICH ARSENAL HOUSING SCHEME AT ELTHAM, KENT

This scheme was the direct outcome of the war. At the beginning of 1915 the land comprising the valley of Shooter's Hill and the Heights of Eltham was for the most part used for market gardens; in less than a year 96 acres of this area was covered with permanent and durable houses having modern sanitary fittings. The work of setting out the roads, sewers and houses was commenced on Feb. 3rd, 1915, and on Dec. 11th of the same year all the roads and houses were handed over complete, ready for a population of 6,491. There were 3.64 miles of roads, and 4.85 miles of sewers constructed. The houses and flats numbered 1,298, and had hollow external brick walls 11" thick and slate roofs. The roads were laid to follow the contours; this insured speed in construction as well as good grades. The average garden space allotted to each householder is 1,100 feet super. The roads are 30' to 40' wide and were paved in advance of occupation of the dwellings.

Figures 37 and 38 are taken from "The Architects and Builders' Journal," Dec. 27, 1916.

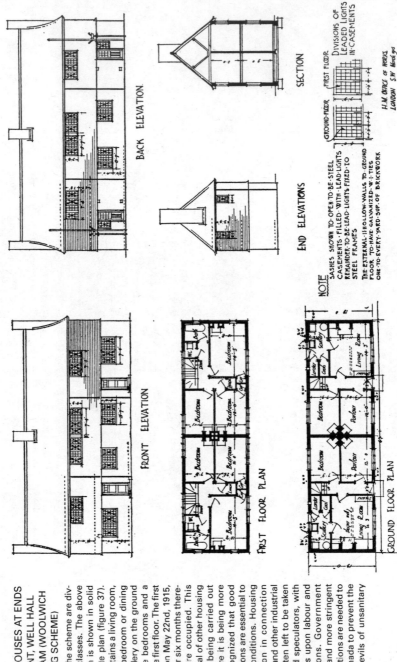

BACK ELEVATION

SECTION

END ELEVATIONS

NOTE

SASHES SHOWN TO OPEN TO BE STEEL
CASEMENTS FILLED WITH LEAD LIGHTS
REMAINDER TO BE LEAD LIGHTS FIXED TO
STEEL FRAMES

THE EXTERNAL HOLLOW WALLS TO GROUND
FLOOR TO HAVE GALVANIZED WI TIES
ONE TO EVERY YARD SUP OF BRICKWORK

DIVISIONS OF
LEADED LIGHTS
IN CASEMENTS

FIRST FLOOR

GROUND FLOOR

H.M. OFFICE OF WORKS
LONDON S.W. Hodges

FRONT ELEVATION

FIRST FLOOR PLAN

GROUND FLOOR PLAN

FIGURE 38 HOUSES AT ENDS
OF CRESCENT, WELL HALL
ROAD, ELTHAM (WOOLWICH
HOUSING SCHEME)

The houses in the scheme are divided into four classes. The above
is class I, which is shown in solid
black on the site plan (figure 37).
Each house contains a living room,
parlour, spare bedroom or dining
room, and scullery on the ground
floor, and three bedrooms and a
bathroom on the first floor. The first
house was let on May 22nd, 1915,
and in little over six months thereafter 1,248 were occupied. This
scheme is typical of other housing
developments being carried out
in Britain, where it is being more
and more recognized that good
housing conditions are essential to
good labour conditions. Housing
accommodation in connection
with munition and other industrial
plants is too often left to be taken
care of by land speculators, with
injurious effects upon labour and
social conditions. Government
aid, guidance, and more stringent
building regulations are needed to
be given in Canada to prevent the
growth of the evils of unsanitary
housing.

industries are extended or are newly established. (Figures 37 and 38.) Nothing has been attempted in this country to deal with this problem, and the warning of Col. Carnegie on this point is one which should be taken to heart at once and not one to consider at the termination of the war. The skill and precision which is being developed in those workers who are employed in making munitions will be one of the most powerful factors in building up Canadian prosperity, if we do not permit physical deterioration of that valuable asset to take place. In so far as careless and disorderly land and building development may cause that deterioration governments are not powerless to avert it. This particular question should not be left to local and private initiative; it is a national problem caused by national needs and requiring comprehensive treatment. The facts pointed out by Col. Carnegie as to the potentialities of the skilled labour to develop new classes of industry after the war will probably not materialize unless we prepare for the development of these industries now; these facts also point to the important part which this skilled labour may take in building up new industrial communities for the purpose of utilizing the unlimited natural resources of the Dominion.

Conclusion

In conclusion it is contended that the important duty of governments is to apply sound principles to the early stages of development of land resources, with the combined object of lessening the evils of speculation during these stages and giving greater scope for individual enterprise in the later stages; that as the Federal and Provincial governments of Canada have the responsibility of directing a vast business enterprise, in the development of the natural resources of the country, they should co-ordinate and improve that part of their administrative machinery which is concerned in the management of these resources so as to secure a more scientific organization of rural life and rural industry than hitherto; that increased responsibility should be placed upon permanent officials to deal with executive details of administration so that members of all classes of government may be able to devote more attention to public policies; that the proposals to strengthen the intelligence departments of the national government and to create new, or secure more co-operation between existing, Federal and Provincial departments is in urgent need of consideration; that government policies should be directed to promote improved methods of land settlement and the utilization of idle or partially cultivated tracts of land near to existing centres of population or means of communication; that departments of municipal affairs should be set up in each province, with skilled advisers, to assist in securing greater efficiency and economy in connection with municipal administration; that more government stimulus should be given to rural manufacturing and mining; and that a constructive policy should be adopted for the purpose of promoting scientific training and improving industrial housing conditions.

CHAPTER VII
GOVERNMENT POLICIES AND LAND DEVELOPMENT

Commentary by Jill L. Grant

Some great thinkers were certainly ahead of their time in the early twentieth century: Le Corbusier proposed towers in the park; Frank Lloyd Wright drew a low-density Broadacre City. Thomas Adams, by contrast, understood and suited his times. While we admire Wright and Le Corbusier as idealists, we appreciate Adams for his pragmatism and common sense. Thomas Adams possessed the perfect template of attitudes and skills for Canada in the 1910s. Despite his abilities and initial enthusiasm for his contribution, however, changing international conditions ultimately undermined political support for planning and the government's commitment to managing land development.

The early years of the twentieth century saw the end of the frontier in America and the last efforts of colonial powers to expand their resource networks in Asia and the Pacific. With the planet mostly settled, the era of rampant economic expansion seemed threatened. Wedded to an economic system that relied on growth, Western nations had no choice but to consider strategies for managing their resources more effectively. Adams defined a role for himself by finding ways to make the development of land more efficient and productive. As a former journalist, he understood how to present ideas to persuade readers of the wisdom of his approach. His chapter on government policies and land development draws on a range of examples to make an effective case for greater government intervention.

We see in Adams' writings his deep concern about the evils of land speculation. Shortly before he arrived in Canada, a major real estate collapse in 1913 had left municipalities holding thousands of acres of subdivided land for which there was no imminent urban use; the failure of developers had left governments deeply in debt and desperate for options. With his background in farming, Adams believed that real value came from working the land, not selling it. His solution for rural areas was to find ways to settle the land for productive farming, mining, industry, or other appropriate uses. Hence, he saw immigration policy and practices as a key to success.

Adams had little time for the railroad companies or for local governments. Governments gave the railways too much land, which then fell subject to land speculation and inefficient development. Local governments lacked the skills and long-term vision to manage land effectively. As a former local councillor, Adams understood the problem: what do grocers and tailors know about planning? he asked. Rampant competition among municipalities looking for investment prevented rational planning. Adams' solution was to suggest installing planning expertise in departments of municipal affairs at the provincial level. Provincial policy could then ensure wise investment and development of resources for the common good.

In the early twentieth century, Canada was still in its metaphorical infancy. Government had a mandate to spread civilization and development throughout the nation. His writings show us that Adams thought that Canada needed to catch up to England. He frequently offers examples of British approaches for better options. For instance, he advises that British municipal institutions are "not only efficient but economical and democratic" (page 274). By contrast, the United States provides the negative exemplar for Canada to avoid in municipal organization. Adams wore the Union Jack on his sleeve, so to speak.

At the time Adams wrote, Canada faced serious social problems. Immigration brought hundreds of thousands of people to Canada every year from diverse backgrounds. Government wanted to get people settled, integrated, and productive. Adams notes the need to find "good quality" immigrants capable of working the land effectively. He cites sources that reflect the racism of his time, sources that suggest that the "pick of the immigrants" came from England, Scotland, and Germany or that English-speaking immigrants might be preferred.

Urban and rural living conditions were poor in Adams' era. Planning derived from the reform tradition that sought to improve housing and sanitation. Proper government policies and regulations would, Adams hoped, reduce opportunities for industry to ignore the needs of workers and prevent workers from building shantytowns with inadequate services. Improving incomes and health conditions would help to keep workers happy and engaged and limit the creeping risk of protest and socialism that threatened industrial societies. Recall that in 1917 the Russian Revolution began with uprisings in February and again in October. Clearly wary of socialism, Adams urged government to avoid subsidies and the "coddling" of industry or individuals. Planning, Adams thought, would give government sufficient tools to manage land and resources in ways that would promote greater security and stability. As Ebenezer Howard argued, planning was the peaceful path to real reform.

Adams' writings indicate that he clearly understood the complexity of the problems planning was asked to address. Like the best thinkers of his time, he tended to take an evolutionary perspective: he saw development as inevitable but believed that progressive interventions might facilitate and enhance the process. He argued that government could achieve its desire for prosperity by employing trained experts versed in scientific methods and with the knowledge to guide growth. His strong faith in scientific expertise resonates throughout his work and exemplifies the philosophy of the Progressive Era (1890-1920).

As a theorist, Adams believed government had an interest in the efficient and orderly development of resources and needed expertise to achieve that mission. Government, he argued, should provide funding to support research and to help industries get started, but it need not subsidize viable industry. It should develop supplies of hydroelectric power and provide the transportation infrastructure to ensure good access to resources and markets. Government should not dispose of land when land values are increasing; better, he argued, to lease the land to avoid speculation. Like many British planners of the period, Adams believed that government should capture the development increment – that is, if government planning or investment improves land values, government should reap the benefit. Canadian legislators failed to follow this advice, allowing private interests to enjoy the rewards of land use changes and creating a political dynamic around land use decisions that encourages unending conflict.

Adams set the template for the pragmatic planner. He believed in an active, interventionist government, one that would use policy effectively to ensure that its wider aims could be met. He argued for a scientific approach to determining the suitability of land for appropriate uses. He advocated trained public servants working for provincial governments in municipal affairs departments providing expertise to rural areas. He criticized excessive regulation as inefficient: his disdain for sixty-six-foot road widths remains as valid today as it was in 1917. As a former land surveyor, he understood the weaknesses of a grid applied unthinkingly to a diverse landscape. He called for compact clusters of development in rural areas with access to public services and transportation networks to create genuine communities. In many ways, his advice seems remarkably modern.

Of course, Adams overlooked some of the issues that trouble contemporary planners. His idea of resource conservation implied protecting resources for human exploitation. No evidence of environmental consciousness, or "design with nature," appears in his writing. He suggests that idle marshlands can be "improved" through proper drainage so that farmers might take advantage of their excellent fertility. He also says little about the growing influence of private automobiles and trucks, although he does discuss the need for road development. Like most commentators in the early twentieth century, Adams thought of roads as a public service: he expected widespread access to motor vehicles to open up possibilities for rural areas that the rail had not. The idea that roads offer public benefits while rail favours private interests remains common today, although transportation policy increasingly acknowledges the need to improve alternative transportation options.

Adams hoped that planning would bring growth and prosperity to rural Canada. He developed strategies to bring industry to small towns and rural areas. He thought that spreading the benefits of hydroelectric power through rural regions would help them to compete with urban areas for jobs and production. Yet by the 1910s, rural Canada had already been left behind as industry concentrated its activities in urban and suburban centres. Decades of planning and millions of dollars in government subsidies and incentives could not reverse the processes of urbanization that Adams witnessed in his years in Canada.

Although Adams was certainly the man for the job, no one could contain or redirect the changes overtaking the nation. Within a few years of the completion of his book, the continuing tension between government control and market logic had brought an end to Adams' civilizing project. As Adams' political supporters such as Sir Clifford Sifton retired, the interests of capital gained strength in Ottawa. It would take another world war before Canada would finally come to recognize the wisdom of Adams' ideas and get serious about the prospects of planning. By that time, conditions had changed and postwar planning focused on urban development.

Many would argue that the early years of the twenty-first century in some ways parallel the times during which Adams worked in Canada. After decades of laissez-faire development, provincial governments have begun to take land development seriously. In some cases, they have adopted smart growth and sustainability policies to manage and shape change. In the last fifteen years, metropolitan amalgamations and provincial land use policies have created a regional planning of the sort Adams and his contemporaries favoured. Current conditions encourage government intervention in land development. Although the mortgage meltdown of 2008 did not represent the risk to local governments that the 1913 real estate collapse did, it has reinforced the governments' belief that planning matters. The unstable pricing regime for fossil fuels and the crisis in the auto industry have served to reinforce land development policies that encourage urban consolidation and intensification. Canadian immigration policy continues to favour "quality immigrants," redefined in contemporary circumstances as skilled workers for an urban economy. Policy on various levels favours urban growth. In a context in which policy-makers see urbanization as a solution to problems of resource decline, efficient service provision, and an aging population, it seems likely that rural areas will continue to be marginalized and "underdeveloped." Were he to return today, Adams would find a Canada that appreciates the bottom line of his message – governments need to plan – without agreeing on many of the particulars of rural planning that made sense in 1917.

CHAPTER VIII

Returned Soldiers and Land Settlement

Land settlement schemes for returned soldiers | Conditions necessary to attract men to the land | Improvement of rural housing and provision of small holdings | Establishment of new towns for returned soldiers

LAND SETTLEMENT SCHEMES FOR RETURNED SOLDIERS

EVERY effort is likely to be made, both by the Federal and Provincial Governments, to make liberal provision for the returned soldiers who desire to settle upon the land. The matter has received the attention of the Federal and Provincial Governments, and a more or less definite policy has been settled by some of the Provincial Governments.

Probably the most advanced and most definite scheme is that which has been prepared by the Government of Ontario. The Ontario Government has established an experimental farm at Monteith, on the Timiskaming and Northern Ontario railway, for the purpose of training soldiers and others in agricultural work. In the description of the buildings and equipment of the farm it is stated that there is abundant water supply, shower baths and modern sanitary conveniences, and that there will be good sized living-rooms with fire-places, reading matter, gramophones and other amusements. We have thus an illustration of the growing importance which is attached to social conveniences and recreation as a means of attracting men to take up country life.

According to a published description of the scheme, the intention of the Ontario Government is to train the soldiers in groups of 20 or 30 at a time and place them on blocks of fertile land, where they will be organized as a community settlement, under the direction of an experienced superintendent.

The forest clearing will be gradually extended from a central community house. The farms will be 80 acres in extent, and each settler will get an 80-acre farm free with 10 clear acres. He will be supplied with machinery, tools, live stock, poultry, etc., up to a maximum value of $500, and will get reasonable assistance in the erection of his house and barn. Repayment of the advances will be deferred for three years, and then will be made by installments payable over a period of twenty years.

In the community headquarters there will be an adequate supply of horses and implements for common use and the Government will assist in marketing such products as pulpwood and in co-operation in purchases and sales. It is also the intention of the Government to provide good roads and to organize social life by means of lectures, moving pictures, etc. As one colony proves successful others will be opened. Men will also be assisted to take up land in old Ontario as well.

The *Toronto Daily News* has expressed the belief that the provincial treasury would make no mistake if it were to set aside $1,000,000 or $2,000,000 from the proceeds of the war tax for the location of time-expired soldiers upon the soil under favourable conditions in the older and newer parts of Ontario.

In other provinces commissions have been at work considering the best means of giving aid to soldiers, and legislation has been under consideration to afford assistance similar to that which has been given in Ontario.

In British Columbia a Returned Soldiers' Aid Commission was appointed as early as November, 1915. This commission has since reported,* and has recommended that the advantages of co-operative farm settlements should be available to all returned soldiers. They argue that the problem of providing for the returned soldiers is of so complex a nature that it should be the object of a Federal enquiry.

A recommendation of the Commission is that a board of commissioners should be appointed to select suitable lands and to direct the preliminary operations in connection with their development; that the board acquire lands to carry out a scheme of co-operative land settlement of at least sixty allotments within easy reach of transportation and markets, and reserving sufficient acreage for a demonstration farm, recreation grounds, etc. All farms are to have easy access to the central organization plant and good roads are to be constructed. Stores, public halls, schools, etc., are to be situated in a central village.

The Commission recommended that a sum not to exceed $500 should be spent on farm implements for each allotment, and that the Government lend up to $1,350 at a low rate of interest for a long term to enable the settler to erect farm buildings, purchase machinery, etc.

It was recommended that the men be trained in farm work, free of cost for all returned soldiers, and that there should be a trained agricultural

---

* *Report of the Returned Soldiers' Aid Commission* (British Columbia) 1916.

adviser for each settlement. The Commission very properly recognized that any scheme prepared for returned soldiers should, as regards its general plan, be available for other settlers.

Legislation has been considered in British Columbia in which the general principles advocated by the commission have been incorporated.

In New Brunswick and other provinces committees have been appointed to enquire into the question of settling returned soldiers in farm colonies where they would have social comfort and co-operation.

The Canadian Pacific Railway Company is offering to provide land under specially attractive conditions for returned soldiers. The company undertakes to provide farms of two kinds, (a) improved farms in distinctive colonies, and (b) assisted colonization farms. The first comprises farms in selected colonies, which are improved by the erection of house, barn and fence, the cultivation of a certain area of land and the providing of a water supply. The assisted colonization farms are first selected by the intending colonist and then improved by him with financial assistance by the company.

A striking fact about all schemes being promoted is the implied acknowledgment that successful agricultural development requires co-operative methods and that provision for social intercourse is considered essential. Great progress has been made in this direction during the past few years, because it has come to be generally admitted that the present system of land settlement, which encourages isolation and makes satisfactory co-operation impossible, cannot be continued if we are to have satisfactory rural progress.

Conditions Necessary to Attract Men to the Land

It is hard to understand why the schemes suggested for dealing with the problem of returned soldiers are mostly of the nature of land colonization schemes. It seems to be assumed that a larger proportion of the soldiers will go back to the land than have come from the land. It is doubtful, however, whether the city dwellers among the soldiers who will take up farming will exceed in number the ex-farmers who will want to follow up the excitement of war with the excitement of city life.

The Parliamentary Committee on the Care of Returned Soldiers was told at Ottawa by Mr. J. B. Kidner, the vocational secretary of the Military Hospitals Commission, that only a very small percentage of the twelve thousand returned men so far handled by the commission was willing to go on the land. Out of 346 soldiers who had returned to Alberta only six had signified a willingness to take up farming, although a number of the returned men had been farmers before they enlisted. Mr. Kidner had personally questioned fifty returned men and only one of them wanted to farm.*

In regard to this matter it is of little use to argue from past experience, for no correct analogy can be drawn between the conditions in this war and in any previous war. What is certain, however, is that the number of men attracted to the land will depend on the conditions of settlement offered to them, and that it will be folly to use pressure or offer financial aid to men who have no liking for farming. It is difficult enough for the man who has capital and experience, and to whom farming is a congenial occupation, to make the business pay under present conditions; and it is not to be expected that the returned soldier who does not possess all these advantages will succeed. To force the pace of land settlement by soldiers who do not want to become farmers will be undesirable both for the soldiers and for the country.

To give a man some capital and training and a free farm in a remote rural area may be a simple way to meet the obligation of the country to the returned soldier. If he turns out a success he may be content and the country will have met its obligation without cost to itself, for a good permanent settler will be worth the investment it has made. If he turns out a failure the country will only have lost what may be regarded as part of the cost of war, but the man will not consider that he has received his due reward. But the problems of the returned soldiers, like that of immigration after the war, cannot be solved in a satisfactory manner unless we first apply more science and intelligence to the problem of land settlement. It is futile to go on with the schemes for placing men on the land without regard to the social and industrial organization which is needed to make land settlement a success. The settlement of land should, however, be dealt with as a distinct and separate problem from any other, and the problem of the returned soldier should not be confused with the question of getting people on the land.

Whatever obligation the country may have to the returned soldier should be determined on principle without regard to whether he is going on the land or to remain in the city. Having determined that principle it may be necessary to make exceptional provisions for the man who wishes to take up farming, *but these should merely be extensions of the kind of provisions available for any good settler.*

As a first duty to all prospective settlers, including the returned soldiers, the system of colonization should be revised so as to make farming more

---

* *Canadian Finance,* March 7th, 1917, p. 209.

profitable. It is conceivable that the giving of free farms to soldiers will only accentuate the evils of haphazard settlement and enlarge the field of speculation, by which the real benefit derived from the free grants of land and money will pass to enterprising and undeserving second parties, and harm instead of good done to colonization.

Until development schemes are made it is not likely that the settlement of isolated groups of returned soldiers in rural districts will succeed, no matter how liberal the terms may be that are offered by the Governments. The areas available for free homesteads are for the most part in remote regions, where success is difficult because of want of proper means of communication. The returned soldier will need social intercourse and good facilities for educating his children, and these must be provided wherever settlement is permitted; they cannot be provided in small artificial colonies, or without closer settlement over wide areas, better roads, and the expenditure of capital in planning and developing large areas of the land.

As an alternative to placing ex-soldiers on isolated farms in territory remote from existing railways and centres of population, consideration should be given to schemes that have been suggested for filling up the available territory nearest to these railways and centres.* In any case we should plan and develop the new territory in such a way as to give the settlers the advantages of accessibility to market centres by road and rail, and the social conditions which they need to make them prosperous and contented. Otherwise we may only succeed either in deadening their initiative and enterprise or in creating a sickening of heart that will drive them back into the cities.

The proposal to settle untrained returned soldiers on the western farm lands is not altogether welcomed by those who speak for the existing settlers. The *Farmer's Advocate,* referring to the matter, says that men should go to that position for which environment and training fitted them. "The farmers in western Canada will meet their responsibility, but it is unfair to the farm and unfair to the returned soldier to attempt to make the farm the solution of the problem that will arise when our soldiers return."

The Trades and Labour Congress of Canada, which met at Vancouver on September 20, 1915, adopted a proposal in which it stated, *inter alia,* that the present system of homesteading was useless for a solution of unemployment difficulties, owing to the prospective settler having insufficient capital and experience. The committee of the Congress

---

*   The Returned Soldiers Employment Commission of Saskatchewan has resolved to
    ask the Dominion Government to select land for returned soldiers near to railways.

recommended that the Government should select land for the proper carrying out of a scheme and be requested "to offer, as an option, to discharge from the army, further enlistment for a period of five years of such men as would be willing to undertake agricultural work under the direction of qualified experts from experimental farms and agricultural colleges; that such men received the regular army pay and allowances with rations on the same basis, suitable accommodation to be provided with quarters for married men and families. After such period of enlistment has expired the men who have thus served should have the option of settlement upon suitable sized allotments of the land so improved, the same to be held on leasehold terms from the Dominion Government."

The Ontario Commission on Unemployment states, in its report, that there was a consensus of opinion among the witnesses who discussed the subject of returned soldiers in favour of action along the above lines.

Mr. Lionel Curtis refers to the importance of the Imperial, Dominion and Provincial Governments co-operating in connection with any scheme of settlement for returned men, and advocates the desirability of securing improved medical service in rural districts, especially in the direction of an equipment of nurses.

Although not so attractive, employment on the land at good wages and with a good dwelling in a well populated area would be a much better means of getting returned soldiers back to the land, unless where they have ample capital, experience and a willingness to undertake pioneer work. But, to accomplish the former, it is first necessary to provide attractive housing conditions in rural districts.

An informal committee, representing the leading agricultural and housing associations in England, has been considering this problem and, while recognizing the advantage of peasant proprietorship and farm tenancies, recorded its conviction that the greater majority of ex-service men desiring a life in the country could only be provided for by employment at wages, and, in order that they could be attracted to the land, wages should be better and houses should be improved. A government policy and legislation to effect these improvements was urged.

IMPROVEMENT OF RURAL HOUSING AND PROVISION OF SMALL HOLDINGS

No serious attempt has been made in Canada to secure an increased supply of labour on improved farms in old settled territory by means of providing attractive homes where a man and his family could live comfortably and enjoy good wages. There is an urgent need for more labour on good farms near to the markets; a good income can be earned on these farms, and the man with small capital and limited experience would find it more profitable to himself to take up employment of this kind than to take up a free homestead in an isolated locality. Although many men prefer to take the risk attached to taking up a farm of their own they should not be encouraged to do so with small capital and without sufficient experience. More encouragement should be given to such men to go on the farms as labourers, and as a first step it is essential that the housing facilities should be improved on existing farms near to the towns. A sufficient area of land should be attached to these houses to enable the farm labourer to be a small farmer on his own account and to be partially independent. The man who can obtain a good house and small holding at a low rent in a good agricultural district, where there is a ready market for his produce, and who can use his spare time in working for the large farmer or in some industrial occupation, can be much better off than in trying to farm 160 acres with inadequate capital.

Arrangements should be made to help farmers to provide houses and small holdings at low rents as a means of attracting more labourers to the improved districts, and also to develop small holdings in immediate proximity to cities and towns. Cities, like Port Arthur, Ontario, which own large sections of suitable land, or which have opportunities to acquire land for the purpose, should prepare colonization schemes for men who would prefer to rent a small improved farm close to a city or town to acquiring a farm in a country district. One of the greatest needs in Canada is to increase production in immediate proximity to large centres of population, and to provide men with alternative means of employment near to such centres. This is one of the best means by which intensive farming and the linking up of manufacture and agriculture can be promoted.

But, after all, in what respect does the problem of placing ex-service men on the land differ from any other problem of land settlement? The country's obligations to the soldier must be met, apart from the business of colonization. In so far as it is sound to organize colonies for soldiers it will be sound to organize colonies for other classes of settlers. In so far as forced and artificial methods of settlement are uneconomic and injurious to ordinary settlers they will prove injurious to returned soldiers, even if schemes are subsidized with government money. In the interests of the whole country we have to get down to the root problem in connection with land development, and get rid of the idea that no matter how we may carve out the land and ignore its proper planning we may afterwards succeed by expenditure of money and time in making sound rural conditions.

In so far as the returned soldiers question can be linked up with the land question it will not be entirely an agricultural problem. It is not so important that we should persuade soldiers to go on the land as it is that we should persuade them to take up the most productive enterprise to which their skill can be adapted. It is not so important that we should keep them out of the cities and towns as it is that we should prevent them from drifting into the ranks of unskilled labour in either town or country.

ESTABLISHMENT OF NEW TOWNS FOR RETURNED SOLDIERS

When all the soldiers who want to go on the land and all those who will take up their own occupations are provided for there must be a great many for whom some sort of organization will be needed to secure that they will devote themselves to productive work. On this point the soldiers will probably have something to say themselves, and will demand that the provision that is made for them will be satisfactory to themselves and the country. As Mr. Neville Chamberlain, Director of National Service of England, has said, they will want a greater share in the distribution of wealth, regularity of employment and *improved conditions both in the factories and homes.* The real problem will be to fit ex-service men into some field of labour where they can produce most and also where they can find congenial environment.

In view of the large number of men who have a taste for industrial pursuits, who have learned discipline and precision, who have seen the advantages of co-operation and social intercourse, it will be essential for some step to be taken to organize the development of new towns or to assist in the extension of existing towns where such men can be provided for. Even those who will want to take up farming will prefer to do so in close proximity to an existing city or town where intensive culture is practicable and better social facilities can be obtained. The success which has been achieved at Letchworth in England, in the building up of a city and agricultural colony combined, affords us the example we require to solve a large portion of the problem of the returned soldiers. Such a scheme involves artificial organization to get it started, but one of the objects of that artificial organization would be to develop a town in which there would be the fullest public freedom for natural growth and individual initiative.

Sites can be obtained close to large centres of population, where towns could be created on land which can be acquired at a reasonable price. The facilities which a government has to enable it to acquire a large block of land at agricultural rates and convert it, by improved transportation, etc., into valuable building land would provide such a scheme with a sound economic basis. The problem of creating such towns is not in the difficulty of acquiring suitable sites, it is in getting sufficient capital to equip the site with such improvements as are necessary to make it adaptable for building a city. In so far as the Letchworth scheme has hung fire during the past fourteen years it has been almost entirely due to lack of sufficient capital at the outset, but in Canada there should be no difficulty in this respect. We are contemplating placing a large number of soldiers on the land, at a cost which may mean that the governments will have to provide, by loans and other forms of expenditure, about $2,000 per family. If we were to apply the same capital to develop a combined industrial and agricultural colony, on scientific lines, for 30,000 people, we would have –at $500 per head – a capital of $15,000,000 for the purpose. The Letchworth scheme was started on a capital of about $750,000,* or less than the cost of the bare site which had to be purchased to build the town. If there had been four or five times the capital available it is certain that the city would have been completely occupied by 30,000 people in a very few years. Owing to the want of capital the development has had to be slow and the city is now about half completed, although it is growing more rapidly than towns of a similar size in England.

In a new development of this kind it is important that the first experiments should be carried out near to existing centres for many reasons, the most important of which is that it is the only way in which the element of risk in obtaining industries and population and securing rapid financial success can be reduced to the minimum. Land can be acquired within a comparatively few miles of the largest cities in Canada at from $150 to $300 per acre. By improving the means of transportation, providing water supply, power and other public services, this land could be converted into building land of a high value which, without any other aid, should alone provide interest and sinking fund on the capital invested. Essential considerations in connection with any such scheme would be:

(1) That a proper plan and scheme of development be prepared and that part of the area acquired, say two-thirds, be set aside permanently as an agricultural estate around the town.

(2) That the land shall be acquired at a reasonable price, having regard to its site and character; and that the site be selected in such a position as to enable attractions to be offered to manufacturers and residents.

---

* The share capital at 30th September, 1904 was $503,460, and mortgages and loans $419,670.

(3) That the scheme should be based on a sound financial footing and that any special advantages offered to returned soldiers should be kept distinct from the business part of the enterprise.

(4) That the dividend payable on capital provided from public and private sources should be restricted to 6 per cent and that all profits in excess of the amount required to pay such dividend be used for the benefit of the town and its inhabitants.

(5) That provision be made to prevent land speculation without unreasonable restrictions of the power to negotiate the sale of land.

Conclusion

In this chapter it is contended that the problem of placing ex-service men on the land does not differ in any material sense from that of placing any other class of settlers on the land; that any system of land settlement which is sound for one class is, generally speaking, sound for another class and should first be determined because of its soundness irrespective of any class; that settlement should not be forced under any conditions, but should be permitted to proceed naturally after the right conditions of land development are laid down; that the obligation of the nation to ex-service men should not be confused with the question of land settlement, but should be determined on its merits as a distinct problem; that government aid to returned soldiers, or others, by means of loans or education, will fail in its object unless there is more scientific organization and planning of the beginnings of development; and that new towns and suburbs combining opportunities for agricultural and industrial employment for returned soldiers should be promoted by government aid in locations where they can be successfully established on economic lines and without artificial pressure.

CHAPTER VIII
RETURNED SOLDIERS AND LAND SETTLEMENT

Commentary by John Devlin

_____

*The problem of placing ex-service men on the land does not
differ in any material sense from that of placing any other class of
settlers on the land ... settlement should not be forced under any
circumstances, but should be permitted to proceed naturally after
the right conditions of land development are laid down ... the
obligation of the nation to ex-service men should not be confused
with the question of land settlement, but should be determined on
its own merits as a distinct problem ... Government aid to returned
soldiers, or others, by means of loans or education, will fail in its
object unless there is more scientific organization and planning
of the beginnings of development; and ... new towns and suburbs
combining opportunities for agricultural and industrial employment
for returned soldiers should be promoted by government aid in
locations where they can be successfully established on economic
lines and without artificial pressure.*

– *Thomas Adams,* Rural Planning and Development, 304

In 1917, Thomas Adams' concern with soldier settlement reflected a pressing
policy problem. As many as one hundred thousand Canadian soldiers were interested in some sort of land settlement upon their demobilization (Jackson
1920, 251). The Soldier Settlement Act of 1917 initiated a settlement program,
and the Soldier Settlement Board was established in 1918 to support the distribution of land to deactivated soldiers through homesteading or the purchase of
existing farms (SSBC 1921, 24). The Soldier Settlement Board could make loans
for the purchase of agricultural land; for the settling of existing debts on farms
that soldiers already owned; for making land improvements; for constructing
buildings and purchasing stock, machinery, and equipment; and for other purposes related to the establishment of a viable farm (Ashton 1925, 494). The
planning problems that the Board faced fell into three general categories: (1)
the identification, procurement, and transfer to returned soldiers of available
land; (2) the management of a large lending portfolio secured by mortgages;
and (3) Adams' central concern, the provision of adequate physical and social
infrastructure to make settlement an economically viable and socially attractive

option for settler families so that they would stay on the land and contribute to the development of viable rural communities.

The land assembly process proceeded with reasonable success. The 1918 survey of Dominion lands indicated that the better land had already been taken up and much was now owned by individuals or corporations for speculative purposes (Ashton 1925, 492). The revised 1919 Soldier Settlement Act gave the board the authority to designate settlement areas and purchase land within those areas at a price set by the board or by the Exchequer Court. The board was also empowered to acquire land on Indian reserves, school lands, and forest reserves, and to reserve for soldier purchase any land offered for sale within fifteen miles of a railway (Morgan 1968, 41). The Soldier Settlement Board was empowered to purchase and resell land up to a value of $5,000 per soldier. The soldier paid 10 percent and obtained the remainder as a mortgage. Provision was also made for additional lending up to $3,000 per soldier for livestock, equipment, and permanent improvements (Ashton 1925, 496). By the end of 1924, soldiers had settled on over 5.8 million acres of land through either purchase or homesteading (DIC 1929, 5). Settlement was most active in the West. Less than 17 percent of soldier settlers receiving loans were settled in Ontario, Quebec, or the Maritime provinces. Roughly the same percentage settled in Manitoba and British Columbia. More than 50 percent settled in Saskatchewan and Alberta (see Table 1).

Table 1

Persons with loans under the Soldier Settlement Act

Province/region	No. of persons	%
Maritime provinces	1,556	6
Quebec	494	2
Ontario	1,972	8
Manitoba	3,715	15
Saskatchewan	6,164	25
Alberta	7,158	29
British Columbia	3,734	15
Total	24,793	100

Note: There were 30,604 soldier settlers but only 24,148 received loans. It is this group of settlers that was tracked by the board.
Source: Canada Yearbook 1951, 1116.

The scale of settlement was small relative to the civilian settlement of the pre-war period. Between 1911 and 1917, there had been 166,000 homestead entries in Manitoba and the provinces to the west (Canada Yearbook 1916-17, 628). The addition of twenty thousand families was not a dramatic increase. But the rates of abandonment were significant. By the end of 1925, over 6,600 of the 30,604 soldier settlers had abandoned their farms. No new applications under the Soldier Settlement Act were accepted after 1924, when the board held over 4,600 farm units that it had not been able to resell (*Canada Yearbook* 1925, 963). Many of these farms passed to civilian immigrants under new settlement programs. In 1923, the Soldier Settlement Board was designated the Land Settlement Branch of the Department of Immigration and Colonization, and the activities related to soldier settlement were merged with more general activities devoted to land settlement (Ashton 1925, 498).

As an agricultural credit institution, the board represented one of the first major state programs for the provision of agricultural credit. Over the course of its operations, it considered over sixty-seven thousand loan applications and made over twenty-four thousand loans. By 1925, the gross value of loans had reached $106 million (*Canada Yearbook* 1925, 962), and by 1931 gross loans had reached $145 million. But repayment problems were common. Much of the initial land purchases by the board had been undertaken during 1919 and 1920, a period of postwar inflation, when land and equipment prices were high. But during the 1920s, agricultural commodity prices fell as European production was re-established and as new land brought under cultivation added to global supplies. As commodity prices fell, loan servicing became difficult, and many soldier settlers fell into arrears. There were calls for ameliorative measures (Hopkins 1922, 283). The Act was amended in 1922 to allow the board to consolidate loans, extend the repayment period to twenty-five years, and grant interest exemption for periods of from two to five years (Morgan 1968, 45). The legislation was followed by the revaluation of land, authorized in 1927. Yet, in 1929, only 50 percent of returned soldiers were meeting their payments in full. Forty percent were making partial payments, and 10 percent were making no payments (DIC 1929, 5-6).

In 1930, a general policy of leniency was adopted on settler loan repayment. Reductions in the valuation of the settlers' land and a corresponding write-off of the debt (principal and interest) owing to the board reached a total value of $50 million between 1922 and 1950 (DVA 1950, 96). Since many of the mortgages ran for a period of twenty-five years and there were many payment delays, it is not surprising that the last official financial entry for the soldier settlement account appeared in 1968 (DVA 1967-68, 47). The lending program had been in effect for fifty years.

Had Adams' warnings about rural economic planning been heeded? Two striking assumptions emerge from the epigraph to this chapter. Adams argues that there is a need for the "scientific organization and planning" of development and that the formation of towns should be stimulated by government aid but in locations where they can succeed under market conditions and without "artificial pressure." The board certainly was aware of these planning concerns. It stated in 1921 that it did not "contemplate the settlement of soldiers as pioneers in remote locations or under isolated conditions, removed from markets, in virgin forest lands, or on lands not cultivable without reclamation or other development" (SSBC 1921, 10). The board did provide extension services to assist farmers with technical issues (Ashton 1925, 496), but the laudable intention of providing the foundation for viable rural communities was not met. As demand grew, soldiers were settled on whatever land was available, even if it was far from physical and social amenities: Kapuskasing in northern Ontario, the Interlake Region of Manitoba, the forest fringe in northern Saskatchewan, the Peace River Country of Alberta, and the British Columbia Interior. These were all remote areas where soldier settlers were poorly serviced by transportation and other infrastructure (Schull 1978, 229; McDonald 1981, 38-40; Koroscil 1982, 70ff.).

The board did not invest in the rural infrastructure that Adams had insisted was necessary for successful settlement. It left the development of municipal centres up to local initiatives and market dynamics. The Porcupine Soldier Settlement, created on two hundred thousand acres of land in northern Saskatchewan in 1919, struggled because "the building of schools, churches, a hospital and any progress made, could be achieved only by their own individual and/or collective effort" (Harris 1967, 7, cited in McDonald 1981, 39). The co-operative soldier settlements established at Kapuskasing in Ontario and in Merville and Camp Lister in British Columbia failed from a combination of inadequate agricultural endowments and excessive distance to urban markets (Schull 1978, 229, 248; Koroscil 1982, 85-87).

Only one example of rational town planning is mentioned in association with soldier settlement. In the community of Prairie River, Saskatchewan, it was reported in 1921 that a new town was being planned on modern town planning lines under the authority of the Soldier Settlement Board. The plan included public reserves and public access to the river, an industrial park with access to the rail line, and a rational organization of urban traffic flows – some of the rational planning approaches discussed by Adams. For reasons that are not clear, however, the plan was not implemented (Morgan 1968, 53-54).

It is certainly consistent with Adams' analysis that many settled soldiers would abandon their land in the face of weak infrastructural support, limited amenities, and limited market access. Soldier settlement was a policy issue that did not generate a development planning response. The perceived need was to stabilize social conditions in the face of the return of over three hundred thousand soldiers from Europe (Morton and Wright 1987, ix). The promise of land was a promise for a better future; the program was a response to social management rather than economic, regional, or rural planning concerns.

The concerns that Adams identified explain much of the overall failure of the soldier settlement program. But soldier settlement was itself merely a minor subplot to the much wider failure of the federal and provincial governments' rural development strategies in the twentieth century. Rural population decline has been a structural consequence of rapid technological change in agriculture. The logic of Adams' analysis was correct. Successful settlement could be made only in areas were farmers could survive on the basis of their competitiveness in agricultural markets or where industrial employment could be created. But policy-makers were not prepared to plan the rural economy. Market forces were expected to determine the allocation of land and labour, and market forces proved to be, not an elixir that supported the vitality of rural communities, but a corrosive that slowly stripped away the rural population as improved agricultural productivity guaranteed the decline of agricultural employment.

Soldier resettlement was an historically specific planning problem. The nine decades that have passed since it was initiated have witnessed the continuous industrialization of agriculture and rural demographic decline. Over that period, rural planners have struggled to follow Adams' dictum and find "new towns and suburbs combining opportunities for agricultural and industrial employment." It is apparent now that the creation of such sustainable rural communities would require a degree of economic planning far beyond that initially envisaged by Thomas Adams.

REFERENCES

Ashton, E.J. 1925. "Soldier Land Settlement in Canada." *Quarterly Journal of Economics* 39, 3: 488-98.
DIC (Department of Immigration and Colonization). 1929. *Land Settlement: Seventh Report of the Soldier Settlement Board of Canada.* Ottawa: The Department.
DVA (Department of Veterans Affairs). 1950. *Report of the Work of the Department of Veteran Affairs.* Ottawa: The Department.
–. 1967-68. *Annual Report, 1967-68.* Ottawa: The Department.
Harris, Herbert R. 1967. *Porcupine Soldier Settlement and Adjacent Areas.* Somme, SK: Shand Agricultural Society.
Hopkins, J. Castell. 1922. *The Canadian Annual Review of Public Affairs.* Toronto: Canadian Annual Review Company.
Jackson, Gilbert E. 1920. "Unemployment in Eastern Canada." *Economic Journal* 30, 118: 245-53.
Koroscil, Paul M. 1982. "Soldiers, Settlement and Development in British Columbia, 1915-1930." *BC Studies* 54: 63-87.
McDonald, J. 1981. "Soldier Settlement and Depression Settlement in the Forest Fringe of Saskatchewan." *Prairie Forum* 6, 1: 33-55.
Morgan, E.C. 1968. "Soldier Settlement in the Prairie Provinces." *Saskatchewan History* 11, 2: 41-55.
Morton, Desmond, and Glenn Wright. 1987. *Winning the Second Battle: Canadian Veterans and the Return to Civilian Life, 1915-1930.* Toronto: University of Toronto Press.
Schull, Joseph. 1978. *Ontario since 1867.* Toronto: McClelland and Stewart.
SSBC (Soldier Settlement Board of Canada). 1921. *Soldier Settlement on the Land: Report of the Soldier Settlement Board of Canada.* Ottawa: King's Printer.

CHAPTER IX

Provincial Planning and Development Legislation

*A draft Planning and Development Act | The term "town planning" |
Planning in Britain | Planning not an end in itself | Need of
legislation | Boundaries of development schemes | Co-operation between
provincial governments and municipalities | Why rural and urban
development should be dealt with in one measure | Details of remedies
reserved for subsequent report | General objects of development schemes |
The principal contents of development schemes in rural areas | Summary
of leading features of planning and development legislation*

A Draft Planning and Development Act

Perhaps the most important work which has been started in the
Dominion with regard to land development is in connection with
the promotion of planning and development legislation and
schemes under the somewhat misleading title of "town planning." This
matter has been the subject of close study by a branch of the Commission
of Conservation for the past two and one-half years. Ever since the
Commission took up the consideration of public health work it has con-
sistently advocated a change in the methods of planning and laying out
land.

The draft Planning and Development Act, which has been prepared by
the Commission, is continually being improved and widened in its scope
to meet new conditions and to make it more workable and effective in
the light of experience which has been gained. Under the name "Town
Planning Acts" there are good measures already in force in Nova Scotia,
New Brunswick, Alberta and Manitoba. Some of these acts need revision
to make them more effective, but without revision they could be used by
the Provincial governments of the above provinces, acting in concert with
the municipalities, to prepare both rural and urban development schemes.
The Nova Scotia Act is the most advanced and complete of any statute
dealing with this question, especially in regard to the provisions relating
to rural development. The novelty of this kind of legislation means that
it will be some time before it can be properly understood and that frequent

modifications will be necessary, as experience is gained, until a satisfactory measure can be evolved.

The Term "Town Planning"

The use of the term "town planning," in connection with legislation dealing with the planning and development of rural and urban land, has led to confusion and misunderstanding, and it is not surprising, therefore, that the suitability of a town planning Act to regulate both rural and urban development has not been sufficiently appreciated even in the provinces where legislation has been passed.

What is called "town planning" is intended by statute to mean urban and rural planning and development. The British Act, which is the precedent for legislation of this character, and some Canadian Acts, are in some respects more applicable to rural than to urban areas and – although their general object is to secure amenity, proper sanitary provisions and convenience in connection with the laying out of land for building purposes – their operation is largely restricted to land that has not already been built upon. Hence they chiefly apply to suburban, semi-rural and rural land "likely to be used for building purposes," and not to the remodelling of portions of towns already built upon.

Planning in Britain

A considerable proportion of town planning schemes in England are being prepared by rural district councils* and most of the land, included in all the schemes being prepared, is rural in character.

In the great majority of cases the English schemes are being prepared by municipal surveyors or engineers, and comparatively little expense is being incurred in connection with their preparation. For instance, the Ruislip-Northwood scheme deals with an area of over 5,900 acres, of which only 437 acres were "in course of development" in 1913. The cost of preparing a scheme of development for this area, in anticipation of the growth for the next 50 or 100 years, was only $5,000. The ultimate estimated cost of carrying out the scheme, namely $150,000, will be spread over the period during which the scheme is being carried out and as assessable value

---

* Out of the 123 planning schemes in progress in England, since 1909, 106, dealing with 157,925 acres, are being prepared by urban authorities, while 17, dealing with 50,230 acres, are being prepared by rural authorities.

increases. It may reasonably be claimed that the Ruislip-Northwood council has, as a result of the preparation of this scheme, laid a foundation for future development which will insure health, convenience and amenity for the community which could not have been obtained by any other method except at prohibitive cost. (Figure 39).

The work being done by the Conference on Arterial Roads in Greater London, which has been at work for the past three years, is an indication of the importance which is attached to the subject of planning and development in England. The conference comprises representatives of 137 local authorities. It has been holding frequent meetings, with a view to determining the best lines of development, particularly in regard to the means of communication by road, for an area of 1,000 square miles within and surrounding the county of London. (Figure 40.) The greater part of this territory is rural in character. Many separate municipalities are preparing schemes for their area, but they are combining together in conference to secure a general plan for their arterial system of highways. The fact that they have been able to join together and present united decisions to the president of the Local Government Board of England shows the value of the services of the Local Government Board in securing effective co-operation. If it is possible for so many authorities to combine surely it should be practicable for the comparatively few who are usually concerned in the control of suburban areas adjacent to large cities in Canada.

In Britain less confusion is caused by the use of the term town planning, because of the broader meaning given to the word town, and because a greater proportion of the rural territory is urban in character. The need for some change in the British Town Planning Act, in order that it may be made more adaptable to rural areas, is, however, being recognized by British authorities, *e.g.*, Mr. Henry Aldridge, in his book, *The Case for Town Planning,* argues that the Act of 1909 should be amended to enable rural councils to prepare a rural planning scheme with the minimum of work and a maximum of practical efficiency. The draft Planning and Development Act of the Commission of Conservation* makes provision for the preparation of simple rural planning (development) schemes in a form which could be made adaptable to British conditions.

PLANNING NOT AN END IN ITSELF

It has to be recognized that a mere plan will not do anything to conserve life or secure industrial efficiency. The plan is only the basis on which a scheme may be made to control development of land. A plan may be

---

*   *Draft Planning and Development Act. Revised Edition, 1917.*

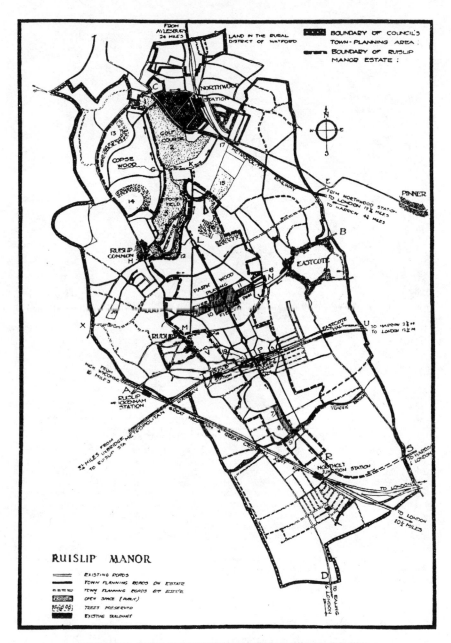

FIGURE 39   RUISLIP-NORTHWOOD TOWN PLANNING SCHEME

The area included in the scheme comprises 5,922 acres. The proportion actually built upon is shown in solid black and only 437 acres are in course of development. The solid lines show the position of the new roads proposed under the scheme and indicate that the greater part of the development was left to be arranged between the local authority and the owners of the land, subject to principles laid down in the scheme.

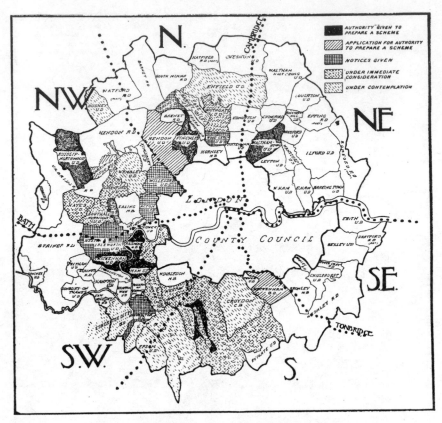

FIGURE 40   MAP OF GREATER LONDON

This map, copied from the "Town Planning Review," shows the area of Greater London, comprising what is known as the Metropolitan district, having an area of 693 square miles. Another 391 square miles of territory outside the metropolitan area is included in districts which have a direct interest in the arterial road system of Greater London. No less than 137 local authorities have jurisdiction in the combined area, and all of these authorities appointed representatives to the Conferences on Arterial Roads in 1913. For that purpose the areas were divided into six sections indicated by the dotted boundaries on the map. These conferences have had frequent meetings and have agreed upon plans of arterial roads for the whole area, a great part of which is entirely rural.

The authorities, while thus combining to determine the skeleton plan of the main highway system, are acting separately in preparing town planning schemes for their own areas. The map indicates the progress made from the passing of the Act in December, 1909, to December, 1913. Since then several schemes have been further advanced, including that of Ruislip-Northwood (illustrated in figure 39), which was completed in 1914.

prepared on paper, but no better result secured than if it had been omitted, because the thing that really matters is the development that follows. "Planning is not an end in itself, but only a means to an end; it is only part of an instrument to guide development and it is of no value unless it guides it aright." *

---

* "Report of Town Planning Adviser." *Eighth Annual Report of the Commission of Conservation.*

It is important that the emphasis should be placed on the character of the development to be achieved under a scheme and not on the preparation of a plan; hence the use of the term "planning and development" throughout this report, instead of "town planning," and the reason for the choice of the title of the draft Act of the Commission of Conservation, namely "Planning and Development Act." The change in terminology is not, however, solely due to ambiguity of previous terms; it also arises from the fact that the same principles which are proving successful in regard to the organization of town life are necessary to be applied to rural life. In other words, the scope of planning and development cannot in practice be limited to urban development if it is to achieve its general object of securing health, efficiency, convenience and amenity.

NEED OF LEGISLATION

Before proper development schemes can be made, it is necessary to have legislation passed in each province, firstly, for the purpose of enabling municipal authorities to prepare schemes for their areas and, secondly, for setting up the provincial machinery necessary to control development in unorganized territory. Such an Act has to make provision for securing effective co-operation between the province, the municipality and the owners of land, and for determining the procedure necessary in connection with the preparation and making of schemes.

In considering any description or text of land planning legislation it has, therefore, to be borne in mind that the measures proposed by the Commission of Conservation, and passed in some of the provinces of Canada, do not give power to the Provincial governments to plan municipal areas, but merely determine the procedure under which municipalities can plan their own areas. There are one or two compulsory elements in the proposed legislation which are necessary to secure uniformity and effective execution, but they do not touch the power of the municipality to control its own expenditure nor to prepare a scheme in accordance with its own ideas so long as it adheres to certain minimum standards which it is desirable to fix for general application.

Among the reasons why new legislation is necessary is the fact that proper development cannot be carried out without some more scientific method in which provision shall be made for the exercise of reasonable discretion. Development schemes in their very nature have to deal with separate, and sometimes opposing, interests, including those of the general public and private owners. It is an essential feature of planning and development legislation that it should provide for effective co-operation between the public authorities and the private owners, and also between adjacent municipal authorities. It is therefore necessary to have a skilled department of the Provincial government to act as a sort of court of appeal in regard to differences which are bound to arise between interested parties and conflicting or co-operating authorities.

BOUNDARIES OF DEVELOPMENT SCHEMES

It may not be practicable in some cases to prepare development schemes within the arbitrary boundaries of one municipal area. For topographical and other reasons one local authority may desire to include part of an area of another local authority in its scheme. In England it has been recognized that arbitrary municipal boundaries must not influence the boundaries of town planning schemes. The city of St. John, New Brunswick, has obtained authority from the Legislature to prepare a scheme for an area of about 20,000 acres, of which about half is outside the city limits. (Figure 42.)

No objection was raised to the inclusion of the outside territory in the area of the scheme by the local authorities concerned, and only one objection was raised by an owner.

The Census Bureau of the United States, in its latest census, has shown that the arbitrary boundaries of cities were little heeded by the growth of population, industry or development generally. Because of this it is necessary that planning and development schemes should embrace a much larger area than is covered by the administrative unit of the city or town, but, if the rural municipality does its duty and prepares schemes for the urban parts of its area, it would not be necessary for the city or town to encroach on the territory outside its boundaries. The development of the agricultural areas adjacent to the city should be considered in relation to the development of the building subdivisions in these suburban schemes.

The entrances and exits of a town are dependent on the planning of the adjacent territory. If one town or district wants to alter the location or levels of roads or railways, the adjacent district must plan to conform to the alteration. Mr. George B. Ford, of New York, has stated that this problem has been realized in Newark, N.J., after four years of endeavour to apply city planning within its area, and recently that city organized a conference on interurban improvement for the purpose of discussing questions relating to the general plan of the territory comprised in some eighteen neighbouring municipalities.

In New York State there has been organized a West Chester County Planning Commission, indicating the first effort on this continent to organize the planning of a county area.

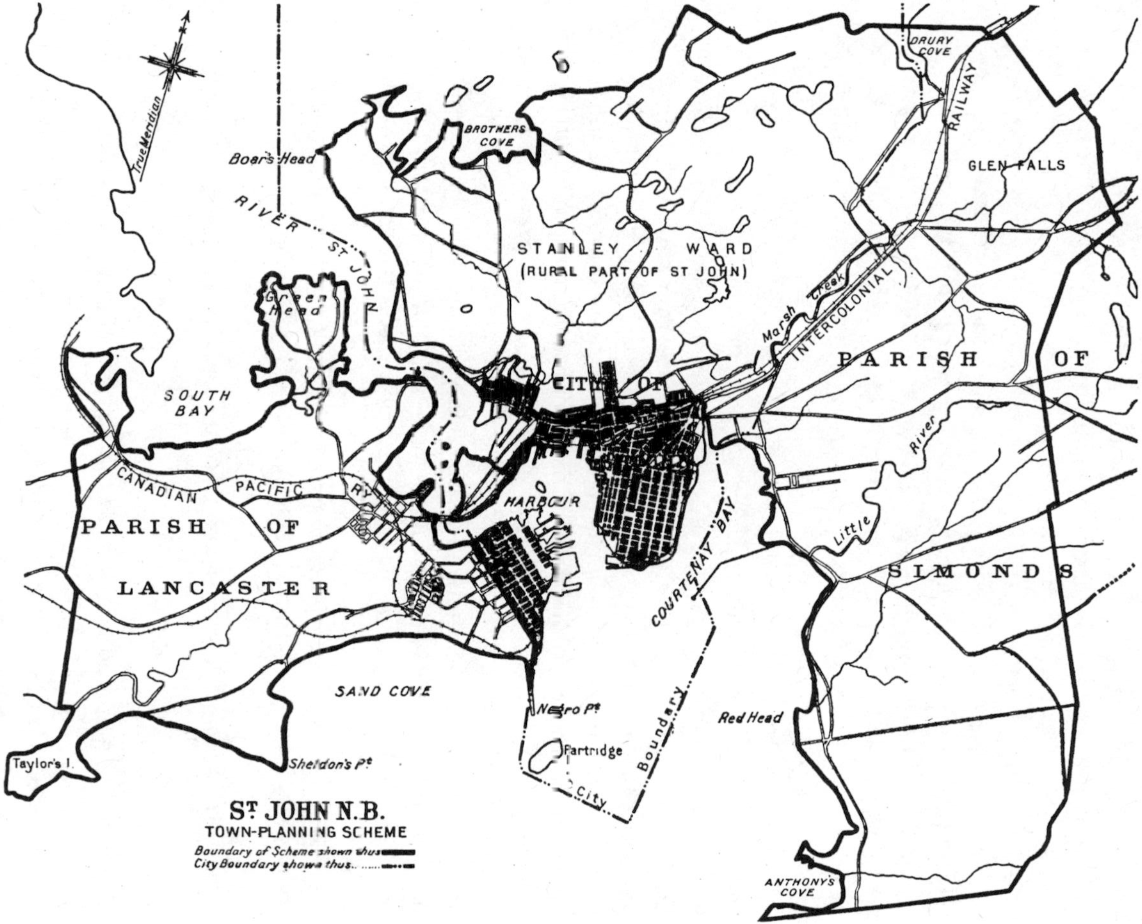

FIGURE 42
MAP OF ST. JOHN TOWN
PLANNING AREA

This copy of Map No. 1 of the St. John Town Planning Scheme shows the boundary of the area authorized to be planned. More than half of the area of the scheme is outside the city boundaries in the county parishes of Lancaster and Simonds, and much the greater proportion, both within and without the city, is rural land. Authority to prepare the scheme has been given to the St. John City Council by the Provincial Government under the New Brunswick Town Planning Act. The County and Parish Councils raised no objection to parts of their areas being included. The inclusion of such a large area will be of great advantage in connection with the preparation of a comprehensive scheme dealing with industrial, residential and agricultural development.

As, therefore, it may be necessary for the success of a scheme that it include land in more than one municipal area this involves that there must be some higher power than either of the two authorities to determine whether or not the area of the scheme should include land outside the area of the council preparing the scheme and questions arising in respect of overlapping jurisdiction. To secure efficient administration of planning and development acts a department of the Provincial government, with skilled advisers, should act both as a bureau of advice and a tribunal of appeal. The former is especially necessary to render assistance to the small municipalities.

There are two other important reasons why new legislation is necessary and why it is found essential in such legislation to provide for co-operation between the Provincial government and the municipalities. In the first place a local authority must have complete control over any building and street development within its area during the period while it is preparing a scheme, and, in the second place, it must be made exempt from spurious claims for compensation which might otherwise be set up during that period. To enable it to have that control, and yet to prevent it from injuring legitimate private interests, it is essential that owners receive adequate notice of the intention to prepare a scheme, that they should have the power and opportunity to object, and that a third party, other than the local authority or the owners, should hear such objections in public. It is important that a public hearing held for such a purpose should be conducted by an expert connected with the Provincial department devoting its attention to the work of planning and development.

Co-operation between Provincial Government and Municipalities

The granting of any additional powers to local authorities to control development of land, which affects property in such a way that the right of eminent domain will be interfered with, involves that certain procedure has to be carried out for the protection of private interests. The provincial authority is the proper one to secure compliance with that procedure. Unless a planning and development act provides for these things it will be largely ineffective. If, on the one hand, it does not enable the local authority to prevent undesirable development taking place while the scheme is being prepared, or if, on the other hand, the method by which this is accomplished unduly injures private owners, the effect of preparing a development scheme would not be likely to be beneficial.

Why Rural and Urban Development
Should Be Dealt with in One Measure

Prima facie it would seem as if the proper way to control rural and urban development would be either to have two acts – namely, a rural development act and an urban development act – or to have one act so framed as to enable urban schemes to be prepared for urban areas and rural schemes to be prepared for rural areas. In practice, however, this would not work out satisfactorily, owing to the absence of any clear division line between urban and rural territory and between urban and rural conditions. Moreover, to suggest a division of this kind would be to emphasize a distinction between the two kinds of areas and their problems which does not exist, although it has erroneously been assumed to exist and has been fostered by many whose one-sided experience has blinded them to the interdependence of urban and rural life. Not only is there no sharp division line between town and country under modern conditions, and no certainty that what is isolated rural territory today may not become the site of a town tomorrow, but the arbitrary divisions between urban and rural municipal areas are such that the conditions and problems on both sides of a boundary line between such areas may be precisely the same.

The only satisfactory method, even if it be somewhat defective, is to have an act which will regulate all *new* settlement and development in all kinds of urban and rural areas. There is, of course, a sharp distinction between the problems that have to be dealt with in areas which are fully built up with substantial and more or less permanent improvements, like those in the central parts of large cities, and other problems in suburban areas where the land is either not built upon or is only in process of being developed. Land which is fully built upon and served by improved streets, which cannot be altered or re-planned except at great cost for reconstruction, is not suitable for inclusion in the area of a development scheme. Even if the planning of such land has been hopelessly bad and the streets have proved to be too narrow and are intersected by dangerous railway crossings, it is hardly practicable to remodel them by a development scheme dealing with large areas of land. The Act and the development schemes prepared under it, intended to deal with both urban and rural conditions, will contain provisions which are applicable to urban and inapplicable to rural territory and vice versa. But there can be no objection to this since, if any provision is inapplicable, no person or interest can be injured thereby. For instance, if a scheme provided for control of building lines, *i.e.,* the distance of set back from the highway boundary

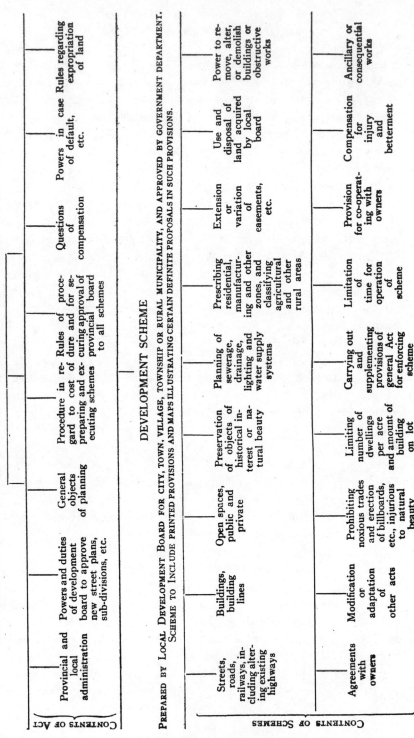

PLANNING LEGISLATURE AND PROCEDURE.

PROVINCIAL GENERAL ACT RELATING TO PLANNING AND DEVELOPMENT OF LAND IN URBAN AND RURAL AREAS.

CONTENTS OF ACT

- Provincial and local administration
- Powers and duties of development board to approve new street plans, sub-divisions, etc.
- General objects of planning
- Procedure in regard to cost of preparing and executing schemes
- Rules of procedure and for securing approval of provincial board to all schemes
- Questions of compensation
- Powers in case of default, etc.
- Rules regarding expropriation of land

DEVELOPMENT SCHEME

PREPARED BY LOCAL DEVELOPMENT BOARD FOR CITY, TOWN, VILLAGE, TOWNSHIP OR RURAL MUNICIPALITY, AND APPROVED BY GOVERNMENT DEPARTMENT. SCHEME TO INCLUDE PRINTED PROVISIONS AND MAPS ILLUSTRATING CERTAIN DEFINITE PROPOSALS IN SUCH PROVISIONS.

CONTENTS OF SCHEMES

- Streets, roads, railways, including altering existing highways
- Buildings, building lines
- Open spaces, public and private
- Preservation of objects of historical interest or natural beauty
- Planning of sewerage, drainage, lighting and water supply systems
- Prescribing residential, manufacturing and other zones, and classifying agricultural and other rural areas
- Extension or variation of easements, etc.
- Use and disposal of land acquired by local board
- Power to remove, alter, or demolish buildings or obstructive works

- Agreements with owners
- Modification or adaptation of other acts
- Prohibiting noxious trades and erection of billboards, etc., injurious to natural beauty
- Limiting number of dwellings per acre and amount of building on lot
- Carrying out and supplementing provisions of general Act for enforcing scheme
- Limitation of time for operation of scheme
- Provision for co-operating with owners
- Compensation for injury and betterment
- Ancillary or consequential works

in a district where no buildings were likely to be erected, this would not be a burden on the farmer, since it would not force or accelerate building development but merely provide for its regulation if and when it took place. If no building took place the provision would remain inoperative. On the other hand – no person or government can foresee where building is going to take place, or where a town site is going to be laid out. Restrictions, which are necessary to regulate development where it is occurring, may, without injury to anyone, be made to apply even where development is unlikely to occur. If such regulations are to be effective they must deal with the possibility and not with the fact.

DETAILS OF REMEDIES RESERVED FOR SUBSEQUENT REPORT

The detailed consideration of the measures necessary to secure the solution of the problems of rural development has to be reserved for a subsequent report because, as this report on rural conditions has to be followed by a report on urban conditions, and as the same measures are proposed in respect of both urban and rural problems, it is necessary to complete the study of both sets of conditions before setting out the details of the remedy applicable to both. This course will prevent a great deal of duplication.

For the above reason only a brief description is given in this report of some of the essential features of planning and development legislation and schemes.

The tabulated statement on the opposite page indicates the relative nature and importance, first, of the enabling and regulating Act required to be passed in each province and, second, the development scheme (or local Act) to be prepared by the municipality. A brief outline of the main features of this legislation is given below under three heads:

(1) The general objects of development schemes.
(2) The principal contents of development schemes in rural areas.
(3) Summary or leading features of planning and development legislation.

GENERAL OBJECTS OF DEVELOPMENT SCHEMES

The main objects desired to be secured in planning land have already been described as:

(*a*) Efficiency and convenience
(*b*) Proper sanitary and hygienic conditions
(*c*) Amenity or agreeableness

All these relate, first, to the town, village or rural municipality as organized communities; second, to the industry or industries, which are the *raison d'être* of each community, and, third, to family, which is the unit of the social life of the community.

(*a*) EFFICIENCY AND CONVENIENCE – To plan for efficiency and convenience in rural land development schemes we have chiefly to consider the questions of transportation and distribution and the location and grouping of farms, residences and factories. It has already been pointed out how many things in connection with the agricultural settlement are dependent for success on proper means of communication and on the planning of the location and grouping of homesteads.

The development scheme will make no direct provision for agricultural co-operation and education, but it will provide facilities for these things in the way it arranges the settlement of land and the means of communication; it will not include any provision for organizing rural credit banks but, having facilitated co-operation, and made the educational and social centre more convenient to the farmer, it will have provided the basis necessary for such banks to be successfully established. It may not include provisions for establishing an industrial village, but it may include a plan for the proper location of such a village and have regard to the conditions – such as the presence of water-power – which are required to establish a healthy village. The development scheme provides the necessary foundation for all these things. It has to consider the waterway, the railway and the highway and how the efficient and convenient means of communication can be secured for the farmer and the manufacturer. Under the present system of planning land no regard is paid to these important problems – the requirements of traffic have to adapt themselves to suit the survey plan of streets instead of the plan being adapted to suit the requirements of traffic.

In regard to harbours and railways, it is unlikely that a development scheme will deal with more than the approaches and with the linking up of these approaches with the industrial or residential areas. A scheme should not be permitted to interfere with the line of railway or any land or building used in connection with the railway, but it might impose restrictions upon the use of land owned by a railway company and intended or likely to be used for purposes of development other than those which had to do with the railway. Railway companies having real estate interests and owning tracts of vacant land in rural or urban areas should be compelled in their own interest to co-operate with the local council in regard to the development of these tracts.

PLATE XIX   SQUARE OCCUPIED BY PUBLIC BUILDINGS AND SURROUNDED BY STORES,
CHARLOTTETOWN, P.E.I.

Under proper development schemes it is practical to get structural and natural beauty
even in the business centres of towns without sacrifice of efficiency or increase of cost over
what is necessary to be spent in development in any case.

PLATE XIX   RESIDENTIAL DEVELOPMENT AT CAULFIELD, B.C.

In rural and suburban development greater cost need not be incurred than at present
to secure pleasant environment to dwellings. The conservation of existing natural features and the
employment of simple forms of architecture produce the most beautiful results.

Perhaps the most important object of convenience in a development scheme is in respect of highways and streets. To secure convenience for traffic as well as economy and efficiency from a municipal standpoint it would be essential in a scheme to permit roads to be of varied width. The absurdity of the present by-law standard of width has already been dealt with. Under a land development scheme roads should be planned to suit the needs of traffic and not to follow a stereotyped rule that fixes a minimum standard without regard to these needs. The 100-foot road should be complementary to the 40-foot road and even the narrow carriage drive of less than 40 feet leading to a few isolated residences should be permitted. (Figure 41.)

Next to highways, and having a relation to their width, consideration has to be given to the fixing of building lines so as to secure that there would be ample space for future widening if such were ever deemed to be necessary, without having to demolish or remove the buildings. Buildings would thus be set back from the boundary line of the road without waste of land and street construction, the distance of the set back being fixed according to the class and width of road. The density of buildings on the lot should also be regulated with due regard to the width of road or street, as this has an effect on the traffic requirements. The character of construction could, if necessary, be determined in a scheme and, if so, would be regulated to suit different classes of road. The apportionment of the cost to be incurred by the province, the municipality and the owner would also be proper matters to be dealt with in a scheme; as well as questions relating to stopping up unnecessary highways and diverting others which may be improved as regards position and alignment. These matters would be largely settled by co-operation between authorities and parties interested in the land affected by the scheme.

In regard to the location of farms, little, if anything, could be done to alter the position of farm buildings already erected in the territory developed for agricultural purposes, but in all undeveloped or unimproved territory the location and grouping of farm buildings so as to secure the closest settlement practicable, the provision of radial highways and the reduction of unnecessary length of roads would be important matters to consider. If it should ever become part of a government policy to encourage re-settlement of abandoned farms, or to reclaim and settle marsh areas in older territory the question of planning the location of new buildings would be part of a scheme. In all such cases regard should be paid to the questions of highway development, the situation of schools, co-operative and distributive facilities, and social centres.

The classification of land should be another important feature in schemes. Before a scheme was prepared for a township, a survey should

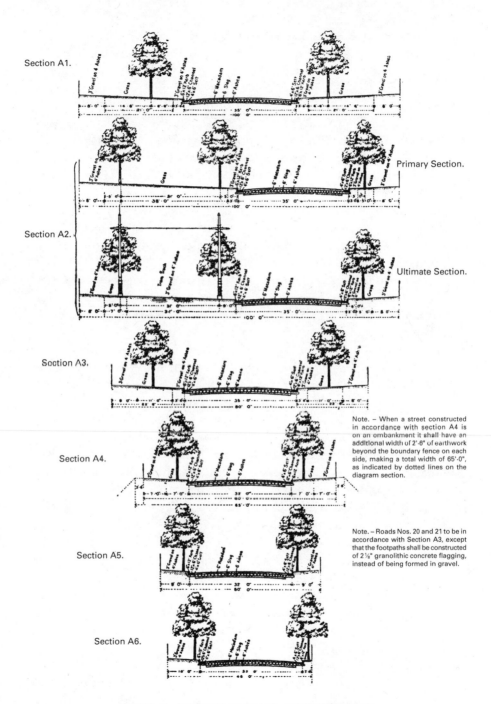

Section A1.

Primary Section.

Section A2.

Ultimate Section.

Section A3.

Note. – When a street constructed in accordance with section A4 is on an embankment it shall have an additional width of 2'·6" of earthwork beyond the boundary fence on each side, making a total width of 65'·0", as indicated by dotted lines on the diagram section.

Section A4.

Note. – Roads Nos. 20 and 21 to be in accordance with Section A3, except that the footpaths shall be constructed of 2⅛" granolithic concrete flagging, instead of being formed in gravel.

Section A5.

Section A6.

FIGURE 41 SECTIONS OF ROADS – QUINTON SCHEME

Sections showing variety of width of roads and streets to be constructed in the Quinton and Harborne town planning area by the Birmingham City Council. The streets vary in width from 45' to 100' to suit different purposes. Streets varying from 20' to 42' in width are also permitted under certain conditions.

be made to ascertain the character of the land included, its suitability for different kinds of farming, or, if unsuitable for farming, whether it should be made a timber or other kind of reserve. The nature of the scheme would be greatly influenced by the facts ascertained in this survey. Areas could also be restricted for residential or other purposes.

A scheme could include provisions for fixing the areas best adapted for the erection of factories and prevent their location in other areas more suitable for agriculture or residence. Incidentally this would have its influence on the width and form of construction of the streets serving such localities. In making such provisions owners of land would have to be consulted, but, even if they objected, they would have no title to claim compensation in this respect, if the Provincial government decided that the restriction was reasonable for the purpose of the amenity of the district.

In many rural districts there are villages and railway depots which suffer from bad approaches, or there is need for consolidation of schools or for provision of co-operative facilities, which are appropriate matters to be dealt with.

(b) PROPER SANITARY AND HYGIENIC CONDITIONS – What is meant by the objects of proper sanitary and hygienic conditions will have been gathered from the facts given and arguments used in preceding chapters regarding the need for improvement of such conditions in rural areas. There are certain matters which come within this category which have also a relation to the object of convenience. For instance, when the widths of roads are fixed to suit the traffic requirements some will be much wider than is demanded under existing by-laws but others, where the traffic needs will be small, may be quite narrow, and, in the interests of economy, should be narrow. In the past such roads have been made wide for the purpose of securing air space to the buildings erected on their frontage. This purpose, however, is much more cheaply and effectively secured by fixing the distances between the buildings and the amount of a lot that can be built upon, than by creating wide streets. It has been shown that the making of wide streets causes the owners of lots fronting upon them to crowd buildings on these lots, with the result that unhealthy conditions are created as a direct consequence of a law that is intended to prevent these conditions. Under a development scheme minimum distances are fixed between the buildings on both sides of a street without regard to the width of the street, so that the air space is not secured at the expense of a wide street. Moreover the density of building on a lot may be prescribed, so that air space is secured at the side and rear of the building as well as on its frontage – a matter which is usually neglected. The objects of sanitation may also be secured by preventing residences being erected on swampy areas or being mixed up in an indiscriminate way with factories. The standards prescribed for height, character, sanitary arrangements, and situation of buildings in a rural area would vary according to the character of development and would naturally differ in purely rural areas and in those areas being developed in subdivisions round cities and towns.

(*c*) AMENITY – Amenity means "the quality of being pleasant or agreeable" – a quality which is of recognized value as an asset in maintaining prosperity in a district, although it has been, and still is, the subject of some scorn on the part of certain people. Whatever is needed to make the development of an area, or the surroundings of the buildings within an area, pleasant or agreeable to the inhabitants would appear to be the object in view under this heading. Frequently a whole district is spoiled by the disorder and unpleasantness introduced into it by one individual, over whose acts the rest of the community have no control.

There is not the objection to the word "amenity" that there is to the word "beauty." It is more comprehensive and refers to a quality in buildings and their surroundings which can be easily defined. A home may be pleasant and agreeable to the general public and to the owner and yet not "beautiful" in the eyes of the artist; but a scheme may provide for the preservation of a fine group of trees as a purpose of amenity which would secure beauty as well as amenity. A local authority may consider that certain restrictions on the height of buildings may be necessary to secure the amenity of part of its district in the interests of the majority of property owners, yet the higher buildings might be the more beautiful. A scheme may require that factories shall only be erected in a certain part or zone of a district, because that is most pleasant and agreeable to the majority of the residents, yet the effect may be to destroy more natural beauty by this restriction than if it were not imposed. Reasonable restriction by a local authority on the use of property may be applied without being deemed to injuriously affect the property – and therefore without being a subject for a compensation claim – but if a scheme involves the acquisition of any property by a local authority, such as the purchase of the site of a historical landmark or an open space, the market price of the property would of course have to be paid.

THE PRINCIPAL CONTENTS OF DEVELOPMENT SCHEMES IN RURAL AREAS

Practically anything connected with the development of land can be included in a development scheme under a planning and development act.

Only by this means can development be planned comprehensively, and its various parts be considered in relation to each other at the same time. Even those matters which are the subject of general provincial statutes or by-laws should be permitted to be varied by the provisions of a scheme. This is an additional reason why the final approval of the scheme must rest with the provincial authority. The following outline gives an indication of some of the matters which may be dealt with:

(*a*) Fixing varied widths of streets and roads; altering or closing existing highways; determining building lines or setbacks of buildings according to a comprehensive scheme for a large area. The relationship between the street and the character and density of the buildings to be erected upon it should be taken into account.

(*b*) Reserving land for new main thoroughfares.

(*c*) Limiting the number of dwelling houses to be erected per acre and prescribing the amount of any lot which may be built upon in order to ensure ample light and air for all buildings and healthy housing conditions.

(*d*) Prescribing zones in urban parts of rural areas within which to regulate different degrees of density and height of buildings, according to local conditions.

(*e*) Classifying land for use for residential purposes, factories, agriculture, timber reserves, etc., and adjusting the system of taxation and the system of planning and constructing local improvements to suit the kind of development permitted under the scheme, to encourage the economic use of the land, and to lessen injurious speculation. Under a scheme land could be permanently dedicated for agricultural purposes and assessed at its value for that purpose, to the advantage of the public and owners alike.

Every scheme can be prepared to deal with local conditions on their merits under any skilled advice that may be employed with the advantage of any local experience.

To be successful, planning and development schemes have to be flexible. One of their advantages is that it dispenses with the necessity of stereotyped by-laws. Certain general principles, such as the amount of space that must be reserved around buildings of different kinds, the width of main arterial thoroughfares, etc., have to be definitely settled, but matters of detail affecting individual properties can be made subject to variation.

One of the purposes of such schemes should be to transfer a larger portion of the burden of making local improvements to the owners of real estate who benefit from these improvements. Among other matters which might be dealt with in rural land development schemes are:

Cancellation and re-planning of subdivisions.

Provision of private and public open spaces for recreation.

Preservation of objects of historic interest or natural beauty.

Planning of sewerage, drainage, and sewage disposal, lighting and water supply systems in advance.

Extension of variation of private right-of-way and other easements.

Planning of community centres and educational institutes.

Protection of rural districts from noxious industries and ugly hoardings.

It is only when these matters are dealt with in a scheme that effective control of land development can be secured on economical lines. When attempts are made to get improvements carried out in respect of individual properties, such as the simple matters of fixing a building line, or diverting a road, much opposition has to be faced, or compensation paid, because the owner is being asked to give up something to comply with a requirement which affects his property only. He has to get compensation not necessarily because he is injured but because he is asked to confer a benefit upon the community which other owners are not asked to confer. In a development scheme the requirements of local authorities are made general throughout its area and in practice what have appeared to be revolutionary proposals have met with little opposition.

In certain schemes large areas of land have been granted free by owners for recreation purposes and for widening roads without cost to the community and without loss to the owners. The fact that the latter contribute by this means to a general scheme of development has meant in such cases that the balance of their property was increased in value as a result of his contribution to the scheme.

The reader who is not familiar with the working of planning and development legislation will probably find many questions arise in his mind regarding the feasibility and benefit of the proposals referred to in the above outline; but experience in the working of such legislation leads to the conclusion that it is the only sound and effective way to control the development of land.

Summary of Leading Features of Planning and Development Legislation

The following summary relates to the proposals of the Commission of Conservation, some of which may not be acceptable in one or other of the provinces. For instance, the compulsory provisions with regard to the appointment of a development board and the preparation of a partial development scheme may be objected to. While it is considered important that these two things should be compulsory this is not essential to the working of the Act, although desirable in the interests of uniformity.

1. ADMINISTRATION. – A new department of the province should be set up, or an existing department strengthened, to undertake all work in connection with planning and development in addition to other work relating to local government. A director of planning and development should be appointed for the province. Each local authority should be required to appoint a development board, or to constitute itself into a development board, in which capacity it would devote entire attention to planning for the future.

2. NEW STREETS AND SUBDIVISIONS. – A development board should approve the plans and particulars of all streets and subdivisions on more comprehensive lines than hitherto. In this connection regulations should provide for dealing with matters connected with the adjustment and alteration of boundaries of land and the cancellation or modifications of plans of subdivisions. Approval of planning the development of unorganized territory should be centralized in, and co-ordinated by, the director of planning of the province.

3. MAIN THOROUGHFARES. – The lines of main thoroughfares should be determined by the provincial government and a map prepared showing the main thoroughfares with which local planning schemes should be linked up and tributary means of communication by road arranged.

4. CO-OPERATION. – The Act should provide for effective co-operation between the adjacent municipalities in regard to the control of highways, sanitation and general planning. Provision should also be made for securing co-operation with owners of land at every stage. These should be requirements of the procedure regulations of the provincial government.

5. SPECULATION ON PUBLIC IMPROVEMENTS. – The Act should provide that when an authority desires to prepare a scheme and sends in its application to the government, no owner or other party can, after the date of application, do anything to contravene the scheme; and power should be given to remove and pull down any buildings erected in contravention to the provisions of the scheme.

PLATE XX   PRESERVING AMENITIES IN STRATFORD, ONT.

Made from a "frog pond" and a dump ground through the enterprises of the Stratford Parks Commission. The making of small towns more attractive is one of the best means of securing the healthy combination of urban and rural development in Canada.

6. Compensation. – In addition to the arbitrary demands for compensation for injury, provision should be made that the local authority can claim half of any increased value which is given to property by the making or operation of the scheme. More important still, it is necessary to include a provision that no claim for compensation can be made against a local authority on the ground that property has been injured as a result of reasonable restrictions applied for the purpose of securing healthy development. In that connection the following subsection is, perhaps, the most important in the Act and without it an Act would be of comparatively little value:

> Property shall not be deemed to be injuriously affected by reason of the making of any provisions inserted in a scheme, which, with a view to securing the amenity of the area affected by the scheme, or any part thereof, or proper hygienic conditions in connection with the buildings to be erected thereon, prescribe the space about buildings, or the percentage of any lot which may be covered with buildings, or limit the number of buildings to be erected, or prescribe the height, character or use of buildings, and which the Department, having regard to the nature and situation of the land affected by the provisions, considers reasonable for the purpose of amenity and proper hygienic conditions.

7. Preparation of Partial Development Schemes. – Under an Act local authorities or their development boards should have the option of preparing complete schemes, but in order to secure some kind of uniformity and to prevent friction by the adjacent municipalities, it is desirable that the Act should make it compulsory for all authorities or boards to prepare a *partial* development scheme.* This partial scheme would be simple in its provisions and not require the preparation of any elaborate provisions or map. Its object would be to generally classify the land and lay down certain principles to guide development. By this means a certain standard of development could be fixed as the minimum. The fact that this is proposed to be compulsory does not mean that the local authority is tied down with regard to the details of the scheme or is compelled to undertake its preparation at considerable cost. The authority would prepare its own scheme and limit its expenditure to the trifling cost of preparation. The latter could be reduced to a minimum by the provincial department preparing a model set of provisions for a partial scheme.

---

* In the Nova Scotia Act the "partial development scheme" is designated "a set of town planning by-laws."

8. Revoking or Altering a Scheme. – When a scheme is deliberately prepared by the local authority and has been approved by the provincial department it should take effect as if it were part of the Act and only be altered or revoked by a subsequent scheme. This is necessary to protect interested parties from having changes made without sufficient reason.

9. Area of a Scheme. – No definite area should be prescribed for a scheme in an Act and the local authority should be permitted to include land outside its own boundaries, if, after hearing objections from the adjoining authority, the provincial department decides to permit the inclusion of such land.

10. Provision of Expenses. – The cost of preparing a scheme should be limited to a certain percentage of the assessable value of the district. *In regard to all expenditure the local authority should have the determining voice whether or not it delegates its power of executing a scheme to a development board.*

11. Procedure Regulations. – The rules of procedure should be drawn up by the provincial department.

12. Expropriation of Land. – The usual powers connected with the expropriation of land in the different provinces should be extended under an Act to simplify the purchase of land especially for open spaces.

13. Powers in Case of Default, etc. – The provincial department should be the superior authority in determining any question which may arise between the different parties interested in giving effect to a scheme and any appeals or representations made under it.

In considering the character and scope of the proposed planning and development legislation we have to bear in mind that it is designed to meet a complex and many-sided problem or series of problems and a variety of contingencies in different kinds of area. Greater simplicity might be possible under conditions where autocratic government were possible; but under our democratic conditions it is essential to impose restraint on bad development and to encourage good development by means which cannot be fairly criticized as an undue and improper interference with the liberty of the subjects. In course of time, experience may show some easier and more direct method of attaining the object aimed at, but until that experience is obtained we should err on the side of protecting such private interests as are not proved to be in conflict with the public welfare.

Conclusion

In conclusion it is contended that proper control of the development of land cannot be secured without the preparation of comprehensive development schemes, in which consideration will be given to all matters affecting public convenience, health and amenity; and that one of the most urgent matters in connection with the conservation and development of land and human resources in Canada is the promotion of planning and development legislation, and its effective administration, in accordance with the objects and principles outlined in this chapter.

CHAPTER IX
PROVINCIAL PLANNING AND DEVELOPMENT LEGISLATION

Commentary by Gary Davidson

It is both enticing and perilous to reflect on the course of rural planning from the vantage point of nearly a century. Thomas Adams' treatise for the Commission of Conservation in 1917 poses such a challenge. Enticing? There is always a natural fascination with the insights of the past. Perilous? Contexts change, and we are all bushwhacked by chaos and complexity. Reading Adams provides not so much an opportunity to pass judgment on his clairvoyance but an occasion to reflect on the tortuous path of rural planning and contemplate the seeds sown by Thomas Adams.

This chapter considers Adams musings on legislation. His main concerns lie in the following areas: types of legislation, the lack of distinction between urban and rural areas, anticipating future trends, the importance of roads, and strategies regarding administration, appeals, and compensation. At the core of his legislative framework, Adams argues for one piece of legislation or act that would combine both urban and rural planning. Almost prophetically, he writes: "The only satisfactory method, even if it be somewhat defective, is to have an act which will regulate all *new* settlement and development in all kinds of urban and rural areas" (page 319). Behind this suggestion is his belief that the purpose of planning in rural areas is the development of rural lands, primarily for urban purposes. In this vein he writes: "The thing that really matters is the development that follows" (page 314).

The position that there is a lack of a clear division between urban and rural lands and that rural lands on the urban boundary will continue to develop in a suburban fashion is the framework for Adams' approach to rural planning and legislation to guide development in rural areas. Two of his comments are worth quoting in this context. In reference to a special Act for rural areas, he writes: "This would not work out satisfactorily, owing to the absence of any clear division line between urban and rural territory and between urban and rural conditions" (page 319). "No person or government can foresee where building is going to take place, or where a townsite is going to be laid out" (page 321).

Adams' approach was to ride the trend, the trend toward building and urban development in a young land with a seemingly endless supply of rural land – rural land waiting for buildings and towns.

This was the Canada that Adams observed in the early 1900s. His overriding concern was not the amount of development or even its location, but its quality.

Slums were a hazard, especially rural slums. He wanted to guide development and improve its quality. To this end, he tried to lay a foundation, through legislation, to improve the quality of suburban growth and the development of new townsites. To achieve these goals, he proposed a comprehensive legislative agenda that included the main elements of planning design, how to administer a planning system, the adjudication of appeals, and the nature of compensation.

One major aspect of his proposed legislation falls under the heading "Efficiency and Convenience." Adams argues that traffic and highway planning are critical: "Perhaps the most important object of convenience in a development scheme is in respect to highways and streets"; "there would be ample space for future widening if such were ever deemed to be necessary" (page 324).

To Adams, planning, be it urban or rural, was about development – buildings, roads, and hard services. The goal was to improve the quality of development as the quantity increased. During the time in which Adams wrote, these were the important needs. From the perspective of the present, however, his ideas started a planning process that had significant negative impacts on rural communities throughout the decades.

Adams also paid attention to how such a planning system could be implemented. His view of planning was "scientific," and this paradigm, so in vogue at the time, tempered his approach to administration. Two central themes informed his administrative concepts – objectivity and co-operation. The rip and tear of politics do not enter his system – nor do the whims of the public.

To start, Adams recommends that a provincial department of planning be set up and a director of planning and development appointed for the province. At the municipal level (local authority), a development board should be appointed that would "devote entire attention to planning for the future" (page 330). Furthermore, he believes co-operation between and among adjacent municipalities and landowners will control "highways, sanitation and general planning" (page 330).

Although co-operation was Adams' watchword, he acknowledges that there will be differences and that appeals to local decisions will occur. In these cases, "the provincial department should be the superior authority in determining any question which may arise between the different parties" (page 333). Because of these differences, Adams proposes that compensation not go to individuals but rather to the local municipality. He suggests that "the local authority can claim half of any increased value which is given to property by the making or operation of the scheme" (page 332).

Adams does not have much to say about planners or the people who would prepare the general plans, or, as he terms them, development schemes. He does, however, venture that "the authority [local municipality] would prepare its own scheme and limit its expenditure to the trifling cost of preparation. The latter could be reduced to a minimum by the provincial department preparing a model set of provisions for a partial scheme" (page 332).

Adams was a firm believer in the need for strong and effective legislation to control the quality of development in rural areas that he saw and hoped would occur. If rural land was to be developed, Adams' cry might have been "let's get it right, especially the roads."

In the decades that followed *Rural Planning and Development*, many of Adams' recommendations made it into provincial legislation throughout Canada. Virtually all provinces followed his suggestions and set up planning sections, usually within a department or ministry of municipal affairs. One of the first tasks undertaken by these planning sections was to offer advice to rural areas and prepare model plans and bylaws that focused on physical land use planning. The idea of local (municipal) development boards also evolved into planning boards that could be found throughout the country. More importantly, Adams' approach to planning in rural areas dominated the thinking of planners for several decades. Rural areas, especially those close to cities, were seen as areas waiting to be developed, and the task was to ensure the efficient and healthy development of these lands.

This approach was Adams' legacy to rural planning. There are two fundamental questions pertaining to this legacy. The first is the extent to which it actually took root, and the second surrounds its efficacy. The first is more interesting, the second more emotionally charged. Much of what Adams proposed ended up in planning legislation, theory, and practices over the next fifty years not because Adams was a genius or a visionary, although he certainly had great insight into planning, but because he summarized the ideas and ideals of his times. His view of scientific planning was the accepted paradigm. A belief in legislative solutions was paramount, and it still resonates today. Because top-down, paternalistic approaches to planning were favoured, Adams' recommendation that the provinces, through their planning departments, should decree what was effective planning and adjudicate appeals, held great appeal. Adams was a planner for his times.

Mostly, however, it was Adams' view that Canada was on the verge of rapid growth that caught the imagination of a young country. Canada had an abundance of land, and that land was ripe for development. Certainly, development schemes abounded. Adams wanted to put some order onto this bursting ambition. He argued for the efficient use of rural land, not its protection. Was he successful? That is too large a question. In some places, his plan worked; in other places, growth swamped all planning considerations. Saskatoon's public land banks were a success, runaway sprawl in the Greater Toronto Area was a failure, and the sanitary facilities throughout the country were a little of both.

Not all of Adams' recommendations were followed in all places. The country was just too big for that. Perhaps one of Adams' weaknesses was his belief that model legislation could be implemented. It is surprising how many of his ideas did have national scope in their application. Probably every municipality in Canada wishes in passing that in these times of downloading services to local government that Adams' recommendations on compensation were commonplace.

The rational land use planning model that Adams proposed started to weaken in the 1970s. During the 1980s and 1990s, it had to make room for social and environmental issues. It took rural areas half a century to grow out of the perspective Adams had enunciated and another twenty-five years to develop their own planning approaches. Although few planners would adhere to a strict land use approach to planning, many of the values that Adams summarized still inform current planning practice. To a certain extent, Adams foresaw this when he indicated: "In considering the character and scope of the proposed planning legislation we have to bear in mind that it is designed to meet a complex and many-sided problem or series of problems and a variety of contingencies in different kinds of areas" (page 333). In this quote, he correctly identifies the complexity of the problems but not the ability of legislation and current planning practice to respond.

Could Adams have done better? Could he have prevented the planning problems we face today? Was he visionary enough? These questions always surface when assessing important people who influenced future events. Time and change overtake everyone. Adams is no exception. Nor did he forecast the future. He assembled the ideas of his time from within its current values. In this, he did well. He had a long run; some would argue, perhaps too long. Systems and legislation often do not change fast enough to keep up and deal with the emerging future. The ability to adapt quickly is particularly important, especially if you're in the business of planning.

CHAPTER X

Outline of Proposals and General Conclusions

*Problems too complex to be solved by simple and one-sided remedies |
Matters requiring attention | Government organization | A comprehensive
survey | Planning and development legislation | Agricultural and industrial
settlements | The problem of the returned soldiers and of social readjustment
after the war | Some final observations*

PROBLEMS TOO COMPLEX TO BE SOLVED
BY SIMPLE OR ONE-SIDED REMEDIES

IT is obvious that there can be no simple and ready solution of the
complicated social questions dealt with in this report, and it is equally
obvious that the adoption of the most perfect system of planning and
developing land will not do more than provide the right foundation on
which to build up a solution by a slow and gradual process. In the degree
in which that foundation is well laid, the ultimate social structure will be
the more stable, and will be the more capable of adjustment to suit altered
conditions from time to time as development proceeds; while, obversely,
in the degree in which the foundation is badly laid the structure will be
proportionately weak, and it will become the more difficult to go back to
the beginning and remedy fundamental defects. Success can only be attained by using skill and exercising patience and vigilance in dealing with
the problem in a scientific way. *Attempts to reach a solution by short cuts and
quick results, as in the past, can only end in failure.*

The fact that this report deals with one essential and preliminary aspect
of the problem is not to be taken as evidence that the importance of other
phases or needs is under-estimated. It is recognized that the solution of
the rural problem is only to be found by means of the application of a
number of remedies. To plan the land for purposes of its proper use and
development is of primary importance, because without that being done,
the other measures – improved educational methods, co-operation, rural
credit, creation of rural indsustries, etc. – cannot be successfully applied;
but it is not an alternative to these measures.

Matters Requiring Attention

As a means of finding and applying the needed remedies, it seems necessary that several lines of activity should be pursued simultaneously. These include:

(*a*) The improving of national, provincial and local government organization in connection with all matters relating to land development.

(*b*) The making of a comprehensive investigation and survey of present conditions and the preparing of detailed topographical maps and reports on rural conditions.

(*c*) The adopting of some system of planning all land for purposes of health, convenience and economic use, and the securing of adequate planning and development legislation and its effective administration by the governing authorities.

(*d*) The creating of agricultural and industrial settlements, free of artificial pressure and on sound economic lines.

(*e*) The formulating of a definite policy in regard to readjustment of social and industrial conditions after the war, particularly in relation to the problem of returned soldiers.

General recommendations in regard to each of these matters are set out below.

Government Organization

The Federal and Provincial Government legislation and machinery for dealing with the control of the planning, settlement and development of land, should be extended and improved.

There should be closer co-operation than hitherto between Federal, Provincial and Municipal governments, and between different branches of the public service, in regard to all matters dealing with land.

The surveying branches of the governments should be strengthened and more comprehensive surveying work assigned to them.

A complete and co-ordinated system of federal, provincial and municipal administration of land resources should be devised, with the whole organization centralized in a department or permanent commission of the Federal Government.

Definite steps should be taken by joint government action to prevent the holding of agricultural land by absentee landlords for purely speculative purposes.

The operations of vendors of real estate should be regulated, so as to prevent misrepresentation and other immoral practices in connection with the sale of land,

and all real estate operators should be licensed by governments under safeguards designed to prevent improper dealing in land.

Provincial governments should reconsider their systems of administering colonization, highways, municipal affairs and public health, with special regard to the need of securing more co-operation and efficiency in connection with land and municipal development than is possible under present conditions and for increasing the responsibilities and powers of municipal authorities, under the advice of a skilled department of local government in each province.

To meet a temporary need, the Federal Government should take an active interest in the housing of workers engaged in munition plants, particularly in government arsenals and in small towns and rural districts where there is lack of strong local government. The Federal Government should either require adequate accommodation and proper sanitary conditions to be provided at a reasonable cost for those who are engaged in the service of the country, or itself assist in making that provision, as is being done in Great Britain and allied countries.

In respect of the last of these matters some reference has already been made to what is being done in Britain. The United States has only recently entered the war; but action is already being taken to deal with the situation created by the establishment of new industrial plants for war purposes. The National Conference on City Planning, which met at Kansas City in May last, passed two resolutions on this subject. One referred to the creation of soldiers' camps, and offered the professional services of its members to advise "as to the various and intricate problems which will arise in connection with the provision of wholesome and sanitary accommodations for the great numbers of men who will be called to the service of the country."

The second resolution passed was as follows:

"Whereas, the United States Government proposes to establish certain plants for the manufacture of armour plate and of other materials which may be required for the effective prosecution of the war, which plants will require the services of a large number of workers;

"Resolved, that the National Conference on City Planning strongly urges the President, the Secretary of War, and any other officers of the Government who may be charged with the location, planning and construction of such plants, to profit by the example of our Allies in providing for the proper housing of the workers in such plants, to the end that their efficiency may be increased to the highest possible degree and that the servants of the country may not be exploited by land speculators and builders, but that decent and sanitary homes may be provided for them at reasonable cost."

This resolution was passed on May 9. Three days later the secretary of the conference reported that the Government had already accepted the services offered, and that twenty members of the conference were then met in Washington.

In regard to land development and public health, we have had a regrettable tendency in Canada to emulate the United States in many respects that have proved to be unsound, but appear to have been slow in deriving profit from her example when it has been good. The importance of civil organization and conservation of economic and human resources for purposes of the war, and as a means of averting bad times after the war, require to be more strongly realized in Canada.

Of all countries engaged in the war Canada has probably most to gain from an active and comprehensive conservation policy, since her vast natural resources are so much out of proportion to the capital and human energy she has available to convert these resources into exchangeable wealth.

Whether in regard to peace or war conditions, the main objects of any improvement in government organization, of rural and of urban conditions, must be to conserve life and to stimulate production. To achieve these objects it is essential, above all other things, that greater activity be shown by governments in protecting public health, in promoting sound systems of education and in controlling land speculation.

The economic loss, due to preventable death and disease in Canada, is briefly alluded to in Chapter VI. An extract from an article by Dr. Chas. J. Hastings, Medical Officer of Health, of Toronto, is given in Appendix D, as a further illustration of the extent of this loss on the continent of America. In addition to the figures quoted by Dr. Hastings we have the further estimate from United States sources that feeble-minded children cost the United States Government $90,000,000 and that crime costs $600,000,000 a year; on this basis the Canadian ratio would be $7,000,000 and $46,000,000, respectively. The feeble-minded child produces the strongest link that connects neglect of social and health conditions with crime.

While these figures are of value in conveying some impression of the importance of the problem of public health, they are, of course, of no value as an indication of the extent of the government responsibility, since the factors necessary to show the proportion of the loss due to individual neglect and the proportion to maladministration must continue to be unknown. Nor are they any guide as to the respective losses caused by overcrowding in cities on the one hand and by isolation and poverty in rural districts on the other hand. But enough is known to make it clear to every student of social conditions that a large share of the responsibility for the deplorable and unnecessary loss of life and physical deterioration on this continent rests with the various governing authorities, who have the powers to regulate land development, and that there are conditions in the rural districts as injurious to health and morals as in the crowded city slums.

At present there is a 'confusion of tongues' as to the desirability, or otherwise, of money and human energy being spent on works that are not absolutely essential to the prosecution of the war. The weight of evidence seems to be in favour of everything being suspended which can be put off without injury to our social and economic life. As conservation of health lies at the root of our social life, and as it is one of the most essential needs as a means of prosecuting the war itself, as well as to make up for the wastage of war and to utilize our natural resources, public health expenditures should be the last to be curtailed. Moreover, whatever public works may be delayed, there should be no delay in thinking out and formulating a policy for future action, having regard to past failures and to the lessons taught by the war.

The importance of carrying out a more aggressive and scientific educational policy in Canada is generally recognized. All that need be repeated here, by way of emphasis to what has already been said on the subject, is that the soundest of policies in regard to education will fail in attaining satisfactory results unless it is pursued simultaneously with improved government organization of land development.

Apart from the question of general education there is need for improvement in the training of those engaged in municipal and sanitary engineering, land surveying, and assessment valuation, in order to qualify a larger body of professional men to specialize in the work of planning and developing land, controlling public health and assessing property values. The organization of municipal and sanitary engineers for purposes of specialized professional training and for the advancement of their particular branch of engineering is needed. In regard to surveyors, few bodies are more highly educated in the practical work of their profession than the land surveyors of Canada; but their course of education should be widened in scope and include principles of valuation and planning of land. Government protection has helped to narrow the scope of the profession, but could equally be used to widen its sphere of usefulness.

Much of the work now being performed by the medical officer of health should be undertaken by the sanitary engineer. The medical officer has full scope for his skill and energy in fields which are essentially his own, and much of the municipal and sanitary engineering work he is doing is a burden of which he would rather be relieved, and which would be more efficiently performed by properly qualified engineering officers giving whole time service.

But until there is a skilled municipal department in each province to advise and help local authorities with engineering advice we cannot expect satisfactory improvement in the status of the municipal and sanitary engineer nor effective local administration of public works and sanitation.

In our Universities, too, we want to see an awakening to a more vital interest in civic problems and in the science of land development and industrial organization. Professor Geddes claims that the Universities in all countries in the passing generation have been strongholds of Germanic thought, with its mechanical and venal philosophy. "The re-awakening movement of the Universities has been slow, timid, blindfold because lacking in civic vision."*

Enough, but not too much, has been said in the preceding pages on the subject of land speculation. It may be added, however, in support of the above recommendations, that this speculation has not only been injurious in its legitimate forms but that it has been accompanied by much dishonest dealing which has caused hardships to numerous purchasers and destroyed a great deal of confidence in real estate investment in Canada. The governments have a special obligation, as the original vendors of the land, and in view of the far-reaching effects of immoral practices in connection with its sale, to employ special means to protect purchasers from such practices. There are numerous obvious steps which should be taken in this respect, including the registration of those engaged in real estate operations and the application of adequate safeguards to protect purchasers.

Government control of land development and the system of assessing and taxing of land should have regard to its use, its non-use, and its abuse as an instrument of production. The economic use of land must be encouraged, the non-use of land hindered, and the abuse of land prevented, by government policies; unless we intend to continue to sacrifice the surplus fruits of production – the only source from which increase of real wealth is derived – for the plaything of speculation.

A COMPREHENSIVE SURVEY

A comprehensive survey of the social, physical and industrial conditions of all rural territory should be made, with the object of ascertaining, first; the main facts

---

* *The Sociological Review*, May, 1917.

regarding the problems of rural life and rural development in territory already settled and organized; and, second, more precise information than is now available regarding natural resources in unorganized territory.

The survey should be so prepared as to enable constructive proposals to be formulated regarding the economic development of the natural and industrial resources of the country, and regarding the location of new towns, railways and highways.

It should include a complete inventory and an additional survey of all lands which have been already surveyed and homesteaded with a view to securing their settlement under proper conditions and to devising means to lessen injurious speculation.

It should deal with questions of taxation and assessment of land and buildings for provincial and local purposes.

Settlement of remote areas should be suspended while the survey is being made; and further Crown lands should not be alienated until after proper plans of development have been prepared and certain preliminary improvements carried out, and only then when it is definitely ascertained that the land can be put to economic use.

Detailed topographical maps showing all existing physical conditions should be prepared for the most valuable and thickly populated parts of the Dominion and the cost distributed over all branches of government.

With regard to the need of an extended topographical survey, this seems to be a matter on which there is only one opinion among leading surveyors.* It is not suggested that the present methods of surveying, indexing and describing the land should be superseded, but that they should be extended so as to utilize topographical information that is contained in the field notes of surveyors. This information could be usefully shown on the maps and used as the basis for proper plans of development. In the different branches of the Department of the Interior consideration is being given to the subdivision of land from other points of view than that of simply obtaining the most accurate system of measurement. For instance, Map No. III is a map of the Dominion, showing the principal drainage areas, practically in accordance with the divisions adopted by the Commission of Conservation in the report on *Water-Powers of Canada*, published in 1911. It will be of great value in connection with the planning of rural territory for purposes both of land settlement and

---

* "I quite agree that our survey is incomplete." — Dr. Deville, Surveyor-General of Canada.

"It is time to improve the methods and further survey the land that was surveyed in the old days ... Our Homestead Act is entirely out of date. It did good work in the start but it has outgrown its past ... In laying out towns the work should be given to expert town planners." — J. S. Dennis, Assistant to the President C.P.R.; President Can. Soc. of C.E., D.T.S. From addresses at the tenth annual meeting of Association of Dominion Land Surveyors.

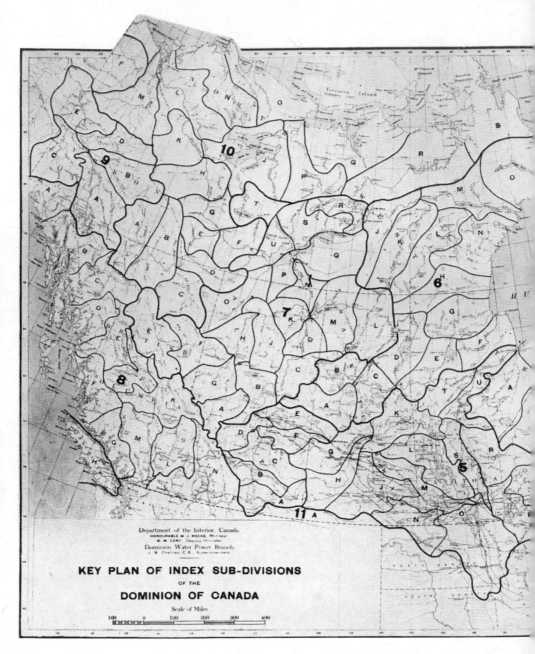

Department of the Interior, Canada.
HONOURABLE W. J. ROCHE, Minister
W. W. CORY, Deputy Minister
Dominion Water Power Branch,
J. B. Challies, C.E., Superintendent.

KEY PLAN OF INDEX SUB-DIVISIONS

OF THE

DOMINION OF CANADA

Scale of Miles

MAP III   WATERSHED SUB-DIVISIONS OF CANADA

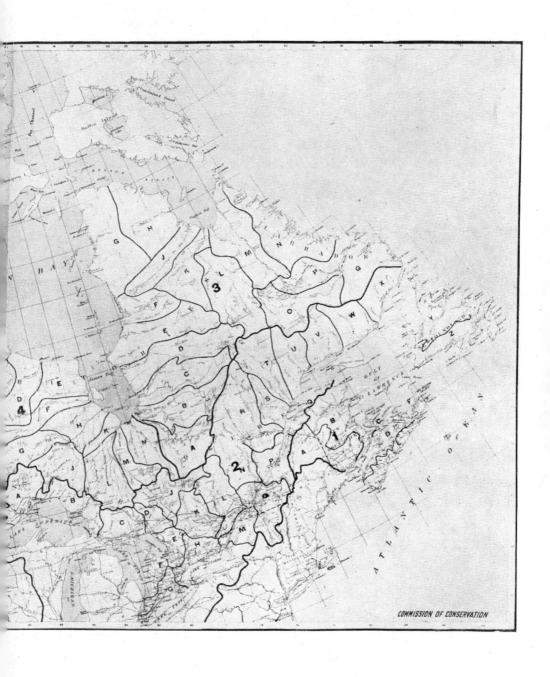

of location of new towns. It shows how greatly the main drainage areas vary from the meridian lines which form the basis of rectangular surveys which are used for purposes of land settlement. It is not advocated that these and other physical conditions should determine the system of planning the land, but it is suggested that they should not be entirely ignored. We are indebted to the Water Power Branch of the Department of the Interior for the use of Map No. III.

Comprehensive surveys are being made of the natural and industrial resources in some of the provinces, including Saskatchewan and Alberta, but, in the absence of a much more elaborate and skilled organization than is available for the purpose, at present, such a survey cannot be made in as complete a form as is necessary.

PLANNING AND DEVELOPMENT LEGISLATION

Comprehensive Planning and Development Acts, corresponding to the draft act of the Commission of Conservation, as briefly described in this report, should be passed in Ontario, Quebec, Saskatchewan, British Columbia and Prince Edward Island, and the Town Planning Acts in the other provinces should be changed in name and widened in scope, so far as may be necessary, to make them applicable to deal adequately with both rural and urban development.

All rural and urban land should be planned and regulated by proper 'development schemes,' prepared under Planning and Development Acts, with a view to securing health, convenience, efficiency and amenity in connection with its use for all purposes.

Provincial regulations, setting a minimum standard of sanitation and housing, building construction and general development, should be agreed to by provincial governments and municipalities in joint conference and under expert advice; and the adoption of such minimum standards by local authorities should be made compulsory.

Development schemes and building regulations should have as one of their objects the prevention of injurious land speculation, in connection with the subdivision and development of land for building purposes; they should define the principles on which future contributions of public money shall be given for constructing local improvements and should aim at limiting these contributions to such improvements as are for the benefit of the inhabitants at large, and at requiring subdividers to meet the cost of a considerable proportion of the local improvements on their own land before it is sold for building purposes.

The character and scope of the legislation proposed is indicated in Chapter IX of this report, and further consideration in detail is reserved for a subsequent report.

Legislation of this kind is constructive and requires qualities of initiative and imagination to be exercised by those who seek to carry it into effect; it is, therefore, in a special degree, true of this class of measure that the mere passing of an Act is of little value unless it is followed by aggressive and skillful administration.

The setting of compulsory minimum standards of sanitation, as above recommended, should not be a local but a provincial requirement. There are degrees of bad sanitation permitted by local authorities which are nothing less than criminal. In order, however, that any proposed minimum standards for general application in each province, shall be reasonable, and shall not be forced on municipalities against the will of the majority, they should be determined in joint conference between the provincial and municipal governments.

AGRICULTURAL AND INDUSTRIAL SETTLEMENTS

Agricultural and industrial settlements should be organized on carefully selected sites, suitable for development on sound economic lines.

Purely agricultural settlements should only be developed on fertile and improved land, having good transportation facilities and accessibility to markets.

New town settlements (garden cities) should be established where there are good facilities for profitable production and distribution, where manufacturing and intensive farming can be successfully carried on, and where advantage can be taken of the tendency to remove industries from crowded centres to rural districts or to establish new industries near water-powers and raw materials.

Government capital, or the guarantee of bonds, should be made available for these settlements and should be made re-payable at a fixed annual rate to cover principal and interest; the benefit of all profits derived in excess of that rate should be spent on improving the settlements.

The increment of land values created by the conversion of cheap agricultural land into a valuable townsite gives to the garden city class of development a special financial stability, which is not possessed by the agricultural settlement.

Although the increase of agricultural production in Canada is essential at the present time yet, in order that over-production in the future may be avoided, it is equally essential to promote the establishment and extension of other forms of industry; so long as the policy pursued has regard to sound economic principles and healthy industrial conditions. If there should be a period of depression after the war it will be less injurious to Canada in proportion as we are able to create a satisfactory equilibrium between agricultural and manufacturing industries.

At the close of the war it seems inevitable that countries like Great Britain which have depended in the past on large imports of foreign produce will, as a result of improved organization and the giving of greater stimulus to agricultural production, greatly lessen their dependence on outside supplies. Legislation has already been passed in Britain to artificially maintain the price of home grown wheat at a level which will enable the British farmer to grow it at a profit for some years after the war. This is certain to reduce the demand for Canadian wheat, for a time at least, and provides a reason why any effort to increase agricultural production should be accompanied by efforts to promote rural manufacturing and thereby to increase the home market for raw materials and food. One of the best means of achieving this object is to create new industrial settlements.

The failures of co-operative forms of agricultural or industrial settlement which have been noted in this report merely suggest what should be avoided in applying co-operative methods, and do not suggest that co-operative enterprise cannot be made successful if rightly applied.

To make co-operative settlements permanently successful care has to be taken to keep them free, on the one hand, from coercive or paternalistic control and, on the other hand, from unbridled speculation. Past failures have not been due to any inherent weakness in co-operative organization but rather to attempt to substitute socialistic for individualistic forms of co-operative enterprise. Co-operation should be stimulated and encouraged by government action, and the facilities for co-operation should be provided by skilled planning – but this should be done without imposing undue restraint on personal initiative or freedom. Co-operative effort should be organized individual effort. In a co-operative scheme artificial control should be limited to the prevention of wrong-doing, including the prevention of such forms of land development as are economically unsound and socially injurious.

For the purposes of agricultural settlements, a county, or counties, in old territory and a few townships in new territory should be taken and an attempt made to apply the best kind of organization and scheme of development that can be devised for each. The capital provided for such schemes should be ample in amount, but as little as possible of it should be given in the nature of a subsidy. A properly conceived scheme should pay its way.

The Commission of Conservation has been engaged for the past two years in making a survey and in preparing a skeleton plan of development for the county of Dundas. The beginnings which have been made with this investigation, and the experience gained in connection with it, should be valuable as a means of indicating what further steps are necessary to re-plan and improve one of the older counties, which would necessarily be a more difficult operation than that of planning and improving new areas.

The recommendation that industrial, or partly industrial and partly agricultural, town settlements be established is apt to be regarded with suspicion by practical men because of its novelty. That novelty has now worn off in England and garden cities and suburbs are no longer looked upon as visionary schemes.

The movement in England has attracted widespread attention in all European countries and in the United States and has caused influential bodies to advocate the establishment of similar communities in these countries.

The following resolution was passed by the United States Senate in the early part of this year, and the inquiry instituted as a result is still proceeding:

> "Whereas, the garden city and garden suburb movement in Europe has made wonderful progress during the first eight years of its existence; and
>
> "Whereas, the object of this movement is to secure permanent and comfortable homes for the people on terms within the reach of the average income, and to combine the advantages of town and country in the same community; and
>
> "Whereas, this movement is contributing materially to the health, comfort, and prosperity of the people who have experienced its benefits, and
>
> "Whereas, the movement, in the estimation of many, points the way to the long-sought goal of a contented, home-owning population; and
>
> "Whereas, a beginning along this line is claimed to have been made in the United States, and
>
> "Whereas, thousands of American citizens have petitioned members of Congress for an investigation of the movement both in Europe and the United States; Therefore be it
>
> "Resolved, that the Senate Committee on Agriculture and Forestry be authorized and requested to hear and consider such testimony as may be produced before said committee in Washington regarding this movement both in Europe, in the United States, and elsewhere, and to report its findings to the Senate."*

It is significant that this resolution was referred for consideration to the Committee on Agriculture and Forestry, indicating that it is the rural

---

* Senate Resolution 305.

rather than the urban aspect of the movement which is being first investigated.

One of the main objects in carrying out the suggestion to create combined agricultural and industrial settlements would be to provide opportunities for the employment of returned soldiers in varied kinds of productive enterprises in both rural and urban areas.

These settlements would also be invaluable as a practical demonstration of town building and land development. Social progress in England during the last fifteen years has been greatly influenced as a result of the one experiment in industrial development and housing which has been carried out at Letchworth.

Before initiating any comprehensive policy to establish new centres of population it might, however, be more prudent to begin by developing one new manufacturing and agricultural town, where systems of rural and urban land development could be tried out, where opportunities for varied kinds of employment could be provided, where the strength and weakness of different methods could be tested, and where there could be evolved, by a process of practical experience, the soundest economic principles on which development should be guided in the future.

The Problem of the Returned Soldiers and Social Re-Adjustment after the War

The reinstating of ex-service men into industrial and social life and otherwise dealing with problems of re-adjustment of employment after the war, should be dealt with by municipalities under the guidance of provincial departments of local government.

Provision should be made for placing ex-service men in suitable and congenial vocations either in rural or in urban localities, wherever their abilities can be put to the best use, where it is reasonably certain that adequate reward can be obtained for their labour, and where facilities for social intercourse and education are available.

The forcing of land settlement should be avoided, particularly for returned soldiers, and proper land development schemes should be prepared in advance of any land settlement.

Any financial aid that may be given as a reward for military service should be determined apart from any other question, and should not be confused with land settlement schemes.

For ex-service men, and others, desirous of taking up intensive farming near to urban centres, where they can have alternative means of employment and congenial social conditions, areas of suitable land should be selected and definitely set apart for small agricultural holdings near these centres. Such areas should either be pur-

chased or, if privately owned, should be delimited under development schemes for agricultural purposes and assessed on an agricultural basis – subject to the payment of an increment tax, if, and when, the land is converted into building land.

In the event of any scheme or schemes being promoted to form town settlements or garden cities, as advocated in this report, opportunities should be provided in these settlements for employment of returned soldiers, including partially disabled men, in factories or on farms, or in industries of a domestic or semi-agricultural character; adequate provision being made for the housing of such men and their families in sanitary and agreeable homes.

Ex-farmers living in cities, who desire to go on the land, but are prevented from doing so owing to their having purchased building lots which cannot be sold at present in the open market, should be assisted in obtaining release of their capital, in order to become producers and to lessen the prospects of unemployment for those returned soldiers who will want to work in the cities.

The scope and variety of opportunity for both ex-soldiers and new immigrants should be widened so as to embrace all classes of rural industry that can be successfully promoted and not agriculture alone; and the combination of free homesteading or artificial pressure with haphazard methods of settlement should be abandoned.

With regard to the recommendation relating to ex-farmers, interesting and important evidence is given by Mr. J. H. T. Falk, in the article which forms Appendix E, showing that there is a considerable number of Slavs in Winnipeg who have capital and experience of farming. The only difficulty is: These people have been speculating in building lots, and, because they still hold these lots, have, therefore, no available funds to enable them to acquire farming land where they can put it to profitable use. A large proportion of the men who came to Canada to farm during the boom in city lands were 'side-tracked' into real estate speculation and became parasites on the community instead of producers. Some plan should be devised to relieve them of their present obligations and to assist them in becoming permanent land settlers.

The fact that we are likely to be faced with a returned soldiers' problem, that the conditions of unemployment which preceded the war may be followed by similar conditions after the war, is, itself, proof of the unsoundness of our system of land development and industrial organization. Properly organized, there should be no limit, within any reasonable estimate of what is probable in the way of increase of population, to the output of human energy that can be employed to develop the vast natural resources of this country. We should, therefore, have no returned soldiers' problem in Canada, apart from dealing with disabled men. Indeed, we should be ready to absorb the ex-service men of other countries with advantage to ourselves and without fear of an overstocked labour market. But, under circumstances and economic conditions likely to be faced in the future, owing to our lack of scientific organization, particularly of our rural life, we may well anticipate the contingency of being unable to conveniently and quickly place even our returned soldiers in productive fields of labour, much less to deal properly with new immigration.

The problem of rural life, as part of the problem of national life, should be faced as a whole and means should be found to remove the difficulties that stand in the way of natural and sound economic development. It is futile to go on ignoring these difficulties and to deal with problems, like that of returned soldiers, by temporary palliatives designed to enable us to get rid of our immediate responsibilities, but without any permanent effect in improving social conditions either for the men presumed to be directly benefited or for the country as a whole.

SOME FINAL OBSERVATIONS

Canada is said to be at the beginning of a new era. In regard to land development it is certainly face to face with a turning point in its history. It is an appropriate time to enquire into past methods and to revise them if they need improvement.

The Chairman of the Commission of Conservation expresses himself thus, as to the ideal we should seek to attain in building up the Canadian democracy in the future:

> "The ideal state is that in which all the citizens, without exception, have the opportunity of living a sane, clean and civilized life, partaking of at least all the necessary comforts provided by modern science, and enjoying the opportunity of spiritual and intellectual improvement."*

He claims that to achieve success we must face facts and get rid of "every false economic standard that militates against the ideal." That is surely true in a special degree of the system underlying the development of land. The false economic standards which have prevailed in connection with land have meant that we have been blind to the futility of those make-believe forms of prosperity and wealth that derive their existence either from unhealthy social conditions or from the license enjoyed by the few to the injury of the many which is misnamed liberty.

False economic standards have been largely responsible for bad beginnings in land settlement, wasteful speculation and unhealthy and haphazard developments of land that stand self-condemned as part of our social

---

* Essay on "The Foundations of the New Era," in *The New Era in Canada,* 1917.

system. Some men have sought to excuse these evils on the ground that they are the outcome of natural laws, whereas they are largely caused by the refusal to recognize the demands of nature, and to apply intelligent direction to what is purely artificial growth.

But probably, on the whole, there is now comparatively little disagreement as to the need for investigation and reform of our rural conditions, the only doubt still prevalent being as to whether the need is great enough to cause disturbance of our minds during the war. On that point there appears to be no doubt in allied countries, in every one of which new principles of land development are being studied and applied. Even in France, where one would think that the urgency of proceeding with the work of reconstruction of devastated areas would prevent careful preparation of plans of development, time is being given to think out and prepare schemes of regional planning with special regard to health and the teachings of modern science. According to the *New York Times* the United States is co-operating with the French people to prepare proper plans for the restoration of the destroyed and injured towns, villages and rural areas of Flanders.

"In France a law has been passed requiring every town and village in that country, whether within the war zones or not, to lay out its future developments according to the principles of modern city planning. To enforce this, there will be a Federal Commission, with a general commission in each of the departments, and under these general commissions community commissions to direct local work. The part the United States will play in the reconstructive work of the towns destroyed or injured in the war necessarily will be chiefly a financial part, but there will be collaboration between French and American engineers and architects, and a thorough knowledge of the problems to the solution of which it will be our privilege to contribute in one way or another, will be obtained by our own experts. The commission of the Red Cross that sailed for France a week or two ago to study the problem of aid for the inhabitants of devastated regions, included highly trained men, among them George B. Ford, consultant in city planning, who already has visited the larger French towns and found work under way in Paris, Limoges, Rheims, Marseilles, and Lyons. Such men will be able to deal efficiently and thoroughly with the new and important reconstruction plans that will call for the best energies to be found in all interested countries."*

---

* *New York Times Magazine,* July 1, 1917.

The work that is being done in France may seem somewhat remote as an object lesson to Canada which, happily, has no areas devastated by war; but as a matter of fact the creative work that has to be done in Canada requires the application of the same principles as are required in connection with the re-creative work that is now forced on the people of France; only we have in Canada the advantage of starting from the beginning. But the chief lesson we may derive from the example of France in this matter is that, although that country is more directly affected than ours by the war, its rulers are not showing indifference to the work of social and economic reconstruction, on the ground that their whole activities should be concentrated on war operations. Indeed they recognize that the very sacrifices which are being made in the war demand, in the interests of continued national stability, that they prepare plans of development which will ensure healthy living conditions and increased efficiency in production in the future. In the degree in which our undeveloped resources in Canada are greater than in France, and to the extent that our hands are at present more free to deal with any necessary re-adjustment of our conditions, we have, in that degree and to that extent, the greater responsibility to apply ourselves, unhesitatingly and at once, to the work of planning for the future, of organizing and co-ordinating our government machinery and of ascertaining the facts regarding our social and industrial conditions in town and country.

In this report an effort has been made to study the causes of social evils from which we suffer in Canada as a result of imperfect methods of land development and rural organization; and to indicate some of our defects rather than our merits in comparison with other countries. The object has not been to describe the extent to which we have achieved comparative well-being in rural Canada but rather to indicate respects wherein we may extend the well-being we already enjoy. The defects of our social life, in any of its aspects, are not serious enough to make us ashamed of them; but, having regard to our opportunities and responsibilities, as a free people and as trustees for posterity, they are serious enough to make it incumbent upon us to find out and apply the needed remedies.

We need not ignore the lessons of other countries, but our first duty is to acquire a thorough knowledge of our own conditions and to formulate and strive for the attainment of our own ideals, in our own way and with the realization of our power to shape our own future.

CHAPTER X
OUTLINE OF PROPOSALS AND GENERAL CONCLUSIONS

Commentary by Wayne J. Caldwell

—————

In 1917, Canada was in the midst of a terrible war, poverty existed in both rural and urban settlements, public health was an issue, and power within the nation was starting to swing from rural to urban areas. In the midst of these issues, the government saw fit through the Commission of Conservation to release what has become a defining moment in the history of professional planning in Canada, the release of Thomas Adams' *Rural Planning and Development in Canada.*

Thomas Adams wrote at a critical point in Canadian history. He was clearly a product of his times, yet he had foresight and vision that has transcended the years. His book is important not only because of what it means for the planning profession but also because of what it means for planning in Canada. In this final chapter, Adams ends with an outline of proposals and general conclusions that build on earlier sections of the book.

What is perhaps most fascinating about the book is its legacy on present-day planning. Adams offers recommendations in five key areas:

1 *Government organization:* improve national, provincial, and local government organizations in connection with all matters relating to land development.
2 *Comprehensive survey:* develop a comprehensive investigation and survey of present conditions and prepare detailed topographical maps and reports on rural conditions.
3 *Planning and development legislation:* adopt some system to plan all land for the purposes of health, convenience, and economic use, and to secure adequate planning and development legislation and its effective administration by the governing authorities.
4 *Agricultural and industrial settlements:* create agricultural and industrial settlements free of artificial pressure and on sound economic lines (i.e., an appropriate and suitable land base).
5 *The problem of returning soldiers and social readjustment after the war:* formulate definite policy for the readjustment of social and industrial conditions after the war, particularly in relation to returned soldiers.

If these issues and recommendations sound familiar, it is not surprising, for they, with the exception of returning soldiers and social readjustment, are core issues for rural communities that the planning profession continues to grapple with nearly one hundred years later. The following reflections draw parallels between Adams' commentary and current planning issues.

Adams calls for greater co-ordination between federal, provincial, and municipal governments. He notes the need for an improved legislative framework and calls for a centralized federal department. A major concern of his time was the holding of agricultural land by absentee landlords for purely speculative purposes. He is also perturbed by the real estate industry and believes the profession should be licensed. His call for provincial governments to reconsider their approach to what we would today identify as municipal affairs was also prevalent. He believed that the planning of roads, municipal affairs, and public health needed to be changed for optimal co-operation and efficiency, including more power for municipal authorities (and a skilled department of local government in each province). Throughout many of Adams' comments, there is an overriding concern about public health – in fact, in the context of the war, he makes the statement that "public health expenditures should be the last to be curtailed" (page 343). Adams also notes the need for enhanced training and education in fields dealing with surveying, engineering, public health, and land assessment and valuation.

In the early part of the twenty-first century, we still grapple with many of these same issues. We continue to muse from a planning perspective on how the public interest can best be served. Although the federal government transcends the regions, we have a constitutional framework that embeds responsibility for planning in the provinces, which in turn delegate it to the municipalities. The result is a variety of schemes and approaches throughout the country. If we look at farmland preservation, for example, provinces such as British Columbia and Quebec have taken an aggressive legislative approach, while others such as Ontario have a policy-led system. In the Greater Toronto Area, the Province of Ontario has adopted greenbelt legislation that municipalities must respect. Numerous other municipal land use decisions are made in the midst of these various approaches. Although there is a general consensus that decisions are best made locally, municipalities sometimes take a relatively narrow view of the public interest. We also continue to strive for the right municipal structure. The restructuring of municipalities in New Brunswick in the late 1960s (Krueger 1970) and more recently in Ontario and Quebec points to this ongoing struggle to get it right (Tindal and Tindal 2008).

In the early part of the twentieth century, Adams argued that there was an absence of quality information on which to base planning decisions. His concerns related to both settled and "unorganized" territory. In particular, he called for a comprehensive survey of the social, physical, and industrial conditions of all rural territory. He wanted to identify the main facts concerning problems of rural life and rural development and called for detailed topographical maps to do so.

Adams' underlying goal was to minimize land speculation and encourage fair taxation and assessment. He also wanted precise information regarding natural resources in unorganized territories. He hoped this information could be used to influence the location of towns, railroads, and highways in the economic development of the natural and industrial resources of the country. Adams even went so far as to call for the suspension of settlement in remote areas until the survey was complete, preliminary improvements were made, and the economic value of the land had been established. One of Adams' more interesting ideas was his plan to use principal drainage basins as the basis for planning. In *Rural Planning and Development,* he presents a map of the country's drainage basins and notes "how greatly the main drainage areas vary from the meridian lines which form the basis of rectangular surveys which are used for purposes of land settlement" (page 348).

The goal of comprehensive surveys continues to challenge the planning field. More recently, largely beginning in the 1960s, Canada accepted the challenge of developing and delivering the type of information Adams had requested. The "Resources for Tomorrow" conference in 1961 was instrumental in launching the Canada Land Inventory. Moreover, new computer-based technologies, environmental assessment processes, and demands for comprehensiveness in planning require detailed and quality information. And, in practice, issues of time, resources, and public expectations often mean that projects go forward without more and better information.

Adams' call for planning based on natural features such as watersheds continues to be an underlying principle of planning practice. Conservation Authorities in Ontario, for example, were established in 1946. There are still struggles, however, to clearly define and implement watershed-based planning. Likewise, we continue to be challenged by the settlement of remote areas. Finally, the economics of a specific proposal can often outweigh the importance of a thoughtful planning review.

Adams was a strong advocate for the adoption of planning and development legislation throughout Canada. In those provinces that already had town planning legislation, he argued that the legislation should be broadened to deal adequately with both rural and urban development. It was Adams' belief that all rural and urban land should be planned and regulated by proper development schemes to secure community health, convenience, efficiency, and amenities. He also lobbied for building, sanitation, and construction standards, and noted that these standards should be provincial requirements, developed in consultation with municipalities. Although the planning system over the intervening years may not have always got this right, the basic direction suggested by Adams remains fundamentally sound.

Although planning and development legislation and minimum building and construction standards exists throughout Canada, the legislative framework and the relationship between the provinces and local municipalities continues to evolve. Society continues to grapple with the issue of individual private rights versus those of the general public. As a result, legislation such as the Greenbelt Act in Ontario or the Agricultural Operation Practices Act in Alberta can generate individual antagonisms that overshadows the broader public benefits that may accompany individual provincial initiatives. Likewise, the balance between the province and the municipality can be a source of tension – who is best able to address a given issue and protect the public interest? In Ontario, Quebec, and Alberta, for example, responsibility for the siting of large livestock facilities has been wrested away from municipalities and assumed by the province. Controversy has accompanied the transition. Some see the measure as being in the best interests of the broader public and of food production and equity for farmers across a province, while others see it as an infringement on the rights of local municipalities to set standards and protect the environment as they see fit.

Adams' core belief was that government should play a strong role in guiding development. Agricultural settlements should only be developed on fertile and improved land with good transportation facilities and access to markets. Likewise, new town settlements (garden cities) should be established only in areas with good facilities for production and distribution, in areas where manufacturing and intensive farming could be successfully carried out. In *Rural Planning and Development,* Adams highlights the opportunity that existed to move industries from crowded centres to rural districts or to establish industries near water power and raw materials. He notes the possibility of using government capital in these settlements and of profits being returned to the community to improve conditions. His industrial development model offered rural communities new opportunities to offset the potential for overproduction in the future (a development that Adams correctly anticipates, along with declining demand from certain European countries). A corollary to this model is Adams' strong support for garden cities and suburbs (building on experience in England and the United States). Although in hindsight we are perhaps more critical of garden cities and certainly see the challenges associated with suburbs, we must also recognize that Adams supported them in response to significant issues of his day.

Over ninety year after Adams wrote his book, the success of governments at guiding development has been mixed. Clearly, Adams witnessed the results of agricultural settlements on the marginal farmlands of the Canadian Shield. He likely would have anticipated the future abandonment of this and similar farmland throughout the country. Likewise, he would have witnessed the withering of communities that were not connected to Canada's rail system. It was probably these failures that encouraged Adams to speak out for a strong government role in directing future development. Despite the wisdom in Adams' arguments, however, certain individuals and property-rights groups continue to resist what they see as an unwarranted intrusion by the state into private matters.

If Adams were with us today and still thinking from a 1917 perspective, he would likely express many of the same concerns as modern-day planners. The protection of vital rural communities would likely be at the top of his list. He would almost certainly acknowledge that some of the original agricultural settlement on lower capability soils or in more challenging climates was problematic and that we should not be surprised at the restructuring in rural economies and communities that resulted (although the casualties could have been avoided). He would be concerned about the so-called rural-urban divide. He would also acknowledge some of the environmental issues that transcend regions and call for a strong federal presence to deal with them.

Adams was far-seeing but constrained by the times in which he wrote *Rural Planning and Development*. The first decades of the twentieth century saw major changes in Canada, including the loss of rural dominance in eastern Canada and initial expansion into the western provinces. Declines temporarily obscured expansion. Urbanization and new technologies were changing Canadian society. Adams could not, however, have foreseen the wide range of issues that currently grip rural Canada: the economic and demographic effects of globalization, the political realities of a diminished rural population, and the exponential influence of technology and climate change. On the other hand, his legacies are his historical account of rural Canada in the early twentieth century and planning prescriptions that are fundamental to current planning practice. Moreover, his work brought a focus to "the rural" that provides the foundation upon which rural planning practice is based and brings insight and understanding that is relevant nearly one hundred years later.

REFERENCES

Krueger, Ralph R. 1970. "The Provincial-Municipal Government Revolution in New Brunswick." *Canadian Public Administration* 13, 1: 51-99.

Tindal, C. Richard, and Susan Nobes Tindal. 2008. *Local Government in Canada*. 7th ed. Toronto: Nelson Education.

APPENDIX A

EXISTING METHODS OF MAKING SURVEYS
AND DIVIDING RURAL LANDS

By H. L. Seymour, B.A.Sc., A.M.Can.Soc. of C.E., D.L.S., O.L.S., etc.

A map of Canada large enough to admit of such features being shown will present numerous small quadrilaterals – or, in many cases, irregular figures with more than four sides. These represent townships, which, for the greater part of Canada that has been surveyed for settlement, may be regarded as the units of land division. The word "township," as originally used in the Old Country, had reference more particularly to the district or territory of a town. In the sense in which it is now used in Canada an early, if not the earliest, record of the term "township" appears in the Ordinances of the Congress of the United States for the year 1786, when provision for the "locating and disposing of lands in the western territory" was made.

Closer inspection of the maps of Canada reveals the fact that, in the earlier settled parts of the older provinces, the townships are generally of all shapes and sizes, lying in no particular direction and exhibiting frequently no apparent correlation. In the newer provinces of Manitoba, Saskatchewan and Alberta the numerous townships that have been laid out appear to be squares and of equal size, the boundaries being north and south lines or east and west lines, which will be found to scale six miles in length. That a definite relation may, or rather does, exist between the townships is readily apparent to the observer as his eye passes over the "checkerboard" superimposed on our western plains.

A history of the township surveys made throughout Canada as a whole would be a very varied one. As might be expected from the irregular shapes and sizes of the townships in the older provinces, many changes in the system, or, as it has sometimes been put, many changes due to lack of system, have taken place there. This is especially true of the province of Ontario, and, to a lesser extent, of Quebec, in which province the prevailing direction of the St. Lawrence river, and the seignorial grants bordering thereon and extending many miles back therefrom, have been determining factors in township surveys. The three western provinces, however, have had the same system of survey, with but minor exceptions, since they were first systematically divided for settlement. There the original survey into townships has been, and still is, under control of the Federal Government.

In general, the earliest surveys might be regarded as an endeavour to apportion in an equitable manner the claims of settlers already on the land. Such surveys became necessary in both Upper and Lower Canada in 1783, "when the United Empire Loyalists scattered and located on the bay of Chaleurs in Lower Canada and along the banks of the St. Lawrence and its lakes in Upper Canada."

A rather close analogy may be traced between these old surveys of the earlier settled parts of Canada and more recent surveys – still occasionally undertaken by the Dominion Government – of lands settled on but located so far from other settlements as not likely to be reached by the regular system of survey for some time. In regard to these "settlement surveys," the *Manual of Instructions for the Survey of Dominion Lands* states in part:

> "Land bordering on any river or lake, or other body of water, or on a public highway, and upon which settlements are in existence, may be laid out and divided into lots of certain frontage and depth in such manner as appears desirable ... a road sixty-six feet in width is laid out across the settlement in the most convenient location, also such further roads of the same width as may be necessary to give access to every settlement lot."

The surveyor is further instructed to endeavour to lay out the land into lots of such size and shape as will best meet the wishes and legitimate claims of the occupants. Such, it may be premised, was also the spirit in which the early surveys were attempted. With the limited facilities townships could not, in any event, have been surveyed regularly. Only the front lots – or lots bordering (as in Fig. A) on a river and required for immediate use by settlers – were laid out. Further rows of lots or "concessions"* were added as settlement, forced further back from the river, required. Thus naturally evolved what is now known in Ontario as the single front system (see Fig. A). Townships surveyed under this system were not necessarily of uniform size or shape, and frequently changes in the widths, depths and area of lots (from 120 to 200 acres) were made, though roads were generally to be 40 feet wide.

---

* The word concession, with such a meaning, originated in the survey of lands granted or 'conceded' to United Empire Loyalists, and in this connection is a word peculiar to Ontario. That row or range of lots nearest the river was termed the first concession; other concessions, as added were termed the second, third, etc.

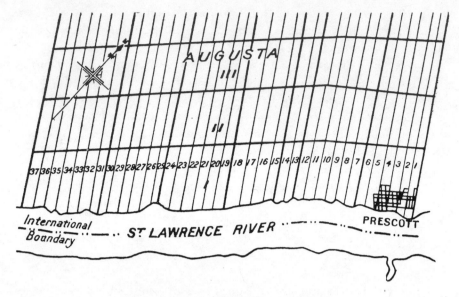

FIGURE A   PART OF TOWNSHIP OF AUGUSTA,
SHOWING EARLY SURVEY OF LOTS BORDERING ON RIVER.

"By royal instructions, dated August 23rd, 1786, to Lord Dorchester, townships fronting on navigable rivers and lakes were ordered to be laid out nine miles in front by twelve miles in depth – subdivided into twelve concessions or ranges, twenty-eight lots each. The lots twenty-six chains by eighty chains eighty links, contain 200 acres each with an allowance of five per cent for highways. These dimensions were adhered to in Lower Canada surveys, but were little regarded in Upper Canada. In Lower Canada it appears that the allowance of five per cent for highways has always been made and the roads have been established in the most suitable places. In Upper Canada road allowances were reserved on the township and concession lines and on certain side lines, but no uniform mode was adhered to in laying out roads in Upper Canada. Many gross errors were made in the old surveys, owing to the use of the magnetic needle and the inferiority of the surveying instruments and the unskillfulness of the surveyor, and especially for want of check or proof lines."*

---

* From a paper on "Different Systems of Township Surveys," read by J. F. Whitson, D.L.S., before the Association of Ontario Land Surveyors, in 1906, to which paper the writer is indebted for much of his information in regard to the early surveys carried out in Ontario.

It is not the intention to trace, in detail, the various methods of land division practised in any province, but the earlier surveys of Ontario and Quebec have been mentioned to emphasize the fact that early Canadian surveys conformed largely to important topographical features, and that an endeavour was made, in some cases at least, to have the roads established in the most suitable places.

As settlement was forced still further back from the rivers or other main determining topographical features the necessity for conformity to topography was not so immediately apparent. Further, some changes were evidently necessary in the grossly inaccurate methods adopted in the original surveys. Various systems were devised, with apparently two primary objects in view. These were to provide settlers with farms of a desirable shape and area and to simplify as much as possible the method of survey. Not much attention was given to topography. In some of the systems roads were given a definite location, irrespective of what the particular or local nature of the country might prove to be. In other cases five per cent of each lot was reserved for road purposes.

"It was impossible in Ontario, Quebec, and the Maritime Provinces, which were wooded countries, and where the settlers selected their locations along the banks of large rivers or lakes, to have any one system of survey for the whole country, and the exigencies of each case had to be met by surveys which would cover the wants of the people. For this reason there has never been any uniform system in these provinces. But where surveys were to be made in a large extent of territory, and the opportunity was had of surveying it ahead of settlement, it became the duty of the government to select such a comprehensive survey system as would obviate all the difficulties arising from irregular systems."*

As to the present methods of making surveys and dividing rural lands in the six eastern provinces, the writer understands that but very little has been done during the war by the provincial governments in this respect. There are still, however, large tracts that could be made available for settlement in Quebec and Ontario.

In Quebec, townships have latterly been surveyed in the shape of a square with sides 10 miles in length, the central line of the township being run north or south astronomically (see Fig. B). From lake Abitibi eastward

---

* From a paper read before the Association of Dominion Land Surveyors in 1885 by Dr. W. F. King, C.M.G., F.R.S.C., late Chief Astronomer, but at the time Inspector of Dominion Lands Surveys.

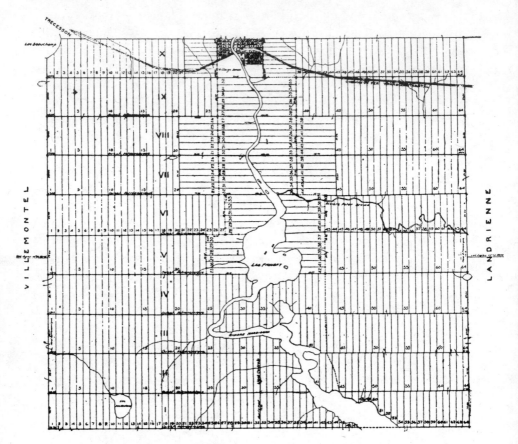

FIGURE B   TOWNSHIP OF FIGUERY, SHOWING SQUARE SYSTEM IN QUEBEC.
Figure 24 (page 103) shows enlarged plan of village Amos.

a strip of territory in the vicinity of the Transcontinental railway has been surveyed into these townships of 10 miles square, which are definitely correlated by the system of survey, though still – as in the case of older townships – designated by unrelated names.

Regular lots in this system are 13 chains in width and 80.80 chains, or a little over a mile, in depth. This gives an area of 100 acres per lot, after allowing five per cent for roads, which, in accordance with the general practice in Quebec, is reserved out of the grant, and may all be used if required for that purpose. During or after settlement roads may be located in the most suitable places; in the past, where the topography admitted, roads were laid out along the lot fronts but only every two miles apart, in which case the mileage of roads to be maintained is minimized. The opinion of Mr. J. E. Chalifour, Chief Geographer of the Department of the Interior, might well be given here in reference to this 10-mile-square township. He finds, in the present system of narrow, long lots, but a continuation of the early system of settlement, with families grouped closely together along the main roads. Such an arrangement was essential for protection against the Indians, but its social advantages have ever been recognized in Quebec where, statistics show, the rural population do not "leave the farms."

In Ontario the two more recent systems of survey have been the "six-mile" and "nine-mile" townships. The former system was first introduced in 1859 and was then apparently a direct copy of the township as laid out in the plains of the United States. Further mention will be made of this system in another connection, but, as modified, the "section" system (see Fig. C) has been in operation since 1874, and was, for a period of ten years, up until 1906, the system exclusively used in Northern Ontario, the townships being definitely related to each other and to certain "base lines" previously located. Lots are 320 acres in area, being one-half mile from east to west with a depth of one mile. There are no road allowances provided in the original survey, but five per cent is reserved out of the area of each lot for roads or highways. By Order in Council, dated April 24th, 1906, the Minister of Lands, Forests and Mines adopted the nine-mile system of surveys (see Fig. 7). An inspection of this plan of Clute township shows that roads are provided around each section of twelve 150 acre lots. This makes it 1½ miles between concession roads and 1⅞ miles between side roads. The dotted lines around the small lakes shown on the plan indicate what is now the general practice in Ontario in such cases, i.e., a public reserve of sixty-six feet around lakes. In Northern Ontario a number of such nine-mile townships have been laid out along the Transcontinental Railway.

The carrying out of township surveys by the Dominion Government under the direction of the Surveyor General of Dominion Lands has not been interrupted to any extent by the war. With the exception of but a few settlement surveys, in round numbers nearly 200,000,000 acres of lands under Federal control have been surveyed since Confederation in 1867, and, what is possibly as noteworthy, all practically under the same system of survey. The Dominion lands system of survey operates in what was originally known as the province of Manitoba and the Northwest Territories, though the provinces of Saskatchewan and Alberta now occupy a large part of what was then the Northwest Territories, into which the boundaries of Manitoba have also extended. The three provinces of Manitoba, Saskatchewan and Alberta may be generally regarded as containing the lands best suited for settlement in the Northwest, but the two

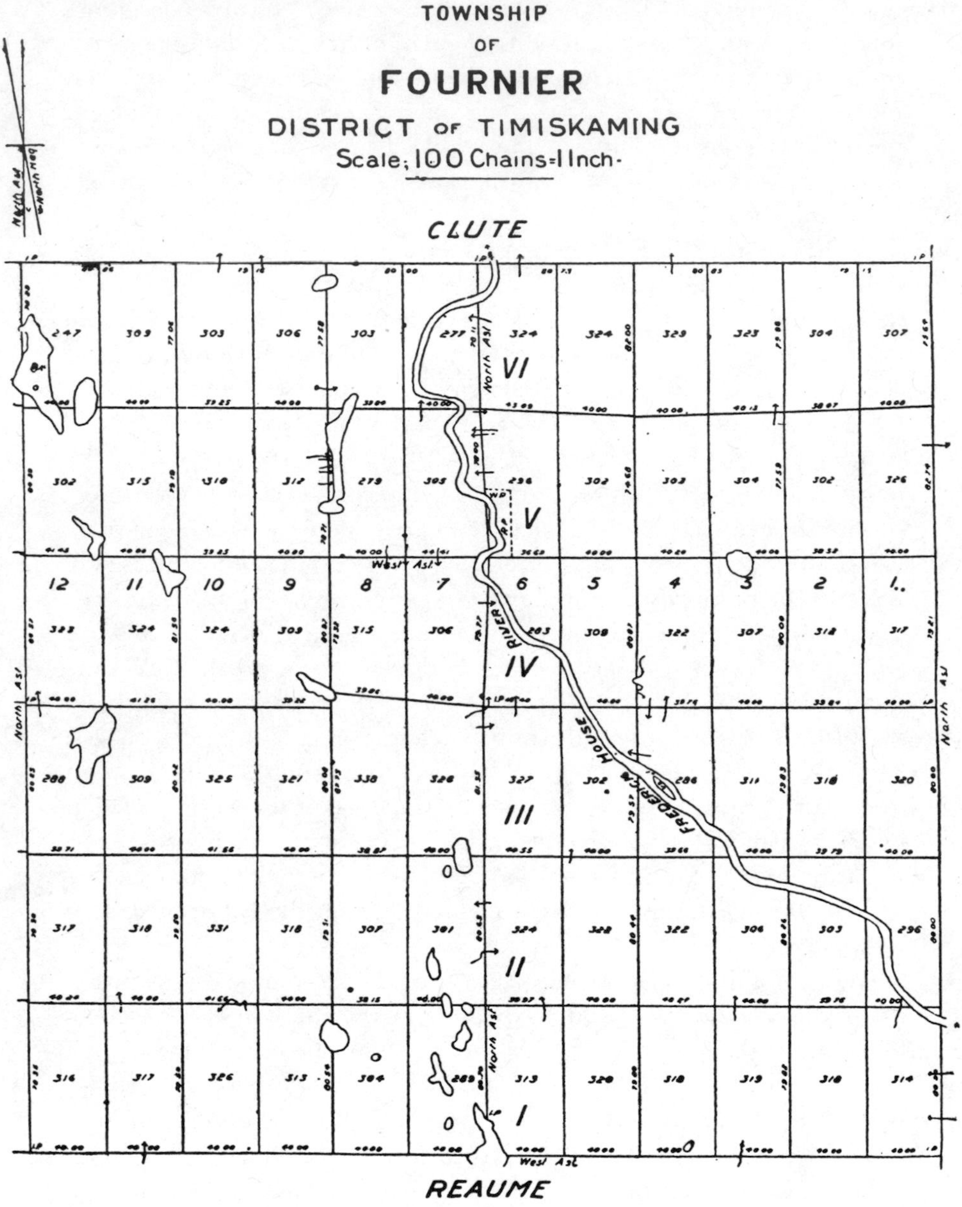

TOWNSHIP
OF
FOURNIER
DISTRICT OF TIMISKAMING
Scale; 100 Chains=1 Inch.

FIGURE C   TOWNSHIP OF FOURNIER,
SHOWING "SECTION" SYSTEM IN OPERATION IN ONTARIO SINCE 1874;
NOW OPERATED BY THE 9-MILE SYSTEM SHOWN ON FIGURE 7 (page 71).

hundred million acres already surveyed represents less than half their combined area.

In 1871 the first *Manual of Instructions for the Survey of Dominion Lands* was issued, and it is very evident, from a study of this and subsequent manuals, that whatever criticism might be made of the system adopted, the endeavour to carry it out in a systematic and scientific manner can not be too highly praised, especially in view of the methods in vogue in the other provinces of Canada and in the United States, from which country the system used in the West was copied.

Charles Mulford Robinson, in his *City Planning*, may be quoted as follows: "In 1785, on the suggestion of Thomas Jefferson, Congress passed a land ordinance which resulted in placing a huge checkerboard of survey lines over all the miles of country north and west of the Ohio river, a checkerboard that was regardless of contours and relentless as fate," and, in connection with such rectangular planning, "law and custom have entrenched a plan which by its own simplicity invited adoption." The ordinance referred to provided for townships 6 miles square, containing 36 sections of one mile square. This system appealed to those in charge of such matters as an admirable one to copy for the great level plains of the Canadian Northwest.

"If the country had been all wooded it is questionable if such a system would have been introduced," says Dr. O. J. Klotz, D.Sc., F.R.S.C., of the Dominion Observatory, who, in the early days, went to Washington in connection with the system of survey to be adopted. The idea of a six-mile rectangular township, with sides lying north and south and east and west, and the words section, township and range, were, it is true, copied from the United States. But from a scientific and mathematical standpoint the system might also be considered a new one. For example, it is understood that the Surveyor General of each state might designate townships by numbers that represented the order in which they were surveyed, rather than being indicative of the locality in which the townships were situated.

For the system that was to operate in Western Canada, however, the advantage of continuity was early and clearly seen. The result is that now each township has an established geographic position, subject, of course, to certain possible inaccuracies in surveying. Given the latitude and longitude of any spot, the section, township and range can be mathematically determined. Such a system was made possible by Lindsay Russell, who, though not Surveyor General at the time, was a remarkable mathematician and scientist. This high tribute is paid by Dr. O. J. Klotz, who gives Mr.

Russell further credit for his ability to recognize these qualities in another man, whom he brought into the services of the Dominion Government, and who, later, was to become, and who is now, Surveyor General of Dominion Lands, namely, Dr. E. G. D. Deville, I.S.O., D.T.S.

In Fig. D is shown a plan of a township surveyed by me in 1910 in Alberta, which is typical of the general system of survey as now carried out.

The regular section of approximately one mile square is ordinarily divided into four quarter sections of 160 acres each, for homesteading or other purposes. Road allowances of one chain, or sixty-six feet, in width are allowed along each section line running north and south, but only along every alternate section line running east and west. Prior to 1881 there were surveyed a number of townships, confined largely to Manitoba or its immediate vicinity, in which the road allowances, unnecessarily wide as it was found, were a chain and one-half (or 99 feet) in width, and were allowed along every section line, whether running east and west or north and south.

When the Canadian Pacific railway was constructed across the continent arrangements were made between the Government of British Columbia and the Federal Government, by which certain lands in British Columbia traversed by the railway were to be surveyed by the latter government. The system, commenced in 1884 for the survey of lands within this "belt" of twenty miles on each side of the C.P.R., is the section system as described, but modified by adding to each quarter section of 160 acres an allowance of three acres for roads, instead of locating this allowance along section lines. Such a modification is very necessary on account of the mountainous character of the Railway belt. The *Manual of Instructions* states: "The directions for the survey of township and section lines may in the mountains have to be departed from, but must be adhered to as closely as the nature of the ground will allow."

Outside of the Railway belt, and a block of 3,500,000 acres in the Peace River country, the survey of Crown lands in British Columbia is under the control of the Provincial, and not the Federal, Government. Where the nature of the country will admit, lands may be surveyed into townships substantially like those laid out in the Railway belt. In many localities the mountainous nature of the country would not permit of a whole township being laid out, and yet certain areas are adapted to settlement. Provision has therefore been made that "All Crown lands may be surveyed into quadrilateral lots, bounded by lines run as nearly as may be true north and south and east and west." Such lots may contain an area of from 40 acres up to 640 acres, and are generally rectangular, though a body of water may form one or more boundaries of a lot.

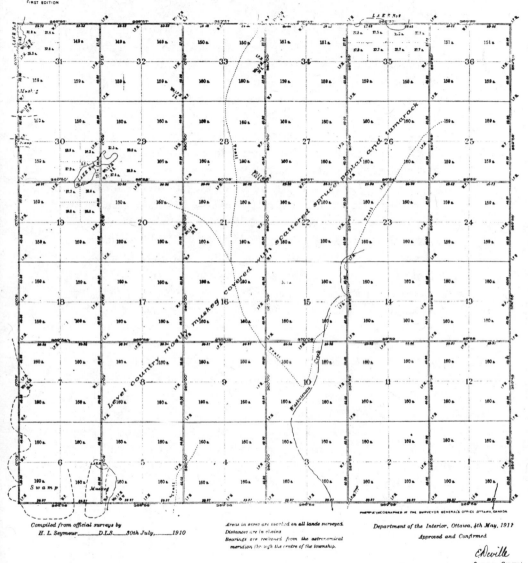

FIGURE D   TOWNSHIP IN SQUARE MILE SECTIONS USED IN DOMINION SURVEYS.

Before concluding this paper, it might be of interest to describe very briefly how the great extent of township surveys in the Prairie Provinces has been accomplished without confusion. The country was first divided into strips approximately 180 miles wide, where bounded on the south by the international boundary. The east and west boundaries of such strips are carefully surveyed lines, known as initial meridians, and, if continued northerly, should all meet at the North Pole, The first of these, which is called the Principal Meridian, is situated in the vicinity of Winnipeg, and the others, with but two exceptions, number west from it. These meridians are connected by base lines, also carefully surveyed, running east and west at a distance of 24 miles, or the depth of four townships, apart. From these base lines the outlines of the intervening townships are projected, and eventually each township is surveyed into sections.

The townships number northerly from the international boundary and in ranges easterly and westerly from the Principal Meridian, easterly from the second meridian east, and westerly from the other meridians. The advantage of this method of numbering is that a very little familiarity with the system will enable anyone to tell from its designation the approximate location of a township. Thus the northwest corner of township 62, range 20, west of the fourth meridian, as shown in Fig. D. is, for practical purposes, 372 miles north of the international boundary, or the 49th parallel of latitude, and 120 miles west of the fourth meridian, which is in longitude 110° west of Greenwich.

In 1915 $1,000,000 was appropriated for 70 survey parties, engaged for the most part in the necessary preliminary surveys of base lines and outlines or in the actual subdividing of townships. In 1916, only 56 parties were in the field. To issue the necessary instructions, check, plot, and reproduce surveyors' returns requires a staff of some 150, most of whom are technical graduates of recognized universities, or men well experienced and qualified in their particular lines of work. This staff is permanently employed at Ottawa, in the Topographical Surveys Branch of the Department of the Interior, under the direction of the Surveyor General. Year by year it has been the endeavour to increase the accuracy of the surveying operations. No more modern equipment exists in America for testing surveyors instruments and tapes than that installed in the Comparator building and in the Surveys laboratory at Ottawa. Levels, as now taken on base and meridian lines and on a number of the section lines in each township, provide useful contour information of the country surveyed. The posts or monuments erected to define the limits of sections or quarter sections have recently been made of a very permanent character. In the early surveys throughout Canada a wooden post was frequently the only monument used. Such a marking soon disappeared, frequently causing confusion and trouble. That now used, a large iron tube filled with concrete and sunk flush with the ground, with four surrounding pits, forms a monument for Dominion Land Surveys that is permanent yet easily found.

Dr. King, in his paper of 1884, previously referred to, says: "For the sake of greater simplicity in making surveys, it is necessary that all boundaries of lots shall be straight lines ... and, as the lots are intended for farms, they should be as nearly square as possible, the squares of all four-sided figures containing the greatest area of land for the length of fencing required, and any other angles than right angles causing inconvenient corners," and in the conclusion of his paper:

> "In this brief paper I have endeavoured to examine into the advantages, and also the defects, of our system of survey, and I have tried to show that the system is as good a one as could have been devised. Now that the surveys have been extended over such a wide extent of country, comprising almost all the prairie regions of the Northwest, we can look at them as a whole, and consider whether a system so perfect in principle has given in practice correspondingly good results. I think the verdict of an impartial observer would be that this has been the case, and that the surveys of the Northwest, as regards accuracy, economy, and the rapidity of their execution, can compare favourably with those of any other country in the world."

In the past various schemes have been devised for the planning and development of a township having particular regard to the establishment of villages or hamlets and of providing thereto suitable means of communication from the surrounding country. It is understood, however, that none of these schemes, chief among which might be mentioned the ingenious arrangement by Sir Wm. Van Horne, have ever been given a practical trial.

It is evident that any general arrangement, however ingenious, might still fail to meet particular topographic or other local conditions. Further, in many such schemes the proposed triangular or otherwise irregularly shaped farms would be a handicap to the settler in working his holding. Considered purely as a problem in geometry, Dr. E. Deville, Surveyor General of Dominion Lands, has recently pointed out that the hexagonal system presents itself as a solution of the hamlet colonization scheme and that the disadvantages of such schemes are by this system reduced to a minimum. Fig. E. represents a township subdivided in accordance with the hexagonal system with twelve farms of 160 acres each radiating from the centre.

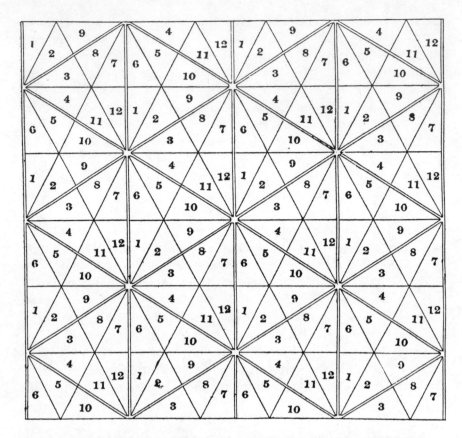

FIGURE E   DIAGRAM OF HEXAGONAL SYSTEM OF LAYING OUT A TOWNSHIP
WITH 12 FARMS OF 160 ACRES EACH RADIATING FROM THE CENTRE.

This diagram has been prepared by Dr. E. Deville, Surveyor General of Dominion Lands.

APPENDIX B

THE COLONIZATION OPERATIONS
OF THE CANADIAN PACIFIC RAILWAY COMPANY

By Allan Cameron, General Superintendent of Lands

The following is a rough outline of the various schemes for colonization adopted by the company since the commencement of our colonization operations:

The original terms of payment for the purchase of company lands, whether for settlement or not, were six equal annual payments with interest at 6 per cent.

To encourage settlement, to make branch lines profitable, and to bring the lands of the company in demand, the following concessions in terms of payment were made:

1. When lands were selling at from $2.50 to $3.50 per acre, the company adopted a policy, to encourage settlement, of giving a rebate of 50¢ per acre for every acre broken. The minimum area per annum on which a rebate was allowed was fixed, and the period for payment of purchase price was six years, throughout which the rebate applied.

2. A policy of assisted colonization was embarked upon in 1888 and kept up until 1901. European immigrants were located in groups in several districts, and furnished with implements and horses to an average amount of $300 each, while a large number of settlers from Ontario and the United States were transported on credit, chiefly to Northern Alberta. The undertaking worked very well. The settlers thus assisted sent word to friends, and soon all available homesteads were taken up and the company's lands were bought, both by the older settlers to increase their areas, and by later arrivals who desired to remain among friends and relatives.

3. During this period a development contract was instituted, which provided that, upon satisfactory proof being furnished of settlement and occupation of land, the second payment, which consisted of an interest payment only, would be waived.

4. Later this was changed, eliminating in the contract the interest payment entirely for the second year of occupation, but a penalty clause was inserted, to the effect that unless the land was occupied and improved the second payment of one-sixth of the purchase price was due and payable at the end of the second year. The penalty clause was inserted so that where lands were not settled upon, the contract might be brought back to the basis of the terms for sale of lands for non-settlement, *viz.*, six equal annual payments.

5. At a later period a settlement contract was adopted, whereby the purchaser declared he was entering on to the land for settlement and development, and payments were divided into ten equal annual installments, extending over ten years. This contract further provided that the second should be a payment of interest only, and in the third and following years a payment of principal and interest became due.

6. In 1909 a crop payment form of contract was adopted, whereby the settler paid one-tenth of the purchase price in cash at the time of purchase. Contract set forth the payments as being due on the ten-year payment plan, but the settler was required to turn over to the company one-half of all crops grown on the land; the amount realized by the company from the crops was then credited to the payment of interest and principal under the contract. The sale of land under the crop payment plan remained in effect until the end of 1912. From 1909 to the end of 1912 the following forms of contract were offered:

> For non-settlement, six equal annual payments, with interest at 6 per cent.
>
> For settlement, crop payment plan, one-tenth cash at time of purchase, balance of payments one-half crop as obtained. Interest on unpaid balance 6 per cent.
>
> For settlement, payments divided into ten equal annual installments; interest 6 per cent.

7. In 1913 the sale of lands was confined to actual settlers only. Terms, 20-year payments, one-twentieth at time of purchase, balance divided over nineteen years, with interest at 6 per cent. To settlers who were married and had sufficient equipment and capital to work the land, a loan of $2,000 was made, for improvements, these improvements to consist of a house, barn, fence and a well, to be erected by the company; cost of same to be added to the contract and payments made concurrently with the payments due under the purchase of the land.

8. From 1910 to date the company has, in certain districts, constructed ready made farms, which consist of house, toilet, barn, well and pump,

fence, breaking and cultivating 50 to 100 acres, and putting in the crops. These farms were sold to married men who entered into occupation with their families, and who had sufficient capital to carry on farming operations; terms of payments were the same as for the unimproved lands for settlement prevailing at the time of purchase.

9. In 1914, 1915 and 1916, loan and improved farms were sold on the basis of one-tenth of the purchase price (value of land and improvements) at time of purchase, interest payment only due at the end of the second year, and balance of principal divided into eighteen equal annual installments at end of each year thereafter.

10. From 1912 to date, settlers who had the necessary buildings for the protection of stock, feed, water and experience, were supplied with cattle, sheep and hogs to the value of $1,000, on lien note.

APPENDIX C

EXTRACT FROM ADDRESS ON THE MANUFACTURE OF MUNITIONS IN CANADA AS A PERMANENT ASSET TO CANADIAN INDUSTRY*

By Colonel David Carnegie
Member and Ordnance Adviser, Imperial Munitions Board

The Standardization of Product

No component part of munitions, however insignificant, has been made or accepted on the old principle of "good enough." Every part has been supplied to drawing and specification, with rigid examination, analysis and test before acceptance.

I think I am safe in saying that there is no industry in Canada which has been occupied in the manufacture of munitions but has passed through a process of refinement, which will leave it in a better condition when it returns to domestic pursuits after the war. If you review the great industries of Canada it will be difficult to find one which has not been actively contributing to the output of munitions.

Industries such as the iron and steel; the metals and metal products; refractory materials and fuels; lumber and timber; leather; textiles; paper; chemicals and other minor industries, have called into being processes and plant which could be adapted for munitions, and have also added new processes, new equipment and new skill where these were required.

In addition to the employment and adaptation of existing industries for munitions manufacture, entirely new industries have been brought into activity. The manufacture of munitions has given an abiding impetus to the mining and subsequent operations in the production of coal, iron, copper, nickel, zinc, molybdenum, antimony, aluminum and other metals.

The chemical industries have been accelerated by utilizing the waste products of the coke ovens for the manufacture of high explosives. These

---

* Extract from an address delivered by Col. Carnegie before the Ottawa Branch of the Canadian Society of Civil Engineers.

waste products, after the war, will be turned, by ingenuity and skill, into valuable domestic products.

The electro-chemical industries, such as the refining of copper, zinc and lead, have been initiated and will remain as a commercial asset. The electro-thermic processes for the production of ferro alloys, such as ferro-silicon, ferro-manganese, ferro-molybdenum, aluminum, magnesium and other metals, have produced standardized products.

It has been a costly, and sometimes bitter, training, but it has been done ungrudgingly and with great patience, and as a result the standard of Canadian products today is greater than ever before.

STANDARDIZATION OF SKILL

The widespread knowledge of new processes, involving the scientific study of metals, the flow of materials, and their physical, chemical and metal-lurgical values, has been such that one can hardly imagine it would have been possible for the universities and technical schools of Canada to have provided such instruction in the course of many years which has been crowded into as many months. Every workshop has been a school of train-ing in standardizing its skill. Every factory in which steel is made and forged is now partly or fully equipped with the means for measuring temperatures and intelligently discovering the value of the materials with which they are working. In every workshop in the different provinces of Canada where shrapnel shells are made, the scientific treatment of steel is known. There is hardly a town of any importance in which the use of precision instruments and gauges for measuring shells and their compon-ent parts does not exist.

It is difficult to assess the value of this skill to Canadian industry, in which over 250,000 workers have become skilled in the art of such pro-cesses and the manipulation of such tools and gauges. It is more surprising still to know that nearly 12,000 workers have become skilled in this work. Never in the history of the world has there been such an incentive to acquire such skill for a purpose the like of which our civilization should be ashamed, but which is nevertheless an asset which will be of great value in the peaceful commercial industries for the expansion of Canada.

CONTRIBUTING FACTOR IN THE STANDARDIZATION OF SKILL

The mental processes which have been silently at work developing char-acter, while the hands of the workers have been acquiring precision in the use of tools and gauges, are factors in the life of the individual worker which cannot be overlooked. Canada has shown a rare capacity during this great war, comparable in some measure with the vastness of its territory.

I have just referred to the great skill and ingenuity displayed by Canadian munition workers with the standard of which you have just cause to be proud. But there has been during the past two and one-half years a growth of character without which all skill and ingenuity would be soulless. I refer to that moral fibre in the character of the worker which has shown such fine courage and unfailing endurance. This fibrous character has through the ages "transformed the malady of thought into a bounding hope." It is this moral fibre which has given courage, energy, patience and unselfishness to the worn-out workers. It has inspired a quality and amount of inventive genius hitherto unknown in Canada. It has fostered harmony in some measure between employer and employee. It has brought our gentle women into touch with the struggles of the toilers and enabled them to understand and share their burdens. It has dignified labour while ennobling the character of those who have made sacrifices to fill the places of our boys who have "crossed the bar."

One morning recently a mother, while working in one of the munition factories, received news that her boy had been killed at the front. For a moment she was stunned, and had the deepest sympathy of her fellow-workers. Instead of collapsing into grief under the shock, and giving up her work, she set her face resolutely and worked with almost supernatural strength. Her employer informed me that she produced more shells that day than on any previous day.

This war, with all its horrors, savagery and sacrifices, has had its ennobling effects, producing absolute and timeless qualities beyond the power of oxidation. Science has discovered no solvent powerful enough for them. They are outside the engineers' specifications and tests. They are engraved on the heart, and beyond the decay of moth and rust. This moral fibre in Canadian industry has provided better conditions in the works, and has brought into prominence welfare work of inestimable value. Signs are not wanting that it will increase facilities for the education of the workers and establish a community of interests between masters and men which exalt humanity above self-interest. If my vision of the future is not distorted, this same moral fibre in both the employer and employed is going to quicken "man's devouring need of liberty." If awakened Canada, with its vast territory, thirty-one times greater than the United Kingdom and with its natural resources of almost immeasurable value, is to utilize its possessions, it must shake off the fetters that bind it to systems which are opposed to a full and free industrial, technical and general education of the people.

APPENDIX D

ECONOMIC LOSS CAUSED BY NEGLECT
OF PUBLIC HEALTH*

On this continent exponents of preventive medicine have recognized the handwriting on the wall and are looking and hoping for a national organization of health, in order that we may efficiently accomplish in the future that which we have in a sense only been touching the fringe of in the past. But this cannot be accomplished without the expenditure of large sums of money and, in order to obtain this money, we must be in a position to show that the expenditure is warranted. Gladstone once said – "In the health of the people lies the strength of the nation." It is a recognized fact that on the efficient solution of the problems of public health depends the comfort and prosperity of our peoples and the future greatness of our nations. But, unfortunately, our civilization has not sufficiently advanced for us to appeal for this on humane grounds alone, therefore, we have to present the economic side of the problem in cold figures of dollars and cents. For this purpose probably the most valuable and most reliable records we have are contained in the *Report of the Committee of One Hundred on National Health*, dealing with the national vitality and setting forth its waste and conservation, as prepared by Prof. Irving Fisher, of Yale. From this report we learn that there are 3,000,000 persons in the United States at all times suffering from some form of sickness (equal to approximately 300,000 in Canada), of whom about 1,100,000 are in the working period of life, three-quarters being actual workers, who must lose at least $700 per year, making an aggregate loss from illness of $550,000,000. The expense of medicine, medical attendance, extra foods, etc., would equal this amount; thus, we have the total cost of illness as approximately $1,100,000,000, of which it is assumed that at least one-half is preventable. The annual loss from preventable deaths has been conservatively estimated at $1,100,000,000. If to this we add the $550,000,000 loss from preventable sickness, we have a total of $1,650,000,000 as the approximate annual

* Extract from article by Dr. Chas. J. Hastings M.D., L.R.C.P.I., Medical Officer of Health, Toronto, in *Conservation of Life,* July, 1917.

monetary loss to these two nations from preventable sickness and death, and these figures are considered by practical and reliable authorities as extremely conservative. Furthermore, no attempt is made here at estimating the loss from the after effects of many of these diseases, that oft times leave the victim handicapped for the balance of his life; no attempt is made to estimate what this enormous amount means in human blood, in agony, pain, sorrow and tears; nor the loss to the children that are left fatherless and motherless. As Prof. Fisher expresses it, "Poverty and disease are twin evils, and each plays into the hands of the other, and from each or both springs vice and crime."

Of the 690,000 who die annually in Canada and the United States from preventable disease, a fitting epitaph for a large percentage would be "Poisoned by sewage-polluted water"; for a still larger percentage "Poisoned by milk," and for a still greater number "Victims of the white plague," resulting from poverty and ignorance.

Of the $1,650,000,000 loss to these nations, over $250,000,000 are expended on medical attendance and medicine in endeavoring to cure diseases that never should have occurred. The United States and Canada are squandering $200,000,000 annually on patent medicines, and less than $5,000,000 on public health and prevention of diseases – they are only tinkering with the problem.

I venture to say, without fear of contradiction, that, if the amount of money spent in the attempt to cure diseases that should never have occurred, plus the amount spent annually on patent medicines, was spent in the organization and administration of a national army of health, in less than one decade preventable diseases would be prevented.

These are hard facts, referring only to the monetary loss. They are black clouds, but it is gratifying to see evidences of clearing all around the horizon, revealing the dawn of the health era, when the money that is now being squandered in endeavoring to cure diseases that never should have occurred is being spent on their prevention. Pasteur assured us years ago that it is within the power of man to rid himself of every parasitic disease. This can only be hoped for by means of efficient appropriation, efficient organization and efficient administration.

APPENDIX E

LAND SETTLEMENT
AND AFTER-WAR EMPLOYMENT PROBLEMS*

POSITIONS FOR RETURNED SOLDIERS CAN BE BEST ENSURED BY NOW
SETTLING, ON VACANT LANDS IN THE WEST, THE MANY THOUSANDS
OF TOWN-DWELLING IMMIGRANTS WHO CAME TO CANADA DIRECT
FROM CULTIVATING OLD-WORLD FARMS

BY J. H. T. FALK
Secy. Winnipeg Social Welfare Commission

Grave doubts exist in the minds of those who have talked with returned soldiers as to whether, no matter how advantageous the conditions, any large number of them will be willing to take up agriculture as an occupation. Production, and production from the land, is looked upon as the one hope of salvation for our after-the-war conditions. Can we not avoid some of our past mistakes and maladjustments in meeting after-war problems?

OUR TOWN-DWELLING FARMERS

In a small office on Main Street, in the City of Winnipeg, one day early in April, 1915, the writer, tired of authorizing grocery and wood orders to be sent to Slav dependent families as relief, because of their unemployment, picked out from the applicants one who seemed capable of acting as an interpreter and started an inquiry into the nature of the occupation of the applicants in their country of origin. Some 255 were interviewed in a short time; of these 70 per cent had owned land, cultivated it, and thereby earned a livelihood in Eastern Europe; 17 per cent had worked

---

* From *Canadian Finance,* June 20th, 1917.

as labourers upon the land of the owner; and 7 per cent had been tenant farmers. Only 6 per cent had earned their livelihood from any other source than by production from the soil.

The writer's thoughts ran thus: "Here we are at war, never before was the necessity from production greater, never before was man power of more value, and here in Western Canada, in its greatest city, money raised primarily for patriotic purposes has been used to keep able-bodied men and their families from starvation, and within 20 miles of the office enough land lay idle, much of it subdivided into 25-foot lots, to have kept all those families self-supporting, and more."

The question was discussed with such authorities as J. Bruce Walker, Commissioner of Immigration; Louis Kon, now Superintendent of Immigration and Colonization for the Provincial Government; J. S. Woodsworth, late of the Bureau of Social Research, and W. J. Black, late principal of the Manitoba Agricultural College. Bruce Walker gave it as his opinion that at that time a Slav immigrant needed $750 to $1,000 in cash to have a fair start on a homestead.

Savings Tied Up in City Real Estate

A more detailed questionnaire was prepared which covered age of the applicant, length of time in Canada and other necessary details. From the very start it was seen that a large number of Slavs in the city had equities, based on the assessment value, of $700 and over, though then without means of bare subsistence or the money to pay their taxes. To conduct the investigation intelligently, it was necessary to tell the applicants something of the idea that they might enter into the spirit of it. The detailed investigation started on a Saturday morning. On the Sunday, for news spreads quickly amongst the Slavs in the North End of Winnipeg, no less than 20 men found the interpreter at his house and said that they had heard that farm lands were being exchanged for city property and wanted to know if they could get in on it. On the Monday, and for the following days, they came not in twos and threes but in tens and twenties. Fifty questionnaires were filled out and a report based on those fifty cases showed that 31 had equities of over $1,000 each in city property, 12 had equities of $700 to $1,000 and only 7 had less than $700.

Comparatively few of these families had sufficient land in the old country to allow of its being the sole support of the family. One or more members of the family worked part of the year for wages for adjoining landowners or at trades in nearby towns. While they understood the production of all the staple crops and the care of stock, only one had any experience with farm machinery beyond the plough and the harrow.

Intended to Take Up Homesteads

Almost all these immigrants learned while still in the old country that they could "buy 160 acres for $10," and almost all before they left had intended to farm as soon as they saved a little from working in the city. The gist of the answer to the question, "Why, when you had enough to make a first payment on a house, did you not use this money to start on a homestead?" was invariably, "I was told that if I bought a house it would increase in value, and then I could sell and would have more money to start on." Some openly admitted that times were too good in the city and that the farm had ceased to appeal to them. Many of them had tried to get loans on their property but were unable to do so. Seven had farms or homesteads at the time the investigation was made but were unable to start on them for want of ready money.

Bearing on Problem of Returned Soldiers

Now if we are right in our first premises, must we not consider the problem of the returned soldiers in the light of other problems? If increased agricultural production means increased manufacturing, and if increased manufacture is the best means of absorbing our returned soldiers, and if our returned soldiers will not readily submit to being placed on the land, then surely we must attack the problem of the returned soldier indirectly – by assisting those who are willing and who can produce from the land to do so, so that their production may indirectly benefit the returned soldier. Slavs and many others who are at present working in our cities in every kind of occupation, will be displaced by returned soldiers to a large extent, but it will indirectly work to the detriment of the returned soldiers if they are allowed to constitute an unemployment problem. If there is an ever present surplus of labour, the general tendency will be to keep the wages down, and this must sooner or later affect the wage of the returned soldier; if, on the other hand, those whom returned soldiers have displaced can be assisted to produce, the surplus of labour will be reduced automatically, while the requirements of the producers purchased from the sale of wheat they produce will offer work for increasing numbers in our cities.

Our Archaic Labour Market System

The study of the methods of marketing labour has been a hobby with the writer for several years. It is almost impossible to realize how archaic is our present system by which labour outside the trade unions is marketed through competitive commercial exchanges.

To the writer one immediate step seems of prime importance. The Dominion Government spent thousands of dollars registering our man power for war-time industry. If this information is not sufficient, then we must at once re-register our man and possibly our woman power for the purpose of readjustment after the war, and, having done this, we must have ready machinery in the form of at least a Dominion controlled system of provincial labour exchanges, so that we may be conscious of the existence and extent of the disease of unemployment and be better able to apply the remedy. The information obtainable through a centralized authority would soon create a public opinion which would demand, if necessary, adjustment of the use of public capital so as to dovetail into the use of private capital

INDEXES

ORIGINAL INDEX

NOTE: This index appeared in the original edition of Adams' text. Page numbers have been adjusted to reflect pagination of this edition.

INDEX FOR INTRODUCTION AND COMMENTARIES

CONTRIBUTORS

Wayne J. Caldwell is Professor of Rural Planning in the School of Environmental Design and Rural Development at the University of Guelph. His research focuses on planning and change in rural and agricultural communities, including planning policy, farmland preservation, rural conflict resolution, and community-based approaches to economic and environmental issues.

Gary Davidson is an independent planner working out of Bayfield, Ontario. He specializes in rural planning and issues impacting rural communities and their economies. Currently, he is a principal researcher for the Canadian Institute of Planners climate change initiative.

John Devlin is Associate Professor of Rural Planning and Development at the University of Guelph where he teaches planning theory and development administration. His research deals with agricultural policy, environmental governance, and the role of the state in development planning.

Len Gertler was Professor of Urban and Regional Planning at the University of Waterloo, later serving as Vice-Chair of Ontario's Environmental Assessment and Appeals Board. As an academic and practitioner, he pursued interests in regional planning, environmental and conservation planning, cultural tourism, and international development in Canada, Europe, and Southeast Asia. Professor Gertler passed away in 2005.

Tony Fuller is an Adjunct Professor at the University of Guelph and is currently a Visiting Scholar at the China Agricultural University in Beijing. His research interests include studying agricultural and migrant labour systems in rural China.

Jill L. Grant is Professor in the School of Planning at Dalhousie University in Halifax. Her current research interests include contemporary development trends (including new urbanism, gated communities, and creative cities), planning practice and theory, and the history of planning.

Hok-Lin Leung is Professor and Director Emeritus, School of Urban and Regional Planning, Queen's University. His areas include urban planning and design, land use planning, infrastructure planning, policy/program evaluation, and China issues.

Michael Troughton was Professor of Geography at the University of Western Ontario where he taught rural and agricultural geography. He was a tireless advocate for the study of landscapes with a strong focus on sustainability, rural resources, and heritage preservation. Although his research was primarily in Ontario and Canada, he was an international leader in the development of agricultural geography. Michael passed away in 2007.

Ian Wight is an Associate Professor of City Planning at the University of Manitoba, where he teaches the regional studio, professional practice, and city-region planning. His research interests include the interrelationship of place, place-making, and planning, and evolving professionalism beyond the status quo, both informed in particular by an integral theory perspective.

Jeanne M. Wolfe was Director of the School of Urban Planning at McGill University from 1988 to 1999, and Professor Emeritus from 2000 until her death in 2009. Her research focused on Canadian planning history, planning practice and housing policy, and the evolution of Montreal's governance structure. She also did extensive research on urban and social issues in developing countries. For her "contributions as a leading scholar and mentor in the field of urban planning in Canada and abroad," she was awarded the Order of Canada in 2009.

Printed and bound in Canada by Friesens

Set in New Baskerville, Univers, and Gisha
by Artegraphica Design Co. Ltd.

Text design: Irma Rodriguez

Copy editor: Lesley Erickson

Proofreader: Stephen Ullstrom